COLLECTED WORKS OF

BERNARD LONERGAN

VOLUME 4

COLLECTION

COLLECTED WORKS
OF BERNARD
LONERGAN

COLLECTION

edited by

Frederick E. Crowe and

Robert M. Doran

Published by University of Toronto Press for

Lonergan Research Institute of Regis College, Toronto

Collection: Papers by Bernard Lonergan

Second edition, revised and augmented, of
Collection: Papers by Bernard Lonergan,
edited by Frederick E. Crowe,
first published by Herder and Herder, New York, and
Darton, Longman & Todd, London, 1967.

Reprinted in paperback 1993

ISBN 0-8020-3438-1 (cloth)
ISBN 0-8020-3439-X (paper)

Requests for permission to quote from the
Collected Works of Bernard Lonergan should be
addressed to University of Toronto Press.

Canadian Cataloguing in Publication Data

Lonergan, Bernard J. F. (Bernard Joseph Francis),
    1904–1984.
    Collected works of Bernard Lonergan

    Vol. 4, 2nd ed., rev. and aug. First ed. (1967)
    published separately.
    Contents: 4. Collection.
    Includes bibliographical references and index.
    ISBN 0-8020-3439-X (v. 4 : pbk.)

    1. Theology – 20th century. 2. Catholic Church.
    I. Crowe, Frederick E. II. Doran, Robert M., 1939–
    III. Lonergan Research Institute. IV. Title

    BX891.L595 1988   230   C88-093328-3

The Lonergan Research Institute
gratefully acknowledges the contribution of
REVEREND HENRY HALL
toward publication of this volume
of the Collected Works of Bernard Lonergan

Contents

A page from File 37 in Batch 2 of the papers in the Lonergan Archives. This file contains Lonergan's notes for the course he gave on the theology of marriage at the College of the Immaculate Conception, Montreal, first in 1941–1942 and again in 1944–1945. To which period does this page belong? The observant eye will notice significant differences between the diagram here and that of the article, 'Finality, Love, Marriage' (page 42 of this volume), which was written in 1943. Thus he came to this problem three times. The published form of the diagram could therefore be a pruning of the one in the Archives, if this is dated in the earlier period; or the published form may be an intermediate stage, and the Archives page a later development. In any case, it is clear that Lonergan's mind never stood still, and it would be worth our while, in order to follow his developing thought, to determine the sequence of his three studies of marriage.

4. De finibus matrimonii

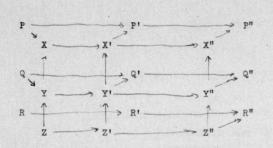

Finis horizontalis matrimonii

Z" Y" X"

Finis lateralis Y' X' circa Z'

Finis verticalis R" Q" P"
      prim.
      secund. P' Q'

Sit Z foecunditas sexualis in homine, quae est pars quaedam
naturae spontaneae in homine (R), quae dirigitur in finem later
per organistica sexus (Z') seu finem lateralem, in prolem procreatam
et nutritam (Z"). Ubi Z' organistica sexus sunt pars quaedam totius
vitae organisticae (R'), et Z" est pars quaedam finis horizontalis
naturae spontaneae (R") qui est "actu vivere speciei".

Sit R natura spontanea hominis, R' huius naturae finis lateralis
nempe organistica vitae spontaneae, et R" huius naturae finis
horizontalis, nempe, actu vivere speciei.

Sit Z pars quaedam naturae spontaneae, nempe, foecunditas
sexualis; Z' pars quaedam organisticorum vitae, nempe actus sexuales;
et Z" pars quaedam R" nempe proles procreata et enutrita. Sequitur
Z ordinari in Z' tamquam in finem lateralem, in Z" tamquam finem
horizontalem. Quae ad R et Z pertinent ratione sui.

Iam vero R et Z includuntur in synthesi superiori vitae rationalis
civitatis terrestre, cuius principium est ratio humana qua humana, Q,
quae ordinatur per finem lateralem amicitiae humanae et pacis, Q',
in finem horizontalem Q" seu bonum commune humanum historice cumulativum.
Proinde rationi competit superordinari inferioribus suis, et
ideo subordinare naturae ordinem inferiorem in actus sibi convenientes.
Quod quidem facit non immutando ordinem naturae inferiorem,
Synthesis enim non destruit partes sui, sed informando, dirigendo,
et elevando in finem superiorem.
Proinde ratio finformat foecunditatem sexualem vinculo contractus,
Y, dirigit organistica vitae sexualis per mutuum adiutorium et amiditiam
maritalem tamquam finem lateralem, Y', et elevat finem Horizontalem
fecunditatis, Z", in finem boni hominis cumulativi per educationem, Y".

Pariter gratia

Pariter ordo gratiae (P) per finem horizontalem caritatis erga
Xtum mysticum (P') procedit in vitam aeternam (P"). Includit vero
in sua synthesi inferiora sexus ratione ordinat, et novam altioremque
superordinationem suam imponit. Vinculum contractus Y informatur
vinculo sacramenti X; amicitia maritalis Y' informatur speciali
ordine caritatis X'; educatio in civitatem terrestrem Y" elevatur
in educationem civitatis caelestis X".

Mysticis
Xtus diligens
ecclesia dilecta
ekta
Eph 5.

Preface

This fourth volume in the Collected Works of Bernard Lonergan is a new edition of the sixteen essays that were published in 1967 under the title, *Collection*. The appearance meanwhile of *A Second Collection* (1974) and *A Third Collection* (1985) had suggested that this one might be renamed now *A First Collection*, but the suggestion met with considerable opposition among those consulted. Lonergan himself, in a letter dated March 18, 1965, at a time when Herder and Herder were proposing to issue two volumes at once, had suggested 'Collection One' and 'Collection Two,' taking the idea from something he read in one of his favorite magazines, *The New Yorker*. Eventually, however, the papers were reduced to one volume, with the title that has been familiar to his readers for twenty years, a title which we therefore retain in the present volume.

The same conservative principle is operative in regard to the text, where editing has been kept to a minimum. We have taken as our basis the text of 1967; Lonergan had reviewed some parts of this himself and given a few general directions for the editing of the rest. But, while he did not complain about the result, and might be said therefore to have implicitly accepted it, our view now is that too much freedom was exercised in the editing. A very simple example: Lonergan's 'It should seem' was changed to the 'It would seem' of New World English. This was quite arbitrary. We know now from the records of the Regis College Library that Lonergan had signed out *The King's English* of H.W. Fowler and F.G. Fowler, and *A Dictionary of Modern English Usage* by H.W. Fowler. Presumably, he had given some thought to his English style, which is in any case his, and quite distinctive. Our aim, then, except where he wished for changes, has been to restore the original Lonergan, though it has not always been possible to determine what he wrote; there are indications, indeed, that prior to the 1967 volume other editors had already 'improved' his style.

We have not, however, surrendered all editorial independence; if we owe readers a faithful reproduction of Lonergan, we also owe it to Lonergan himself to attend to the mechanics of bringing sixteen disparate essays into a volume, and inserting that volume into a set of Collected Works. But our main governing principle has been that we are dealing with a thinker of great stature, who will not be read for his literary style, however elegant that may be, but rather for his ideas, expressed in his own way. The expression is not therefore to be lightly tampered with.

Still, there are the mechanics we have mentioned. Where does one draw the line? We feel bound to inform our readers of our policy here, though it means going into some rather tedious detail. In the matter of spelling and punctuation, and minor points of grammar, we have not scrupled to introduce uniformity and needed changes; our authorities here have been for the most part the *Oxford American Dictionary* and *The Chicago Manual of Style*. We have, however, left intact any expressions that might be a clue to Lonergan's ideas, or procedures of thought, or personal history, even when those expressions might seem, from one viewpoint or another, to be flawed. This involved a good many prudential decisions: in the simple matter of commas, for example, we had often to decide whether Lonergan's use was idiosyncratic or expressive of a more or less important nuance.

In other areas our governing principle was easier to apply. There was no question, then, of changing language that would be regarded now as noninclusive, or of discreetly removing statements that are less ecumenical in tone than we would wish. To come down to some of the minute details of chapter 1, we did not alter the phrase, 'both have a common form'; the logic is faulty, but it may be important for some researcher, somewhere, sometime, to know that Lonergan thought that way. Nor did we decide whether he should use 'Mr' or 'Professor' in referring to Joseph; his usage here is data on his acquaintance with, or ignorance of, the British academic scene, data which some historian, somewhere, sometime, might wish to investigate. On the other hand, when he wrote that 'the symbolism not only expresses the minor premise ...

but also its implication,' we corrected his word order, which seemed to be a matter merely of grammar. Sometimes Lonergan's own marginal notations to earlier printings of his work enabled us to make corrections in the present edition with greater surety.

There are points that require further comment: for one example, the difficult question of what to do with foreign words, phrases, and quotations. Our rules have been these. When longer foreign-language quotations appeared in the text, we substituted a translation and transferred the original to a footnote (such a combination, then, regularly means that the translation is ours). We did this in such a way, however, as not to change the numbering of Lonergan's own notes. This forced us to use asterisks for new notes in chapter 11, though in chapters 3 and 13 we merely added new numbers. Words and shorter phrases in modern languages are not translated in the text, nor are any foreign-language quotations translated in the notes.

The major problem had to do with words and shorter phrases in Latin and Greek. Lonergan's writing is studded with Latin, and the *Collection* of 1967 had often given the English in brackets after the foreign phrase. But that had a rather jarring effect on the reader, so in this edition we have eliminated most (not quite all) of these bracketed phrases; instead we have drawn up a lexicon of Latin and Greek words and phrases, and included it at the back of the volume. To be noted, however: Lonergan himself sometimes gave English and Latin in the text, bracketing one or the other. Our rule, then, has been to use round brackets for his translations, and square brackets for the few of ours that remain. In fact square brackets in text or footnote will regularly signal an editorial addition; any exceptions will be clear from the context.

Another point regards numbering and headings. Lonergan's essays were nearly always constructed with great care for divisions and sequence. Sometimes he expressed this care (or a previous editor did – we cannot now be sure about this in every case) in the numbers and subtitles used. It seemed helpful to do the same more systematically for the whole volume; subtitles and numbers have been added, therefore, to most of the essays, and indications of this have been given in the Editorial Notes.

We have felt somewhat freer in dealing with lesser matters. Thus a special feature in the original form of chapters 8 and 13 was the 'hierarchy' of typefaces: some paragraphs in smaller, some in larger type; this seems to have been editorial, and has not been reproduced. Again, we have made minor additions and changes, without noting the fact, in Lonergan's footnotes. Regularly, we have filled in page numbers for his 'f.' or 'ff.' Often we have enlarged his references, adding data on publishers and the like. We chose to use arabic numerals in references to Thomas Aquinas (except where roman numerals occur in the title of the Thomist work – e.g., *In IV Sent.*), but we retained the traditional roman numerals for references to Aristotle (*Metaphysics*, VII, 17). We have indicated titles of the Leonine edition of Aquinas, but have used our own abbreviations – of course, when Lonergan quoted a particular edition (Mandonnet, Wyser, etc.) we used the title of that edition – and added numbers from the Marietti editions of Thomas Aquinas where that was helpful; further, we counted paragraphs (as Lonergan himself often did) in the Leonine manual edition of the *Summa contra Gentiles*. We have checked the Bekker and Stephanus references for Aristotle and Plato (in the latter changing *Banquet* to the more common *Symposium*). As for references to Lonergan's own works (in his writings or in our notes), sufficient bibliographical information may be found in the list provided at the end of the Editorial Notes, pp. 313-316. On his use of scripture, our rule has been to leave Lonergan's quotations the way he wrote them; to change them to the uniformity of a single translation of the Bible might well result in missing his point. But any scripture we have added is taken from the *Revised Standard Version*.

What the reader has from Lonergan in this volume is therefore very close to what Lonergan originally wrote and what the reader of *Collection* had in 1967. But in what the reader has from the editors now, there are some major differences. There is omission of the biographical section of the original introduction. At the time of the previous edition Lonergan was still not well known, and the diversity of topics treated (indicated by the very title of the volume) seemed to call for some account of the person who wrote the essays and of the unitary vision of his lifework. That is less necessary now. In any case the volume is to be evaluated in its new context, which is that of the Collected Works. Students of Lonergan's thought will eventually have all his major work available with the single items carefully dated, and the whole set carefully indexed – in that context the focus is less on a general introduction than on establishing relations for each particular item with the whole.

Another major difference regards the notes on the several chapters. These formed part of the general introduction in 1967, and gave only a general context for each chapter. They still give the context, but also

add specific notes on particular phrases. These notes are indicated un-
obtrusively in the text – by letters, where Lonergan's own notes are
indicated by numbers. The whole batch of Editorial Notes is then gath-
ered together out of the way at the back of the volume.

The essays do seem to require comment, at least for the reader who
is meeting Lonergan for the first time. They span nearly a quarter of a
century of his life, beginning with one that looks back to his student
days, and ending with one that looks forward to the radical rethinking
of theology his method calls for. It was a period of enormous development, in which he wrote his study of Thomist cognitional theory,
produced *Insight*, provided manuals of Latin theology for his students,
continued to work on his crowning achievement of *Method in Theology*,
and laid the foundation for his last great effort in economics. To edit
these essays without relation to this multifaceted activity would be a bit
like removing sixteen disparate details from a painter's masterpiece and
expecting them to make sense. Still, the need for annotation is temporary, and the function of the Editorial Notes limited; that is the point
of keeping them separable at the back of the volume where they can
easily be dropped from future editions.

There remains the duty, so pleasant that the word 'duty' is hardly in
place, of thanking those who contributed to the work of publication.
Very helpful advice was given by several of our editorial consultants,
namely, John Carmody, Walter Conn, Peter Drilling, Tad Dunne, Charles
Hefling, Arthur Kennedy, Matthew Lamb, Richard Liddy, William Loewe,
Sean McEvenue, Philip McShane, Ben Meyer, Desmond O'Grady, Quen-
tin Quesnell, Philip Boo Riley, Terry Tekippe, and Michael Vertin. Vin-
cent MacKenzie, Librarian of Regis College, has given material assistance,
as has Walter H. Principe, of the Pontifical Institute of Mediaeval Studies.
Thanks are due also to Marcela Dayao, who very efficiently put the whole
volume onto computer for the printer, and to the editorial staff of the
University of Toronto Press who saw the volume through the next stages.
And we thank those who released previously held publishing rights;
fifteen of the essays had been published elsewhere before the 1967 *Collection*, and the original publisher is indicated in the notes to the several
chapters.

A special word is reserved for Robert M. Doran, who conceived the
idea of the Lonergan Research Institute three years ago, proposed as
one of its first aims publication of the Collected Works of Bernard
Lonergan, did the larger part of the work in planning and preparing

the Collected Works, and has topped all this by taking on the tedious side of editing this volume: the hundred and one trips to the library to check footnotes, the thousand and one decisions to be made on commas, hyphens, capital letters, and the like. Although I have written this Preface and the Editorial Notes, I have not agreed to have my name appear alone as editor of the volume; it is simple honesty to declare, as the title page does, that we are its coeditors.

F.E.C.
August 20, 1987

COLLECTION

Papers by Bernard Lonergan

1

The Form of Inference

Mr Joseph's thorough *Introduction to Logic*[a] consistently opposes the idea of reduction. In convincing analysis are set forth the three or four figures and nineteen moods of syllogism. But the admission that moods of the fourth (or indirect first) figure need validation is canceled by the contention that these moods never occur in actual thinking. The second and third figures are found not only to conclude in their own right but also to involve distinctive processes of thought; their reduction, at times easy and at others ludicrously cumbrous, is always superfluous. A similar position is maintained with regard to other formal types of inference. If a hypothetical argument contains only three terms, it can be reduced to syllogistic form; but it may contain more than three, and then reduction is a useless *tour de force*. Occasionally mathematical reasoning is syllogistic, as when a Euclidean proof appeals to an earlier theorem; but such appeals arise only when insight into the data is imperfect, and in general the mathematician has perfect insight.[1] If, finally, one cares to complete the brief against reduction, one need only turn from Mr Joseph to Cardinal Newman. By definition the latter's illative sense[b] proceeds along ways unknown to syllogism from a cumulation of probabilities – too manifold to be marshaled, too fleeting to be formulated[c] – to a conclusion that nonetheless is certain.

I have recounted these views not because I hope to refute them but

---

1 See H.W.B. Joseph, *An Introduction to Logic,* 2nd ed. (Oxford: Oxford University Press, 1931) 330, 339, 341, 545.

because I wish to present a problem. Is the human mind a Noah's ark of irreducible inferential forms?[d] Is there no general form of all inference, no highest common factor, that reveals the nature of the mind no matter how diverse the materials on which it operates? Is everything subject to measure and order and law except the mind which through measurement and comparison seeks to order everything with laws? One has only to raise such questions to grasp how paradoxical it is to deny reduction. But if this point is granted, there immediately follows another. Neither Cardinal Newman nor Mr Joseph has attacked reduction as such. Their sole contention is that a particular reduction, reduction to syllogism, does not fit the facts. Thus it remains to be seen whether there exists some other type of formally valid inference that possesses both the radical simplicity and indefinite flexibility necessary to embrace all other types within itself.

1   Inference and Language

Any language has a number of syntactical forms that are peculiarly inferential. Most obvious is the causal sentence, because A, therefore B, where A and B each stand for one or more propositions. Next comes the concessive sentence, although A, still not B, which is the natural instrument of anyone ready to admit the propositions, A, but wishing to deny that A implies B. To meet such denial, to give separate expression to the implication of B in A, there is the host of conditional sentences, if A, then B, which may be past or present, proximate or remote future, particular or general, actually verified or the pure interconnection grammarians call contrary-to-fact. It is not hard to see that these three syntactical forms are peculiarly inferential. Just as 'so that' and 'in order that' express the relations of efficient and final causality, so also 'because,' 'although,' and 'if' are the special tools of reasoning man.

Closely related to these linguistic tools is the transition from informal to formal inference. It appears a fact that spontaneous thinking sees at once the conclusion, B, in apprehending the antecedents, A. Most frequently the expression of this inference will be simply the assertion of B. Only when questioned do men add that the 'reason for B' is A; and only when a debate ensues does there emerge a distinction between the two elements in the 'reason for B,' namely, the antecedent fact or facts, A, and the implication of B in A (if A, then B). Thus the transition from informal to formal inference is a process of analysis: it makes explicit, at once in consciousness and in language, the different elements of thought that were present from the first moment. For when B simply is asserted, it is asserted not as an experience but as a conclusion; else a question would not elicit the answer, B because of A. Again, when this answer is given, there would be no meaning to the 'because' if all that was meant was a further assertion, A. On the contrary, the causal sentence (because A, therefore B) compresses into one the three sentences of the formal analysis (if A, then B; A; $\therefore B$).

No doubt these considerations throw some light both on the prevalence of enthymeme and on the awkwardness of a logical theory that overlooks the normal syntax of inference to design a Procrustean bed with predication. But at any rate it is from the syntactical forms that the logician derives his simple hypothetical argument. This is of the type

If A, then B

But A

$\therefore B$.

Its indefinite flexibility is apparent: A and B each stand for one or two or any number of propositions; the propositions may be categorical, disjunctive, or hypothetical; and there is no reason why any of them should be forced into the mold of subject, copula, and predicate. No less apparent is the radical simplicity of this type. Every inference is the implication of a conclusion in a premise or in premises: the conclusion is B; the premise or premises are A; the implication is, if A, then B. Thus a study of language has given us a working hypothesis: the form of inference is the simple hypothetical argument.

2   Symbolism and Illative Sense in Relation to Inference

2.1 Symbolism

What language suggests, symbolism[e] confirms. For if one analyzes a symbolism, one finds two distinct elements. First there is abbreviation: eight hundred and thirty-seven reduces to 837, a paragraph is compressed into the equation, sin $i = m$.sin r, and at least a page into any expression involving the nabla operator. But symbolism is much more than abbreviation. Of the millions who would have no difficulty in finding the square root of 1764,[f] not a few would be at a loss if required to use roman numerals in performing the same operation. Why? Not because 1764 is shorter than MDCCLXIV, but because they work by rule of thumb and have never grasped the algebraic theorems underlying the rules of thumb. Their understanding has been short-circuited. Like adding machines which do not understand addition, like integrating machines which never were puzzled by the calculus, they have acquired through classroom drill not an intellectual insight into arithmetical operations but an ability to get answers.

Now these two elements in symbolism correspond to the two elements in the simple hypothetical argument. Because symbolism is abbreviation, it gives a terse expression to the minor premise, the data, A. But because it is more than abbreviation, because it involves pattern, association, convention, and rule of thumb, the symbolism expresses not only the minor premise, A, but also its implication, if A, then B. Indeed, only because machines and schoolboys possess the implications in automatic routines are they capable of obtaining right answers without understanding what they are doing. Nor is there any other explanation of the fact that the inventive mathematician, who is at once master and schoolboy, occasionally finds his symbolism taking the initiative and leading to theorems or methods that otherwise would not have occurred to him. Between the crucial experiments of these extremes, both of which are somewhat abnormal, there is the everyday function of symbolism, the function of reducing to a compact routine the use of multitudinous theorems which the mathematician has understood, which now he wishes to employ, but which he wishes to employ without retracing the countless steps that once for all were taken in the past.

2.2 The Illative Sense

A further point is to be made by adverting to the limitations of symbolism. The mathematician deals with ideal entities, with things that are exactly what he defines them to be; this makes it possible to abbreviate without falsifying. Again, the mathematician studies correlations that not only are universally valid but also are employed over and over again; this makes it worth while to reduce these correlations to habitual patterns of thought and to automatic routines of notation and operation. But at the opposite pole to such inquiry stands Newman's illative sense. Thus a general will estimate his own and the enemy's resources, opportunities, preparedness, methods, drive, staying power, to conclude principles of strategy, the merits of different dispositions of forces, the measure of success and the ulterior effects of given lines of action. In another field the diplomat studies persons, problems, movements to predict reactions

to given policies. In still another field the broker examines both general
trends and the actual position of, say, Broadcast Bounty, Inc.,^{g} to foresee
that Broadcast Bounty will rise. In such inferences the data are not ideal
but real; they are known not by the decision of a definition but only by
the intimate familiarity of longstanding experience; and so far are they
from admitting abbreviation of statement that they tend to be too multitudinous, too complex, too nuanced to be stated in any adequate fashion. Similarly, the implication of the conclusion in the data is not any
general principle or rule. It arises from the intuition of the moment; its
ground is the objective configuration of the moment as interpreted through
the accumulated insights of experienced judgment; its value is just the
value of that judgment; its only court of appeal is the event, and when
the event has come then, except on a theory of identical historical cycles,
its day of usefulness is over forever. To attempt to apply symbolism to
such inferences would be to misunderstand symbolism. The data can
hardly be stated, much less abbreviated. The implication is not a general
correlation to be employed repeatedly but the unique coincidence of a
complex objective configuration and a complex subjective interpretation
and judgment.

But however vast the interval that separates mathematical and concrete
inference, both have a common form. Both proceed from data through
implication to conclusion; and so both are of the type

If A, then B

But A

$\therefore B$.

It may be that only the conclusion, B, can be stated in a concrete inference. But this does not prove that there are no data, A, or no implication,
if A, then B. Again, such conclusions are usually probable and only in
limiting cases certain; but this is irrelevant to formal logic, for the form
of the inference is exactly the same whether one diffidently concludes,
'probably B,' or downrightly asserts, 'certainly B.' On the other hand,
the mathematician regularly states his data, A, and with equal regularity
omits the implication, if A, then B. Still, the implication is an essential
moment in his thought or in the routines of his symbolism, nor does it
make the slightest difference whether the implication be obvious, as in
the step

$A = B$

$B = C$

$\therefore A = C$

or not so obvious, as in the stride

$$y = \sin t$$
$$x = \cos t$$
$$\therefore dy/dx = -\cot t.$$

For the function of formal logic is not to make explicit the elements of thought that are not obvious to everyone; its function is to make explicit all the essential elements whether they are obvious or not.

3   Comparisons (1): With Nonsyllogistic Types

If the simple hypothetical argument appears a plausible form of inference from the syntax of language, the significance of symbolism, and the structure of Newman's illative sense, it still has to undergo comparison with the other formally valid types recognized in manuals on logic. Deferring syllogism to the next section, we here examine the *modus tollens* of the simple hypothetical argument, the dilemma, the disjunctive argument, the compound hypothetical argument, and the hypothetical sorites.

From the hypothetical premise, if A, then B, one can always draw two and sometimes draw four conclusions. Always, if one affirms A in the minor, one can affirm B in the conclusion. Always, if one denies B in the minor, one can deny A in the conclusion. Sometimes one can deny A or affirm B in the minor and so deny B or affirm A in the conclusion. This last case arises when A is the unique ground of B: thus all organisms and only organisms are mortal; hence, if the major premise is

If X is an organism, X is mortal

one can argue that a stone is not an organism and so a stone is not mortal, or again that men are mortal and so men must be organisms. However, in the general case, the antecedent, A, is not the unique ground of the consequent, B, but only one of many possible grounds; if Fido were a man, he would be mortal; Fido is mortal and yet not a man. Hence, in the general case, it is invalid to argue through a denial of the antecedent or an affirmation of the consequent. On the other hand, 'if A, then B' always implies 'if not B, then not A,' because the absence of B proves the absence of all grounds of B; hence it is always valid to argue through a negation of the consequent to a negation of the antecedent. Thus the very justification of the *modus tollens* reveals it to be an implicit form of the *modus ponens*. One can argue

If A, then B

Not B

$\therefore$ Not A

not because of a special form of inference but because the explicit major implies the major of the *modus ponens*, because 'if *A*, then *B*' necessarily implies 'if not *B*, then not *A*.'

The disjunctive argument yields to analysis in similar fashion. For the disjunctive premise

Either *A* or *B* or *C* or *D* or ...

is ambiguous. It may have only the minimal meaning that at least one of the alternatives is true, that is,

A, if neither *B* nor *C* nor *D* nor ...

B, if neither *A* nor *C* nor *D* nor ...

Etc.

But it may also mean that the truth of any alternative is incompatible with the truth of any of the others, and that gives the additional bases of argument

If *A*, then neither *B* nor *C* nor *D* nor ...

If *B*, then neither *A* nor *C* nor *D* nor ...

Etc.

If follows that the *modus tollendo ponens* is always valid, that the *modus ponendo ponens* is sometimes valid, and that in either mood the real argument is in virtue of an implicit premise and so in the *modus ponens* of the simple hypothetical argument.

Perhaps it will suffice to deal only with the most symmetrical forms of the dilemma, trilemma, tetralemma, etc. These employ a series of hypothetical propositions to proceed from one disjunction to another; thus from the major

If *A*, then *P*; if *B*, then *Q*; if *C*, then *R* ...

one may argue constructively by adding

Either *A* or *B* or *C* ...

∴ Either *P* or *Q* or *R* ...

or destructively by adding

Neither *P* nor *Q* nor *R* ...

∴ Neither *A* nor *B* nor *C* ...

In these instances it should seem that one has simply a combination of several simple hypothetical arguments and so no solid reason for affirming a distinct form of inference.

The compound hypothetical argument is a particular case of the hypothetical sorites; the type is

If *A*, *B*; if *B*, *C*; if *C*, *D*; if *D*, *E*; ∴ if *A*, *E*

where the premises may be any number greater than one. Illustrations of such argumentation abound in mathematics, in which the data, *A*, are transformed to B, C, D, and finally E which is the solution; and, as anyone familiar with mathematics is aware, much more complex patterns than the single track of the sorites are common. But the question arises, Are we to suppose an implicit premise

If 'if A, B; if B, C; if C, D; if D, E,' then 'if A, E'

and so reduce the sorites to the simple hypothetical argument, or should one say that sorites by itself expresses the whole process of thought? We think the former alternative preferable: the implication of the conclusion in the premises is distinct from the set of implications that constitute the premises, as may be made evident by constructing a fallacious sorites; the function of formal logic is to make explicit all the elements of thought essential to the conclusion, and therefore even the awkward implicit premise stated above.

4   Comparisons (2): With Syllogism

4.1 Denotational Interpretation of Syllogism

Syllogism is open to different interpretations. Thus we have Euler's circles in vivid illustration of the view that syllogism concludes in virtue of the coincidence or noncoincidence of the denotations of its terms. Only on such a view can one have the conversion of propositions, rules regarding distribution, the argument showing that there are nineteen and only nineteen valid moods, and the reduction of the imperfect figures by means of converting propositions or of substituting contradictory premises. Hence, if arguments from denotational coincidence never occur elsewhere, at least they occur in books on logic. What then is the form of such inference?

It seems to be enthymematic. No one can consistently advance that the argument

$A = B$
$B = C$
$\therefore A = C$

is an enthymeme which fails to express a factor in the mental procedure, while the argument from denotational coincidence

All S is some M
All M is some P
$\therefore$ All S is some P

is not an enthymeme but formally complete. It should seem evident that both arguments suppress the statement of the implication and, indeed, that the implication is less obvious in the denotational coincidence or noncoincidence than in the geometrical argument.

4.2 Connotational Interpretation of Syllogism

On a second possible interpretation of syllogism, the denotations of the terms are considered quite irrelevant. The inference arises from the connotational relations between a middle, M, and a predicate, P. Thus either M implies P, or M excludes P, or P implies M, or P excludes M. If these four cases are combined with the merely material fact that the subject, S, may be distributed or undistributed, there result the eight direct moods of the first two figures of syllogism. When M implies P, the mood is Barbara or Darii; when M excludes P, it is Celarent or Ferio; when P implies M, it is Camestres or Baroco; when P excludes M, it is Cesare or Festino.

However, this connotational interpretation, no less than the denotational, leads to the hypothetical argument as the form of inference. In the first place, a purely connotational relation between M and P cannot be expressed in the categorical propositions, all M is P, no M is P, all P is M, no P is M, for the subject of a proposition is meant materially or in denotation and not formally or in connotation. The same point may be put differently by asking the logician, 'If when you say that all organisms are mortal, you do not mean to speak of "all organisms" but of the nature of "organism," then why on earth do you say "all organisms"?' To that query I have never heard a sensible answer, and on the present hypothesis of connotational interpretation there is no answer possible. Thus one is forced to replace Barbara and Darii by

If S is M, S must be P; S is M; $\therefore$ S is P

If our enemies are men, they must be mortal; they are men; therefore they must be mortal

If some capitalists are fraudulent, they ought to be punished; some are fraudulent; they ought to be punished

Celarent and Ferio by

If S is M, S cannot be P; S is M; $\therefore$ S is not P

If angels are pure spirits, they cannot have bodies; angels are pure spirits; they cannot have bodies

If some employers demand evil, they are not to be served; some do; therefore some are not to be served

Camestres and Baroco by the *modus tollens*

> If *S* were *P*, it would be *M*; *S* is not *M*; ∴ *S* is not P
>
> If John had a vote, he would be twenty-one; but he is not twenty-one; therefore he has no vote
>
> If all guests were to enter, they all would have tickets; but not all have tickets; so not all are to enter

or by the *modus ponens*

> If *S* is not *M*, it is not *P*; *S* is not *M*; ∴ it is not *P*
>
> If John is not twenty-one, he has no vote; etc.
>
> If not all guests have tickets, not all are to enter; etc.

Cesare and Festino by the *modus tollens*

> If *S* were *P*, *S* would not be *M*; *S* is *M*; ∴ *S* is not *P*
>
> If hydrogen were a compound, it would not be an element; but it is an element; so it is not a compound
>
> If all aquatic animals were fish, none would be mammals; but some are mammals; so not all are fish

or by the *modus ponens*

> If *S* is *M*, *S* is not *P*; *S* is *M*; ∴ *S* is not *P*
>
> If hydrogen is an element, it is not a compound; etc.
>
> If some aquatic animals are mammals, they are not fish; etc.

Now the foregoing reduction is not merely a *tour de force* in the interests of a theory on the form of inference. If a connotational interpretation of the first two figures of syllogism is possible at any time and sometimes actually occurs, then it has to be expressed in the hypothetical form for the very good reason that categorical expression would be saying what is not meant; there is no reason why so daintily precise a person as a logician should speak of 'all men' and 'all frauds' and 'all voters' when he is thinking of the connotational aspect of humanity, fraudulence, and the right to vote. Further, the reduction to hypothetical form reveals the exact significance of the reduction from second-figure to first-figure syllogisms. A glance at the examples given above will show that Cesare and Festino in the *modus ponens* are identical with Celarent and Ferio; thus these instances of syllogistic reduction are really a transition from the *modus tollens* to the *modus ponens*; and such reduction is easy because, if *P* excludes *M*, as in Cesare and Festino, then *M* must exclude *P*, as in Celarent and Ferio. In other words, connotational incompatibility is a mutual relation. On the other hand, if one wishes to substitute the direct movement of thought from *S* through *M* to *P* for the roundabout movement from *S* to *P* through *M* back to *P* in the moods Camestres and Baroco, then the substitution of a *modus ponens* for a *modus tollens* is perfectly simple, while a syllogistic reduction is an almost incredible feat of denotational acrobatics. The reason for this is plain from the more ultimate reduction to hypothetical form, for that reduction reveals that there is no first-figure mood identical with the *modus ponens* of Camestres and Baroco; if P implies M, then it does not follow that M implies P, while it is false that M excludes P; what does follow is that not-M implies not-P, which denotationally is the acrobatic contrapositive but hypothetically the quite obvious and natural premise, if S is not M, S is not P.

4.3 A Third Interpretation of Syllogism

A third interpretation of syllogism is partly connotational and partly denotational. The classic formula of this view is the *dictum de omni et nullo*, namely, that what is true of a class of objects is true of all the members of that class. Here both the subject, S, and the middle, M, are taken in denotation while the predicate, P, is connotational. This seems to provide the most natural interpretation of third-figure syllogisms, for, as Professor Joseph has observed, the third figure is an appeal to an instance in refutation of a hasty generalization. Thus when the revolutionary calls for the confiscation of all property, the heckler asks, 'What about savings?' The argument is in Felapton
> No savings are to be confiscated
> All savings are property
> ∴ Some property is not to be confiscated.

But really one may doubt that the argument is as described; for if it is true that the subject of a proposition is to be taken denotationally and the predicate connotationally, then the above syllogistic expression implies that the subject of the argument, property, is at once both connotational and denotational. It should seem much more plausible that the expression is mistaken than that the thought is confused, and so again we are led to the hypothetical form
> If all property is to be confiscated, then savings are
> But savings are not to be confiscated
> ∴ Not all property is to be confiscated.

The hypothetical major gives the implication of the revolutionary thesis; the minor premise gives the bourgeois antithesis; and the conclusion gives the bourgeois answer. I submit that that is the real process of thought, and anyone caring to make the induction will find that arguments in Felapton, Ferison, and Bocardo are expressed unambiguously and naturally by the *modus tollens*

> If S were P, M would be P; M is not P; $\therefore$ S is not P
>
> If all domestic animals had horns, cats would have horns; but cats have no horns; so not all domestic animals have horns (Ferison)
>
> If all ruminants had horns, all goats would have horns; but some goats have no horns; etc. (Bocardo)

while Darapti, Disamis, Datisi are in the *modus tollens*

> If S were P, M would not be P; M is P; $\therefore$ S is not P
>
> If no woman could be a statesman, Maria Theresa was not; but she was; so a woman can be a statesman (Darapti)
>
> If no quadrupeds had horns, no goats would have them; some have; etc. (Disamis)
>
> If no revolutionary is intelligent, no communist is intelligent; but some communists are intelligent; therefore some revolutionaries are (Datisi).

It will be objected that the hypothetical form is longer than the syllogistic. But this objection merely confirms our position, for in actual thinking these arguments are always enthymemes, and what is omitted is the hypothetical major premise; such omission is natural, since 'because A, therefore B' is equivalent to the formally complete 'if A, then B; but A; therefore B'; on the other hand, the exponents of categorical syllogism have still to explain why at least one of their premises is always omitted in actual thinking.

The forms we have given for the third figure are in the *modus tollens*; if they are reduced to the *modus ponens*, there result arguments in the first figure as interpreted by the *dictum de omni et nullo*. This is not equivalent to the connotational interpretation of the first figure, which makes the middle term, M, not a class of objects but an attribute or meaning. However, in all cases except the moods Bocardo and Disamis (in which M neither implies nor excludes P), it is possible to rethink the argument from denotational coincidence to connotational implication. Thus one can conceive 'savings' as an attribute of some property and as excluding the further attribute 'deserving of confiscation.' This rethinking will give as *modus ponens*

> If some property is savings, it is not to be confiscated ...

instead of giving through the *dictum de omni et nullo*

> If savings are not to be confiscated, some property is not ...

The difference between the two is obvious. The latter is an argument from denotational coincidence; the former is what Aristotle calls scientific thinking, in which the middle term is the *causa essendi* of the predicate: savings precludes confiscation; the argument turns on the meaning of terms and not on their denotation. Such rethinking of the third-figure moods is possible even when the middle term is an individual; thus the appeal to the instance in

If a pious man is a sissy, Jogues was a sissy ...

becomes scientific in the form

If a pious man is a Jogues, he is not a sissy ...

This, I submit, reveals a rather obvious difference between the *Posterior Analytics* and the pseudoclassical *dictum de omni et nullo*. But the revelation comes through the form we have found in all inference, the hypothetical argument.

So much for syllogism. Three distinct interpretations of it have been considered, and all have led away from syllogism to the hypothetical form. There are other interpretations of minor importance, such as the view that syllogistic inference is a matter of second intentions, with S a logical part of M and M a logical part of P, so that S must be a logical part of P, as is evident from Porphyry's tree. No doubt one can perform an inference in this or in various other fashions if one makes up one's mind to do so. But the mere existence of so many different interpretations of syllogistic thought is proof that the mind really is proceeding in virtue of some more general and ultimate law that can be given a variety of less general interpretations.

Conclusion

To conclude, our aim has been an empirical investigation of the nature of inference. Just as the physicist working out a theory of light will not repeat the established experiments on reflection, refraction, color, interference, spectral lines and the like, but rather will accept the results of such prior investigations in an effort to discover their ultimate unity, so too we have taken as our empirical basis not particular instances of inference but generally recognized types, and from them as starting point we have worked to the ultimate unity of the simple hypothetical argument. Thus our conclusion has to do with the nature of the human mind. We have not sought the reduction of one inferential type to another because we thought one more valid or more obviously valid than the other. On the contrary, we assumed all to be valid, and our concern with reduction has been a concern with the one law or form of all inference.

We have not considered inductive conclusions.[h] To correlate the movement from data through hypothesis to verified theory with the movement from implier through implication to implied, and both of these with the more ultimate process from sensa[i] through intellection to judgment, is indeed a legitimate inquiry; but it is more general than the present and presupposes it. For the same reason we have not aimed at explaining inference but rather at finding the highest common factor of inferences no matter how they are explained. Indeed, it is precisely in our attitude towards the explanation of inference that we differ from the approach of the more traditional manuals on logic; the latter presupposes an explanation of conceptualization and of inference; we on the contrary have aimed at taking a first step in working out an empirical theory of human understanding and knowledge.[j]

2

Finality, Love, Marriage

In the recent fermentation of Catholic thought on the meaning and ends of marriage,[1] the basic component of novelty would seem to be a development in biological science. Quite other factors, no doubt, account for the intense and widespread interest aroused; but the ground of the intellectual problem must be placed, I think, in a new scientific insight. To this Dr H. Doms has given full prominence, and I cannot but agree that, if Aristotelian biology was aware of a distinction between fecundity and sex, it did not admit any systematic elaboration and application of that distinction.[2] On the other hand, modern biology makes such elaboration and application inevitable. There results more than a suggestion that, as fecundity is for offspring, so sex has a personalist finality of its own.

To Dr Doms this implies that the theologian is confronted with the

1 For a bibliography, see J.C. Ford, s.j., 'Marriage: Its Meaning and Purposes,' *Theological Studies* 3 (1942) 333–34.
2 Dr Herbert Doms, *Du sens et de la fin du mariage* (Paris: Desclée de Brouwer, 1937) esp. 72–76; 'Amorces d'une conception personnaliste du mariage,' *Revue thomiste* 45 (1939) 755–57; for Aristotelian biology, Doms refers to Albert Mitterer, 'Mann und Weib nach dem biologischen Weltbild des hl. Thomas und dem der Gegenwart,' *Zeitschrift für katholische Theologie* 57 (1933) 492–98. [Doms' book was written in German, *Vom Sinn und Zweck der Ehe* (Breslau: Ostdeutsche Verlagsanstalt, 1935); an English translation appeared in 1939, *The Meaning of Marriage* (New York: Sheed and Ward). Lonergan's references are to the French translation.]

task of thinking out afresh the theory of marriage.[3] Now if one cannot avoid suspicion of new beginnings, at least one can agree with Fr Ford[a] in desiring the assimilation of new insights into the traditional theoretical framework.[4] However, Fr Ford's own discussion of 'Marriage: Its Meaning and Purposes,' though notably constructive, was more positive and doctrinal than analytic and explanatory; and if the former approach is more important to us as Catholics, it is the latter that is more relevant to the solution of problems. Nonetheless, it remains a large and long task, in which it is convenient to distinguish two stages: first, a preliminary general outline of a modified theoretical position; second, the systematic elaboration of definitions, theses, proofs, that normally is the cumulative product of a succession of professorial notes and handbooks.

The present paper is concerned with a preliminary speculative outline; it aims at no more than a brusque occupation of strategic theoretical points on finality, on love, and on marriage. On finality is affirmed, besides the absolute reference of all things to God and the horizontal reference of each thing to its commensurate motives and ends, a vertical dynamism and tendency, an upthrust from lower to higher levels of appetition and process; thus are provided the empty categories of the ultimate solution, since horizontal ends are shown to be more essential and vertical ends more excellent. Next, an account of the nature of love is attempted, and this opens the way for a discussion of the 'primary reason and cause of marriage' mentioned in the papal encyclical, *Casti connubii*.[5] Here the argument draws upon Aristotle's classic on friendship and Aquinas' transposition of Aristotelian analysis,[6] and it endeavors to formulate an ascent of love from the level of two-in-one-flesh[7] to the level of the beatific vision. Finally, there emerges the problem of inserting

3 Doms, 'Amorces ... ' esp. 754, 762–63.
4 Ford, 'Marriage ... ' 373–74.
5 Pope Pius XI, *Acta Apostolicae Sedis* 22 (1930) 548; or see Henricus Denzinger, *Enchiridion symbolorum definitionum et declarationum de rebus fidei et morum*, 2232. [In the revised edition by Adolfus Schönmetzer (Freiburg im Breisgau: Herder, 1965) 3707; the Schönmetzer edition henceforth will be referred to as DS.]
6 So manifold is the dependence of Aquinas that an understanding of the *Summa theologiae* on charity (2–2, qq. 23–27) is attained most easily by reading first the eighth and ninth books of the *Ethics*.
7 Dr Doms' *Zweieinigkeit* is, of course, scriptural: Genesis 2.24; Matthew 19.5,6; Ephesians 5.31; 1 Corinthians 6.16. Aristotle appears to have coined the somewhat similar adjective, *syndyastic*, 'two-together-ative.' *Ethics*, VIII, 12, 1162a 17; see the praise of *erôs* in Plato, *Symposium*, 189c–193d.

the vertical tendency of love from sex to divine charity into the horizontal process from fecundity to offspring; and such insertion has to be made on the background of the general field of human process. For it is only in the cosmic breadth of a simultaneous context of nature, history, and grace, that appear at once the justice and the assimilative capacity of the, on the whole, traditional view that the most essential end of marriage is the procreation and education of offspring but its most excellent end lies on the supernatural level of personalist development.

1   Vertical Finality

The common instances of finality fall into two classes: the response of appetites to motives, and the orientation of processes to terms. But if we are to formulate the notion of vertical finality,[b] it is extremely important to break away from instances and to conceive things generally. First, then, the mere fact of response or of orientation does not constitute finality. Any positivist will admit that appetites do respond to motives, that processes are orientated to terms. Quite coherently, any positivist will deny final causality since, beyond such concomitance and correlation, causality requires that appetite respond because of motive, that process be orientated because of term. Moreover, causality is not yet final causality. If appetite responds because motive moves, if process is orientated because an intelligent agent envisages and intends a term, there is causality indeed; but it is efficient and not final. No doubt, in the concrete, such efficiency is connected intimately with finality. But rigorously one must maintain that there is final causality if, and only if, appetite responds because the motive is good; if, and only if, process is orientated because the term is good.

For the final cause is the *cuius gratia*, and its specific or formal constituent is the good as cause. Under this formal constituent may be had either of two material differences: the good may be cause as motive for the response of appetite or as term for the orientation of process. But with regard to the formal constituent itself, it is necessary to distinguish between *qui* and *quo*, between the good thing which is motive or term and the mode of motivation or termination. Now in our hierarchic universe God is at once absolute motive and absolute term: 'omnia appetunt Deum';[8] 'omnia intendunt assimilari Deo.'[9] On the other hand, the mode

8 Thomas Aquinas, *De veritate*, q. 22, a. 2.
9 Thomas Aquinas, *Summa contra Gentiles*, 3, c. 19.

in which the different grades of being respond to God as motive or attain him as term is always limited; this remains true even in the beatific vision, in which the infinite as motive is apprehended finitely and as term is attained finitely.[10] Further, the ground of such limitation is essence: remotely it is substantial essence; proximately it is the essence of an ontological accident, the essence, say, of sensitive appetite, of rational appetite, of infused charity; for it is essence that limits, that ties things down to a given grade of being, that makes them respond to motives of a given type, that assigns them their proper and proportionate ends. Finally, there are many grades of being, each with its defining essence and its consequent and commensurate mode of appetition and process; accordingly, one has to think of the universe as a series of horizontal strata; on each level reality responds to God as absolute motive and tends to him as absolute term; but on each level it does so differently, for the limitation of essence reappears in the limitation of the mode of appetition and response, of process and orientation.

Thus the application to the hierarchic universe of the notional distinction between *finis qui* and *finis quo*[d] has given two distinct types of finality: the absolute finality of all things to God in his intrinsic goodness;[11] the horizontal finality of limiting essence to limited mode of appetition and of process. But now attention must be drawn to a third type of finality, that of any lower level of appetition and process to any higher level. This we term vertical finality. It has four manifestations: instrumental, dispositive, material, obediential. First, a concrete plurality of lower activities may be instrumental to a higher end in another subject: the many movements of the chisel give the beauty of the statue. Second, a concrete plurality of lower activities may be dispositive to a higher end in the same subject: the many sensitive experiences of research lead to the act of understanding that is scientific discovery. Third, a concrete plurality of lower entities may be the material cause from which a higher form is educed or into which a subsistent form is infused: examples are familiar. Fourth, a concrete plurality of rational beings have the obediential potency to receive the communication of God himself: such is

10 ' ... actu aliquo finito infinitum ad modum infiniti finito modo videtur.' Henricus Lennerz,[c] *De Deo uno* (Rome: Gregorian University Press, 1931), §184, p. 131.
11 See the two articles by Philip J. Donnelly, s.j., 'Saint Thomas and the Ultimate Purpose of Creation,' *Theological Studies* 2 (1941) 53–83; and 'The Vatican Council and the End of Creation,' *Theological Studies* 4 (1943) 3–33.

the mystical body of Christ with its head in the hypostatic union, its principal unfolding in the inhabitation of the Holy Spirit by sanctifying grace, and its ultimate consummation in the beatific vision which Aquinas explained on the analogy of the union of soul and body.[12]

If the existence of such vertical finality has always been recognized,[13] its ground and nature have hardly been studied. Partly this neglect may be explained by an unduly apologetic conception of *finis operis*; for if one defines *finis operis* as resulting from the abstract nature of the thing, then necessarily one restricts finality to horizontal finality, absolute finality becomes a difficulty, and vertical finality subjectively inconceivable. But not only is such a restriction arbitrary; it cannot claim even the sanction of tradition, which defines *finis operis* not in terms of abstract nature but as *hoc ad quod opus ordinatum est ab agente*.[14] However, a perhaps stronger reason for the neglect of vertical finality lies in the fact that modern science throws a great deal of light on its nature. Straightforward metaphysics suffices for a knowledge of absolute and of horizontal finality: the former results from the idea of an absolute good; the latter results from the theorem of essence as principle of limitation. But vertical finality seems to operate through the fertility of concrete plurality.[15] Just as the real object tends to God as real motive and real term, just as the essence of the real object limits the mode of appetition and of process, so a concrete plurality of essences has an upthrust from lower to higher levels. But just as this fact is shrouded in the mists of Aristotelian science[e] – and here we generalize Dr Doms' complaint against Aristotelian biology – so it is most conspicuous to one who looks at the universe with the eyes of modern science, who sees subatoms uniting into atoms, atoms

12 Thomas Aquinas, *Super IV Sententiarum*, 4, d. 49, q. 2, a. 1; *Summa contra Gentiles*, 3, c. 51.
13 For example, Genesis 1.29–30; Thomas Aquinas, *Summa contra Gentiles*, 3, c. 22, 'In actibus autem ... '
14 For example, Thomas Aquinas, *Super II Sententiarum*, d. 1, q. 2, a. 1 c.
15 The *per se* results from the essence of either ontological substance or ontological accident; it remains that the *per accidens* results from the interplay of a plurality of essences. Such interplay as interference is prominent in Aristotelian and Thomist thought, as previously I had occasion to point out (*Theological Studies* 3 [1942] 387–91); but besides interfering, different essences may complement one another; it is the latter possibility that is the ultimate root of vertical finality. [The section referred to is entitled 'The Essence of the Idea of Application'; see *Grace and Freedom: Operative Grace in the Thought of St. Thomas Aquinas*, ed. J. Patout Burns (London: Darton, Longman & Todd, and New York: Herder and Herder, 1971) 76–80 (CWL 1).]

into compounds, compounds into organisms, who finds the pattern of genes in reproductive cells shifting, *ut in minori parte*,[16] to give organic evolution within limited ranges,[f] who attributes the rise of cultures and civilizations to the interplay of human plurality, who observes that only when and where the higher rational culture emerged did God acknowledge the fulness of time permitting the Word to become flesh and the mystical body to begin its intussusception of human personalities and its leavening of human history.

The difference of vertical from absolute and from horizontal finality is quite clear. Absolute finality is to God in his intrinsic goodness: it is universal; it is unique; it is hypothetically necessary, for if there is anything to respond to motive or to proceed to term, then its response or tendency can be accounted for ultimately only by the one self-sufficient good.[17] Horizontal finality results from abstract essence; it holds even when the object is in isolation; it is to a motive or term that is proportionate to essence. But vertical finality is in the concrete; in point of fact it is not from the isolated instance but from the conjoined plurality; and it is in the field not of natural but of statistical law, not of the abstract *per se* but of the concrete *per accidens*. Still, though accidental to the isolated object or the abstract essence, vertical finality is of the very idea of our hierarchic universe, of the ordination of things devised and exploited by the divine Artisan. For the cosmos is not an aggregate of isolated objects hierarchically arranged on isolated levels, but a dynamic whole in which instrumentally, dispositively, materially, obedientially,[g] one level of being or activity subserves another. The interconnections are endless and manifest. Vertical finality would seem beyond dispute.

But if one acknowledges that the same thing, besides its absolute reference to God, may have one finality horizontally and another vertically, there arises the question of systematic comparison between the latter two types of end. First, then, a horizontal end is more essential than a vertical end: for the horizontal end is the end determined by the essence of the thing, while the vertical end is had only by escaping the limitation of isolated essence through the fertility of concrete plurality. On the other hand, a vertical end is more excellent than a horizontal end: for

16 There is a noteworthy affinity between modern statistical law and the *contingens ut in maiori parte*, between modern 'chance variation' and the *contingens ut in minori parte*.

17 See James E. O'Mahony, *The Desire of God in the Philosophy of St. Thomas Aquinas* (Cork: Cork University Press, 1929) 159–61.

the horizontal end is on the lower level of being but the vertical on some higher level; and from the very concept of hierarchy the higher is the more excellent. Inversely, one cannot say that the vertical end is nonessential or that the horizontal end is not excellent. For the vertical end, though it escapes the limitation of isolated essence and its abstract *per se*, nonetheless results from the same essence when in concrete combination with other essence. Again, though the vertical end is more excellent, still it is so only relatively; all finality is ultimately to the absolute good, and all is limited in mode of appetition or of process, so that the difference in excellence between higher and lower is never more than a difference in mode with respect to the absolute good.

With perfect generality this establishes hierarchic criteria of more essential and more excellent ends. Universally, the horizontal end is more essential, the vertical end is more excellent. Thus the essential end of oxygen is to perform the offices of oxygen as oxygen; but its more excellent end is its contribution to the maintenance of human life, and this end oxygen attains not in isolation nor *per se* but in combination with other elements and within the human biological process. Similarly, we have to establish the contention of Aquinas that the most essential good of marriage is the child but its most excellent end lies on the supernatural level.[18]

2   The Concept of Love

2.1 Four Aspects

The difficulty of conceiving love[h] adequately arises from its essential concreteness and from the complexity of the concrete.[i] Even on a preliminary analysis there are at least four simultaneous aspects. For any activity is at once the act of a faculty[j] and the act of a subject. As act of a faculty (*principium quo*) love is, in the first instance, the basic form of appetition: it is the pure response of appetite to the good, *nihil aliud ... quam complacentia boni*,[19] while desire, hope, joy, hatred, aversion, fear,

---

18 ' ... proles est essentialissimum in matrimonio, et secundo fides, et tertio sacramentum' (*Super IV Sententiarum*, d. 31, q. 1, a. 3 = *Supplementum*, q. 49, a. 3 c.). ' ... primus finis respondet matrimonio hominis, inquantum est animal; secundus, inquantum est homo; tertius, inquantum est fidelis' (ibid. d. 33, q. 1, a. 1 = *Supplementum*, q. 65. a. 1).

19 Thomas Aquinas, *Summa theologiae*, 1–2, q. 25, a. 2 c.

sadness are consequents of the basic response and reflect objective modifications in the circumstances of the motive good.[20] But again, as act of a faculty, love, besides being the basic form of appetition, is also the first principle of process to the end loved,[21] and the whole of the process is thus but the self-expression of the love that is its first principle. Further, love is the act of a subject (*principium quod*), and as such it is the principle of union between different subjects. Such union is of two kinds, according as it emerges in love as process to an end or in love in the consummation of the end attained. The former may be illustrated by the love of friends pursuing in common a common goal. The latter has its simplest illustration in the ultimate end of the beatific vision, which at once is the term of process, of *amor concupiscentiae*, and the fulfilment of union with God, of *amor amicitiae*.[22]

2.2 Tensions and Contradictions

So much for a general scheme: love is the basic form of appetition; it is the first principle of process; it is a ground of union of different subjects both in their process to a common end and in the consummation of the end attained. But besides this multiplicity of aspects, to be verified in any instance of love, there also is a multiplicity of appetites and of loves generating within a single subject tensions and even contradictions. Inevitably, such objective tensions obscure the nature of love, and a clarification is our next task. For there seems to be some confusion as to the meaning of the tag, *appetitus tendit in bonum sibi conveniens*. This, I think, means no more than the specialization of appetite: there are many appetites, but not any one responds to any motive; each has its proper object, to which it is specially fitted, and to that alone does it respond. Certainly, I cannot grant that the tag contains some facile and obscure metaphysic of selfishness. For appetite as appetite is indifferently egoistic or altruistic: my hunger is for my good; but maternal instinct is for the good of the child; and rational appetite, with the specialized object of the reasonable good, moves on an absolute level to descend in favor of self or of others as reason dictates. Just as food suits hunger,

20 Ibid. q. 25, aa. 1, 2; q. 27, a. 4; q. 28, a. 6.
21 '... principium motus tendentis in finem amatum' (ibid. q. 26, a. 1).
22 The terms, *amor concupiscentiae, amor amicitiae*, vary somewhat in connotation in St Thomas; contrast: *Summa theologiae*, 1–2, q. 26, a. 4 c. & ad 1m; q. 27, a. 3 c.; q. 28, a. 2 c.; 2–2, q. 23, a. 1 (Aristotle, *Ethics*, VIII, 2, 1156a 4).

just as care of her child suits a mother, so the reasonable good suits rational appetite; on the other hand, being unreasonable is what suits mistaken self-love.

2.3 Friendship

This contention is fundamental, but it is not new. As Aristotle saw with remarkable clarity and set forth in a famous chapter of his *Ethics*, the opposition is not between egoism and altruism but between virtue and vice. The wicked are true friends neither to themselves nor to others.[23] On the other hand, a wise and thorough egoist will take to himself what is best; but that is knowledge and virtue; and as he attains these, he becomes the opposite of what is meant by a selfish man. Thus only by being a true friend to oneself can one be a decent friend to others; and the value of one's friendship,[k] from any viewpoint, rises only with an increase in true friendship to oneself.[24] But what is true friendship? The question touches a methodological defect in Aristotle's thought. Intent on a practical goal, he defined virtue empirically and ruled out discussion of an absolute good. In this manner he excluded what really is the logical and the ontological first in his ethical theory: for it is only in a tendency to an absolute that one can transcend both egoism and altruism; and such transcendence is implicit in the Aristotelian notion of true friendship with its basis not in pleasure nor in advantage but in the objective lovableness of the virtuous man.[25] For objective lovableness involves an absolute good, and so what is implicit in Aristotle became explicit in Aquinas when he affirmed that man and, as well, all creatures according to their mode naturally love God above all things.[26] And, of course, this love of God above all is only a particular case of the general theorem that absolutely all finality is to God.

2.4 Selfishness

It remains that the true account of selfishness[l] be given, for it is necessary for an understanding of love and, still more, of the ascent of love. In beatitude, then, which is the ultimate consummation of love in union,

---

23 *Ethics*, VIII, 4, 1157a 16–19; IX, 4, 1166b 2–29; IX, 8, 1169a 12–15.
24 Ibid. IX, 8; see 4.
25 Ibid. VIII, 3–7; esp. 1156b 7–23.
26 *Summa theologiae*, 1–2, q. 109, a. 3 c.; *Quaestiones quodlibetales*, 1, a. 8 c. & ad 3m.

there is a simultaneous and full actuation of all potencies, but in the process to consummation the very multiplicity of appetites gives rise to an inner tension. In this tension the rational part of man is at a disadvantage,[27] for natural spontaneity takes care of itself while knowledge and virtue have to be acquired. Things were otherwise before the fall: then reason had its preternatural gifts and grace a full abundance, so that man's inner justice and rectitude were in a stable equilibrium, with reason totally subjected to God and lower appetites to reason.[28] Now it is the loss of this rectitude that underlies the familiar opposition between the idealism of human aspiration and the sorry facts of human performance.[m] 'The spirit indeed is willing but the flesh is weak' (Matthew 26.41). 'It is not what I wish that I do, but what I hate, that I do' (Romans 7.15). To quote the philosopher: 'Most men will what is noble but choose what is advantageous.'[29] To quote the theologian: 'Even without grace man naturally loves God above all things but, from the corruption of nature, rational will seeks self.'[30]

2.5 Dialectic

But the point to which we would particularly draw attention is the dialectical and social aspect of this tension[n] and opposition. For while it may happen that after each failure to carry out ideal aspiration man repents and reasserts the primacy of the ideal over the real, of what ought to be over what is, it may also happen that after repeated failure man begins to rationalize, to deform knowledge into harmony with disorderly loves. Such rationalization may involve any degree of culpability, from the maximum of a sin against the light which rejects known truth, to the minimum of precluding such futurible advance in knowledge and virtue as without even unconscious rationalization would have been achieved. Moreover, this deformation takes place not only in the individual but also and much more convincingly in the social conscience. For to the common mind of the community the facts of life are the poor perfor-

27 Thomas Aquinas, *Super I Sententiarum*, d. 39, q. 2, a. 2, ad 4m. This line of thought I developed in an earlier article in *Theological Studies* 3 (1942) 69–74. [The section referred to is entitled 'The General Nature of Habits'; see *Grace and Freedom* 41–46.]

28 Thomas Aquinas, *Summa theologiae*, 1, q. 95, a. 1.

29 Aristotle, *Ethics*, VIII, 13, 1162b 35.

30 Thomas Aquinas, *Summa theologiae*, 1–2. q. 109, a. 3 c. [The quotation here is *ad sensum*.]

mance of men in open contradiction with the idealism of human aspiration; and this antithesis between brutal fact and spiritual orientation leaves the will a choice in which truth seems burdened with the unreal and unpractical air of falsity. Thus it is that a succession of so-called bold spirits have only to affirm publicly a dialectical series of rationalizations gradually to undermine and eventually to destroy the spiritual capital of the community; thus also a culture or a civilization changes its color to the objectively organized lie of ideology in a trans-Marxian sense, and sin ascends its regal throne (Romans 5.21) in the Augustinian *civitas terrena*. To pierce the darkness of such ideology the divine Logos came into the world; to sap its root in weak human will he sent his Spirit of Love into our hearts; and in this redemption we are justified, rectified, renewed,[31] yet never in this life to the point that greater justification, rectification, renewal ceases to be possible.[32] Finally, just as there is a human solidarity in sin with a dialectical descent deforming knowledge and perverting will, so also there is a divine solidarity in grace which is the mystical body of Christ; as evil performance confirms us in evil, so good edifies us in our building unto eternal life; and as private rationalization finds support in fact, in common teaching, in public approval, so also the ascent of the soul towards God is not a merely private affair but rather a personal function of an objective common movement in that body of Christ which takes over, transforms, and elevates every aspect of human life.

3   The Primary Reason and Cause of Marriage

3.1   Casti connubii

It is in this complex field of human struggle that the encyclical *Casti connubii* places the primary reason and cause of marriage. It quotes the Roman Catechism to the effect that conjugal love is to be a pure and holy love, not such as the mutual love of adulterers, but such as the mutual love of Christ and his church. This divine charity, it asserts, is to be effective as well as affective, to be proved by deeds and, above all, by mutual support in a continuous development of the Pauline 'interior man,' so that through their life in common husband and wife progress

---

31 Ibid. q. 113; *De virtutibus in communi*, a. 10, ad 14m.
32 Denzinger, *Enchiridion symbolorum* ... 803 [DS 1535].

daily in virtue and most of all in charity towards God and their neighbor. As though anticipating the objection of the pseudorealist,° the encyclical goes on to insist that Christ our Lord is not only the complete model of sanctity but also a model set before all by God himself; that this model is to be imitated by all, no matter what their station or state of life; that, as the example of the saints confirms, all can and should strive with God's help to attain the very summit of Christian perfection. Finally, according to the encyclical, it is this mutual influence toward development, this sustained effort of common improvement, that rightly is acknowledged by the Roman Catechism as even the primary reason and cause of marriage; though in this context marriage is to be understood, not strictly as an institution for the proper rearing of children, but broadly as two lives at one till death, lived in intimacy, lived in pursuit of a common goal.[33]

3.2 Ascent from Nature to Beatific Vision

If I have paraphrased this passage fairly, I think there can be no doubt that the encyclical is speaking of a process of development through conjugal love to the very summit of Christian perfection. Now such a process cannot but be an end (*finis operis*) of Christian marriage. For if we prescind from the mind of God, then first there must be the objective ordination which is presupposed by the universal exhortation of the encyclical; second, there will be actual desire of attainment in some individuals; third, there will be some measure of actual attainment. Of these the first is *finis operis*, the second *finis operantis*, the third efficient causality. But what the encyclical is concerned to affirm is the first, the objective ordination, the duty of husband and wife to advance together in the spiritual life.[34] But how can this be so? How can a natural insti-

---

33 See note 5 supra.
34 Fr Ford ('Marriage ... ' 372) argued from the authority of Fr Hürth and from the explicit reference of the encyclical to the Roman Catechism that the intention of the encyclical was to speak not of an end (*finis operis*) but of a motive (*finis operantis*). Three questions may be distinguished: first, the mind and intention of theologians employed in the composition of the encyclical; second, the objective meaning of the document; third, the implication of the document. I am inclined to regard the first question as only remotely relevant. As to the second, neither the encyclical nor the catechism mentions any specific type of causality; they speak of reasons and causes; they do not state whether the causes are material,

tution have a supernatural end? The general answer lies in our already formulated category of vertical finality: all Christians are called to the imitation of Christ, to the summit of Christian perfection; but from marriage there is a dispositive upward tendency giving a new modality to that high pursuit, for husband and wife are called not only to advance but to advance together. Such is the generic answer. To make it specific one has to set the complex nature of love in the empty category of vertical finality; one has to study the ascent of love from the level of nature to the level of the beatific vision.

---

formal, efficient, or final; much less do they distinguish different kinds of final cause. As to the third, three types of implication may be distinguished, namely, formal, material, scientific. I have failed to discern in either document a formal implication of some specific type of causality; on the contrary, each is concerned with its essentially doctrinal function, and neither seems to have theoretical preoccupations or the intention of settling some speculative issue. On the other hand, there is, of course, material implication of specific types of causality, for the causes assigned must, as a matter of fact, belong to some specific type. Thus the beauty of the bride and the size of her dowry are motives (*Catechismus Romanus* [*Catechismus ex decreto Concilii Tridentini ad Parochos Pii v. Pontificis Max. et deinde Clementis* XIII. (4th ed., Rome: Sacred Congregation for the Propagation of the Faith, 1907)], II, viii, 14); the procreation of children intended by the Creator from the beginning is an end (ibid. 13); sexual impulse seems an efficient cause (ibid.); the hope of mutual aid is a motive (ibid.); the requirement that husband and wife be joined in a pure and holy love, such as Christ's for his church, is a precept presupposing an objective ordination and so a *finis operis* (ibid. 24). However, though such material implications exist, properly they do not pertain to the document but to a reader's use of philosophic categories in interpreting the document; and so to argue, in virtue of a parallelism, from the material implication of one document to the material implication of another seems remote enough to be doubtful. This doubt is confirmed by the fact that the encyclical begins by referring to q. 24 in the catechism and, without changing its topic, ends by referring to q. 13 [see *Acta Apostolicae Sedis* 22 (1930) 548]; but the former deals with a precept which presupposes an objective ordination and so an end, while the latter deals with a motive; such ambiguity of material implication, besides accounting for current difficulties of interpretation, also shows that the material implications lie outside the attention and intention of the document. Nor is it altogether irrelevant to recall both that the encyclical notably expands and develops the idea of the catechism and that its *primaria causa et ratio* is a much stronger phrase than the latter's *prima igitur est*. Finally, even if it were certain that the encyclical were speaking of a motive, there would remain the possibility of a scientific implication of an end. Such a deduction we make in the text.

On any level, then, love has a passive aspect (A) inasmuch as it is response to motive good, an immanent aspect (B) inasmuch as it is a perfection of the lover, and an active aspect (C) inasmuch as it is productive of further instances of the good. But on the level of reason there is superposed on each of these three aspects a fourth of reflection and freedom (D), inasmuch as rational love examines and selects its motives (A), deliberately wills its own immanent perfection (B), and freely proceeds to effect further instances of the good (C). Now in man this rational process is embedded in a field of natural spontaneity and infused virtue. On the level lower than reason, appetition, in its triple aspect of passivity, immanent perfection, and activity, is very obviously the work of God, who implants in nature its proper mode of response and orientation.[35] But on the level of reason itself, there is an antecedent spontaneity to truth and goodness through which God governs the self-government of man.[36] And on the highest level of grace, there is a heightening or elevating transformation of the rational level's antecedent spontaneity, so that the truth through which God rules man's autonomy is the truth God reveals beyond reason's reach, and the good which is motive is the divine goodness that is motive of infused charity.[37] Finally, these three levels are realized in one subject; as the higher perfects the lower, so the lower disposes to the higher; and it is in this disposition of natural spontaneity to reinforce reason, of reason to reinforce grace – for all three come from and return to God[38] – that is to be found the ascent of love that gives human marriage a finality on the level of Christian charity and perfection. Such is the thesis. We proceed to verify it, considering first love as passive; second, love as immanent; and third, love as active.

3.2.1 Ascent and the Passive Aspect of Love

In the first place, then, love is passive response (A) to motive good. But motive good is either God himself or else some manifestation of divine perfection. If the former, God may be apprehended by reason, by faith,

35 Thomas Aquinas, *Summa theologiae*, 1, q. 103, a. 1, ad 3m.
36 Ibid. a. 5, ad 3m.
37 For a fuller statement, see Bernard Lonergan, 'St. Thomas' Thought on Gratia Operans,' *Theological Studies* 3 (1942) 576 [*Grace and Freedom* 142–43].
38 Cf. O'Mahony, *The Desire of God* 62–65.

or by vision. If the latter, the motive may be the excellence of a person, of a state of affairs such as peace or a happy family, or finally a thing. Superposing the reflective aspect of freedom (D) upon the multiplicity of motives for the passive aspect (A), we arrive at the question of the right order of loving. Now God, the ground of all excellence, is to be loved absolutely: 'Thou shalt love the Lord thy God with thy whole heart, and with thy whole soul, and with thy whole mind' (Matthew 22.37). As Aquinas elaborates the precept, God is to be loved above all things,[39] more than self,[40] as good in himself more than as good to us,[41] because of himself (whether the 'because' is understood of the formal cause, for God is goodness itself, of the final cause, for God is the end of all, or of the efficient cause, for God is the cause of all good);[42] God is to be loved immediately,[43] totally,[44] and without measure or limit.[45] On the other hand, creatures are to be loved according to the measure of their excellence, which also is the measure of their proximity to God by assimilation. Still, such proximity and assimilation may be actual or potential, and so we may love others not only according to the assimilation they already possess but also according to the assimilation we wish them to have.[46] But whence that wishing? It is the insertion of other proximity and love into the order of divine charity. It is the vertical upthrust, the ascent, that crosses from lower to higher levels of appetition and process. Not only is it true that man should love other objects in virtue of his love of God; it is also true that he can love God only in an ascent through participated to absolute excellence. Thus love of others is proof of love of God: 'If we love one another, God abides in us and his charity is perfected in us' (1 John 4.12). Hatred of others is proof of hatred of God: 'If anyone says, "I love God," and hates his brother, he is a liar. For how can he who does not love his brother, whom he sees, love God, whom he does not see?' (ibid. 4.20). Now towards this high goal of charity it is no small beginning in the weak and imperfect heart of fallen man to be startled by a beauty that shifts the center of appetition out of self; and such a shift is effected on the level of sensitive spontaneity by *erôs*

39 *Summa theologiae*, 1–2, q. 109, a. 3 c.
40 Ibid. 2–2, q. 26, a. 3.
41 Ibid. ad 3m.
42 Ibid. q. 27, a. 3.
43 Ibid. a. 4.
44 Ibid. a. 5.
45 Ibid. a. 6.
46 Ibid. q. 26, aa. 4–13, esp. aa. 4, 7, 8, 13.

leaping in through delighted eyes and establishing itself as unrest in absence and an imperious demand for company.[47] Next, company may reveal deeper qualities of mind and character to shift again the center from the merely organistic tendencies of nature to the rational level of friendship with its enduring basis in the excellence of a good person.[48] Finally, grace inserts into charity the love that nature gives and reason approves. Thus we have a dispositive upward tendency from *erôs* to friendship, and from friendship to a special order of charity.

3.2.2   Ascent and the Immanent Aspect of Love

In the second place, love is an immanent perfection (*B*) with three formal effects: a moral effect, a relative effect, and a unitive effect. It has a moral effect, for as our loving is orderly or disorderly, we make ourselves virtuous or vicious; just as technique makes a good job, so virtue makes a good person.[49] Thus, as we have pointed out already, true love of self is love of virtue, while to love self wrongly is to hate self. But consequent to this moral effect there is a relative effect: a good person is a lovable person; and it is only the friendship based upon this lovableness that Aristotle considered worthy of the name.[50] But when love is habitual and reciprocated, there emerges a third formal effect: then love unites; it makes lovers parts of a larger unit[51] with each to the other as another self, a *dimidium animae suae*.[52] Now in the union that is the mystical body of Christ, we are all 'severally members one of another' (Romans 12.5), parts of a larger unit in which we are to love our neighbors as ourselves (Matthew 22.39). But in fallen man this objective unity of the mystical body runs ahead of its appetitive component of love; and much the same is true of man's objective unity in a common humanity with its historical

47 See Aristotle, *Ethics*, IX, 5, 1167a 3–7; VIII, 4, 1157a 7–11.
48 Ibid. VIII, 3–7.
49 Ibid. II, 6, 1106a 14–23.
50 Ibid. VIII, 3, 1156a 17, b 7.
51 Thomas Aquinas, *Summa theologiae*, 1–2, q. 109, a. 3; 2–2, q. 26, a. 3; see Aristotle, *Politics*, 1337a 29; 1253a 20. The idea of friends as parts of a larger unit is closely connected with the idea that all friendship is in a κοινωνία (*Ethics*, VIII, 12, 1161b 11).
52 Thomas Aquinas, *Summa theologiae*, 1–2, q. 28, a. 1; Aristotle, *Ethics*, IX, 12, 1171b 33; see ibid. VIII, 12, 1161b 29; IX, 4, 1166a 32; IX, 9, 1169b 7; 1170b 6.

solidarity, and even of the objective unities of states and nations, of occupations, of time and place.

On the other hand, in marriage the initial drive is not in an intellectual apprehension of objective unity calling for its appetitive component but precisely in the appetitive component itself. Husband and wife are made for one another by sexual differentiation and are brought to one another by sexual attraction. Moreover, this bringing together is such as to involve a full realization of the existence of another self: for there is no reasonable basis for marriage except the basis of a contract that holds for life, while the self-surrender to a life partner in that contract is also no more than the rational form, postulated by man's rational being, of the mutual self-donation contained in the marriage act itself.[53] Both on the level of spontaneity and on the level of reason, marriage is the real apprehension, the intense appetition, the full expression of union with another self. Again, what holds of husband and wife holds equally though differently of parents and children: for children do not come as distinct selves but, as Aristotle observed, as parts of self that gradually become distinct.[54] Finally, not only does marriage concretely unfold the meaning of love, the meaning that there are other selves, on the levels of natural spontaneity and reflective reason; it also does so on the level of grace. What Adam saw in Eve taken from his side,[55] what Christ our Lord confirmed,[56] has been transposed to another and higher order by the very fact of incorporation in the body of Christ. For now it is 'because we are members of his body, made from his flesh and from his bones. For this reason a man shall leave his father and mother, and shall cleave to his wife; and the two shall become one flesh' (Ephesians 5.30–31). As fornication has taken on the note of sacrilege,[57] so marriage has become the sacrament of the union of Christ and his church. It is the efficacious sacrament of the realization of another self in Christ, and its ascending

53 See Doms, *Du sens et de la fin ...* 61–67.
54 *Ethics*, VIII, 12, 1161b 18; see IX, 7, 1167b 17 to 1168a 8.
55 'Wherefore a man shall leave father and mother, and shall cleave to his wife and they shall be two in one flesh' (Genesis 2.24).
56 'What therefore God has joined together, let no man put asunder' (Matthew 19.6).
57 'Do you not know that your bodies are members of Christ? Shall I then take the members of Christ and make them members of a harlot? By no means. Or do you not know that he who cleaves to a harlot, becomes one body with her?' (1 Corinthians 6.15–16).

finalistic drive, its primary reason and cause, is to the very summit of Christian perfection in which in due order all members of the mystical body are known and loved as other selves.

3.2.3 Ascent and the Active Aspect of Love

This goal is to be attained by love under its third, its active aspect (C). In this activity and productivity love looks back to the motive good (C_1), it actuates its own immanent perfection (C_2), and it moves towards its ultimate end and consummation (C_3). With respect to its motive good, active love is productive in four ways. Seeking its own self-perpetuation, it effects contemplation of the motive good. Seeking its own self-expression, it effects imitations and reproductions of the motive good. Separated from the motive good, it seeks possession of it. And if the motive good itself is merely a project, love endeavors to produce it. These four types of love active with respect to its motive good are enumerated not because they are always distinct, but only because they may be distinct. Further, of the four, three are too obvious to need comment; but the self-expression of love is an idea that may benefit from illustration. Such self-expression, then, is the aspect of volitional efficiency in the principle, *bonum est sui diffusivum*:P its primary instance is God manifesting his perfections by creation,[58] and to this corresponds the effort of all creation to attain ever greater assimilation to God,[59] whence the precept, 'You therefore are to be perfect, even as your heavenly Father is perfect' (Matthew 5.48). But the same movement of self-expression, which is quite distinct from willing means for ends,[60] has innumerable other instances of which

58 Denzinger, *Enchiridion symbolorum* ... 1783 (DS 3002).
59 Thomas Aquinas, *Summa contra Gentiles*, 3, c. 19.
60 Means are willed, not at all for their own sake, but only for sake of the ends. On the other hand, what is loved in love's self-expression is loved in itself though as a secondary object and from a superabundance of love towards the primary object which is imitated or reproduced. Thus God loves creatures not as mere means but as secondary objects; similarly, Christian charity is to love one's neighbor for the sake of God, yet this is not to make a mere means of one's neighbor, but to love him in himself and for himself as a manifestation, actual or potential, of the perfection of God. Parallel to this position in the volitional order, there is a similar position in the ontological order. There the mere means is represented by the mere instrument; but the mere instrument emerges only from a limited viewpoint. Reality is either act or potency: as act, it is end; as potency, it is what is for the end. The mere instrument is

the most relevant is that of the family; there the mutual love of husband and wife effects reproductions of its motive in children, and the filial love of children responds to parental education in seeking assimilation to the parents.

Next, active love, besides looking back to the motive good, also reflects and actuates more fully the immanent perfection of love (C_2). Contemplation, expression, possession, or achievement of a motive good is also an actuation of true or false self-love according as the right or wrong motive is loved and in the right or wrong measure; simultaneously, it is an increase or decrease in the lovableness of the lover and so an elevation or debasing of the union of friendship. But this last and most relevant aspect may best be approached from another angle. For just as habitual and reciprocated love has the formal effect of constituting a union, of setting up mutual other selves, so a common end, defined by a common motive and sought in the common effort of friends sharing a common life, actuates the common consciousness of mutual other selves. On the plane of marriage this is the *totius vitae communio, consuetudo, societas* of which the encyclical speaks; but the same idea in its proper generality is worked out by Aristotle in the following manner. The basic principle is that, as a man is to himself, so also he is to his friend. Now a man is to himself in consciousness of his being, and he is conscious of his being through activity; hence, to be to his friend as he is to himself, the common consciousness of mutual other selves has to find a common activity; and since activity results from response to motive, this common activity presupposes a coincidence of views, profound or superficial, on the meaning of life, on what makes life worth while and sets a goal to human striving. Hence, whatever it is that men value in life, 'in that they wish to occupy themselves with their friends; and so some drink together, others dice together, others join in athletic exercises or hunting, or in the study of philosophy, each class spending their days together in whatever they love most in life.' Now this expansion of a common consciousness in a common life cannot but be, as we have indicated already, also an expansion and development of a common conscience. For one's ideas on

---

had only inasmuch as the act of lower potency subserves the act of higher potency in another subject; and this is from a limited viewpoint, since the act of lower potency is the perfection and end of that potency before it is instrumental to higher act; the plane is built to fly and only consequently to its actual attainment of flying does man fly. Hence, it is gravely misleading to term means and instrument whatever is not primary end.

life, one's moral conscience, one's deeds, the expressed ideas of others near one, and their deeds, all are linked together in a field of mutual influence and adaptation for better or for worse. So Aristotle continues, 'The friendship of bad men turns out an evil thing (for because of their instability they unite in bad pursuits, and besides they become evil by becoming like each other), while the friendship of good men is good, being augmented by their companionship; and they are thought to become better too by their activities and by improving each other; for from each other they take the mould of the characteristics they approve – whence the saying "noble deeds from noble men".'[61]

Evidently enough, such an expansion of conjugal love into a common consciousness and conscience the church protects by the Pauline privilege, by the impediments of mixed religion and disparity of cult, and, in cases of utter failure, by the *separatio a mensa et thoro*. However, our point is not merely such recognition of fact but the dynamic ascent of love, the upward finality from love on a lower level to more perfect love on a higher level. Now already, in discussing love as passive (A) and as immanent (B), we have indicated such ascents; but if by ascent one understands development, then from the nature of the case the ascent of love comes only from love as active (C). Further, we have implied that such ascent is a dispositive influence: the lower is not the mere instrument of the higher, nor material from which it is educed, nor obediential potency for it; but granted several levels of activity and love, then there is an intensification[62] of the higher by the lower, a stability resulting not from mere absence of tension but from positive harmony between different levels, and, most dynamic, the integration by which the lower in its expansion involves a development in the higher. Thus *erôs* leads to company; but company reveals deeper qualities of mind and character to set up a human friendship; a human friendship cannot but intensify the mutual charity of members of the mystical body; finally, it is in charity to one another that, in truth and reality, as St John so clearly taught, people come to the love of God. But next, sexual differentiation makes man and woman complementary beings for the living of life: it sets up spontaneously a division of labor not only with regard to children but

61 *Ethics*, IX, 12, 1171b 33 to 1172a 14. The two sentences in quotation marks are from Ross's translation (London: Oxford University Press). The rest of the passage I have expanded.

62 Aquinas recognizes two grounds of love: the excellence of the object and our proximity to it; to the former he attributes the species of love; to the latter its intensity (*Summa theologiae*, 2-2, q. 26, a. 7; see aa. 8, 9, 11).

also with regard to the whole domestic economy; each partner is part of a larger whole, invited to fit into that whole, and so intense is the intimacy of that common life, so serious its responsibilities, that reason seals it with an inviolable contract and grace with a sacrament. Now in that contract and sacrament, consummated in the flesh, another self is most intensively apprehended, loved, realized. So married life is launched, but the human and infused virtues that already exist will be tested by the life in common; they will be heightened by the almost palpable responsibility of children; they will develop in the midst of trials faced together; they will be purified in the serenity of old age, when perforce the self becomes selfless as the field of enjoyment contracts to joy in the enjoyment of others, in the romping vitality of grandchildren. This educative process is objective; it comes whether willed or not; but if, as should be, at some time people begin to cooperate with the scheme of things, then their hearts turn and settle on the real meaning of life; their goal will be not just fun but, here below, the humanistic goal of the Aristotelian good life, and supernaturally the beatific vision. Then their mutual actuation of a common consciousness and conscience will be a rejection of the world's dialectical rationalizations, a focal point in the stream of history for the fostering of growth in the mind and heart of Christ, a pursuit of the highest human and eternal ends. Such, surely, is the meaning of the encyclical when it affirms that marriage, considered broadly as *totius vitae communio, consuetudo, societas,* has as its primary reason and cause a mutual influence, a sustained effort of common improvement, tending to the very summit of Christian perfection. Any insertion of spontaneous union or human friendship into charity, which is friendship in Christ, has not the ground of supernatural excellence achieved but the end of such excellence to be achieved.[63] It follows that the compenetrating consciousness of lives shared by marriage is dynamic and reaches forth to will and to realize in common the advance in Christian perfection that leads from the consummation of two-in-one-flesh to the consummation of the beatific vision.

4   The Hierarchy of Ends in Marriage

4.1 Context: General Hierarchy in Human Process

The hierarchy of ends in marriage can be understood only in the context of the more general hierarchy in human process. Man has three ends:

63 See ibid. a.7.

life, the good life, and eternal life. Now by man is meant not an abstract essence nor a concrete individual but the concrete aggregate of all men of all times. Thus, as in current physics, the viewpoint is four-dimensional; or, as in medieval philosophy, the viewpoint is eternal, seeing *omnia simul*; for though the things seen are at different times in their internal temporal relationships, still it is possible and proper for the human intellect to imitate the divine and by abstraction stand outside the temporal flow in which really, though not of necessity intentionally, it is involved. The importance of adopting this viewpoint arises from a difference in man's three ends. The emergence and maintenance of human life is repetitive. But the attainment of the human good life is a historical development, a unique process, not repeated for each individual, as is life, but a single thing shared by all individuals according to their position and role in the space-time solidarity of man. Finally, the end of eternal life stands completely outside both the measurable time of repetitive life and the ordinal time of progressive good life. Such differences make it imperative that we view human process not in the distorting cross-section of any particular instance of time but from outside time.

Corresponding to the three human ends – life, the good life, and eternal life – are three levels of human activity: there is the level of 'nature' understood in the current restricted sense of physical, vital, sensitive spontaneity; there is the level of reason and rational appetite; and there is the level of divine grace. Throughout, nature is characterized by repetitiveness: over and over again it achieves mere reproductions of what has been achieved already; and any escape from such cyclic recurrence is *per accidens* and *in minori parte* or, in modern language, due to chance variation. But in contrast with this repetitiveness of nature is the progressiveness of reason. For if it is characteristic of all intellect to grasp immutable truth, it is the special property of the potential intellect of man to advance in knowledge of truth. Nor is it merely the individual that advances, as though knowledge were classically static, a fund whence schoolboys receive a dole. On the contrary, to the historian of science or philosophy and still more to the anthropologist, the individual of genius appears no more than the instrument of human solidarity; through such individuals humanity advances, and the function of tradition and education is to maintain the continuity of a development that runs from the days of primitive fruit gatherers through our own of mechanical power on into an unknown future. But not only are nature and reason contrasted as repetitive and progressive. There is also a contrast between the organistic spontaneity of nature and the deliberate friendships of reason. By 'organistic' spontaneity I would denote the mutual adaptation and automatic correlation of the activities of many individuals as though they were parts of a larger organic unit. This phenomenon may be illustrated by the antheap or the beehive; but its more general appearance lies in the unity of the family, a unity which nature as spontaneously and as imperiously attains in the accidental order as in the substantial it effects the unity of the organism. Now it is not by organistic spontaneity but by mutual esteem and mutual good will that reason sets up its comparable union of friendship; and in accordance with our eternal viewpoint we may note that human friendship is to be found not only in the urbanity and collaboration of contemporaries but much more in the great republic of culture,[q] in contemporaries' esteem for the great men of the past, on whose shoulders they stand, and in their devotion to men of the future, for whom they set the stage of history for better or for worse. A third contrast between nature and reason is in point of efficiency. While nature with the ease of a superautomaton pursues with statistical infallibility and regularly attains through organistic harmonies its repetitive ends, the reason and rational appetite of fallen man limp in the disequilibrium of high aspiration and poor performance to make the progress of reason a dialectic of decline as well as of advance, and the rational community of men a divided unity of hatred and war as well as the indivisible unity of fraternity and peace. Last of all, the process of divine grace contrasts with the characteristics both of nature and of reason. Of itself it is neither repetitive as nature nor progressive as reason but eternal and definitive. It is not the statistical spontaneity of nature, nor the incoherent liberty of man, but the gratuitous action of God. It is the transrational spontaneity of revelation and faith and intuition, the transorganistic efficacy of the mystical body of Christ, the uniqueness of eternal achievement: God with us in the hypostatic union, God holding us by the theological virtues, God and ourselves, face to face, in the beatific vision.

Now the correspondence of these three levels of contrasting activity with the three ends of man is only essential. Nature sets its goal in the repetitive emergence and maintenance of life; reason supervenes to set up the historically cumulative and so, on the whole, ever varying pursuit of the good life; grace, finally, takes over both nature and reason to redirect both repetitive spontaneity and historical development to the supernatural end of eternal life. From such integration there result projections from one level of activity to another: what essentially is natural or rational or of grace receives secondary elements from projection and transference. Thus nature is spontaneous but reason makes it rational by a host of juridical entities: things become property; they are subjected to laws and regulations; they are enmeshed in a web of human creations. Again, reason seeks its goal of the good life not only in the purely rational pursuits of knowledge and virtue, the Aristotelian beatitude,[64] but also in a greater excellence added to nature's pursuit of life; and so it is that by arts and crafts, by applied science and technology, by economics and medicine, by marriage and politics, reason transforms the natural *nisus* towards life into a rational attainment of a historically unfolding good life. In like manner grace takes over both nature and reason. The purely rational pursuit of philosophy is made into an instrument as the handmaid of theology; reason itself as reasonable faith is elevated to the level of grace; virtuous living is transformed into merit unto eternal life; repetitive preaching becomes the space-time multiplication of a unique revelation; repetitive doing is elevated into sacraments and liturgy. Inversely, the distinctive eternity of the order of grace is submitted to human progress inasmuch as grace sets up a human society or a human science or human advance in virtue; and it is submitted to natural repetitiveness inasmuch as it embraces even the recurrent aspects of human existence.

Now we have been engaged in establishing a basic system of reference for the discussion of any hierarchy of human ends. For such a basic system will prescind from all secondary elements by transference and projection to attend only to the three contrasting types of activity and their three essentially correlated ends. Diagrammatically, then, our system is

P to P' to P''
Q to Q' to Q''
R to R' to R''

where on the level of grace the movement is from the mystical body on earth (P), through further communication of sanctifying grace (P'), to the triumphant mystical body in heaven (P''); on the level of reason the

64 Aristotle, *Ethics* x, 6–9.

movement is from the life of knowledge and virtue (Q), through advance in knowledge and virtue (Q'), to man's attainment of the historically unfolding good life (Q''); and on the level of nature the movement is from physical, vital, sensitive spontaneity (R), through the actuation of such spontaneity (R'), to the emergence and maintenance of human life (R'').

4.2 Marriage in the Context of Human Process

Next, within this skeletal structure of all human process have to be placed the various elements of marriage. As is to be expected, some of these elements are primary, that is, integral parts of the basic types of activity, while others are secondary, that is, byproducts of the substantial unity of man and of the integration of human activities.[65] Thus, on the level of nature, there are fecundity and sex (Z), their actuation in the organistic union of man and wife (Z'), and their horizontal end of adult offspring (Z''); now these are all primary elements, for they are part of the spontaneous tendencies (R) that terminate in the emergence and maintenance of human life (R''). Again, on the level of reason, there is the friendship of husband and wife (Y) and the marriage contract (Y'); and these are not primary but secondary elements, for they are not necessarily part of the life of knowledge and virtue but conditioned integrations of organistic union within the life of reason.[66] Further, as a result of such

65 Hence marriage may be specifically human, as Dr Doms rightly insists (*Du sens et de la fin* ... 17–18 and passim), without being a primary element on the rational level of human process, without resulting from the life of reason as such. Inversely, when Aquinas attributes the *bonum prolis* as pertaining to marriage inasmuch as man is an animal (*Super* IV *Sententiarum*, d. 33, q. 1, a. 1 = *Supplementum*, q. 65, a. 1), there is no necessary implication that marriage is not specifically human.

66 It is practically to confine the ends of marriage solely to the generation of offspring, to assert with St Augustine and St Thomas that woman was given man as a helpmate in the work of generation and that in any other work another man would be a greater help (see Doms, *Du sens et de la fin* ... 226, note 31). But there is this kernel of truth in the old position, that marriage is not a primary element in the life of knowledge and virtue; *per se* one does not marry to become a philosopher or an ascetic; were the contradictory true, the counsel of virginity would invite us to forsake not only the life of spontaneous nature but also the life of reason for the sake of the life of grace. [With regard to the diagram on p. 42, note that in the original (*Theological Studies* 4 [1943] 501), one of the arrows was misplaced.]

integration, there is the subsumption of the finality of fecundity to off-spring under the finality of reason to the historical expansion of the good life; so that while the actuation of fecundity (Z') is for adult off-spring (Z''), the end of marriage (Y') is a procreation and education of children (Y'') that make the historical process continuous. Finally, on the level of grace, there is the special order of charity between husband and wife (X) and the sacramental marriage bond (X'); and these are not integral parts of the process of grace but rather incorporations of the human friendship and contract on the supernatural level; and as reason redirects the finality of fecundity to offspring into a finality to educated offspring for the sake of the historical process, so grace effects a further redirection to Christianly educated offspring (X'') that the mystical body of Christ may grow to full stature. Hence, as a preliminary scheme, we have the following, in which the symbols have the meanings already assigned and arrows denote horizontal and vertical finalities.

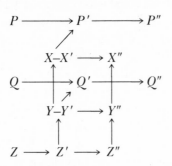

First of all, then, from the viewpoint of marriage, the relevant part of natural spontaneity (R) is bisexual fecundity (Z). Fecundity offers no difficulty. As far as human operation is concerned, it is primarily on the level of nature, and its ultimate term is the repetitive emergence of adult offspring. But sex is more complex. Not only is it not a substance but it is not even an accidental potency as intellect or sense. Rather, it is a bias and orientation in a large number of potencies, a typical and comple-mentary differentiation within the species, with a material basis in a difference in the number of chromosomes, with a regulator in the se-cretions of endocrinal glands, with manifestations not only in anatomical structure and physiological function but also in the totality of vital, psychic, sensitive, emotional characters and consequently, though not formally, in the higher nonorganic activities of reason and rational appetite. But for all its complexity sex remains on the level of spontaneous nature, and there, clearly, one may easily recognize that in all its aspects it definitely, if not exclusively, has a role in the process from fecundity to adult offspring. For elementally sex is a difference added to fecundity, dividing it into two complementary semifecundities and so obtaining for offspring the diversity in material cause sanctioned by the impediment of consanguinity. More prominently, sex is the principle of reunion of the divided semifecundities, bringing together on the level of sensitive attraction and local motion what had been separated and placed in different beings on the level of physiology. Finally, sex unites not only the semifecundities of spermatozoon and ovum but also their bearers: it makes male and female complementary beings, postulating their life in common, automatically setting up a division of labor in this life, and automatically providing offspring with a home, that is, with an environmental womb for infancy, childhood, and adolescence. Thus, from one viewpoint, sex is but an aspect of an elaborate process of fecundity. Simple fission in an amoeba gives another adult amoeba. But the more complex the life form, the more elaborate the process from fecundity to adult offspring. Sex is the elaboration of the process.

Still, what from one viewpoint is merely instrumental may from another be act and perfection and therefore end. The science and skill of the doctor are mere means to my health yet not mere means to the doctor, in whom they are actuations and perfections at the basis of his vocation, his professional status, his social role, his lifetime occupation. In general, all act is end: it is what potency is for; and though the actuation of a potency may be mere means from some limited viewpoint, always it is at least a material end to the actuated subject. Thus sex as a differentiation of fecundity is merely an instrument of fecundity in the latter's process to adult offspring. But at the same time, it is a quality and capacity of subjects or persons. To them its actuation is at least a material end, that is, an end that can and ought to be integrated with higher ends. Further, the actuation of sex involves the organistic union of a concrete plurality, and as such it has a vertical finality. Such an upward drive follows from our general theory. In the vegetal and animal kingdoms it has its verification in the measure of truth that may be attributed to theories of evolution in terms of statistical laws and probabilities regarding combinations of genes through random mating.[67] But in man the upward drive is to the human and personalist aspects of

67 For a professional but nonmathematical account of this theory, see A.F. Shull, *Evolution* (New York: McGraw-Hill, 1936), chapters v–x.

marriage, to projections from fecundity and sex to the levels of reason and grace. For if the human family was not left to the invention of reason, if its root lies in sexual differentiation, its release in the attraction and compulsion of *erôs*, its repetitive fulfilment in a mutual actuation that reabsorbs husband and wife back into the elemental rhythms of the biosphere, its autumnal glory in the spontaneous devotion of parents to each other and to children, of children to parents and to one another, nonetheless the human family is never merely such spontaneity, repetitiveness, organisticity. Man is rational. Even if often reason is no more than the mere servant of irreflective appetite, even then the actuation of bisexual fecundity is a friendship of pleasure and mutual advantage. But, as Aristotle observed, husband and wife have only to be decent people for their friendship to be one of virtue,[68] that is, one based upon the objective lovableness of qualities of mind and character. Here it is remarkable to note that Aristotle counted the friendship of virtue something rare,[69] so that a minimum of virtue, simple decency, obtains for husband and wife what only exceptional virtue obtains elsewhere. Such, then, is the dispositive upward tendency of sex to human friendship, an upthrust that is realized when even a mediocre life of knowledge and virtue (Q) sets up a human friendship (Y) to incorporate on the level of reason an actuation of *erôs* and sex (Z'). But in like manner the life of grace (P) embracing this friendship (Y) effects a further projection to the supernatural level, namely, the special order of charity (X) that obtains between husband and wife.[70]

Next, both of these projections have upthrusts of their own. The human friendship of virtue (Y) finds in married life an educative process and so has a tendency not merely to the expansion of the friendship but also to advance in the whole human life of knowledge and virtue (Q'). In like manner, the special order of charity (X) has an upthrust to advance in the whole of Christian perfection, of which the principal part is sanctifying grace (P'). For in both cases there is, in love as active, the expansion of a common consciousness and conscience and, if it is more usual to think of people advancing in human perfection and working out their salvation under the conditions of married life, it is no less accurate to think of married life as the matrix of conditions that supplies an upward tendency to advance in human and supernatural perfection.

68 *Ethics*, VIII, 12, 1162a 25.
69 Ibid. VIII, 3, 1156b 24–25.
70 Thomas Aquinas, *Summa theologiae*, 2-2, q. 26, a. 11.

Indeed, there is a special appropriateness in the latter viewpoint: as we have seen already, human development is a personal function of an objective movement in the space-time solidarity of man, and married life a series of steps upward through love of one's neighbor to the love of God.[71]

But were this the full analysis one would have to accept a position somewhat similar to that of Dr Doms. Marriage would have its center in the organistic union (Z'); on the level of nature it would have a horizontal finality to the biological resultant of offspring (Z''); and it would have a vertical finality to personalist ends in friendship (Y) and advancing virtue (Q'), in a special order of charity (X) and the whole of Christian perfection (P'). However, it is only generically that a human friendship and a special order of charity satisfy the upward tendency of bisexual fecundity. Unlike the more facile life of ignorance and selfishness, the life of knowledge and virtue incorporates on the level of reason not merely organistic union but also the whole process from bisexual fecundity to adult offspring. Now this difference happens to correspond to the distinction drawn in the encyclical between marriage in a broad sense and marriage in a strict sense: the former is a human friendship – totius vitae communio, consuetudo, societas[72] – to which sex as unitive disposes; the latter is the contractual bond that incorporates on the level of reason the concrete totality of sex, both its unitive tendencies and its horizontal finality in the process from fecundity to adult offspring.

Here three points are to be observed. First, marriage is the rational form, the incorporation on the level of reason, not of the child nor of the fecundity of parents, but of sex and of the finality of sex to the child. Not the child, for it advances to the level of reason by divine action, by the infusion of the soul. Not the fecundity of parents, for the marriage is valid even though the parents are sterile. It incorporates sex, for the sexual deficiency of impotence is a diriment impediment; and it incorporates the finality of sex to the child, for the object of marital right is actus per se apti ad prolis generationem. In the second place, marriage is more an incorporation of the finality of sex than of sex itself. Of course, it is just the opposite that seems true to phenomenologist scrutiny, for that ignores the metaphysical principle that what is prior quoad se is posterior quoad nos,[r] and that the more ultimate final cause enters more

71 See pp. 26–27, 36–37 supra.
72 Acta Apostolicae Sedis 22 (1930) 548–49.

intimately into the nature of a thing than the more proximate.[73] But, as we argued above, on the essential or horizontal level of natural spontaneity, sex is but a differentiation of fecundity and a means to the adult offspring that is the end of fecundity. If, then, reason incorporates sex as sex is in itself, it will incorporate it as subordinate to its horizontal end, and so marriage will be an incorporation of the horizontal finality of sex much more than of sex itself; nor is this to forget vertical finality, for vertical and horizontal finalities are not alternatives, but the vertical emerges all the more strongly as the horizontal is realized the more fully. Third and last, the incorporation of natural finality to adult offspring involves a redirection of that finality to higher ends. The life of reason and rational appetite has its end, here below, in the historical unfolding of the human good life (Q''); the life of grace has its end in the triumphant mystical body in heaven (P''). Hence, when the finality to adult offspring (Z'') is incorporated on the level of reason, it becomes a finality to edu-

---

73 See Thomas Aquinas, *Super Librum De causis*, lect. 1. This, I think, touches upon a fundamental methodological error in the analysis presented by Dr Doms. I agree that sex is to be distinguished from fecundity, as impotence from sterility. I agree with the validity of the question, What is the ontological significance of bisexuality? It is only a terminological difference when he asserts that the meaning of marriage is union and I say that the act and end of bisexuality is union, or when in different ways we both place two ends beyond this union. But when he speaks of this meaning of union as immanent, intrinsic, immediate, I distinguish: in the chronological order of human knowledge or of the development of human appreciation, the union is first; but in the ontological order the ordinations to the ends are more immanent, more intrinsic, more immediate to the union than the union itself. For what is first in the ontological constitution of a thing is not the experiential datum but, on the contrary, what is known in the last and most general act of understanding with regard to it; what is next, is the next most general understanding; etc. Thus the proximate end of bisexuality is union; but of its nature, bisexuality is an instrument of fecundity, so that the end of fecundity is more an end of bisexuality than is union; similarly, bisexual union has a vertical finality to higher unions of friendship and charity; and these enter more intimately into the significance of bisexuality than does the union on the level of nature. See my note on *immediatio virtutis,* in 'St. Thomas' Theory of Operations,' *Theological Studies* 3 (1942) 376, for references to this line of Thomist thought [*Grace and Freedom* 64–65]. As to the difficulty that frequently procreation is objectively impossible and may be known to be so, distinguish motives and ends; as to motives, the difficulty is solved only by multiple motives and ends; as to ends, there is no difficulty, for the ordination of intercourse to conception is not a natural law, like 'fire burns,' but a statistical law,[s] which suffices for an objective ordination.

cated adult offspring (Y''); and when it is incorporated on the level of grace, it becomes a finality to Christianly educated offspring (X''). The latter subsumption and redirection of lower under higher finality is clearer than the former. Christian parents are the representatives and the instruments of Christ and his bride, the church, and so they generate children to have them regenerated in Christ, and they educate them for their eternal role in the triumphant mystical body in heaven. But just as the life of grace wills offspring for the full expansion of the mystical body, so also the life of reason wills offspring for the continuity of reason's own historical unfolding of the human good life. It is this elevation of lower finality that makes the end of marriage not only the procreation but also the education of children, with the former the material and the latter the formal condition of historical continuity; further, the relativity of history accounts for the relativity in the obligation of parents to educate. But as theologians, let alone parents, rarely think of the historical process, it must be noted that we speak not of a *finis operantis* but of a *finis operis* and that we do so in its most general terms. No one will find a motive in the historical process as such. What moves men and women is some concrete aspect of history, a national destiny, the maintenance of a cultural tradition, the continuity of a family; and even this will be apprehended by parents, not in its abstract generality, but concretely as the good of bringing into the world and leaving in it behind them others like themselves.[74]

This brings us to our main analytic conclusion. The process of bisexual fecundity (Z, Z', Z'') is in man integrated with the processes of reason and of grace. Such integration takes place by projection, by the incorporation of the lower level of activity within the higher. The incorporation on the level of reason is generically a friendship (Y) and specifically a contractual bond (Y'); the latter has a horizontal finality to the procreation and education of children (Y''), but the former has a vertical dynamism tending to advance in human perfection (Q'). Similarly, the incorporation on the level of grace is generically a special order of charity (X) but specifically a sacramental bond (X'); the latter has a horizontal

74 Aristotle in his *Politics* (1252a 27–30) considers this motive so natural as not to be a matter of choice. He exaggerates, but at least reveals implicitly the strength of the tendency of educated parents to have educated children. [We are indebted to C.G. Arevalo for the correct Bekker reference; see *Philippine Studies* 15 (1967) 719, note 4. The original publication had an erroneous reference, not corrected in the *Collection* of 1967.]

finality to the procreation and Christian education of children (X''), but the former a vertical dynamism tending to advance in Christian perfection (P').

4.3 Conformity with Traditional Doctrine

Now if this analysis satisfies the exigencies of modern data and insights, it is no less true that it leads immediately to the traditional position on the ends of marriage. For the criteria of more essential and more excellent ends may be applied in three ways, to the organistic union (Z'), to the marriage contract (Y'), and to the sacrament (X'). The first application gives the traditional position on polygamy: the horizontal finality of organistic union to offspring is more essential than the vertical finality to monogamous marriage; hence, under special circumstances, divine providence might permit polygamy for the sake of the more essential end and find other means to secure the more excellent personalist end. The second and third applications to monogamous marriage itself, whether contract or sacrament, are parallel: in both cases the horizontal finality to procreation and education of children is more essential than the vertical finality to personal advance in perfection; and if we take the terms 'primary' and 'secondary' in the sense of more and less essential,[75] we have at once the traditional position that the primary

---

75 Objection to the use of the terms 'primary' and 'secondary' has this much justification, that considerable care is required to use them properly. Most commonly, they are used in a nonscientific sense: 'primary' means 'more important'; and this greater importance is known through the unanalyzed type of inference Newman termed the illative sense. But they may also be the instruments of systematic thinking, and then they are of themselves generic to be determined specifically in the context. Such possible specifications are numerous. Above, we used 'primary' and 'secondary' of more and less essential ends; previously, we used them to denote elemental and resultant factors in human process. In *De veritate*, q. 22, a. 2, Aquinas called the end of the first cause primary and that of secondary causes secondary. In his commentary on the *Sentences* (*Super IV Sententiarum*, d. 33, q. 1, a. 1 = *Supplementum*, q. 65, a. 1), he distinguished between an actuation and its byproduct as primary and secondary: the primary end of eating is health, the secondary end is feeling fit for work. But I would not say that another specific meaning is to be found in *Quaestiones quodlibetales* 5, q. 10, a. 19, ad 2m (see Doms, *Du sens et de la fin* ... 89 [where the reference is found in this form; but what Doms refers to as ad 2m is in the corpus of the article, the para-

end of marriage is the procreation and education of children. Further, our less essential vertical finality corresponds at least roughly with the traditional secondary ends of *mutuum auxilium* and *honestum remedium concupiscentiae*. For mutual aid is the spontaneous division of labor in the organistic union; it is the companionship and the good deeds of friendship; it is mutual support in spiritual advance to Christian perfection; it is all three, not isolated on the levels of nature, reason, and grace, but integrated and inseparable in the expansion of love into a common consciousness and conscience in the pursuit of life, the good life, and eternal life. The virtuous remedy for concupiscence would seem but the reverse aspect of the same thing. For if the virtuous remedy is sometimes understood narrowly as a legitimate outlet for sexual impulse, still such a view hardly squares with the fact that there is much more than sex in sexual impulse. The sexual extravagance of man, unparalleled in the animals, has its ultimate ground in St Augustine's *Fecisti nos ad te, Domine, et inquietum est cor nostrum donec requiescat in te.*[t] The ignorance and frailty of fallen man tend to center an infinite craving on a finite object or release: that may be wealth, or fame, or power, but most commonly it is sex. Thus marriage, not merely by the outlet of intercourse but in all its aspects, is a virtuous remedy: the manifold activities of the home drain off energies that otherwise would ferment; the educative process of the life in common and the responsibility of children develop character and mature wisdom; the pursuit of Christian perfection establishes a peace of soul that attacks concupiscence at its deepest root. In this fashion it would seem that the traditional secondary ends may be identified with the vertical upthrust to friendship and charity, to human and Christian perfection.

4.4 A Qualification

It remains that the strength of this upthrust is not to be exaggerated. An integral part of Catholic thought on marriage is the doctrine that virginity is preferable to marriage, widowhood to second marriage, temporary abstinence to use within marriage (1 Corinthians 7.25–40). The precise implications of this doctrine are not too clear. Because of his

---

graph beginning 'Circa secundum ... ']); the ultimate disposition to a form does not precede but results from the infusion or emergence of the form (e.g., *Summa theologiae*, 1–2, q. 113, a. 8).

position on original sin, the Pelagians charged St Augustine with a rejection of Christian defense and praise of marriage.[76] St Augustine answered that marriage was good but concupiscence evil, indeed a disease to be tolerated only for the sake of children.[77] Now it is quite certain that by concupiscence St Augustine does not mean simply the spontaneous tendencies by which two beings are invited to function as parts of the larger unit of the family; along with that natural phenomenon he also means an effect of original sin, a constituent in original sin, an instrument in its transmission, and in fallen nature a fecund cause of actual sin.[78] Such global and concrete thinking was alone possible in the fifth century. It does not admit direct transference to the more elaborate conceptual field of later theology – though, as was lamentably conspicuous in the case of Baius and Jansenius, a realization of the illegitimacy of such direct transference has not always been had. Account, then, must be taken of later development, and in this the main factor would seem to have been the theorem of the supernatural[u] and its concomitant position that Adam's immunity from concupiscence was not natural but preternatural. Now, since in the lifetime of Aquinas this theoretical advance was still in process of development,[79] it would be easy to attach too much significance to his maintenance in the *Sentences* of the essentially Augustinian position of an *excusatio matrimonii et copulae*.[80] In any case

76 Augustine, *De nuptiis et concupiscentia*, I, 1 (*Corpus scriptorum ecclesiasticorum latinorum*, XLII, p. 211).

77 Ibid. VIII, 9 (220–21) and passim.

78 E.g., ibid. XXIV, 27 (239–40), where almost all these aspects are united in a single passage.

79 The general movement I have outlined in an earlier article, 'St. Thomas' Thought on Gratia Operans,' *Theological Studies* 2 (1941) 301–306 [*Grace and Freedom* 13–19]. On Adam's immunity from concupiscence, contrast *Super II Sententiarum*, d. 20, q. 2, a. 3 c., and *Summa theologiae*, 1, q. 95, a. 1. The former passage distinguishes between a natural and a gratuitous original justice to place the subjection of the body to reason in natural justice; the latter passage makes the subjection of the body to reason an effect of grace.

80 *Super IV Sententiarum*, d. 31, q. 1, a. 1; q. 2, aa. 1–3 = *Supplementum*, q. 49, aa. 1, 4–6. For the parallel position of St Thomas' master, see John J. Clifford, 'The Ethics of Conjugal Intimacy according to St. Albert the Great,' *Theological Studies* 3 (1942) 1– 26. The intermediate character of this position might be illustrated by a comparison of extremes. Thus St Augustine, who did not envisage the hypothetical state of *natura pura*,[v] argues from the phenomena of concupiscence to original sin (*De nuptiis et concupiscentia*, v, 6 to VII, 8 [216–20]); but Christian Pesch, in his very representative *Praelectiones dogmaticae* (Vol. 3, Freiburg

that rigorous view seems to have been dropped by moral theologians,[81] while the dynamic Thomist position[82] would take its basis not in the explicit argument of the *Sentences* for the *excusatio*, namely, the eclipse of rational control in orgasm, but rather in broader considerations of different states of human nature. Fundamental would be the position that in the state of integral nature virginity would have been neither praiseworthy nor virtuous.[83] Hence, absolutely, what is best for man is the full actuation of all his capacities. But in the disequilibrium of fallen nature, with lower spontaneity taking care of itself, with reason apt to be misled by the historical aberrations of the *civitas terrena*, with the wisdom of God appearing folly to man, man's best is not full actuation of all potentiality but rather concentration on the higher levels of activity. Such concentration is commended to all, though in the triple form of virginity,[w] widowhood, and temporary abstinence in marriage. So understood, the counsel does not imply any negation of an objective upward tendency from organistic union to a common pursuit of Christian perfection, though indeed it does emphasize the limitations of such an upthrust under actual circumstances and the need of supplementing it by an opposite procedure. Excellent is the instrumentality of husband and wife to Christ and his bride, the church – an instrumentality that participates the love of the principal causes and brings forth to them the children that extend to full stature the mystical body. Excellent is the Christian home, a focal point that turns aside the influences of the world to rear children in an atmosphere of wholesome fear and love. But the bulwark of that excellence, the palpable proof of its ever doubted possibility, is the greater excellence that rises, not through organistic tendency but immediately, to concern with the one thing necessary, our eternal embrace with God in the beatific vision.

---

im Breisgau: Herder, 1899, §196), maintains the same phenomena to be natural. But I fear I am rushing through a very large and complex historical question. May I say that the views so briefly expressed here do not pretend to settle any issue, but only to indicate that the vast questions involved account not a little for the difficulties of the past in arriving at a satisfactory theory of marriage.

81 See Ford, 'Marriage ... ' 369.

82 For a timely insistence in this matter on the distinction between Thomism as a vital school of thought and Thomist history, exegesis, apologetic, see M.-Benoît Lavaud, o.p., 'Sens et fin du mariage: La thèse de Doms et la critique,' *Revue thomiste* 44 (1938) 760.

83 Thomas Aquinas, *Summa theologiae*, 1, q. 98, a. 2, ad 3m.

Conclusion

With this note of qualification, I may end. The purpose of the paper has been, as stated at the outset, a speculative outline that would manifest some of the assimilative capacity of traditional views. Necessarily, an outline is lacking in definition and in detail, for it is not a treatise. Much less can I claim to have fitted into it all that ancient and modern theorists have contributed to the subject. But if I have succeeded in hitting upon some pivotal points, perhaps I may hope that this labor will merit the scrutiny, the corrections, and the developments of others.[x]

3

On God and
Secondary Causes[1]

This work on the Thomist doctrine, *Deus operatur in omni operatione naturae et voluntatis*,[a] is at once historical, philosophic, theological, and controversial. As a historian, the author argues for a modification and development of Stufler's position.[b] As a philosopher, he advances that the view at which he arrives historically is in itself demonstrable and so should replace other theories current in textbooks. As a theologian, he contends that his philosophic position is compatible with Catholic and with Thomist doctrine on grace. Finally, the interests and distractions of controversy are everywhere evident in the work and, in my opinion, detract from its value.

1   Efficient Causality and the Causal Series

To grasp the author's position, it is necessary, even at the cost of considerable space, to find a more general viewpoint than he presents. The fundamental issue is the nature of the reality of efficient causality; that is, What is the reality which, if existent, makes the proposition, *A* is the efficient cause of *B*, true, but which, if nonexistent, makes it false? There are two answers. One may affirm that the desired necessary and sufficient condition is a causally efficient influence proceeding from *A* to (the

---

1 A review of E. Iglesias, *De Deo in operatione naturae vel voluntatis operante* (Mexico, D.F.: Buena Prensa, 1946).

subject of) B. On the other hand, one may consider the foregoing either a mere *modus significandi* or else sheer imagination, to affirm that the required necessary and sufficient condition is a real relation of dependence in B with respect to its ground and source, its *id a quo*, A. In this view, the reality of efficient causality is the relativity of the effect *qua* effect; one also may say that it is the relative element in the Aristotelian *actio, actus huius ut ab hoc*; that is, B is an act pertaining to A inasmuch as it is from A.

1.1 Efficient Causality as Influx

When one thinks of efficient causality as influx and attempts to analyse the causal series (A is efficient cause of B, and B is efficient cause of C), one may arrive at any of three opinions. First, one may say that in such a causal series there are two and only two instances of influx and so two and only two real instances of efficient causality: from A to B, and from B to C; but there is no third influx from A to C; accordingly, mediate causality is not a true species of causality but merely a name for the combination of two other instances. However, one may dislike this conclusion and desire to make the mediate cause[c] really and truly a cause. Hence, secondly, one may say that in the causal series there are, at least at times, three instances of influx and so three instances of efficient causality: not only from A to B, and from B to C, but also a third from A to C; simultaneously both A and B exert an influx to produce C. Now while this makes A the efficient cause of C not only in name but also in reality, it does so by making A the immediate cause of C; mediate causality is not saved. Hence, thirdly, one may say that there is a real difference between B as effect of A and B as cause of C, and this real difference is what explains the reality of mediate efficient causality; first, an influx from A gives B'; secondly, an influx from A gives B''; thirdly, an influx from B'' gives C. Thus efficient causality thought of as influx yields three views of the causal series, and one may note that there is some resemblance between these three views and the views respectively of Durandus, Molina, and Bañez.[d] I shall not say that Durandus, Molina, Bañez, or any of their followers arrived at their positions in the foregoing manner. I am not engaged in history but in listing theoretical possibilities, and merely draw attention to a resemblance among three possibilities and three historical opinions.

1.2 Efficient Causality and Relation of Dependence

As there is an alternative view of efficient causality, so also there is an alternative analysis of the causal series. Distinguish between the series properly so called and the merely accidental series: the latter is illustrated by Abraham begetting Isaac, and Isaac, Jacob, where evidently Abraham does not beget Jacob; the former is illustrated by my moving the keys of my typewriter, and my typewriter typing out these paragraphs, where evidently I am more a cause of the typed paragraphs than the typewriter is. Now in the accidental series there are only two real relations of dependence on an *id a quo*: B depends on A, C depends on B; but the relation of C to A is not of causal dependence but of conditioned to condition. On the other hand, in the proper causal series, there are three real relations of dependence with respect to an *id a quo*: B depends on A, C depends on B, and C depends on A even more than on B. Since there are three real relations of dependence, there are three real instances of efficient causality, and, as it appears, the instance of merely mediate causality (which causes such trouble when thinking is in terms of influx) turns out to involve more dependence, and so more causality, than the apparently immediate instance. This leads to an examination of the notion of immediacy. What is it? A first answer is in terms of space and time; but this necessarily is irrelevant, for there are causes and effects outside space and time. A second answer is in terms of proximity in the enumeration of terms in the causal series; but terms have their place in the series inasmuch as they are causes of what follows and instruments or means with respect to what precedes; and so we are brought to the etymology; the 'immediate' involves a negation of a *medium*, a middle, a means; and such a negation may be either 'not being a means' or 'not using a means'; what is not a means may be termed immediate *immediatione virtutis*; what does not use a means may be termed immediate *immediatione suppositi*; the former is what has first place in the proper causal series; the latter pertains in turn to each preceding term in the proper causal series.

Now with this analysis of the causal series, different views may arise when one asks the grounds of affirming that God, any created cause, and the created cause's effect form a proper causal series. Three sets of grounds have been offered; the first regards only immanent acts and so from its lack of universality has fallen into desuetude; the second regards all created causes and, indeed, as causes; the third is equally universal, for it regards all created causes, but it regards them, not as causes, but as conditioned. An argument for the first view may be put as follows: When I see, I act and so am an efficient cause; but when I see, I add to my own ontological perfection; to enable me to make such an addition, I must receive a physical premotion; and only God can be the cause of such premotions in the general case. The second view proceeds more generally: Only absolute being is the sufficient ground for the production of being; hence, insofar as it produces being, every created cause must be an instrument; further, this instrumentality affects the created cause as cause, for there is a real difference between *potentia agendi* and *ipsum agere*, and that real difference is in the created cause as such; but it cannot be produced by the created cause, for nothing can add to its own perfection; and it must be attributed to God, for it involves the production of being, and only God is proportionate to that.

The third view regards the created cause, not as cause, but as conditioned.[e] As in the second view, only infinite being is the proportionate cause of being, of the event as event, of the actual emergence of the effect, of the exercise of efficiency; hence, all finite causes are instruments, naturally proportionate to producing effects as of a given kind, but not naturally proportionate to producing effects as actual occurrences. However, this limitation is operative, not through some entitative and remediable defect in the created cause (for the only remedy would be to make it infinite), but through the manifest fact that finite causes are all conditioned. Since no finite cause can create, it must presuppose the patient on which it acts, suitable relations between itself and its patient, and the noninterference of other causes. Over these conditions the finite cause has no control, for the conditions must be fulfilled before the finite cause can do anything. Next, though the conditions are finite entities and negations of interference, though the conditions of the efficiency of one finite cause may be fulfilled by suitable operations and abstentions on the part of other finite causes, still it remains that all the other finite causes equally are conditioned. Hence, appeal to other finite causes can do no more than move the problem one stage further back; it can do that as often as one pleases; but never can it solve the problem. The only solution is to postulate a master plan that envisages all finite causes at all instants throughout all time, that so orders all that each in due course has the conditions of its operation fulfilled and so fulfils conditions of the operation of others. But since the only subject of such a master plan is the divine mind, the principal agent of its execution has to be God. Demonstrably, then, God not only gives being to, and conserves in being, every created cause, but also he uses the universe of causes as his instruments in applying each cause to its operation, and so is the principal cause of each and every event as event. Man proposes, but God disposes.

1.3 Critique of Views on Efficient Causality

Such are six views on the issue. I believe that the first three are easily refuted, that the fourth and fifth involve fallacies, that the sixth is demonstrated validly. The troublesome question for anyone who would defend any of the first three views is whether the influx is a reality. If it is not a reality, then efficient causality is not a reality but only a thought or, perhaps more accurately, a bit of imagination. But if the influx is a reality, it would seem that there must be an infinity of influences for each case of efficient causality. For if the influx is a reality, it must be produced itself; that production would involve a further influx, and that influx a further production. One might wish to say, *Sistitur in primo*.[f] But why? Either the influx is or it is not really distinct from what it produces. If it is, there is an infinite series. If it is not, then influx is just another name for the effect. At this point, the defender will urge that the influx is indeed a reality, that there are not an infinity of influences for each effect, and the reason is that the influx is a different type of reality from the effect – the type that eliminates the infinite series. But what type is that? I know only one, the real relation. There is no real efficient causality of efficient causality, and so on to infinity, because the reality of efficient causality is the reality of a real relation, and 'relatio relationis est ens rationis.'[g] It should seem that the first three views, while they differ profoundly on the reality of mediate efficient causality, have in common the source of their differences, namely, a failure to think out what is the reality of efficient causality as such.

The fourth view (the first on the second concept of efficient causality) involves a fallacy. When I see, it is true that I act in the sense that grammatically 'I' is subject of a verb in the active voice. But that does not prove that ontologically I am the efficient cause of my own seeing. Nor is it likely that anyone will find a proof that I am. For both Aristotle and Aquinas, external sensation has its efficient cause in the sensible object. Again, for both, 'intelligere est pati.' Again, for both, 'appetibile apprehensum movet appetitum,' and in later Thomist doctrine of the will, the act of willing an end is effected *quoad exercitium actus* by God.

The fallacy of the fifth position lies in affirming that the real difference between *potentia agendi* and *ipsum agere* is a reality added to the agent as agent; in fact, that reality is the effect, added to the patient as patient (*motus est in mobili, actio est in passo*), and predicated of the agent as agent only by extrinsic denomination; it has to be so, for otherwise either metaphysical laws have exceptions or else a *motor immobilis* would be a contradiction in terms; nor is it possible to demonstrate that, while action as action is predicated of the agent by extrinsic denomination, still created action as created is predicated of the agent by intrinsic denomination; what alone is demonstrable about created action as such is that it is conditioned, and that happens to be the premise of the sixth view.

2   Iglesias on God and Secondary Causes

Now it is to the sixth view that the author approximates. On that ground he naturally may be assured of my full admiration and esteem. But I have indulged in this long preamble because I cannot give any blanket approbation to the author's position and because I wish to point out just where we differ and where I believe his thought might be improved. His analysis of the nature of efficient causality I find inadequate. Indeed, it seems to me that he compromises between the two alternative notions of the reality of efficient causality, so that lower causes are causes because they exert an influx, whereas higher causes are causes although they do not. What is certain is that repeatedly (pp. 30, 70, 72) he states that, whereas the higher cause really is a cause, nevertheless the *agere in virtute alterius* of the lower involves no activity of the higher, either on the lower as acting or on its effect.

2.1 General Philosophic Position

What can the author mean by *activitas, actio, actio physica*? It should seem that an entity not found in every case of efficient causality has nothing to do with the metaphysical analysis of efficient causality: metaphysical laws have no exceptions. Again, if one takes *actio* as *actus huius ut ab hoc*, then the higher cause certainly does exert *actio* both on the means as means and on the effect, for *actio* is precisely the means as means and the effect as effect. On the other hand, if one takes *actio* in some other sense, the argument already given shows that the notion of efficient causality has not been examined adequately. While the author has gone further than most writers on the subject to untangle the issue, I cannot say that he has gone far enough.

Rightly the author insists on the relevance of final causality with regard to divine operation in the operations of creatures. But I believe that he attributes to God as final cause more than that notion can bear, and again the root difficulty is inadequate analysis. The final cause is the good as cause, the *cuius gratia*: just as efficient causality is a real relation of dependence on an *id a quo*, so final causality is a real relation of dependence on a *cuius gratia*. But there is a catch in the notion of the final cause. An end may be considered in two ways: simply as end, or as apprehended end; the former is the end as in *ordo executionis*; the latter as in *ordo intentionis*; the former is *finis operis* and the latter *finis operantis*, though it is safer to avoid the last pair of terms since moralists and even metaphysicians are prone to pay those words extra, so that they then mean what one pleases. Now there are two peculiarities of the end as apprehended. First, without it there would be no final causality at all: things do not tend to ends unless an intellect apprehends the ends and directs the things to them; secondly, the end as apprehended is the efficient cause of the act of appetition: *appetibile apprehensum movet appetitum*. Now the author has recognized these peculiarities, but not in the sense that the end as apprehended is properly, not a final, but an efficient cause; on the contrary, he has argued from that fact to the conclusion that final causes generally are movers. Such a generalization is unwarranted, but from it follow two further consequences: first, since the final cause is a mover, yet exerts no *actio physica*, a mover need exert no *actio physica*; this is correct, provided *actio physica* means some imagined and unintelligible influx, but not for the reason assigned; secondly – a graver consequence since it involves a general distortion of the theory of divine operation – as on the plane of pure theory the author injected efficiency into final causality, so on the plane of applied theory he has God as final cause exerting the efficient causality of a mover; in other words, while in fact every finite entity has two real relations of dependence – one on God as *id a quo* and the other on God as *cuius gratia* – the author appeals to God as final cause to fill up lacunae in his theory of God as efficient cause of all events.

So much for the author's general philosophic position. Its main tendency is, I believe, quite correct. But I also believe that it should undergo a very thorough revision before it can be recommended for the role of supplanting theories current in textbooks. I have indicated as well as I could the basic points of disagreement. I pass over all other points on which I also disagree, except one, namely, the summary treatment of the problem of sin. No doubt this problem has not on the sixth theory the acuteness so evident on the second, third, fourth, and fifth. Still, even on the sixth theory, it is a real problem and, so far from solving it, the author does not give evidence of having grasped it.

2.2 Historical Aspect of the Work

Let us turn to the historical aspect of the work. Judged by traditional standards of works *ad mentem divi Thomae*, the author is to be credited with an exceptionally sound instinct for history; thus he refuses to take it for granted that Aquinas carefully studied Suarez or John of St Thomas; on the contrary, about the first third of his work is devoted to determining the medieval meaning of technical terms and the medieval *status quaestionis*. But while this plan of operations is excellent, its execution, if judged by the absolute criteria of the logic of positive investigation, is extremely defective. The list of terms examined by the author does not include *actio, operatio, potentia activa, potentia passiva, procedere*; yet these terms, because of different strata in his sources and in his own development, are used ambiguously by Aquinas; these ambiguities tend to become systematized confusions in the commentators; and without clearing up the whole matter it is impossible to discuss intelligently either Thomist or Thomistic views[h] on efficient causality. Secondly, the investigation generally is based upon a minimum of texts; now quoting a few passages is only sampling but can yield rough lines for further study; it can substantiate negative conclusions, but cannot establish exact and positive information on what a thinker meant. Logically, the interpretation of a writer is a matter of formulating a hypothesis, working out its presuppositions and its implications, and verifying in the text the presuppositions, the hypothesis itself, and the implications. Deductions of what a writer must have meant are just so much fancy; in reality they are deductions from the hypothesis assumed by the interpreter; and whether that hypothesis is correct can be determined only with probability, a probability that increases only with the extent and the variety of the verification. Now, while Fr Iglesias is to be given credit for having derived his ideas from the text of St Thomas instead of merely using the text as a sort of cement to make a wall of a private heap of stones, it remains that his appetite for positive investigation is never keen, that instead of following out a search for historical fact, he would prefer to anticipate the objections of some not too enlightened controversialist. Accordingly, while I am in wholehearted agreement with Fr Iglesias in his contention that neither Molinism nor Bannezianism is an interpretation of Aquinas, still I find his own views on what Aquinas meant too briefly elaborated and too thinly substantiated to be interesting. For what Aquinas held was not some purely philosophic view: Avicenna had combined neo-Platonist emanationism with Aristotelian cosmic theory;[i] Aquinas modified this mixture to his own purposes. I believe that the essence of Aquinas' position can be given a purely philosophic statement that is strictly demonstrable. But I also believe that it is quite impossible to tell anyone what Aquinas meant while omitting mention of the historical origin and the nature of the blocks which he pieced together. To take a single instance of the result of neglecting the historical background, repeatedly the author informs us that the higher cause was denominated a cause because of its *praestantia ontologica formae*. In fact, higher causes like lower causes are causes if and only if they produce effects; their immanent perfections reveal what they could do but not what they actually do; finally, what lends color to the author's statement is simply that, on the assumption of Thomist cosmic theory, immanent perfection is at times a *ratio cognoscendi*, though not a *ratio essendi*, of efficient causality; for in that hierarchic universe, God and the *corpus caeleste* respectively have all subordinate beings as their instruments.

Formally theological but materially historical is the discussion of the Suarezian censure that *concursus immediatus*[j] has been the doctrine of all scholastics with the solitary exception of Durandus. Against this the author rightly points out that a number of early scholastics would not admit God to be the cause of the sinful act, where the thesis against which they argued was not that God was the immediate cause but simply that God was the cause of all acts. This alone suffices to require a qualification of the Suarezian censure. But the author also claims that the very question of immediate *concursus*, as later understood, was raised for the first time by Scotus or perhaps Giles of Rome. On this point I think further investigation is desirable: even if the general lines of the author's position would remain unaltered, at least more delicately exact history can be attained. The author fails to mention St Albert's *virtus divina creata*, which would seem a promising candidate for the role of immediate *concursus*. He also passes over the fact that Aquinas not only rejected the *virtus divina creata* but moreover took to task some censor who had objected to a theological proposition on the ground that it did not make God a more proximate cause than free will. Rather harshly, though far from unjustly, Aquinas wrote: 'As to the slanderous objection that God is more the proximate cause than free choice is, that is utterly frivolous, for God is the proximate cause according to the efficacy of the action and not according to the order in which causes are listed.'[2] It should seem that the frivolity, or to use Aquinas' expression, the utter frivolity, of insisting on unqualified immediacy began earlier than the author suspects. God really, and not in name merely, is the efficient cause of every event; God is the immediate efficient cause in the sense that God never is a means, not in the sense that he can never employ a means. But to my mind, what causes trouble is that immediacy and causality are not conceived but merely imagined; when that occurs, then one will argue that, unless God is the immediate efficient cause of every event, then he is a cause, not really, but only in name; such argument, of course, is frivolous, but at least Aquinas did not think frivolity impossible. Again, when controversialists assume that, if a certain theory of divine operation is not that of Molina or of Bañez, then it must be that of Durandus – Fr Iglesias has an appendix on this argument against Fr Stufler – then their attitude is explicable to me only on the assumption that they wish causality to be an influx they can imagine but no one can conceive. Finally, if I may voice a suspicion or suggest a hypothesis, it is this intrusion of the imagination, before as well as after Aquinas, that underlies what the author argues to be a post-Thomist shift in the *status quaestionis*.

3   Iglesias and Thomas Aquinas

The last third of the work deals mainly with the Thomist theory of grace. It is introduced, not for its own sake, but to buttress the philosophic position. On the whole I think the author would have done better to

2 *Declaratio centum et octo dubiorum ex commentario Fr. Petri de Tarantasia in Sententiis ad Magistrum Generalem*, q. 74, in S. Thomae Aquinatis, *Opuscula Omnia*, Vol. 3, ed. P. Mandonnet (Paris: Lethielleux, 1927) 235: 'Quod vero obiciens calumniatur, quod Deus est magis causa proxima quam liberum arbitrium, omnino frivolum est: est enim Deus causa proxima secundum efficaciam actionis et non secundum ordinem enuntiationis (Parma: enumerationis) causarum.' [The Mandonnet edition is the one cited by Lonergan; the Leonine title for the same work is *Responsio ad Magistrum Ioannem de Vercellis de 108 articulis*.]

omit it. He reads the Thomist text objectively enough but not widely enough. He bases himself almost exclusively on the final questions in the *Prima secundae*, so that he writes without awareness of the great development of Thomist thought on actual grace. Further, he writes with a controversial intent; he wishes to exclude *concursus immediatus*; and with this negative goal dominant, his own positive work suffers as, for the same reason, that of Fr Stufler suffered. Finally, he is unaware of the nature of Thomist theory of the will. Up to the *Pars prima* inclusively, the will, for Aquinas, was a passive faculty moved by an intellectual apprehension of the good: 'appetibile apprehensum movet appetitum.' In the *De malo* and in the *Prima secundae*, the intellectual apprehension of the good is the efficient cause only of the specification of the act; the exercise of the act of willing a means has its efficient cause in the will actuated with respect to an end; the exercise of the act of willing an end has its efficient cause in an external mover who is God. At no time did Aquinas advance or suppose that an immanent act has to be caused efficiently by the faculty in which it occurs though, of course, it is possible to construct arguments to the contrary based upon the equivocation of the terms *actio* and *operatio*, which sometimes mean efficient causality and sometimes simply second act, ἐνέργεια. Of all this the author seems unaware. His assumption with regard to immanent acts leads him to exclude a priori that the *voluntas mota et non movens*[k] of *Summa theologiae*, 1–2, q. 111, a. 2, is what it claims to be, a passive act produced in the will by God without any efficiency exerted by the will itself. It is true that in later Thomist doctrine not only is such passivity incompatible with freedom, but also that the act of willing an end is not free.[1] Nonetheless, it is a vital, immanent, voluntary act, just as the act of understanding in the *intellectus possibilis* is a vital, immanent, intellectual act, though *intelligere est pati*. Next, the significance of the argument against acts of charity produced in the will without a habit of charity is not that the will must be an efficient cause and God cannot be an immediate efficient cause. God is the external mover who *immediatione virtutis et suppositi* causes all acts of willing an end, whether natural or supernatural, *quoad exercitium actus*. The significance of the argument on the necessity of a habit of charity is the same as that of the argument on the necessity of an *intellectus possibilis*: for an act to be the act of a subject, the subject must be in potency to the act; else it is not his act. Just as Averroës' man cannot understand without an *intellectus possibilis*, so St Thomas' man cannot elicit supernatural acts of love without a habit of charity; absence of potency – and in both cases it is passive potency that is absent – means that the subject cannot be actuated in a given way. With these basic differences between the author and myself, it is plain that points of disagreement on his treatment of grace are too numerous to be treated in detail. I wish to say that I think he is right in acknowledging a problem with regard to the gratuitous character of acts preparatory remotely to justification, but his outlined solution in terms of a *forma fluens*, of a habit that is not habitual, neither takes advantage of the indications Aquinas himself gave nor is satisfactory as independent thinking. Again, actual grace after justification is not merely the general theorem of divine operation in the operations of creatures; it includes divine causation of the act of willing the end and so divine control over willing means; and the act of willing the end, as caused gratuitously by God, is supernatural not only extrinsically in virtue of the end envisaged but also intrinsically as the actuation of supernatural habit; finally, since any habit is only a *per se* principle of the occurrence of acts and so of their occurrence only *in maiori parte*, special divine intervention to secure perseverance is an additional need.

4   Bañez and Molina

The controversial element in the work is pervasive and, to me at least, distracting from better things. It takes a pure form in the systematic refutation of *concursus simultaneus* and *praemotio physica*,[m] which the author argues not only to lack intrinsic proof but also to involve contradiction. The precise argument he advances for the latter contention is difficult to evaluate because argument and counterargument can follow one another indefinitely unless there is a very searching and thorough elaboration of fundamental concepts; as I have already stated, such basic elaboration is lacking. However, the former contention by itself is quite enough, and I believe it to be quite true; no Bannezian has ever demonstrated his position to a Molinist, or Molinist his to a Bannezian; and I agree with Fr Iglesias that both are right in finding one or two of the other's arguments fallacious.

Conclusion

To conclude, Fr Iglesias has confronted a very large problem courageously. The urgency of confronting it is only going to increase in the future, for today medieval studies are flourishing in a manner unknown in the past; and this involves, I believe, not only the discredit of baroque procedures but also an unexpectedly quiet funeral for a once celebrated and very passionate debate. Sooner or later there will be an evidently empty place at the philosophic and the theological tables, and Fr Iglesias' effort to meet that future contingency is an act of intelligent foresight. However, one has the feeling that he did not quite realize the magnitude of the task he set himself, but was more concerned to surpass the requirements of the average product of the past than to meet the exigencies of the future; that, while he regularly comes to grips with the real issues, still he struggles with them rather in the dark. I have given my reasons for not considering the work definitive. I do not believe it should be recommended to minds more inclined to accept than to criticize what they find in print. But, for all that, it possesses the value of calling attention to real issues and of indicating a direction of solution that I believe sound.

4

The Assumption and Theology

My terms of reference set forth three topics: (1) the death of our Lady; (2) theological discussions concerning the assumption; (3) the assumption as a defined doctrine. If these topics are transposed into questions and taken in reverse order, their unity will be immediately apparent. The last topic is the question, Could our Lady's assumption be defined as a matter of faith? The second topic, namely, the discussions of theologians, gives the question, Why could the assumption be defined as a matter of faith? Finally, the first topic raises the question, Might our Lady's death be included in a definition of the assumption?

1   Could the Assumption Be Defined?

The answer undoubtedly is affirmative. From the seventh century to the present day the affirmation of the assumption has increased in clarity and in unanimity in the church of God. In the Dark Ages there existed doubts about the fact of the assumption and consequent obscurity regarding the object of the feast.[1] In the medieval period obscurity was

1 See Martin Jugie, A.A., *La mort et l'Assomption de la Sainte Vierge*: *Etude Historico-Doctrinale* (Vatican City: Biblioteca Apostolica Vaticana, 1944) 274–85. This monumental work is an invaluable source of historical information. However, the author's scholarship is frequently put to the service of theological opinions of little or no probability. The latter tendency in the work unfortunately has led to not a little obscuration of its great merit and utility.

removed mainly through the influence of St Albert the Great,[2] while the scholarship of the Renaissance removed the grounds of doubt that had lingered in the liturgy from the Dark Ages.[3] As prior to the Renaissance the assumption was not denied, so since then it has not been doubted.[4] Finally, from 1869 to 1941 vast numbers of petitions for the definition of the assumption have been addressed to the Holy See. To select the most significant of these petitions, namely, those from residential episcopal sees, an incomplete survey reveals that from 820 sees 1332 patriarchs, archbishops, and bishops have sent 1859 petitions asking that our Lady's assumption be defined as a matter of faith.[5] While this leaves 299 residential episcopal sees unrepresented, that is, some 27% of the total, it provides very serious grounds for expecting the agreement of all the rest.

Such a practically universal agreement and consent both down the centuries and throughout the church provides the theologian with sufficient ground for affirming that the assumption can be defined. Were the assumption not truth but error, then one would have to admit what no Catholic can admit, namely, that God has not promised preservation from error to the church.[6] Moreover, though the recent petitions are appreciated differently by theologians,[7] it should seem that they imply not only that the assumption is true and certain but also that it is definable as a matter of faith. For the teaching office of the church is exercised by the bishops throughout the world; and they preponderantly affirm the assumption to be definable as a matter of faith. Such is the conclusion drawn by notable theologians in authoritative positions;[8] and while one

2 Ibid. 395.
3 Ibid. 424–30.
4 For the inevitable qualifications of so sweeping a statement, see ibid. 437–60.
5 G. Hentrich and R.G. de Moos, *Petitiones de Assumptione corporea B. V. Mariae in caelum definienda ad S. Sedem delatae* (2 vols., Rome: Typis Polyglottis Vaticanis, 1942), Vol. 2, 836. I am citing F.S. Mueller, 'Petitiones de Assumptione corporea B. V. Mariae in caelum definienda,' *Gregorianum* 27 (1946) 112.
6 Thus, prior to the publication of the petitions, Henricus Lennerz, *De Beata Virgine*, 3rd ed. (Rome: Gregorian University Press, 1939) 100.
7 Jugie (595–600) advances nine considerations against giving much weight to the petitions.
8 'Des pétitions moralement unanimes de l'épiscopat catholique du monde entier, il résulte donc que la définibilité de cette prérogative mariale est

might add qualifications and reservations with regard to this or that consideration they advance, I do not see how their ultimate conclusion could effectively be reversed.

2   Why Can the Assumption Be Defined?

I thought it best to begin with the argument from authority, first, because in matters of faith we normally know what is true before we know why it is true and, secondly, because an initial account of theological discussions and disagreements might easily be misleading, for it might lend an impression of confusion and doubt that would be quite ungrounded. The assumption of our Lady is one thing; the reasons, apart from the ultimate argument from authority, are quite another. The former is proximately a matter of faith; the latter are not; and it is with the latter that now I have to deal.

2.1 Assumption Implicitly Revealed

Why, then, can the assumption be defined as a matter of faith? Evidently, the one sufficient reason for this is that it pertains to the deposit of faith, that it is a truth revealed by God. But in what manner is it revealed? Is it contained explicitly in holy scripture? Or is it an explicit, oral, apostolic tradition? The answer to both these questions would seem to be negative. Very few have been those who claimed that the assumption was explicitly revealed in scripture.[9] A more frequent contention has been for the existence of an explicit, oral, apostolic tradition.[10] It remains that the predominant view among theologians at present is that the assumption was revealed not explicitly but implicitly.[11] Three very broad facts mil-

---

chose certaine et que la note théologique, qu'on devra désormais (en attendant la dogmatisation) donner à la thèse de l'Assomption, sera à tout le moins "proximum fidei".' – E. Druwé, 'Vers la définition dogmatique de l'Assomption: A propos d'une publication récente,' *Recherches de science religieuse* 33 (1946) 477. Similarly, F.S. Mueller, 'Petitiones ... ' 135; R. Garrigou-Lagrange, 'De definibilitate Assumptionis B. Mariae Virginis,' *Angelicum* 22 (1945) 72; C. Balić, 'De definibilitate Assumptionis B. Mariae Virginis in caelum,' *Antonianum* 21 (1946) 33.

9 Jugie, *La mort* ... 474–75.
10 Ibid. 475–79.
11 Ibid. 480. 'Veritas Assumptionis dicenda est formaliter revelata, non quidem, ut videtur, explicite, sed implicite et confuse ... ' Thesis defended at the Pontifical Gregorian University in the presence of nine

itate against the existence of any explicit revelation either in scripture
or in tradition. The first is the silence of the early centuries. The second
is the diversity of views that appeared, notably in the Apocrypha, when
attention first turned to our Lady's death.[12] The third is the long per-
sisting doubts existing in the Western church,[13] of which the most notable
found expression in the Martyrology of Usuard that was read from the
ninth century to the sixteenth and advanced that on the question of the
assumption the sobriety of the church preferred pious ignorance to
frivolous and apocryphal doctrine.[14] These three broad facts of an initial
period of silence, a second period of naive speculations, and a third
period in which doubts were countenanced, are, on the one hand, just
what would be expected were revelation only implicit and, on the other
hand, extremely difficult to reconcile with the existence of explicit
revelation.[15]

---

cardinals and uncounted other dignitaries, December 12, 1946.[a] See
'Disputatio solemnis de definibilitate Assumptionis B. Mariae Virginis,'
Gregorianum 27 (1946) 640, thesis 4. Similar positions are adopted by
Druwé, Mueller, Garrigou-Lagrange, Balić, in the articles cited in
note 8.

12 Observe that the early silence includes such statements as St Augustine's
'Unus resurrexit, non moriturus ... Christus' (*Enarratio in psalm.* CXXVI,
7, J.-P. Migne, *Patrologiae cursus completus ...,* Series Prima [PL], Vol. 36,
col. 1673); the reference is in Jugie, *La mort ...* 67 [where Lonergan
found Augustine quoted in a slightly different form, 'Unus resurrexit,
iam non moriturus, Christus']. On the Apocrypha, see ibid. 103–71; also
Alfred C. Rush, 'The Assumption in the Apocrypha,' *American Ecclesiastical Review* 116 (1947), 5–31. On St Epiphanius and on Timothy of
Jerusalem, see Jugie, *La mort ...* 70–81, and also Otto Faller, *De priorum
saeculorum silentio circa Assumptionem B. Mariae Virginis* (Rome: Gregorian
University Press, 1946) 27–43.
13 Jugie, *La mort ...* 276–85, 371–78, 389–91, 437–52.
14 Ibid. 208, 428.
15 From the viewpoint of apologetics, this point is very important. No theologian would deny that the assistance of the Holy Spirit enabled the
apostles to understand the full implications of divine revelation. But it is
quite another matter to affirm an explicit, oral, apostolic tradition when
there is not sufficient evidence to justify such an affirmation. J. Coppens
expresses a legitimate concern when he concluded a rather unsatisfac-
tory article with the remark: ' ... évitons, en toute hypothèse, de parler
ou d'écrire comme si nous voulions obtenir de l'Eglise, ou comme si
l'Eglise elle-même envisageait, de sanctionner, sur le plan de l'histoire,
une doctrine comme remontant à l'âge apostolique, alors que toute base
historique solide, à parler humainement, semble lui faire défaut.' 'La
définibilité de l'Assomption,' *Ephemerides theologicae lovanienses* 23 (1947)
35. The argument that the later consent of the church presupposes the

If the assumption, then, is revealed not explicitly but implicitly, a further question arises, namely, What is the precise nature of the implication? This question is the center of theological discussion. Accordingly, I shall set forth very summarily, first, an illustration of scriptural implication, secondly, an outline of the argument from holy scripture for the assumption, thirdly, an evaluation of the certainty of this argument, and fourthly, an account of its sufficiency for dogmatic definition.

2.2   Nature of Scriptural Implication of Assumption

2.2.1   Illustration of Scriptural Implication

First, then, what is meant by a scriptural implication? In the twenty-fourth chapter of St Luke[b] there occurs the account of the two disciples who had lost faith in our Lord, did not credit reports of his resurrection, and so on the first Easter Sunday set out for a town named Emmaus some sixty furlongs from Jerusalem. As you know, a stranger fell in with them on the way, asked the cause of their dejection, upbraided them for being 'foolish and slow of heart to believe in all the things which the prophets have spoken' (Luke 24.25), and then proceeded to explain to them the messianic prophecies of the Old Testament. As he spoke, the faith of the faltering disciples was enkindled anew, their hearts burned within them, and the eyes of their understanding were opened; they began to see in divine revelation what had been there all along, even though previously they had not seen it. We have, then, in this story an instance of scriptural implication. The mystery of the redemption through the suffering and death of our Lord is contained in the Old Testament. But still that mystery does not lie on the surface. To grasp it one must, as we say, put two and two together; one must begin, as did our Lord with the disciples, from Moses and then proceed through all the prophets; but Moses and the prophets treated of very many things, and so

---

previous existence of an explicit, oral, apostolic tradition is valid only on the erroneous supposition that there is no such thing as implicit revelation or the development of dogma. E. Druwé denies that any nugget of tradition is to be extracted from the Apocrypha ('Vers la définition ... ' 473). A. Rush ('The Assumption in the Apocrypha' 29–30) suggests that the Apocrypha may exhibit the first attempts to formulate Christian thought on the death of Mary; he denies that they presuppose necessarily some apostolic or patristic tradition. Still, see O. Faller, De priorum saeculorum silentio ... 43–63.

from them one must select just the right passages; finally, one has to piece together these many passages into a single, intelligible pattern. By this selection and piecing together there is effected a development of understanding, an opening of the eyes of faith, upon what had been long revealed but what had not, from lack of understanding, been apprehended.

Just as our Lord taught the disciples to discover in the Old Testament the doctrine of the redemption, so down the ages has the church in the development of dogma brought forth from the deposit of faith both old things and new. My next step, then, will be to indicate the scriptural sources for the doctrine of the assumption and the manner in which one may proceed from those sources to the assumption itself.

2.2.2 Argument from Scripture for Assumption

Scriptural sources for the doctrine of the assumption lie in the account of man's fall through Adam and his redemption through Christ. There are two solidarities: a first in Adam through sin to death; a second in Christ through death to resurrection. Adam sinned, and through his sin death entered into the world. This death was threefold: there was the spiritual death of the loss of sanctifying grace in the soul; there was the metaphorical death, the curse of Adam, so vivid to us today in the host of the moral and physical evils of the world; finally, there was the material death of the grave where dust returns to dust. Now Christ, the Son of God, knew not sin; still he died, but only to rise again; and as he died for the remission of sin, so he rose again to give us grace (Romans 4.25). For it is the risen Christ that is the vitalizing spirit of the mystical body,[16] and to that body of Christ we belong ever more fully as progressively we die to rise again. First, there is baptism in the death of Christ by which our souls rise again to live to grace and sanctity (Romans 6.2–4). Secondly, there is the metaphorical death of mortification, in which the reign of sin over us and in us is crushed and we live with our members as instruments of justice unto God (Romans 6.11–14). In the third place, death is swallowed up in victory (1 Corinthians 15.54), when 'in a moment, in the twinkling of an eye ... the trumpet shall sound and the dead shall rise again incorruptible ... For this corruptible must put on incor-

---

16 1 Corinthians 15.45. On this and connected matter, see F. Prat, *La théologie de saint Paul*, 17th ed. (Paris: Beauchesne, 1933), Vol. 2, 250–54, 66–78, 203–13.

ruption, and this mortal must put on immortality' (ibid. 15.52–53). 'As in Adam all die, so also in Christ all shall be made alive' (ibid. 15.22).

Such, then, is the general scheme of things. It is through Christ the transfiguration of death, from a death of soul and body in consequence of sin, to a dying with Christ as a prelude to resurrection of soul and body. Nor is the resurrection of the body merely a charming incidental, an added attraction. Rather it is the triumphant goal to which all else proceeds and in which all is contained. 'By the envy of the devil death came into the world' (Wisdom 2.24) and contrariwise, it was 'through death he [Christ] might destroy him who had the empire of death, that is to say, the devil' (Hebrews 2.14). Again, 'Jesus Christ … hath destroyed death' (2 Timothy 1.10), yet because 'the enemy death shall be destroyed last' (1 Corinthians 15.26), 'the expectation of the creature waiteth for the revelation of the sons of God … For we know that every creature groaneth and travaileth in pain, even till now. And not only it, but we ourselves also, who have the first fruits of the Spirit: even we ourselves groan within ourselves, waiting for the adoption of the sons of God, the redemption of our body' (Romans 8.19–23). There have been those who found fault with St Paul for exclaiming: 'If … I fought with the beasts at Ephesus, what doth it profit me, if the dead rise not again? Let us eat and be merry, for tomorrow we shall die' (1 Corinthians 15.32). But the emphasis of holy scripture on things spiritual is not its exclusive emphasis; nor does our good Lord expect us, his creatures of flesh and blood, redeemed by the flesh and blood of Christ, fed on his flesh and blood in the Eucharist, to look forward to a beatitude out of the body or to count Christ's victory over Satan and sin complete without an eternal triumph of sense and sensibility, of flesh and of feeling, over the miseries of this life and the catastrophe of the grave.

Such is the general perspective presented explicitly to our faith by holy scripture. But where in this picture stands Mary, the virgin blessed amongst women, the Mother of God? As Christ rose from the dead and ascended into heaven, was she too assumed, soul and body, into heaven? Or does she still await, with sinners, the trumpet of an angel to be summoned from death to life? If there have been Christians who felt they had not the grounds to affirm the first alternative with certitude, there have been none to venture to affirm the second. Too clearly, Mary's position is a position of privilege: full of grace, she never for an instant was under the dominion of Satan or stained by sin; ever a virgin, still she was a mother, the Mother of God; and she became a mother without the pangs of motherhood, for those pains were the curse of Eve (Genesis 3.16) and she was blessed amongst women (Luke 1.42) to be called blessed by all generations (ibid. 1.48). Who but she could be the woman spoken of in Genesis: 'I will put enmities between thee and the woman, and thy seed and her seed: she shall crush thy head, and thou shalt lie in wait for her heel' (Genesis 3.15)? But can all this be granted, and yet the assumption be denied? Can one say that the fruits of the redemption were anticipated to preserve the soul of Mary from original sin but not anticipated to bring her body to heaven? Can one say that she was freed from the empire of Satan, inasmuch as that empire was sin, but not inasmuch as that empire was death? Can one say that she adores in heaven the body to which she gave birth, yet is without the body that gave it birth? Can one invent some metaphysical law or some principle of divine justice that overrules the best of sons' love for the best of mothers, that permits the Sacred Heart to be a living heart but forces the Immaculate Heart to be a dead heart, that calls a halt to privilege after the immaculate conception, divine maternity, and perpetual virginity, to consign our Lady's body to the grave? Can one deny that the assumption would be a grace, or that Mary is full of grace? The more one thinks about it, the more numerous the aspects one considers, the fuller becomes the evidence and the greater its cogency.

2.2.3 Certainty of the Argument

Such, then, is the implication of the assumption in the teaching of scripture. But is that implication absolutely certain? Are not affirmative answers born more of sentiment or enthusiasm or loyalty than of cold logic?[17] Probability is one thing, but certitude is quite another. Un-

17 The question is raised by J. Coppens, 'La définibilité de l'Assomption' 20. H. Lennerz cuts various theological arguments down to probability. See *De Beata Virgine* 101–11. M. Jugie denies efficacy to arguments other than the one he invented. See *La mort* ... 626, 638, 641, 647. The elementary point to be born in mind – it does seem to be overlooked – is that our understanding of the mystery of the redemption cannot be perfect and cannot yield the type of necessary implication familiar from metaphysics or mathematics; this is no less than the doctrine of the Vatican Council (Sess. 3, c. 4, Denzinger, *Enchiridion symbolorum* ... 1796 [DS 3016]). A further point to be noticed is that it is not an implication

doubtedly there is a good case for the assumption. One may even admit
that there is, at the present time, an overwhelming case for the assumption; if one understands scripture in the manner outlined above, one
cannot consider any other alternative; but understanding is a tricky
thing, the parent of endless theories and hypotheses that have their day
and then are relegated to the dustbin of outmoded thought.

There are three steps in the answer to this difficulty. The first is to
point out that the development of Christian doctrine is not subject to
the revolutions that are part and parcel of the development of science;
the reason for this is ultimately that the development of understanding
in science regards sensible data, while the development of understanding
in Christian doctrine regards, not sensible presentations which intellect
has to raise to the order of truths, but a divine revelation which already
is in the order of truth. The second step is to observe that, in the present
instance at least, not only the truths to be understood but also the general
lines of the understanding itself are revealed; we do not have to construct
the whole picture; the whole is something given; all that we have to do
is to determine from the shape of the whole the place to be assigned to
a part. Finally, the third and conclusive step to observe is that the implication of the assumption is not the fruit of individual human understanding; the understanding that is relevant is the understanding of man
illumined by faith and moved by the grace of the Holy Spirit; it is not the
understanding of this or that man, nor of this or that age, but of the
church; and ultimately, certitude rests not upon judgment proceeding
from merely human understanding but upon the judgment of the church
to whom God has promised infallibility in matters of faith and morals.

2.2.4 Sufficient Basis for Dogmatic Definition

There remains a final question. Did God reveal the assumption of our
Lady? Can it be a matter of faith? We have admitted that the assumption
was revealed not explicitly but only implicitly. Still, not every implication
of scripture, not every conclusion theologians can spin out from scripture, thereby is a matter of faith. On the contrary, the Vatican Council
is quite strict, teaching that 'the doctrine of faith, revealed by God, has

___

as such but the affirmation of an implication that is true or false, certain
or probable; this distinction underlies the distinction drawn by John of
St Thomas (see note 32 infra) between the inference made by human
intellect and the affirmation made with the assistance of the Holy Spirit.

not been presented to human talent to be perfected as though it were some philosophic discovery'; that 'it has been entrusted to the church, the spouse of Christ, as a divine deposit, faithfully to be guarded and infallibly to be declared.'[18] There does exist a development of understanding, knowledge, and wisdom both in individuals and in the whole church; but it must be true to type and without change of dogma, of meaning, or of doctrine.[19]

As is apparent, there are definite limits to the development of dogma, but for a more precise account of them we have to go to the theologians. Here we are met with a variety of opinions. In a recent article Fr Garrigou-Lagrange, o.p., affirmed that the majority of theologians require what is termed 'formally implicit' revelation for a doctrine to be of faith; his point appears to have been that, since the bishops could not in conscience follow a minority opinion, their petitions for definition of the assumption imply that they consider the assumption to be formally implied in revelation.[20] In an even more recent article Fr Charles Balić, o.f.m., advanced that to require formally implicit revelation was to sabotage the movement for a definition of the assumption,[21] that the commission that prepared the definition of the immaculate conception was hampered by no such criterion as formally implicit revelation,[22] that Melchior Cano, who presumably was, had maintained that the church could never define the immaculate conception as a matter of faith.[23] If representatives of the Dominican and Franciscan theological institutes in Rome disagree, one can quote Jesuits from either side of the fence. In 1930 Fr Francis Mueller wrote a book to prove that the assumption was revealed implicitly and formally.[24] In reviewing it, Fr Adhémar d'Alès advanced that, as far as he could see, formal implicit revelation was not necessary, and in any case what Fr Mueller called 'formal implication' was no more than

18 Sess. 3, c. 4, Denzinger, *Enchiridion symbolorum ...* 1800 [*DS* 3020].
19 Ibid.: 'Crescat igitur ... et multum vehementerque proficiat, tam singulorum quam omnium, tam unius hominis quam totius Ecclesiae, aetatum ac saeculorum gradibus, intelligentia, scientia, sapientia: sed in suo dumtaxat genere, in eodem scilicet dogmate, eodem sensu, eademque sententia.'
20 R. Garrigou-Lagrange, 'De definibilitate Assumptionis ... ' 70 (see 68). On the same point see also F.S. Mueller, 'Petitiones ... ' 130–33.
21 C. Balić, 'De definibilitate Assumptionis ... ' 16.
22 Ibid. 20–24.
23 Ibid. 53.
24 F.S. Mueller, *Origo divino-apostolica doctrinae evectionis Beatissimae Virginis ad gloriam caelestem quoad Corpus* (Innsbruck: Rauch, 1930.)

a virtual implication.[25] As this disagreement manifests, the problem involves not only whether formal implication is necessary for definition but also what precisely formal implication is.

I think not a little light is thrown on this subject if one leaves the field of contemporary theology and goes back to the initiators of the discussion. The original question was whether one could believe by divine faith a conclusion resulting syllogistically from two premises, one of which was revealed by God, while the other was known with certainty by merely human science. For example, we know from the gospel that our Lord changed water into wine at Cana; we know from chemistry that ordinary water is largely H_2O; is it, then, or could it be a matter of faith that our Lord changed into wine what mainly was H_2O? That is a perfectly clear question; it was given different answers. Molina held it never could be.[26] Vasquez advanced that already it was a matter of faith.[27] Suarez straddled: unless it is defined, it is not; but if it were defined, then it would be.[28] De Lugo followed Suarez.[29] John of St Thomas held the church would not define a mere theological conclusion such as the above.[30] The *Salmanticenses* agreed with him.[31] Now the point to be observed is that this discussion throws no doubt on the definability of the assumption. For the assumption is not a theological conclusion in the sense defined above; it depends exclusively upon divine revelation; it draws no premises from philosophy or physics or chemistry or biology or any other merely human department of knowledge. On the contrary, the argument outlined above for the assumption meets exactly the requirements of the rigorous school as represented by John of St Thomas.[32]

25 In *Recherches de science religieuse* 21 (1931) 240–41.
26 *In I* [*In primam divi Thomae partem*], q. 1, a. 2, disp. 1 and 2. I cite Lennerz, *De virtutibus theologicis* (Rome: Gregorian University Press, 1938) 81. The old writers did not, of course, discuss the example given in the text, but the equivalent, *homo est risibilis*.
27 *In I* [*In primam partem Summae theologiae*], q. 1, a. 2, disp. 5, c. 3 (Venice: Baretium Baretium & Socios, 1600) 23–24; Lennerz, ibid.
28 Francisco Suarez, *Tractatus de fide*, disp. 3, sect. xi, nn. 1, 6, 7, 11 (*Opera omnia*, Vol. 12, Paris: Vivès, 1858) 95–100.
29 Joannis de Lugo, *De virtute fidei divinae*, disp. 1, sect. xiii, §1, nn. 261, 269–70 (*Disputationes scholasticae et morales*, Vol. 1, Paris: Vivès, 1891) 123–28.
30 Joannis a Sancto Thoma, *Cursus theologici, In quaestionem I primae partis*, disp. 2, a. 4 (Solesmes ed., Vol. 1, Paris: Desclée, 1931) 357–62.
31 *Collegii Salmanticensis cursus theologicus*, Vol. 11 (Paris: Palmé, 1879) 58, 65–71 (*De fide*, disp. 1, dub. iv, §§ 4, 6, 7, nn. 124, 139–42, 143–52).
32 Joannis a Sancto Thoma, ibid. §10, p. 360: 'Respondetur negando quod propositiones definitae ab Ecclesia non sint immediate revelatae a

But if this is so, why is there the contemporary disagreement? I should say that it is occasioned by a shift of viewpoint. In the seventeenth century the basic issue was an accurately defined theological conclusion which was called a virtual implication. In contemporary writers the foreground is occupied with an account of formal implication, and for reasons which are not our present concern, hardheaded and clear accounts of formal implication are not broad enough to fit the facts,[33] while loose and obscure accounts of formal implication fit the facts by dodging the issue.[34] If one wishes to go to the root of this theological problem, one has to get beyond conceptualism[c] and give a central role in thought to the act of understanding. But I see no reason why the definition of the assumption should be delayed until this problem in speculative theology is solved.[35]

Deo: licet revelatio illa sit implicita et occulta nobis, et ideo per discursum attingatur, et eodem discursu Ecclesia disponat et praeparet ipsam inquisitionem veritatis; tamen cum venitur ad diffinitionem, discursus ipse et disputatio humano modo facta non est ratio definiendi et credendi, sed quia *visum est Spiritui Sancto*: non quidem de novo revelanti illam veritatem, sed occultam revelationem factam illuminanti, et manifestanti legitimum sensum occultum; iuxta quod dicitur (Luc. xxiv, 45), quod *Dominus aperuit sensum discipulis, ut intelligerent Scripturas*, et ad hoc promisit Spiritum Sanctum Ecclesiae ut *doceret* illam *omnem veritatem*. Et sic per auctoritatem Ecclesiae veritas immediate revelata transit ab occulta ad manifestam, non a revelata mediate ad revelatam immediate.'

33   Such a hardheaded account is represented by the list of formal implications – definition in the defined, essential physical parts in the whole, particular proposition in the universal, conclusion in its premises (Lennerz, *De virtutibus theologicis* 67). In his *De Beata Virgine* the same author recalls his criteria (101), shows the difficulties of certainty regarding the assumption as revealed (101–109), and finally proposes as possible solutions that the assumption was revealed implicitly in the corporeal integrity explicitly revealed as perpetual virginity, or again as part of the victory over Satan explicitly revealed with regard to sin, implicitly with regard to death (110–11). It would seem, then, that the assumption is an *essential physical* part of a kind of corporeal integrity that includes the assumption or, again, of a victory over Satan.

34   It has been maintained that the assumption is a conclusion following from two explicitly revealed premises and therefore itself revealed formally and implicitly. See R. Garrigou-Lagrange, 'De definibilitate assumptionis ... ' 71–72. With regard to the putative syllogism so offered, one can only say that the conclusion does not follow syllogistically from the premises; and if the premises are so modified that the conclusion does follow rigorously, then the premises will be found not to be formally and explicitly revealed.

35   Fr Balić, 'De definibilitate Assumptionis ... ' 18, expresses the same view. Fr Mueller, 'Petitiones ... ' 132, comes round to it.

3   Our Lady's Death

If our Lady died, then she died at some determinate place and time; she died from some assignable cause; and one would expect that there were witnesses of the event. But contemporary documentary evidence is totally lacking. Nor do the fathers add much to our information. Her death was mentioned incidentally as an assumed matter of fact, certainly by Saints Ephraem and Augustine, probably by St Ambrose, perhaps also by St Gregory of Nyssa.[36] There are dubious suggestions that she was thought never to have died, in St Epiphanius and in a sermon by Timothy of Jerusalem.[37] On the other hand, the Apocrypha, which began to be compiled towards the end of the fifth century,[38] take the death of our Lady as the central fact of their narrations. Further, at the end of the sixth century, veneration was paid to our Lady's tomb at Jerusalem though when that veneration began we hardly know.[39] In subsequent centuries Fr Martin Jugie has unearthed two writers whose words might possibly be taken to express a doubt or denial of our Lady's death.[40] On the other hand, Fr Jugie has run to ground an alleged list of theologians supposed to have denied her death; it turns out that the list never existed.[41] All in all, until one reaches the speculations of Canon Arnaldi in the nineteenth century, an unmistakable denial of our Lady's death does not seem to have been found.

These speculations cannot be allowed any weight. They are to the effect that Adam, because he was created in grace, had the privilege of immortality; similarly, since our Lady was conceived immaculately, she had either the privilege itself or, in Fr Jugie's modification, the right to the privilege of immortality. The summary answer is that privileges are

---

36 See Jugie, *La mort* ... 59–70.

37 Ibid. 70–81. Also Faller, *De priorum saeculorum silentio* ... 27–43.

38 Jugie, *La mort* ... 108.

39 Ibid. 681–87. Also Faller, *De priorum saeculorum silentio* ... 44–60.

40 In the eighth century, Tusaredus; in the fourteenth, Francis of Mayron (*La mort* ... 275, 402).

41 This list attributed to Macedo is mentioned by A.M. Lépicier, *De Beatissima Virgine Maria* (Paris, no date, but after August, 1901) 251. [Thus in Lonergan's text; but in the 5th ed. (Rome: Ex Officina Typographica, 1926) 361.] Also by J. Bellamy, 'Assomption de la Sainte Vierge,' *Dictionnaire de théologie catholique*, Vol. 1 (Paris: Librarie Letouzey et Ané, 1931), col. 2128. See Jugie, *La mort* ... 515.

freely bestowed.[42] The fuller answer is contained in three statements: one may grant that Fr Jugie establishes an abstract possibility that our Lady did not die; in the second place, such abstract possibilities are not very relevant to matters of fact; in the third place, the church has not doubted that our Lady did die – and that agreement is final for the theologian.[43] I need not add that the scientific historian would not think of asking whether a human being who lived nineteen centuries ago has died.

But there is a further question: Is the death of our Lady capable of definition along with the assumption? On this issue the recent petitions already mentioned offer nothing decisive. Out of 3019 petitions of what may be termed the teachers in the church, 2344 do not mention the issue, 5 seem to doubt our Lady's death, 24 seem to affirm her death but do not do so clearly, 434 (including 264 residential bishops) affirmed that our Lady died, do not wish her death defined but rather placed in a preambulatory argument or exposition; finally, 212 (including 154 residential bishops) wish her death included in the definition itself of the assumption.[44]

Theological opinion reveals a parallel division. Fr Balić argues that the death of our Lady could be defined as a dogmatic fact in virtue of its connection with the doctrine of the assumption as that doctrine has been understood by the church.[45] Other theologians, while not disputing such a position as Fr Balić's and while casting no doubt whatever on the fact of our Lady's death, insist on the point that the assumption does not necessarily presuppose the death of our Lady (she can be in heaven body and soul, even though her soul never was separated from her body); they further point out that the arguments for the assumption and for the death of our Lady are distinct, that they differ in character, in their guarantees of certitude, in the manner in which they could be objects of faith; in consequence, they favor a simple affirmation of our Lady's death and devote their efforts to showing that the assumption itself,

42 P. Charles, review of M. Jugie, *La mort ...* , in *Nouvelle revue théologique* 69 (1947) 885. More fully, Balić, 'De definibilitate Assumptionis ...' 45–53.
43 Lennerz, *De Beata Virgine* 59.
44 Hentrich and de Moos, *Petitiones de Assumptione ...* , Vol. 2, 715–25. I am citing from Mueller, 'Petitiones ...' *Gregorianum* 27 (1946) 122.
45 Balić, 'De definibilitate Assumptionis ...' 53–59.

taken in a rigorous sense, could be defined as an object of faith.[46] This second view suffers from a certain complexity; on the other hand, it is content with a minimum with which, at present, all could agree.

Conclusion

In conclusion I recapitulate what has been said. The assumption of our Lady to heaven could be defined as a dogma of divine and Catholic faith. Though not explicitly revealed in holy scripture nor, as far as we know with certitude, in any explicit, oral, apostolic tradition, still it is revealed implicitly. That implication is grasped as human understanding, illumined by faith and aided by grace, penetrates the economy of man's fall and redemption and settles our Lady's place in it. That implication is certain because of the longstanding and widespread agreement existing in the church. That implication is certainly not a theological conclusion in the classical sense, for it is grasped without appealing to any merely human science as a premise; whether one chooses to name it a formal or a virtual implication will depend on one's definition of those terms; but the manner one chooses to define those terms will not alter the one important fact, that the implication of the assumption is of the type that has sufficed for previous dogmatic definitions. Finally, doubts about the fact of our Lady's death are unjustified; whether, however, our Lady's death should be asserted as a preamble or included in a definition, are points on which theological thought has, as yet, not crystallized.

---

46 This position advanced by Mueller, *Origo divino-apostolica* ... , seems to have been adopted in the theses defended at the Pontifical Gregorian University on the occasion mentioned above, note 11.

5

The Natural Desire
to See God

My purpose is clarification. I am concerned with the concept and the affirmation of a natural desire to see God,[a] and I shall indicate some of its presuppositions and implications. While it is my opinion that the position to be presented is that of St Thomas Aquinas, still that historical issue lies outside my terms of reference.[1]

1   Thesis

The desires of human intellect[b] are manifested in questions; and all questions reduce to the pair, *an sit* and *quid sit*.[2] But to put these questions is natural: it supposes no acquired habit, as does playing the violin; it supposes no gift of divine grace, as do faith and charity. Hence, since the questions are natural, the desire they manifest must also be natural. There exists, then, a desire that is natural to intellect, that arises from the mere fact that we possess intellects, that is defined by the basic questions, *an sit* and *quid sit*.[c]

Next, the question, *quid sit*, expresses a desire to understand, to know

1 For a general history, see Victorinus Doucet, o.f.m., 'De naturali seu innato supernaturalis beatitudinis desiderio iuxta theologos a saeculo xiii usque ad xx,' *Antonianum* 4 (1929) 167–208. On Aquinas, see William R. O'Connor, *The Eternal Quest* (New York: Longmans, Green and Co., 1947).
2 Thomas Aquinas, *In Aristotelis libros Posteriorum analyticorum*, 2, lect. 1. [Our usage henceforth will be: *In 11 post. anal.*]

the cause, and especially to know the formal cause.[3] When we ask why light refracts, we ask for an explanation of refraction. When we obtain that explanation, we are able to assign the nature and cause of refraction. Then and only then are we able to state what refraction is. Until then, we can do no more than assign a nominal definition which tells, not what refraction is, but what we mean by the name, refraction.

Thirdly, natural fulfilment of the natural desire to understand is of two kinds, proper and analogical. Proper fulfilment is by the reception in intellect of an intelligible form or species proportionate to the object that is understood. Analogical fulfilment is by the reception in intellect of some lesser form or species that bears some resemblance to the object to be understood and so yields some understanding of it; the same species, however, also differs from the object to be understood and so must be complemented by the corrections of a *via affirmationis, negationis, et eminentiae*[d] as in natural theology or in the mathematical procedure of taking the limit.

Fourthly, the limited understanding of the mysteries of faith, attained through the connection of the mysteries and the analogy of the mysteries with nature, is a further instance of analogical fulfilment. However, this fulfilment is not simply natural, for it presupposes revelation and faith. Similarly, the desire that is fulfilled is not simply natural, for the theologian needs grace to know of the existence of the Blessed Trinity though he needs no further grace to ask what the Blessed Trinity is.

Fifthly, analogical fulfilment is fulfilment only in an improper sense. It does not satisfy our intellects. It goes part of the way but not the whole way. It answers some questions but raises others. Fulfilment by analogy is a matter of decreasing returns, for the further one pushes the issue, the clearer it becomes that there is much we do not know. On the other hand, proper fulfilment really satisfies; but it can be had naturally only with respect to material things; for we can understand directly and properly only what first we can imagine, and so the proportionate object of our intellects in this life is said to be the *quidditas rei materialis*.

Sixthly, besides their proportionate object, our intellects also have their adequate object,[e] namely, the transcendental, *ens*. Because the proper fulfilment naturally attainable is limited by the proportionate object, it

3 See my article, 'The Concept of *Verbum* in the Writings of St. Thomas Aquinas,' *Theological Studies* 7 (1946) 360–64 [In book form, *Verbum: Word and Idea in Aquinas*, ed. David B. Burrell (Notre Dame: University of Notre Dame Press, 1967) 12–16 (CWL 2)].

might seem that the proper fulfilment naturally desired is limited in the same fashion. The facts are otherwise. We are not content to ask *quid sit* solely with regard to material things, and we are not content with merely analogical knowledge of immaterial things. We keep on asking why, and we desist ultimately not because we do not desire but because we recognize our impotence to satisfy our desire. Even the Kantian, who denies to speculative intellect any knowledge of God, nonetheless appeals to some transcendental illusion to account for our desire. The fact seems to be that, just as the natural desire expressed by the question, *an sit*, has its range fixed by the adequate object of intellect, so also the natural desire expressed by the question, *quid sit*, has an equal range. Since, then, acts are specified by their objects, and the object of natural desire is the transcendental, *ens*, we may say that the desire of our intellects is natural in origin and transcendental in its object.

In the seventh place, the question, *quid sit Deus*,[f] expresses a desire that arises naturally as soon as one knows the existence of God. This is but a corollary of the twofold affirmation that the desire to understand is natural and transcendental. Moreover, analogical knowledge of God does not satisfy this desire completely: not only is this clear a posteriori from the fact that natural theology and Trinitarian theory are not completely satisfying but only what we have to take because we cannot do better; it also is evident a priori since analogical knowledge is knowledge not only of similarity but of difference as well, and so of the limitations inevitably resulting from the difference. Hence, it is only proper knowledge of God that fully can meet the question, *quid sit Deus*. But proper knowledge is an act of understanding in virtue of a form proportionate to the object; hence proper knowledge of God must be in virtue of an infinite form, in virtue of God himself; such knowledge is beyond the natural proportion of any possible finite substance and so is strictly supernatural; it is what Aquinas called 'videre Deum per essentiam' and is identical with the act commonly named the beatific vision.

Eighthly, this conclusion is theological. It can be thought only because one has the faith, knows the fact of the beatific vision, and so must accept its possibility. A philosopher operating solely in the light of natural reason could not conceive that we might understand God properly; for understanding God properly is somehow being God; and somehow being God is somehow being infinite. How could a creature be conceived to receive the *ipsum intelligere* that is identical with *ipsum esse?* Theologians speak of a quasi reception of a quasi formal cause; but their speech does not elucidate the mystery; it merely provides an orderly expression for their faith; such systematized faith is not philosophy. The best that natural reason can attain is the discovery of the paradox[g] that the desire to understand arises naturally, that its object is the transcendental, *ens*, and that the proper fulfilment that naturally is attainable is restricted to the proportionate object of finite intellect.

Such, then, is the thesis. There exists a natural desire to understand. Its range is set by the adequate object of intellect. Its proper fulfilment is obtained by the reception of a form proportionate to the object understood. This natural desire extends to understanding God. In that case its fulfilment is the beatific vision. Still, only the theologian can affirm a natural desire to see God; a philosopher has to be content with paradox.

2   Presuppositions of the Thesis

The thesis rests on two presuppositions. On the objective side it involves the rejection of a static essentialism that precludes the possibility of natural aspiration to a supernatural goal. On the subjective side it involves the rejection of a closed conceptualism that precludes the possibility of philosophy being confronted with paradoxes which theology can resolve. Since debate on the natural desire to see God is basically debate upon these two presuppositions, something must be said about them. Though what I can say will be very inadequate, still it will serve to indicate fundamental lines of cleavage.

The static and essentialist view conceives finite natures as prior to world orders. God knows all things in his own essence; but first of all he sees there the possibility of finite natures, of men and horses and cows and dogs and cats; only secondly and derivatively does he see possible world orders, for a possible world order is a possible combination of finite natures, and even God has to have the idea of what he combines before he can have the idea of the combination. Further, since finite natures are prior to world orders, since they are the ultimate element into which all else must be reduced, it follows that there are two parts to a world order, namely, a necessary part which meets the exigences of finite natures, and a contingent part that may or may not be present for it embraces God's free gifts over and above the exigences of nature. Finally, corresponding to this split in world order, there is the distinction between philosophy and theology: philosophy deals with the necessary part by the light of natural reason; theology deals with the contingent part; the former is properly a science; the latter is basically a catalogue of revealed truths though, by means of philosophy, the theologian can deduce the consequences of revelation.

Now I am more than ready to grant that it is rather difficult to hold the foregoing view and yet defend the existence of a natural desire to see God. But I fail to see any solid reason for supposing that Plato's Ideas are in the divine mind pretty much as the animals were in Noah's ark. At any rate I would affirm that world order is prior to finite natures, that God sees in his essence, first of all, the series of all possible world orders, each of which is complete down to its least historical detail, that only consequently, inasmuch as he knows world orders, does God know their component parts such as his free gifts, finite natures, their properties, exigences, and so on. Coherently with this position I would say that the finite nature is the derivative possibility, that it is what it is because of the world order, and that the world order is what it is, not at all because of finite natures, but because of divine wisdom and goodness. Thus the world order is an intelligible unity mirroring forth the glory of God. Because of this intelligible unity lower natures are subordinate to higher natures, not merely extrinsically, but also intrinsically, as appears in chemical composition and in biological evolution. Again, because of this intelligible unity finite natures are sacrificed for the greater perfection of the whole; thus there are extinct species, and the toleration of many physical evils. Finally, the intelligible unity of the existing world order may be known in three ways, imperfectly by philosophy, less imperfectly by theology, but satisfactorily only as a result of the beatific vision.

Complementary to the rejection of static essentialism, the rejection of a closed conceptualism is presupposed by the affirmation of a natural desire to see God. What is a closed conceptualism? Well, conclusions result from principles. In turn, principles result from their component terms. But whence come the terms? The conceptualist view is that they are had by an unconscious process of abstraction from sensible data. It follows that all science is a matter of comparing terms, discovering necessary nexus, and setting to work the cerebral logic machine to grind out all the possible conclusions. It is the sort of science for which a symbolic logic is an essential tool. Moreover, it is the sort of science that is closed to real development: objectively there either exists or does not exist a necessary nexus between any two terms; on the subjective side either one sees what is there to be seen or else one is intellectually blind and had best give up trying. It will be observed that static essentialism and closed conceptualism are very similar: the essentialist posits the ideas of finite natures in the divine mind; they are whatever they happen to be, and all else is to be explained in terms of them; with a similar basic arbitrariness the conceptualist posits ideas in the human mind; he affirms that they are there by an unconscious process of abstraction over which we have no control; our conscious activity is limited to seeing which terms are conjoined by an objective, necessary nexus and thence to deducing the implications that are there to be deduced.

Alternative to a closed conceptualism, there is an open intellectualism.[h] Again, conclusions result from principles, and principles result from their component terms. But the terms are expressions of acts of understanding. The selection of certain terms as basic, the elucidation of their precise meaning and import, the validation of such choice and determination are all the work of wisdom;[4] and wisdom is the cumulative product of a long series of acts of understanding. Hence it is that the nexus between terms is not at all evident to a person who understands nothing, more or less evident to a person who has attained some greater or less degree of understanding, but perfectly evident only to a person who understands perfectly. Hence it is that there exists a natural desire to understand, the development of understanding, and the consequent development of science, philosophy, and theology. Hence it is that any finite wisdom must expect paradox; only perfect wisdom can understand and order everything satisfactorily. Finally, no matter how stouthearted a conceptualist one may be, one cannot as a philosopher escape paradox in the existing world order; one may deny the possibility of a natural desire to see God; but one cannot deny that man by nature can demonstrate the precepts of the natural moral law, and one cannot affirm that without grace man can long observe the precepts of the natural moral law.

Such in briefest outline are the intellectualist, dynamic,[i] existential[j] presuppositions of the affirmation of a natural desire to see God. Let us now consider specific objections.

3   Objections Considered

1 Must not a desire and its fulfilment have the same object? If so, how can the desire be natural and the fulfilment supernatural? If not, how can the fulfilment be fulfilment of the desire?

4 Thomas Aquinas, *Summa theologiae*, 1–2, q. 66, a.5, ad 4m.

The desire and its fulfilment must have the same material object. But a desire to understand cannot have the same formal object as the fulfilling act of understanding. A desire to understand is specified by what we already know. The fulfilling act is specified by what as yet we do not know. Thus the object of the natural desire is transcendental; but the object of the fulfilling vision is supernatural.

2 St Thomas, as Fr O'Connor testifies, does not speak of a natural desire for the beatific vision.

This is quite correct. A desire for the beatific vision is a supernatural act of hope or of charity. The natural desire is to know what God is. That natural desire neither includes nor excludes the Blessed Trinity. It supposes knowledge that God is. It asks to know what God is. It asks it, no matter what God may prove to be, and so it is fulfilled only by an act that is identical with the beatific vision.

3 If there is a natural desire to see God, there cannot be a beatitude natural to man; for beatitude implies the fulfilment of all natural desire.

On the essentialist position, this is invalid. On the opposed position one answers that perfect beatitude satisfies all desire because it fulfils all potentiality; but such fulfilment involves the pure act that is God, and so it can be natural to no one except God. The beatitude natural and proportionate to a finite nature is imperfect. It excludes all sorrow, all regret, all wishing that things were otherwise. But it does not exclude the acknowledged existence of paradox that seems an inevitable consequence of finite nature and finite wisdom.

4 What about the axiom, *Nihil in natura frustra?*

If nature is taken as world order, the principle is certainly valid, for there is no possible world order that is not in accord with divine wisdom and divine goodness, and whatever is in accord with that wisdom and goodness is not in vain. However, since divine wisdom and goodness are beyond the competence of our judgment, it does not follow that we can account for everything either in the existing world order or in other possible world orders.

On the other hand, if nature is taken as simply some particular finite nature, the axiom is not to be admitted without qualification; for parts are subordinate to the whole, and particular natures are subordinate to the divine plan which is realized in world order. Hence there are extinct species; there are the physical evils of the world; and such things can be accounted for only by appealing to the common good of world order. Finally, such qualification is hardly contrary to Aristotle's intention, for

Aristotle defended his view of human well-being by urging us to reject the popular opinion that men should think in human terms and mortals in terms of mortality.[5]

5 Is a state of pure nature, a world order in which no one receives grace, a concrete possibility?

This is a distinct and very large question; no more than an indication of an answer can be offered; and that perhaps will be effected most expeditiously by considering the validity of various types of argument.

First, all things are possible to God, on condition that no internal contradiction is involved. But a world order without grace does not involve an internal contradiction. Therefore, a world order without grace is possible to God and so concretely possible. The major premise is common doctrine and certainly the position of St Thomas. The minor premise stands until the contrary is demonstrated, for the onus of proof lies on anyone who would limit divine omnipotence.

Clearly this argument is valid. Further, since possible world orders are a topic that lies beyond our range of understanding, it is not likely that convincing proof of contradiction can be produced. Hence the argument seems to be not only valid but also definitive.

Still, it might be objected that a world order without religion is an absurdity, that a world order without grace would be a world order without religion, and so a world order without grace would be an absurdity. The major will be admitted and the minor proved as follows. Religion is a personal relationship between man and God; a personal relationship with God regards God, not as man may conceive God naturally, but as God is in himself; hence religion is necessarily supernatural.

In reply one may grant that it is extremely difficult for us to conceive positively, concretely, and convincingly just what religion would be like were it not supernatural; for in the existing world order true religion is supernatural; data on merely natural religion are doubtful; and without data we cannot understand properly. However, this limitation on our knowledge cuts both ways; if it precludes a convincing account of religion without grace, it equally precludes a convincing refutation of the possibility of religion without grace. In particular, the argument just advanced seems fallacious; merely natural religion would not be so intimately personal as is supernatural religion; but it does not follow that it would

5 *Ethics*, x, 7, 1177b 31–34.

not be a personal relationship. To treat with God as he is known by us naturally is to treat with the real God and not with some fiction. In somewhat similar fashion other objections against the possibility of world order without grace can be met.

However, there are other arguments in favor of the concrete possibility of a world order without grace. The one most commonly adduced may be put as follows. A concrete possibility is constituted by a finite nature and the satisfaction of its exigences. But grace does not pertain to any finite substance or to any of its exigences. Therefore a concrete possibility is constituted by a finite nature without grace.

Clearly this argument is not only valid but also peremptory on the essentialist supposition that finite natures are prior to world order. Indeed, this argument is simply a statement of the essentialist view which splits world order into two parts, one of which is necessary and the other contingent; just as one can unhook the trailer and drive off in the motorcar, so one can drop the supernatural out of the existing world order and have a possible world order left.

However, precisely because this argument is connected so closely with essentialist assumptions, it is received with marked frigidity by those who reject those assumptions. To them it seems that a concrete possibility is constituted by the concrete and not by that splendid pair of abstractions, finite nature and the satisfaction of its exigences. More pertinently, concrete possibility is constituted by a world order complete down to its least historical detail. Concrete possibility is not constituted but only participated by finite natures, by their exigences, and by the satisfaction of their exigences. Because certain parts of an undetermined and indeed unmentioned whole do not necessarily include grace, it does not follow that there must be cases in which the whole does not include grace. Further assumptions must be introduced, e.g., that the parts in question determine the whole, that finite natures are prior to and determine world order. On that assumption the argument becomes valid; but, of course, it is precisely the assumption that is denied. Need I add that it is denied not by nominalists but by those who agree with Aquinas that the *ordo universi*[6] is a whole and that the whole is prior to its parts.

In addition to the argument from the gratuity of grace, there some-

---

6 See R. Linhardt, *Die Sozialprinzipien des heiligen Thomas von Aquin*, §10: Die Universumidee (Freiburg im Breisgau: Herder, 1932) 67–80.

times is advanced an argument from the special liberality of God in bestowing grace. Were there not a possible world order without grace, God would be free not twice but only once; he would be free to create, but if he created then he would have to give grace. But God is perfectly free not once but twice; he is free to create; and then he is free either to give grace or not to give it. Therefore a world order without grace is concretely possible.

The argument is formally valid but its suppositions are open to question. In one act of will there seems to me to be no more than one freedom of exercise and one freedom of specification. Further, the number of divine acts of will seems to me to be quite independent of possibility or impossibility of world orders without grace, and directly to depend upon the number of objects that are willed. Hence there will be only one act of will, one freedom of exercise, and one freedom of specification if, as God knows all existing things by knowing one concrete world order, so also God wills all existing things inasmuch as he wills one concrete world order. What I fail to see is any contradiction in affirming both that God wills the existing concrete order by a single act and that God could will another world order in which there was no grace. Hence I suspect that this argument is simply an anthropomorphic attempt to state what Aquinas puts exactly by his distinction between *ex simplici voluntate* and *ex ordine etiam aliarum causarum*.[7]

To conclude, I believe that a world order without grace is a concrete possibility. But I suggest that this possibility is not a central doctrine but merely a marginal theorem. It is a central doctrine if it can be demonstrated from the gratuity of grace and from the liberality of God in bestowing grace; the suppositions, usually concealed, of such demonstrations seem to me to be highly questionable. On the other hand, the possibility of a world order without grace is a marginal theorem if its truth is on the same footing as the truth of any other possibility, namely, it contains no internal contradiction. In confirmation of this position may be adduced the fact that, since Aquinas never explicitly mentioned the possibility of a state of pure nature, it can hardly be maintained with plausibility that Renaissance theologians discovered a central Thomist doctrine. What is plausible is that they discovered a marginal theorem which, in virtue of suppositions not entertained by Aquinas in my opinion, they magnified into a central doctrine. Finally, at the present time,

---

7 *Summa theologiae*, 1, q. 19, a. 5, ad 3m.

it seems to me that the real issue does not lie in the possibility of a world order without grace; the real issue, the one momentous in its consequences, lies between the essentialist and conceptualist tendency and, on the other hand, the existential and intellectualist tendency.

6

A Note on Geometrical Possibility

In the preliminaries to his *Elements*, after assigning twenty-three definitions and before adding five common notions,[a] Euclid listed five postulates. Of these the first three are practical: they ask to join points, to
produce straight lines, and to draw circles of any size about any center.
But the other two postulates are theoretical: they ask not the performance of operations, but the truth of propositions, namely, that all right
angles are equal and that under certain conditions two straight lines will
meet.[1]

These theoretical postulates have stimulated considerable speculation.
Geometers began by seeking substitutes and ended by developing non-
Euclidean geometries. Logicians began by trying to define their precise
status and function, and have ended with a technical analysis that clas-
sifies types of axioms and lists what combinations of what types will yield
what geometries.[2] But there is also a metaphysical question of possibility.
It is distinct from the geometrical and logical issues and, to some extent,
independent of them. I do not think it has been discussed frequently,
but Fr Hoenen in his *Cosmologia* adverts to it and contends that only
Euclidean three-dimensional extension is known as possible.[3]

1 Sir Thomas L. Heath, *The Thirteen Books of Euclid's Elements*, trans. from
   the text of Heiberg, with introduction and commentary, 2nd ed. (Cambridge: Cambridge University Press, 1926), Vol. 1, 154–55.
2 See Henry George Forder, *The Foundations of Euclidean Geometry* (Cambridge: Cambridge University Press, 1927).
3 Peter Hoenen, *Cosmologia* (Rome: Gregorian University Press, 1931),

I think the issue is of interest, both because of the light it may bring to problems of integration, the so-called *quaestiones annexae*,[b] and also because of the opportunity it provides for working out a concrete application of the Thomist theory of intellect and science. The latter aspect interests us more directly; and we shall find, I think, that Fr Hoenen's own contributions to Thomist intellectual theory[4] can be developed into a broader view on geometrical possibility than he has admitted.

It will be simpler to base the discussion on Euclid rather than his modern correctors. Euclid is generally familiar, and, once one is aware of his slips from rigor,[5] allowance may easily be made for them. On the other hand, not only is the work of modern analysts not generally familiar, but also it is not altogether successful in handling the problem of consistency of foundation propositions;[6] and, further, consistency is a little less than the positive intelligibility that grounds possibility. In due course the nature of this type of analysis should be examined; but, I think, a study of Euclid himself is a very useful, if not necessary, preliminary.

1   The Division of Definitions

Our basic assumption is that science primarily is understanding, that only secondarily in virtue of self-scrutiny and self-appraisal is scientific

---

Nota III, 443–54. The 1945 edition does not seem to modify this note but places it some ten pages later. [The 1945 edition was the third edition; it places this note at pp. 453–64; the 1936 second edition places the same note at pp. 447–58.]

4 Peter Hoenen: 'De origine primorum principiorum scientiae,' *Gregorianum* 14 (1933) 153–84; 'De philosophia scholastica cognitionis geometricae,' ibid. 19 (1938) 498–514; 'De problemate necessitatis geometricae,' ibid. 20 (1939) 19–54; 'De problemate exactitudinis geometricae,' ibid. 321–50. See also Fr Hoenen's *La théorie du jugement d'après St. Thomas d'Aquin* (Rome: Gregorian University Press, 1946, Analecta Gregoriana 39) [In English, *Reality and Judgment according to St. Thomas*, trans. Henry J. Tiblier (Chicago: Regnery, 1952).] The present writer has dealt with allied questions in the first four articles of the series: 'The Concept of *Verbum* in the Writings of St. Thomas Aquinas,' *Theological Studies* 7 (1946) 349–92; 8 (1947) 35–79; 404–44; 10 (1949) 3–40 [*Verbum* 1–181].

5 See the discussions in Heath, *The Thirteen Books* ... 242–43, 249–50, 280–81.

6 I think the difficulty is no more than that mathematicians as mathematicians cannot treat consistency as such, and so have to assume its existence in some simple case to which all others are reduced.

understanding expressed in definitions, postulates, deductions. It follows that definitions are expressions of understanding and may be divided by differences in what is understood. But it is one thing to grasp the language proper to a science; it is quite another to grasp the nature of the object investigated in the science. Hence, definitions will be of at least two kinds, namely, nominal and essential.[c] Nominal definitions express one's understanding of a linguistic system, of how terms are to be employed, of what employed terms must mean. Essential definitions express one's understanding of a real system, of the necessary and possible and impossible relations of things, of why things are just what they are.[7] In both cases the understanding itself is real; but in nominal definitions the understood has only the reality of names; while in essential definition the understood has the reality of what names name.

The foregoing emphasizes the difference between nominal and essential definitions. But it is equally important to observe how intimately the two are related. In Aristotelian language one may say that essential definition expresses form in matter while nominal definition expresses the matter presupposed by the form.

It is for this reason that nominal definitions are inevitable. For essential definitions are of essences; and material essences are not pure forms, but composites of form and common matter. It may happen that this common matter is another material essence; but in that case it will be composed of another form and other common matter. This may be repeated a number of times, but it cannot be repeated indefinitely. There must be, then, common matter that is not an essence, that cannot be defined essentially itself, yet will be included in the essential definitions of other things, that accordingly will itself need some definition. It seems to follow that nominal definitions have the function of determining the residual common matter involved in essential definition.

But this conclusion may be declared paradoxical. Nominal definitions have been characterized as understanding not realities, but names. Clearly common matter is an element in realities and not merely a name. The paradox is resolved quite easily by the distinction between the empirical and the intelligible. One does not understand everything that one knows; what one knows without understanding, prior to understanding, is the empirical; what one knows over and above the empirical, and precisely

7 Heath mentions Aristotle's knowledge of causes in its relations to definition, but fails to identify it with real definition; see ibid. 143, 149.

inasmuch as one understands, is the intelligible in the strictest sense of that term. Now, nominal definitions involve no understanding of reality, but it does not follow that they involve no knowledge of reality; they do involve empirical knowledge of reality; and we have such empirical knowledge precisely because, besides strictly intelligible forms, there is also common matter to be known.

Since the sensible is empirical and since the intelligibles we know are the intelligibility of empirical and mainly sensible data, one may cast the argument for the inevitability of nominal definitions in another form. Essential definitions express an understanding of things; prior to being understood, the things are known empirically and, in the present discussion, by sense. Now an understanding of sensible data regularly is a grasp of intelligible unity in sensible multiplicity. It follows from the priority of the sensible that there will be an inevitable residue of sensible elements that are not themselves unifications of lower elements, but only the common matter of all higher unifications. Such residual elements may be generalized by nominal definitions; but they cannot become universalized in the sense that an essence is universal, for they are not essences, but only the common matter of essences.

Nominal definitions, then, suppose no understanding except the understanding of names; but they suppose empirical knowledge which is of things; in geometry this empirical knowledge is sensible; but it admits a generalization, as distinct from universalization,[d] in virtue of the understanding involved in understanding names; finally, in metaphysical terms, the object of such generalized empirical knowledge is the common matter that is mere common matter and not an essence composed of form and other common matter.

It may be well to indicate at once an incidental function of nominal definitions. It has been noticed that one cannot imagine a Euclidean point:[e] one can imagine a minute speck, but if the speck really has no parts and no magnitude, then one's image disappears. Similarly, one cannot imagine a Euclidean line: one can imagine a very, very fine line, but if one imagines length from which all breadth is eliminated, one imagines nothing at all. Again, one cannot imagine the indefinitely produced straight lines of the definition of parallels: insofar as they are actually imagined, they are not indefinitely produced. On the other hand, one cannot do geometry without imagination and solely by using concepts. For the abstract straight line is unique; there are not two of them to run parallel to each other; and similarly whenever there is question, and perpetually there is question, of more than one geometrical entity of a kind, it is necessary for intellect to convert to phantasm.[f] The solution to this anomaly is the symbolic image,[g] that is, the image that stands for things it does not resemble. The geometer boldly imagines blobs and bars but understands them and thinks of them as Euclidean points and lines. The geometer does not bother producing lines indefinitely; he produces them a bit but understands them and thinks of them as indefinitely produced. He can do this because in between his images and his understanding there intervene his definitions, which settle for understanding and thought what the images stand for, no matter what they resemble.[8]

Let us now turn to essential definitions. They presuppose nominal definitions of common matter at least symbolically represented in imagination. They proceed from acts of understanding[h] in which is grasped the intelligible form of the common matter. The essence that is defined is the compound of form and common matter. Conversely, the form is the *propter quid* that functions as middle term between common matter and essence. Why are these bones and this flesh a man? What is the middle term between the empirical data of bones and flesh and the conceived essence, man? It is the formal cause of a man, that is, his soul.[9] Or, to take an illustration from geometry, why is this symbolically imagined uniformly round plane curve a circle? What has to be grasped to effect the transition from empirically given uniform curvature to the essentially defined circle? It is the formal cause of the circle,[i] what grounds both the circularity of the circle and, as well, all its demonstrable properties. But such a formal cause is the equality of all radii in the circle.[10]

8 The distinction between sensible and intelligible matter is perhaps relevant here. See Thomas Aquinas, *In librum Boethii de Trinitate, Quaestiones quinta et sexta,* ed. Paul Wyser, o.p. (Fribourg: Société Philosophique, 1948), q. 6, a.2, p. 64, lines 1–13. [The Leonine title is *Super Librum ...*]
9 Aristotle, *Metaphysics,* vii, 17, 1041a 9 to 1041b 32; Thomas Aquinas, *In metaphysicam Aristotelis commentaria,* lib. vii, lect. 17 (ed. Cathala, Turin: Marietti, 1935), §§1649–61) [Leonine: *Sententia libri Metaphysicae*; henceforth our usage will be *In vii Metaphys.*]; Lonergan, 'The Concept of *Verbum* in the Writings of St. Thomas Aquinas,' *Theological Studies* 7 (1946) 360–64 [*Verbum* 12–16].
10 Strictly the formal cause is not equal radii *qua* equal but *qua* intelligible ground of consequents. There is a more fundamental ambiguity lurking in the context: a soul is a natural form; equal radii refer to an intelligible form. The analogy is that intelligible form stands to sensible matter

If all radii are equal, the plane curve must be round; if any are unequal, it cannot be round; and similarly for the other properties of the circle. The 'must' and the 'cannot' reveal the activity of understanding; and what is understood is not how to use the name, circle, but circularity itself. Further, not only does understanding intervene, but it intervenes with respect to sensible data; the necessity results from the equality of all radii, but only sense knows a multiplicity of radii; the abstract radius is unique. Finally, from the understanding of sensible data, there results the definition: without understanding one can repeat the definition like a parrot; but one cannot discover the definition, grasp what it means, without understanding equality of radii as the ground of circularity.

It is of obvious importance to distinguish between this grasp of formal cause, of intrinsic ground, of *propter quid*, and, on the other hand, the verbal form in which it happens to be expressed. Aristotle adverted to this when he pointed out the equivalence of essential definition and scientific syllogism.[11] Both assign the *propter quid*. But what the essential definition expresses in one proposition, the scientific syllogism[j] expresses in three propositions. From the viewpoint of an analysis of science in terms of understanding, the number of propositions is utterly irrelevant. What is significant is exclusively the fact that the *propter quid* has been grasped, assigned, and made operative in the deductions of a science.

This point has a bearing, I believe, on the interpretation of Euclid's theoretical postulates. Had Euclid defined the circle, not essentially by appealing to the equality of radii, but only nominally by affirming circles to be uniformly round plane curves, this nominal definition would prevent him from later introducing his essential definition and so would lead him to presenting the theoretical postulate that all the radii in the same circle are equal. On the supposition we are making, it is quite simple to state the nature of such a theoretical postulate; for clearly it comes to the same thing whether the equality of radii is affirmed in the essential definition of the circle or in a theoretical postulate added to a nominal definition of the circle. Naturally enough this raises the question

---

as natural form stands to natural matter. The difference is that knowledge of intelligible form is prior to essential definition and judgment of possibility, while knowledge of natural form is due to metaphysical analysis consequent to judgment affirming actuality. Since we are dealing with knowledge of possibility in this paper, regularly we shall be speaking of intelligible form and sensible matter.

11 Thomas Aquinas, *In II post. anal.*, lect. 6–8.

whether the theoretical postulates, which Euclid did posit, assign the *propter quid* of geometrical entities that had been defined only nominally.

2   Euclid's Definitions

It would be unnecessarily tedious to examine all thirty-three terms defined by Euclid in his preliminaries. With the exception of the circle, they are given only nominal definitions. A sufficient paradigm for investigating the others will perhaps be had if we consider the definitions of the straight line and of the right angle.

The fourth definition reads: 'A straight line is a line which lies evenly with the points on itself.'[12] Sir Thomas Heath in his commentary, while admitting that Euclid's wording is quite obscure, contends that there need be no doubt about his meaning. A straight line is a line that involves no irregularity differentiating one part or side from another.[13] Clearly, this is very much like saying that a circle is a uniformly round plane figure; it enables one to use the name, straight line, correctly; it does not tell what makes straight lines straight; and it does not provide 'a premise for deductions about straight lines. It is a nominal definition.

The tenth definition reads: 'When a straight line set up on a straight line makes the adjacent angles equal to one another, each of the equal angles is right, and the straight line standing on the other is called a perpendicular to that on which it stands.'[14] This cannot be an essential definition, for an essential definition is a premise to properties, just as an essence is a ground whence properties naturally result; despite the above definition Euclid had to postulate that all right angles are equal;[15] if he had had an essential definition of right angles, he would have demonstrated and not postulated their equality. This is confirmed by examining the definition itself. It appears that Euclid is saying no more than that a right angle is half of a straight angle, where a straight angle is the angle in any plane between two different but continuous segments of a straight line. Because the straight line is defined nominally, the straight angle is defined nominally; and because the straight angle is defined nominally, the right angle is defined nominally.

But combine the nominal definitions of the straight line, the straight

12 Heath, *The Thirteen Books* ... 153.
13 Ibid. 167.
14 Ibid. 153.
15 Ibid. 154.

angle, and the right angle with the theoretical postulate that all right angles are equal. It becomes apparent that the postulate assigns the *propter quid* of the straight line. For if all right angles are equal, then all straight angles are equal; if all straight angles are equal, straight lines must be absolutely straight; they cannot bend in any direction, for if they did, the straight angle on the side of the bending would be less than the straight angle on the opposite side. Conversely, if any right angles were unequal, straight lines could not be truly straight. Thus the equality of right angles is the necessary and sufficient condition of the straightness of straight lines, just as the equality of radii is the necessary and sufficient condition of the roundness of circles. The equality of right angles is just as much a *propter quid* as the equality of radii. But while the latter could be expressed in the essential definition of the circle, the former could not be expressed in an essential definition of the straight line; for the nominal definition of the right angle presupposed the nominal definition of the straight line; and once the straight line was defined nominally, since two definitions would be anomalous, its *propter quid* had to be assigned in a theoretical postulate.

What accounts for the fourth postulate will be found to account for the fifth. Euclid's fifth postulate[k] is that, 'if a straight line falling on two straight lines make the interior angles on the same side less than two right angles, the two straight lines, if produced indefinitely, meet on that side on which the angles are less than the two right angles.'[16] The postulate states conditions under which straight lines will meet. It omits, however, explicit mention of the necessary condition that initially the two straight lines must lie in the same plane. On adding that condition, the postulate appears as a correlation in the plane surface of angles and straight lines.

Now this correlation is intelligible. Down the centuries it has been claimed to be evident to intellect. Nor has the fact of intellectual evidence been disputed. What has been disputed is only the precise nature of the evidence. From that dispute one prescinds in affirming the fifth postulate to present an intelligible correlation.

On the other hand, the material correlated is the material of the nominally defined plane surface. The definition reads: 'A plane surface is a surface which lies evenly with the straight lines on itself.'[17] This

16 Ibid. 155.
17 Ibid. 153.

definition is nominal: it enables one to distinguish a plane surface from other surfaces; it does not form a premise to deducing, for example, the measurement of plane areas, though plane areas are either constituent or properties of plane surfaces. Now the material of the nominally defined plane surface consists in the straight lines lying evenly in the surface. Within the field of vision, so to speak, some of these straight lines intersect and so make angles with each other. The fifth postulate is a correlation that enables one to argue from given intersections and angles to other intersections and so, through theorems to be established, to other angles and to areas.

In the light of our analysis it seems reasonable to say that the fifth postulate stands to the nominally defined plane surface as does formal cause to common matter. A formal cause is an intelligible correlation or unification. Common matter is the correlated. Combine the two and there result necessary properties which, in the present instance, are the properties of the Euclidean plane surface. As the equality of radii stands to the circle, as the equality of right angles stands to the straight line, so the parallel postulate stands to the Euclidean plane surface. There are differences; but in each of the three cases the first term is related to the second as formal cause to the essence it constitutes.

It follows that the evidence of the parallel postulate is the evidence of a (virtual) essential definition. It is evident that all radii in the same circle must be equal, else there would not be a circle. It is evident that things equal to the same thing are equal to one another. But while the latter proposition normally is taken as stating a necessary consequence, the former does not state a consequence but defines a starting point; it defines a starting point because it assigns the first step, namely, the step from the material and nominal to the formal and essential. Further, the fact that it is a first step does not mean that it is a step in the dark, a step taken without evidence, for it is quite evident that all radii in the same circle are equal. Nonetheless, the fact that it is a first step does imply that it is a step taken without necessity. From nominal definitions there follow necessary, though only nominal, consequents. From essential definitions there follows the demonstration of necessary and real properties. But the transition from the material and nominal to the formal and essential cannot be necessitated by the former, else the distinction between them would be illusory; and it cannot be necessitated by the latter, for the latter is not prior to the transition. Just as ontologically an essence is a possible, so psychologically an essence has the evidence proper to a possible. Accordingly, we agree with those who consider the parallel postulate evident, and we agree with those who do not consider it evidently necessary.

The foregoing squares with the conclusion of modern geometers that the parallel postulate is independent[18] of other geometrical definitions and postulates. However, it supplies a theoretical context that seems to obviate Fr Hoenen's objection[19] that there may exist some unconsidered definition or really evident axiom whence the parallel postulate might be deduced. Such an excursus into hypothetical unknowns can be shown, I think, to lead nowhere. The issue is not whether the parallel postulate is or is not the best possible selection as logical first whence other correlations of straight lines and angles (and areas) in plane surfaces are to be deduced. The issue is whether or not the (nominally) defined plane surface is an essence with the parallel postulate its consequent property. Let us turn to illustrative parallels. Because bodies have souls, they are alive. Because animals are composite, they are mortal. Both 'soul' and 'composite' are middle terms that assign a *propter quid*. But bodies need not have souls, and so some bodies are not alive. Animals, on the other hand, must be composite and so must be mortal. In terms of this illustration, the issue is not whether the parallel postulate is like 'composite' or like 'mortal'; the issue is whether the parallel postulate is like 'soul' or 'alive' or, alternatively, like 'composite' or 'mortal.' Once one grants that the parallel postulate is independent of known definitions and axioms, automatically one grants that it resembles neither 'composite' nor 'mortal' for both of them are deducible from 'animal,' and so one grants that it must resemble either 'soul' or 'alive' since neither of them is deducible from 'body.' It follows that the nominally defined plane surface stands to the properties Euclid establishes concerning plane surfaces, not as essence to its properties, but as common matter to properties that accrue only when a form is added to the common matter to constitute the relevant essence. In other words, Euclid's fifth postulate is the equivalent of an essential definition, and the essence in question is the Euclidean plane surface. Moreover, the same will be true of any substitute fulfilling the functions of Euclid's fifth postulate.

18 Hoenen, *Cosmologia* 449; 1945 ed. 459; Forder, *The Foundations* ... 213; see 138, 302.
19 Hoenen, *Cosmologia* 450–51; 1945 ed. 459.

3   Possibility[1]

As the actuality of any X is known in the true judgment that X is, so the possibility of X is known in the true judgment that X can be. For *veritas logica est formaliter in solo iudicio*,[m] and *veritas logica consistit in adaequatione intellectus ad rem*.[n]

The grounds of true judgment of possibility are twofold. There is the consequent ground of known actuality: *ab esse ad posse valet illatio*. There is the antecedent ground that, as the unintelligible is impossible, so the intelligible is possible. It is with this antecedent ground that we are concerned, and we note that, as possibility is ontologically antecedent to being, so intelligibility is cognitionally antecedent to true judgment; for true judgment is rational, and one cannot rationally affirm the unintelligible.

Broadly, the intelligible is whatever can be understood. But strictly and primarily, the intelligible is only what is knowable about the understood inasmuch as one is understanding. Understanding itself is an irreducible experience like seeing colors or hearing sounds. It is what is rare in the stupid and frequent in the intelligent. It is the goal of inquiry, emerging upon the empirical, grounding the formation of concepts, definitions, hypothetical systems, pure implications. It is the grasp of unity (Aristotle's *intelligentia indivisibilium*)[o] in empirical multiplicity,[p] and it expresses itself in systematic meaning. Strictly and primarily, the intelligible is the grasped unity; and it is only by their relations to that unity that other instances of the intelligible are intelligible.

Thus the unity is the unity of the unified.[q] But the unified is the common matter, and so common matter is intelligible by information. Again, unity and unified together are the essence, and so the essence is intelligible by inclusion. Thirdly, unity and unified are universal, but the universal and the particular are correlative, so that individual matter is intelligible tangentially. Fourthly, the particular essence is the possibility of a contingent existence, so that contingent existence is intelligible again tangentially. Fifthly, since the primary intelligible as such is not necessarily the intelligibility of something else, since it does not necessarily presuppose matter, since it has not intrinsic opposition to particularity, there can be pure forms that are identical with particular essences. Finally, since not all existents can exist contingently, there must be, if anything exists, a simply intelligible existent, and in it pure form and existence will coincide.

Now the ground of possibility is intelligibility,[r] and intelligibility reduces to the strictly and primarily intelligible, to what is known inasmuch as one is understanding. To this criterion of possibility the more familiar conceptualist criterion may be reduced. A thing is said to be possible if its notes not merely are not opposed but positively cohere. What is this positive coherence of notes? It is the reappearance of the unity in multiplicity that is known by understanding.

However, one must distinguish two different types of the strictly and primarily intelligible and consequently two different types of possibility. Substantial essence is essence *simpliciter*, but accidental essence is essence *secundum quid*;[20] both types of essence can be defined; and both types of definition proceed from acts of understanding. But while the substantial essence is defined in terms of what it itself is, the accidental essence can be defined only by introducing what it is not; 'snubness' cannot be except in a nose, yet 'snubness' is not a nose.[21] Thus the intelligibility of the accident involves a duality: on the one hand, there is the grasp of its proper *ratio*, say, of the curvature that makes snubness snubness; on the other hand, there is the grasp of its necessary dependence, of the *in alio* that pertains to the accident as accident. It follows that the possibility of the accidental raises a twofold question: there is the initial question of the possibility of the accident as a *ratio*; there is the further question of the possibility of the substance in which such an accident might inhere. This has an obvious bearing on our question. As a *ratio* or intrinsically, an N-dimensional curved 'space' might be possible; yet the only possible substances might have properties that excluded more than $(N-1)$ dimensions or that excluded curvature. In that case the geometry in question would be possible *secundum quid*, as a *ratio*, but not *simpliciter*, for a fully possible accident supposes as possible its substance. Unfortunately, a discussion of the possibility of substances cannot be crammed into this paper,[22] and so our account of geometrical possibility must be limited to possibility *secundum quid*.

A first point to be made is that the consistency or coherence of nominal definitions is not directly relevant to geometrical possibility. For suppose

20 Aristotle, *Metaphysics*, VII, 4, 1030a 28 to 1030b 13.
21 Ibid. VII, 5, 1030b 16–37.
22 The possibility of a substance is the possibility of an *unum per se*; it implies the possibility of its proper accidents which naturally result from it and the possibility of a 'world' in which its operations would occur *ut in maiori parte*; it seems to follow that *quoad nos* the possibility of a substance is the possibility of its accidents and of their conjunction.

such consistency to be lacking. Necessarily there will result verbal contradictions. Probably there will result more than mere verbal contradictions: for the incoherence or inconsistency of the language will provide
a constant occasion, almost an invitation, for error about things. Meth-
odologically both are deplorable. But the issue before us is not methodological. We are not concerned to ensure that geometers speak
coherently or that they avoid mistakes in geometrizing. We leave to the
symbolic logicians the problem of coherent speech and to the geometers
themselves the business of avoiding geometrical blunders. When both
have done their work, there remains the question of geometrical possibility.

A second point regards sense and imagination.[5] They have a role to
play, but it is a minor role. Possibility as known has its ground in the
primarily intelligible which is neither sensible nor imaginable yet of the
somehow sensible and somehow imaginable. There must be empirical
elements to be unified and correlated intelligibly; such elements must
be in the sensible and imaginable order, else they would not be merely
empirical. Still, a virtual image will suffice, as when Euclid only virtually
imagines indefinitely produced straight lines; and a symbolic image will
suffice, as when Euclid imagines lines with breadth as well as length but
understands them and thinks of them as without breadth. This privilege
of using virtual and symbolic images cannot be granted to Euclid and
denied to other geometers. Moreover, it is a broad privilege; what cannot
be imagined formally often can be imagined virtually; and what cannot
be imagined virtually always can be imagined symbolically, for symbols
stand for whatever one assigns them to stand for.

Directly, then, the limitations of sense and of imagination are not
limitations to our knowledge of possibility. But indirectly, and this is our
third point, they give rise to a difficulty that can be turned only at the
expense of some complexity. Initially the act of understanding is an
insight into sensible or imagined data; but to be understood, the data
must be presented or represented; hence, in the measure that virtual
and symbolic images fall short of representation, in the same measure
they fail to provide the agent objects that cause insights. This has its
effect upon the development of the science: in systems in which the
common matter can be represented imaginatively, there is an ever present tendency for insights not acknowledged in postulates or axioms to
creep surreptitiously into the argument; on the other hand, in systems
in which the images are mainly or entirely symbolic, logical rigor prevails
(at least, once the assumptions of the symbolism have been investigated

carefully), and for purposes of inspiration thinkers are prone to desert the symbols and appeal to imaginable models of their common matter.

However, what concerns us is the bearing of this absence of insight upon knowledge of possibility. The relevant distinction seems to be between the apprehension of intelligibility and the certitude of the judgment of possibility. There is an apprehension of intelligibility no less with respect to the symbolically imagined than with respect to the representatively imagined; for to apprehend intelligibility is to grasp the one in the many and the many through the one; and such a grasp may be had by using concepts and purely symbolic images. But from the grasp of intelligibility there follows, on the principles we have laid down, a judgment of possibility. In theory that is true. But when one comes to apply the general principle to particular cases, one finds oneself hesitant. For our intellects operate upon concepts eked out with symbolic images pretty much as do our senses in the dark: we may be more or less familiar with the terrain; but we are never certain that things are exactly as we think them to be. The ground of this uncertainty is that the *per se* infallibility of intellect resides in the insight into sensible data; when we proceed by insight, we may be presupposing more than we are aware and we may be proving very much less than we think; but there is no doubt that we have got hold of something; rigorous analysis may reduce it to very little, but not to nothing.

Our conclusion is, then, that as knowledge of possibility rests on knowledge of intelligibility, so certain judgment affirming possibility rests on the *per se* infallibility of intellect grasping intelligibility in representative images. In other words, it is the intuitively possible that basically, though not exclusively, is the certainly possible.

This reveals the significance of techniques of reduction. It has been objected that one does not establish the possibility of the definition and properties of a non-Euclidean plane surface by showing that they are exactly parallel to those of a Euclidean curved surface. While that is true enough, still the objection falls when one distinguishes between the intelligibility of the non-Euclidean plane surface and, on the other hand, our grounds of certitude concerning that intelligibility. One knows the intelligibility of the non-Euclidean plane surface because knowing it is understanding; for to define essentially, to deduce properties, to grasp the many through the one, is to understand; and to understand is to know the intelligible. Still, knowledge of that intelligibility, though it is understanding, nonetheless is hesitant. To dispel doubts and bring in certitude, the technique of reduction is invoked. What the infallibility of insight secures for the representatively imagined, the technique of reduction secures for the symbolically imagined. One knows intelligibility because one understands; one is certain one knows intelligibility either because of the infallibility of insight or because of the successful use of a technique of reduction; and certain knowledge of intelligibility is sufficient ground for the judgment of possibility. Hence, while granting that the technique of reduction does not establish intelligibility or possibility, we would maintain that it gains certitude for an intelligibility that already has been apprehended in nominally defined and symbolically represented objects.

In applying our conclusion a series of distinctions is needed. Euclidean geometry deals with objects that are possible, for it deals with certainly intelligible essences and their properties. Next, the Euclidean object is only possible; for the essences with which it deals are finite, and no finite essence is necessary. Thirdly, the Euclidean object is not uniquely possible; just as the Euclidean circle is not the only possible plane curve, so the Euclidean plane surface is not the only possible plane surface; besides the Euclidean correlation of straight lines and angles in the plane surface, there are other intelligible correlations yielding formally different plane surfaces, and the intelligibility of these correlations is certain. Fourthly, turning from possibility to actuality, we can be certain only that the geometry relating bodies in our space either is Euclidean or else approximates to Euclidean; this follows from the admission that Euclidean geometry neither is necessary nor uniquely possible, from the rejection of essentialism which would conclude from possibility to actuality, from the fact of a margin of error in all observation, a margin large enough to leave a slight curvature undetected.

Accordingly, we meet with a distinction Fr Hoenen's claim that an equivalent of Euclid's parallel postulate belongs to extension as we know it. We admit that such an equivalent, a continuum of directions, is evidently possible in extension as we know it; but we deny that it is evidently necessary. For what is extension as we know it? It is (1) the extension presented to sense, (2) the extension conceived by the nominal definition, *id quod habet partes extra partes*, (3) the extension conceived by the essential definition that involves some geometry. Neither the sensible datum nor the nominally defined object is necessarily Euclidean, while the defined finite essence necessarily is only a possible. It is true that the Euclidean object has the greater simplicity and has to be conceived first from certain viewpoints; but such considerations are not proof of actuality. Similarly, we would meet with a distinction Fr Hoenen's claim that we do not know whether or not N-dimensional spaces are possible: we do not know whether they are possible *simpliciter*, but it would seem that we do know that they are possible *secundum quid*.[23]

As a final word, may I say that I suspect there exist in this paper a number of failures to hit things off with complete accuracy; I present it in the hope that I have noted some worthwhile points and that others will be moved to complete and perfect my treatment.

23 It is not doubted that N independent variables are possible, but only that N independent spatial variables are possible. Whether there is a significant difference between the two depends on one's notions on space.

7

The Role
of a Catholic University
in the Modern World

Within the limited space assigned, I shall endeavor, first, to set forth a somewhat incomplete but at least concrete and dynamic notion of the good,[a] and then to place within that framework both the human situation, named the modern world, and the Catholic university.

1   The Human Good

As human knowing rises on three levels, so also the good[b] that men pursue contains a threefold aspect.

There is to our knowing an experiential component constituted by the data of sense and of consciousness. Secondly, there is an intellectual component constituted by insights and consequent definitions, postulates, systems. Thirdly, there is a reflective component constituted by the weighing of evidence and the rational utterance of judgment.

But as we experience data, so also we experience the tendencies, the drives, the unrest of our spontaneities. Empirically, then, the good is the object of desire.

Again, as we understand the unities that are things and the systematic correlations that explain their operations, so also men grasp and formulate technological devices, economic arrangements, political[c] structures. These too are instances of the good, but they stand as higher syntheses that harmonize and maximize the satisfactions of individual desires. Intellectually, the good is the good of order.

Finally, as speculative theorizing is cut short by judgment of fact, so also practical deliberation upon courses of action reaches its term in judgments of value and in choices. Thus judgments of value set the good of order above private advantage, subordinate technology to economics, refer economics to social welfare, and, generally, mete out to every finite good both appreciation and criticism. As appreciation is a spring of action, so criticism is a source of restraint;[d] and as only the infinite good is beyond all criticism, radically man is free.

2   Community

Men are many. Their lives are not isolated but solidary. In the pursuit of the good they communicate, and so three levels of community[e] follow from the three components of knowing and of the good.

Corresponding to experience and desire, there is intersubjective community. Its basis is spontaneous tendency. Its manifestation is an elemental feeling of belonging together. Its nucleus is the family. Its expansion is the clan, the tribe, the nation.

Corresponding to intellectual insights and the good of order, there is civil community. It is a complex product embracing and harmonizing material techniques, economic arrangements, and political structures. The measure of its development distinguishes primitive societies from civilizations.

Corresponding to judgments of value, there is cultural community. It transcends the frontiers of states and the epochs of history. It is cosmopolis,[f] not as an unrealized political ideal, but as a longstanding, nonpolitical, cultural fact. It is the field of communication and influence of artists, scientists, and philosophers. It is the bar of enlightened public opinion to which naked power can be driven to submit. It is the tribunal of history that may expose successful charlatans and may restore to honor the prophets stoned by their contemporaries.

3   The Dialectic of History

Intellectually and morally, individually and socially, men are subject to ambiguous change, to development-and-decline.[g]

As the question, *Quid sit?* directs us from data to their intelligible form, so also practical intelligence moves from particular objects of desire to the schemes, structures, systems of civil community. As intellectualists and positivists dispute whether the real is the intelligible form or the merely given, so also there is an ambiguity of the good. For men to be truly practical is for them to favor the common good of order at the expense of private advantage; but in fact, to be practical is taken to mean that one is cool and calculating and, when necessary, moderately unscrupulous in getting what one wants. Finally, as mastery of the science is a cumulative product of many insights, so also civil communities are the cumulative products of many acts of practical intelligence; and as there is a test of the sciences in experimental verification, so also the validity of civil communities stands revealed in their histories. Genesis and development, improvement and achievement, parties and factions, privileged and depressed classes, political realism and revolution, dissolution and decay, all have a common origin in the commonly undecipherable ambiguities of human practicality.

As the question, *An sit?* directs us from theory to fact, from possibility to actuality, so the ambiguity of civil community releases the publicly expressed reflection, appreciation, criticism, constitutive of cultural community. But as human intellect can wander through the philosophic labyrinth, so also cultural community has its proper ambiguity: *video meliora proboque* ...[h] The pronouncements of rational reflection are splendid, but they lack efficacy. In another universe things could be different, but in the existing universe man suffers from moral impotence. This fact leads men to question the hegemony of reason, to relegate its precepts to some isolated academic or ecclesiastical sphere, to develop 'realist' views in which theory is adjusted to practice and practice means whatever happens to be done. It follows that, besides the succession of higher syntheses characteristic of intellectual advance, there is also a succession of lower syntheses[i] characteristic of sociocultural decline. Protestantism rejected the church but kept revealed religion. Rationalism rejected revealed religion but acknowledged the supremacy of reason. Liberalism despaired of rational agreement but respected the individual conscience. Totalitarianism ridicules the bourgeois conscience to conquer and organize mankind on an artificial intersubjective level.

4   The Modern World and the University

This rough outline suffices for an adumbration of our basic terms, namely, the modern world and the university.

The modern world is the present human situation. It is the cumulative product of centuries of ambiguous change. It is the threatening precipitate of civil and cultural development-and-decline, solidified in assumptions, mentalities, interpretations, philosophies, tastes, habits, hopes, fears. Precisely in the measure in which man's incomprehension of his situation makes appropriate action impossible, the modern world is involved in a major crisis. Inversely, in the measure in which man can be brought to comprehend what he has not understood, to criticize what he has valued blindly, to do what he has neglected to do, what otherwise would be a major crisis is transformed into a task commensurate with available power and resources.

A university is a reproductive organ of cultural community. Its constitutive endowment lies not in buildings or equipment, civil status or revenues, but in the intellectual life of its professors. Its central function is the communication of intellectual development. Nor is the significance of that function obscure. For it is the *intus legere* of intelligence in act that alone grasps many truths in comprehensive synthesis, that holds ranges of concepts in the unity of their intelligible relations, that moves back and forth freely between the abstract and the concrete, the universal and the particular, the speculative and the practical. Without developed understanding, explanations are of hypnotic drugs by their *virtus dormitiva*,[j] truths become uncomprehended formulas, moral precepts narrow down to lists of prohibitions,[k] and human living settles into a helpless routine without a capacity for vital adaptation and without the power of knowledge that inspires and directs the movement from real possibility to concrete achievement.

5   The Catholic University

Catholic and secular universities exercise the same function, but they do so under different conditions and with different problems. Common to both is the task of communicating intellectual development, nor can anyone suppose that a second-rate Catholic university is any more acceptable to God in the New Law than was in the Old Law the sacrifice of maimed or diseased beasts. Still, this identity of essential function is overlaid with profound difference. The secular university is caught in the ambiguities of civil and cultural development-and-decline; it may lag in consenting to aberrations but in the long run it has to yield, for it recruits its students and their professors from the sociocultural situation that exists. No doubt the same situation constrains the Catholic university and the Catholic community. But the latter is armed against the world.

The supernatural virtues[1] of faith, hope, and charity are named theological because they orientate man to God as he is in himself. Nonetheless, they possess a profound social significance. Against the perpetuation of explosive tensions that would result from the strict application of retributive justice, there is the power of charity to wipe out old grievances and make a fresh start possible. Against the economic determinism that would result were egoistic practicality given free rein, there is the liberating power of hope that seeks first the kingdom of God. Against the dialectic discernible in the history of philosophy and in the development-and-decline of civil and cultural communities, there is the liberation of human reason through divine faith; for men of faith are not shifted about with every wind of doctrine.

But if the Catholic university, because it is Catholic, enjoys liberation from the ambiguity of practicality and from the ambiguity of human culture, still, as a university, it is involved in an ambiguity of its own. From the schools of Alexandria and Antioch, through the medieval universities, to *Pascendi* and *Humani generis*, Catholic intellectuals have been discounted as doubtful blessings. Praise is given St Thomas because of his merits; it is concentrated upon him because one finds it a little difficult to be outright in praising so many others. Indeed, the misadventures of Catholic intellectuals could be taken as a counsel to wrap one's talent in a napkin and bury it safely in the ground, were not that conclusion clean contrary to the gospel, which demands, beyond capitalist expectations, one hundred percent profit. Such then is this third ambiguity: Catholic intelligence is to be used to the limit; yet so complex, so arduous, so excellent is the task confronting it that failure is both easy and disastrous.

6   The Catholic University in the Modern World

If our age is full of deep foreboding, still 'only with the fall of twilight does Minerva's owl take wing.' As real principles exerting real influence are not enunciations in books but intelligences in act,[m] so also it is not pure logic, exercised unerringly by an electronic calculator, but concrete events and palpable consequences that bring light and conviction to rational animals. The vast anxieties and insecurities of the modern world both make it rich in lessons for mankind and, no less, tend to make men ready to learn them.

Though a Catholic university does not dispense the grace of God,

though it is not entrusted with Christ's mission to teach, though it must
see to the conservation and transmission of acquired knowledge before
it can turn to its extension and development, still it is the normal center
in which both the need for intellectual integration is felt and the way
towards that integration is prepared. But upon this large and intricate
question we must be content with three brief remarks. First, then, integration presupposes a purification, for human change is ambiguously
good; it is development-and-decline; the aberrations of man's practical
and speculative intelligence neither invalidate, nor admit integration
with, his real achievements. Secondly, the purifier must be pure, for
purification itself is a human change and so is subject to ambiguity; one
cannot remove the mote in another's eye when there is a beam in one's
own; the true intellectual has to be humble, serene, detached, without
personal or corporate or national complacence, without appeals to contemporary, let alone archaist, bias or passion or fads. Thirdly, there
exists for the modern Catholic thinker a new and distinct problem of
integration[n] that owes its existence to the development of the empirical
sciences of man. Not pure nature envisaged by philosophy but man as
he exists is the object of empirical anthropology and psychology, of
economics and sociology, of the existentialisms, of explanatory histories
of civilizations and cultures, of religion and dogma. But man as he has
existed and exists is man as subject to moral impotence; it is man as the
cooperative or uncooperative recipient of divine grace. Hence, the integration of sciences that deal with man concretely has to be sought not
in philosophy but in theology. The old maxim that theology is the queen
of the sciences has been given a new relevance and Newman's *The Idea
of a University* a fresh significance.

8

Theology and Understanding

I   General Exposition of Beumer

Reverend Fr Johannes Beumer's *Theologie*[a] *als Glaubensverständnis*[1] calls for more than a review. The author began contributing articles on the issue some fifteen years ago; he is acquainted with the extensive French and German literature that has been accumulating for a far longer period; and to come to what alone is important, he has succeeded in hitting off a fundamental feature of theological thought in a manner that seems to demand but a single though somewhat complex reservation.

The central portion of the book[2] is an exposition of the familiar paragraph in the *Constitutio de fide catholica*[3] on the existence of an extremely fruitful but imperfect understanding of the mysteries of faith. After outlining the opposed positions of fideists and traditionalists, of Hermes and Frohschammer, and especially of Günther, he sets forth the history of the text from the initial *schema* through its various modifications to the final form adopted by the Vatican Council in its third session. He then presents a detailed account of its meaning under five headings that may be indicated by quoting the phrases: (1) *ratio fide illustrata* [reason illuminated by faith]; (2) *sedulo, pie, sobrie; Deo dante* [diligently, reverently, moderately; with the favor of God]; (3) *ex eorum quae naturaliter*

---

1 Johannes Beumer, *Theologie als Glaubensverständnis* (Würzburg: Echter-Verlag, 1953).
2 Ibid. 121–203.
3 Concilium Vaticanum, sess. 3, c. 4; Denzinger, *Enchiridion symbolorum* ... 1796 [*DS* 3016].

cognoscit analogia [from the analogy of those things it knows by natural means]; (4) *e mysteriorum ipsorum nexu inter se et cum fine hominis ultimo* [from the way the mysteries themselves cohere with one another and bear on the ultimate end of man]; (5) *fructuosissimam* [extremely fruitful]. He concludes this main section with an estimate of the significance of the decree both in its nineteenth-century setting and in its relevance to a general theory of knowledge and method in theology.

The first part of the work[4] prepares the reader for the conciliar decision. The *gnôsis* of Clement of Alexandria and of Origen, the *crede ut intelligas* of Augustine and Anselm, the *intellectus fidei* of William of Auxerre and of Henry of Ghent, the connection that mystical writers, notably Josephus a Spiritu Sancto, acknowledge between the habit of theology and acquired contemplation, are so many stages in a continuous development that culminated in the Vatican Council's *intelligentia mysteriorum*.

A final section[5] deals with results. While Franzelin, Bilz, Congar receive their meed of praise, Scheeben is singled out as the theologian that based his methodical principles and his practice on the Council's doctrine. In contrast, G. Koepgen's *Die Gnosis des Christentums*[6] is accounted incompatible with the conciliar position. Between the extremes there lies the mass of theologians, and it is not left to inference that, if more had followed Scheeben's lead, not only should we be closer to attaining a methodical speculative theology, a theology within the layman's grasp, and a reinvigorated positive theology, but also we should have heard far less about *Verkündigungstheologie, charismatische Theologie, betende Theologie, eine heilige Theologie der Überlieferung*, and perhaps even *une nouvelle théologie*.

No one will find fault with Fr Beumer for wanting a theology based on the Vatican Council. Nor do I believe a good case can be made out against the substance of his interpretation of its decree. But considerable misgivings will be felt over his views on St Thomas and on the relations between Thomist thought and *Glaubensverständnis*. This is the complex issue I referred to in my first paragraph, and now I must attempt to state its terms.

2   Understanding and Science of Faith

Fr Beumer distinguishes between an understanding of the truths of faith (*Glaubensverständnis*) and a science of the truths of faith (*Glaubenswissen-*

4 Beumer, *Theologie* ... 25–120.
5 Ibid. 205–36.
6 2nd ed., Salzburg, 1940.

schaft). On his view the two should be complementary components of the same reality: the science of faith refers to the method of theology; the understanding of faith assigns its end and goal. Because the method is science, syllogisms and theological conclusions are indispensable. Because the goal is an understanding of faith, the conclusions are concerned primarily, not with the more or less remote implications of the truths of faith, but with a positively intelligent apprehension of the truths of faith themselves.

This apprehension is the *intelligentia mysteriorum*. It is not an act of assent nor a motive for assent, for the assent to the truths of faith is the act of faith, and the motives for the assent are the motives of faith. It is not a merely defensive or a merely negative activity devoted to refuting adversaries or to establishing the absence of inner contradiction. It is something like insight, for it is a heightening of clarity in the object and a developed capacity to contemplate in the subject. Still, it is not insight in the sense of Günther's *spekulative Idee*, which would demonstrate the necessity of the Blessed Trinity, of the act of creation, and of the incarnation and redemption. Such a notion the Council wished not merely to repudiate but also to replace, and so it affirmed an *intelligentia mysteriorum* that remained obscure and imperfect in this mortal life, yet nonetheless was a positive and most fruitful enlightenment. Its obscurity and imperfection imply that one does not understand the mysteries in their internal content or substance. Its element of positive enlightenment lies in a grasp of relations that stand in an analogy of proportion with naturally known truths and link the mysteries to one another and to man's last end.

As Fr Beumer argues for a science of faith that heads towards an understanding of faith, so he argues against a notion of theology that conceives the science of faith to head away from the truths of faith into other realms. On this opposed view, revealed truths provide the initial premises of theology; they are to be defended; they are to be shown free from inner contradiction; but they do not constitute the object or objective of theology as science. For science is deductive, and the theologian's proper business is to proceed from the revealed truths which he takes on faith to other truths which as a scientist he demonstrates.

The issue, then, is precise. Fr Beumer is not denying the essential role of deduction in theology. He is not denying that theologians validly draw conclusions that have not been revealed. But he claims that the central significance of deduction in theology is to reach, not new certitudes, but a fuller understanding of what already is known with the certitude of faith. Moreover, he regards this view not as a mere matter of opinion but as a traditional Catholic position crystallized in a conciliar definition. Finally, while he grants that Aquinas was right in drawing upon Aristotle to give the notion of *intelligentia fidei* an exact scientific context, he also feels that this context was not adequate and that it led Aquinas and his followers away from a proper distribution of emphasis and a fully satisfactory determination of objectives in theological thought.

Here again Fr Beumer's position is nuanced. He finds Aquinas' earlier works to lie well within the Augustinian and medieval tradition of *intelligentia fidei*. But he is not altogether certain that as much can be said for the *Summa theologiae*. He cites the evidence that earlier views still survive and the contrary evidence that would favor the contention that the importation of Aristotelian notions reduced the understanding of faith to the negative content of an absence of inner contradiction. He rather clearly inclines to the opinion that Aquinas does not represent a pure gain in the forward march of Catholic thought on the nature of theology from Clement of Alexandria to the Vatican Council; and in this utterance he feels supported by the fact that the Thomistic school gradually restricted its concern for an understanding of faith to concentrate ever more exclusively on the science of faith.

3   Aquinas on Theological Understanding

I believe these hesitations and doubts about the *Summa theologiae* to rest upon an inadequate analysis. In the first place, for St Thomas theology is neither the understanding of faith nor the science of faith, neither Fr Beumer's *Glaubensverständnis* nor his *Glaubenswissenschaft*. The subject of Thomist theology is not a set of propositions; it is not even a set of truths; it is a reality. *Deus est subiectum huius scientiae.*[7]

In the second place, it seems to me a grave mistake to suggest that there is some opposition between understanding and Aristotle's syllogism. Syllogism fulfils a twofold function. It is obviously an instrument for exhibiting the grounds of a judgment on the conclusion: if the premises are true, the conclusion must be true. But it is also an instrument of developing understanding, and it is this aspect of syllogism that comes to the fore in Aristotle's lengthy discussion of the συλλογισμὸς

7 Thomas Aquinas, *Summa theologiae*, 1, q. 1, a. 7 c.

ἐπιστημονικός, the *syllogismus faciens scire*. Moreover, St Thomas was fully aware of the significance of explanatory syllogism: he conceived reasoning as simply understanding in process, as moving from principles to conclusions in order to grasp both principles and conclusions in a single view.[8] Plainly, Aristotle and Aquinas formulated with technical precision the very relations between understanding and science that Fr Beumer advocates.[9]

In the third place, since science is understanding in process, the possibility of a science of God runs parallel to the possibility of an understanding of God. Now precisely because understanding is *quo est omnia fieri*, its object is not any restricted genus of being but being itself.[10] Because its object is being, it is impossible for understanding to be fully in act without its being God.[11] Because the full act of understanding is God, there arises the apparent[12] antinomy that every created intelligence naturally desires to know God by his essence[13] yet none can attain such a fulfilment by its natural powers.[14] Finally, though the fulfilment can and in fact does occur, still the occurrence does not pertain to this life: ' ... there are two ways of seeing God. One is perfect vision, in which the essence of God is seen. The other is imperfect; though in this vision we do not see what God is, we do see what he is not. And, in this life, the better we understand God to transcend whatever is grasped by intellect, the more perfectly also do we know him.'[15]

In the fourth place, our present impossibility of participating God's understanding of himself implies that any understanding that we do

8 Ibid. q. 14, a. 7; q. 79, a. 8; 2–2, q. 8, a. 1, ad 2m. See J. Peghaire, Intellectus *et* Ratio *selon s. Thomas d'Aquin* (Ottawa: Institut d'Etudes Médiévales, and Paris: Vrin, 1936).
9 Beumer, *Theologie ...* 240.
10 Thomas Aquinas, *Summa theologiae*, 1, q. 79, a. 7 c.
11 Ibid. a. 2 c.
12 I have indicated my reasons for saying that the antinomy is merely apparent in a note, 'The Natural Desire to See God,' *Proceedings of the Eleventh Annual Convention of the Jesuit Philosophical Association*, Boston College, Boston, Mass., April 18, 1949, 31–43 [included as chapter 5 in this volume].
13 Thomas Aquinas, *Summa theologiae*, 1, q. 12, a. 1 c.
14 Ibid. a. 4 c.
15 Ibid. 2–2, q. 8, a. 7 c.: ' ... duplex est Dei visio. Una quidem perfecta per quam videtur Dei essentia. Alia vero imperfecta per quam, etsi non videamus de Deo quid est, videmus tamen quid non est; et tanto in hac vita Deum perfectius cognoscimus quanto magis intelligimus eum excedere quidquid intellectu comprehenditur.'

attain is negative, that is, a refutation of objections or a grasp of the absence of inner contradiction.[16] On the other hand, though we do not understand God in any positive fashion, this does not imply that we do not understand revealed truth in any positive fashion. In the very question in which the gift of understanding in this life is affirmed to be a matter of understanding that we do not understand God, there is also the statement, ' ... with regard to what is proposed to faith for acceptance, there are two requirements ... The first is that intellect should penetrate or grasp it; and this pertains to the gift of understanding ... '[17]

In the fifth place, there are at least three distinct manners in which one may express the possibility of understanding the revelation of a reality that itself is not understood. First, one may speak of the *donum intellectus* and then one refers to an understanding that is connected not with schools and books but with sanctifying grace.[18] Secondly, one may speak of a fruitful yet essentially imperfect understanding of the revelation, and then one adopts the traditional, nontechnical language that has inspired Fr Beumer's study and for obvious reasons would be preferred by a council of the church. Thirdly, one may speak of a *scientia subalternata* of the reality that is God, and then by a single technical phrase one conveys (1) that the subject of theology is not a set of propositions or a set of truths but a reality, (2) that theology itself is an understanding, for science is a process towards a terminal understanding, (3) that this understanding is not of God himself, for then the science would be not subalternated but subalternating, and (4) that an understanding of the revelation cannot be adequate, for the revelation is about God and God himself is not understood.

In the sixth place, it is true that St Thomas speaks of theology as a science that deduces conclusions from the articles of faith. But it is also true that this statement has to be understood in the light both of Aristotle's theory of science and of Aquinas' theological practice.

Now Aristotle was not content to distinguish between explanatory and merely factual syllogisms. He also drew attention to the difference between explanatory middle terms that assigned the *causa cognoscendi* and others that assigned the *causa essendi*. Thus the phases of the moon are

16 Ibid. a. 2 c.
17 Ibid. a. 6 c.: ' ... circa ea quae fidei proponuntur credenda, duo requiruntur ... Primo quidem, ut intellectu penetrentur vel capiantur: et hoc pertinet ad donum intellectus ... '
18 Ibid. a. 5 c.

the cause of our knowing that the moon is a sphere, but the sphericity of the moon is the cause of its phases being what they are. Moreover, the *causa cognoscendi* is also *prior quoad nos*, and so it is first in the *via* or *ordo inventionis*; but the *causa essendi* is *prior quoad se*, and so it is first in the *ordo doctrinae* or *disciplinae*. Nor is this merely a bit of irrelevant, antiquarian lore. If one compares a history of chemistry with a textbook on chemistry, one finds that the course of discovery runs from sensible data to ever more recondite theoretical elements while the arrangement for teaching and learning begins from the theoretical elements[b] and gradually shows how they may be constructed into explanations of all known phenomena.

Let us now turn from Aristotle's theory to Aquinas' practice. It is easy enough to see that the articles of faith are the theologian's *causae cognoscendi*, that they provide the *priora quoad nos*, and that they are first in the *ordo inventionis*. But the complementary terms are not so easily imported into theology. God is always the *causa essendi* but in this life we do not reach a positive understanding of God. Even the expression, *priora quoad se*, cannot be employed universally, for in the Blessed Trinity there is *nihil prius aut posterius*. Accordingly, our inquiry into Aquinas' practice has to be restricted to the question, Did he attach any importance to the *ordo doctrinae* or *disciplinae*?

First, one may note that commonly enough in the *Contra Gentiles* Aquinas proceeds from theoretical premises to conclusions that are confirmed by texts of scripture. His argument is not from revelation to theological conclusions that are distinct from revelation but from nonscriptural premises to conclusions that are coincident with scriptural statements. Moreover, one cannot maintain successfully that in such cases Aquinas was essentially a philosopher and accidentally interested in conformity with revealed truth. The general indications are that Aquinas never considered himself a philosopher and that he regarded mere philosophers as pagans or, at least, as non-Catholics. Again, he explicitly stated that his intention in writing the *Contra Gentiles* was to manifest the truth professed by the Catholic faith and to refute contrary errors.[19] Finally, even when issues lie entirely outside the range of philosophy, he was capable of introducing texts of scripture not to supply himself with

19 *Summa contra Gentiles*, 1, c. 1, §§ 2–3. [§§ 2–3 refer to the second and third paragraphs, which we have counted in the Leonine manual edition. This was Lonergan's own practice, which we shall follow throughout the volume.]

premises but to confirm and illustrate his conclusions.[20] The argument is summary but it more than suggests that the *Contra Gentiles* was intended as a theological work but was composed not in the *ordo inventionis*, which moves from revelation to conclusions that have not been revealed, but in the *ordo disciplinae*, which moves from the conclusions of the *ordo inventionis* to a systematic presentation of the truths that have been revealed.

Secondly, as the reader will recall, St Thomas justified his *Summa theologiae* on the ground that the ordinary run of books on the subject were loaded with useless questions and articles, that they did not follow the *ordo disciplinae* but the exigencies of the text they were commenting or the opportunities that arose for debating, and finally that they kept treating the same issues over and over until students became weary and confused. Now in this indictment the one positive point is the *ordo disciplinae*. To follow that order, one presumes, will be to eliminate the irrelevant, to prevent mere repetitions, and to provide an alternative to the commentary and to the free debate.

Thirdly, a concrete instance of this order is offered by the questions in the *Summa theologiae* on the Blessed Trinity, for they open with the preliminary remark that in the *ordo doctrinae* one begins from the processions, goes on to the relations, and in the third place treats of the divine persons. Now this arrangement is strikingly different not only from the magnificent disorder of the *Scriptum super Sententias*[21] but also from the conspicuous order of the *Contra Gentiles*[22] and from the still different order of the *De potentia*.[23] It would seem that Aquinas had conducted a rather elaborate experiment in theological method, and while even an outline[24] of his successive essays cannot be attempted here, it may be worth while to indicate schematically just how the *ordo inventionis* and the inverse *ordo doctrinae* are related in Trinitarian theory.

20 Thus in the *Summa contra Gentiles* (4, c. 11, §§9–11, 13–17), there are eight successive paragraphs that proceed through conceptual construction to terminate with the phrase, *Hinc est quod* ... , introducing a passage of scripture.
21 *Super I Sent.*, dd. 2–34.
22 *Summa contra Gentiles*, 4, cc. 2–26.
23 *De potentia*, qq. 2, 8, 9, 10.
24 I attempted an outline from the present viewpoint in 'The Concept of *Verbum* in the Writings of St. Thomas Aquinas, v. *Imago Dei*,' *Theological Studies* 10 (1949) 380–88 [*Verbum* 206–15]. A profitable study of sources and development has appeared recently: Paul Vanier,[c] *Théologie trinitaire chez saint Thomas d'Aquin* (Montréal: Institut d'Etudes Médiévales, and Paris: Vrin, 1953).

Anyone who has attempted to find rigorous proof for Trinitarian theses[d] will agree, I think, that the most effective procedure is to begin from the dogmatic affirmation of three consubstantial persons and to argue (1) that, since the persons are consubstantial, their real distinctions cannot be grounded on distinct absolute perfections and so must be grounded on relations, (2) that the relevant relations, if they are to ground distinctions, must not presuppose them and so must be relations of origin, (3) that relations of origin presuppose processions, and (4) that the only processions we can conceive in God are analogous to the processions of human rational consciousness. But clearly, in such a procedure one is operating in the *ordo inventionis*; one argues by setting dilemmas and eliminating the more obviously unacceptable alternatives; one concludes to the existence of relations (*quia sunt*) and one first obtains an inkling of their nature (*quid sint*) when one argues further to the existence of processions; similarly, one determines something about the nature of the processions only when one moves to a further argument on the existence of an analogy.

Inversely, if one aims at generating in pupils the limited understanding of mystery that can be attained in this life, one directs one's attention not to demonstrations of existence but to the synthetic or constructive procedure in which human intelligence forms and develops concepts. First, one works out in detail the notion of God without asking any Trinitarian questions. Then one inquires, not whether the Son proceeds from the Father (which would be to presuppose the notion of person), but whether there are processions in God. Though this question is not *quid sit* but *utrum sit*, still it involves one in the necessity of determining in what sense we can speak of processions in God; and such a clarification is all that we can attain, for as we do not understand God himself, so we do not understand the processions identical with God. Next, the clarification of the notion of the divine processions leads to a clarification of the divine subsistent relations. Finally, from three mutually opposed subsistent relations we can advance to some understanding of the truth that there are three really distinct yet consubstantial persons.

Such is the procedure of the *Summa theologiae*. As has been noted already, it cannot claim to be based on any *priora quoad se*, for in the Blessed Trinity nothing is prior or posterior. But it is the order of the genesis in our minds of our imperfect *intelligentia mysteriorum*; and by identity it is the order of Aquinas' *scientia subalternata* presented in the *ordo doctrinae*.

4   Consequences of the Thomist Position

My disagreement with Fr Beumer's interpretation of St Thomas tends not to weaken but to reinforce his basic contention. So far from opposing his view that the *intelligentia mysteriorum* is a fundamental concern of speculative theology, I have been engaged in transforming an objection against his position into an argument in its favor.

Moreover, that transformation is somewhat more significant than a merely additional argument. Fr Beumer himself has acknowledged that the notion of a *Glaubensverständnis* is lacking in clarity and precision and so runs the risk of encouraging merely enthusiastic nebulosity.[25] He considers it to have been the role of Aquinas to endow theology with the spirit of scientific exactitude.[26] Yet he has to concede that this benefit to theology is not a benefit to his *Glaubensverständnis* since he believes it to be regrettable yet necessary to drop the old Aristotelian and scholastic views on the nature of science.[27]

Accordingly, when I argue that the understanding of the mysteries was a notion that Aquinas not only grasped fully but also placed in a profound and rich theoretical context, I also am endeavoring to supply for a deficiency of which Fr Beumer is aware. Still, to make this point somewhat clearer, I venture to add a few indications of the manner in which the context of Thomist thought enables one to relate speculative theology to the truths of revelation, to the illumination of reason by faith, and to the teaching authority of the church.

From revelation come the premises of the *ordo inventionis*, and on the truth of the premises rests the truth not only of their conclusions but also of the subsequent development of the *ordo doctrinae*. It follows, as Fr Beumer contended, that the theologian's labors in this field do not offer new motives for the assent of faith but, on the contrary, stand upon the assent of faith. Indeed, one may add that the deductions of the *ordo inventionis* are all the more secure if not only the initial premises are revealed but also the conclusions are confirmed by revelation, and inversely, the more extensive such confirmation, the greater the section of revealed truth that is unified in the *ordo doctrinae*. Finally, it is to be observed that the distinction between *ordo inventionis* and *ordo doctrinae* is to be drawn, not by ascertaining which truths are revealed, for the

---

25 Beumer, *Theologie* ... 55, 243.
26 Ibid. 93.
27 Ibid. 241.

same truths admit different arrangements, not by inquiring into the chronology of discovery, but by discriminating between arguments that settle matters of fact and arguments that throw some light on the nature of things.

Secondly, the deductions of the *ordo inventionis* offer a twofold illumination of reason by faith. Thus while it is true that natural reason can arrive at a correct philosophy, it also is apparent that very commonly it fails to do so. Because, then, the *ordo inventionis* yields series of theological conclusions excluding series of philosophic alternatives, theology expedites reason's efforts in the pursuit of reason's proper goals. Further, because revelation is supernatural, its implications present reason with truths that otherwise it could not know, and the analysis of these truths leads to the discovery of the theoretical elements that (1) stand beyond the confines of man's natural knowledge, (2) possess something like an immanent systematic structure of their own (*nexus mysteriorum inter se*), and (3) may be approximated through the analogies offered by scientific knowledge in the natural and the human fields.

I have spoken not of two illuminations but of a twofold illumination, and by this I would suggest both the unity of the subject and the unity of the goal. A man has but one intelligence, and it would grasp all in a single view; moreover, the truths of revelation are in harmony with the truths of reason; and so the first mentioned illumination is to be regarded as producing the necessary dispositions for the second. Just as grace is beyond nature yet perfects nature, so faith is beyond reason yet perfects reason. The olive branch is grafted on the oleaster, and it is the signal merit of the Thomist synthesis that its *ordo doctrinae*, conveying an *intelligentia mysteriorum*, seems ever a vital outgrowth in which, often enough, it is not too easy to show just where philosophic analysis has ended and theological understanding has begun. Nor, finally, is the philosophic component within the total view to be regarded as a perhaps necessary but regrettable intrusion. If such an opinion follows from Fr Beumer's concept of theology as *Glaubensverständnis*, it is quite incompatible with the Thomist position that the subject of theology is God primarily but secondarily includes all things in their relations to God.

Thirdly, one misses the whole point of the *ordo doctrinae* if one mistakenly expects its syllogisms to offer not expressions of limited understanding but evidence for indisputable certitudes. There exists certitude, but it is derived from the certitude of faith, and the derivation is exhibited in the *via inventionis*. There is no additional certitude generated by understanding itself, for our understanding of the mysteries is imperfect. To convey that imperfect understanding is the function of the *ordo doctrinae*, and one only betrays one's incomprehension if, on the one hand, one pretends to find evidence for certitude where such evidence does not exist or, on the other hand, one dismisses *argumenta convenientiae* as proofs that do not prove.[e]

Still, though it generates neither new certitude nor perfect understanding, the *ordo doctrinae* is most fruitful. With some approximation to a single view it gives rise to an apprehension of the exact content and the exact implications of the many mysteries in their many aspects. That single view both simplifies and enriches one's own spiritual life, and it bestows upon one's teaching the enviable combination of sureness of doctrine with versatility of expression. Finally, the single view remains, for it is fixed upon one's intellectual memory. So we find that non-Catholic clergymen, often more learned in scripture and the fathers, preach from their pulpits the ideas put forward in the latest stimulating book or article, while the Catholic priest, often burdened with sacerdotal duties and administrative tasks, spontaneously expounds the epistle or gospel of the Sunday in the light of an understanding that is common to the ages.

Fourthly, the issue of certitude has another aspect. The *via inventionis* concludes with the theoretical elements which, in the *ordo doctrinae*, understanding will combine into principles and science will expand in deductions. But unless the formulation of the theoretical elements is both accurate and complete, the whole structure of the *ordo doctrinae* will suffer from a hidden vice. Nor is the occurrence of such a radical structural defect unknown for, as has often been remarked, heresy may be almost defined as the selection of some but not all the relevant elements from the sources of revelation. At this point, then, one must invoke St Thomas' doctrine that wisdom[f] is above both understanding and science. The conclusions of science depend upon the grasp of principles by understanding. The principles of understanding depend upon the terms that they unite. But the validation of the selection of the terms and so the validation of both understanding and science is the work of wisdom.[28]

It would be a mistake to say that the speculative theologian is either devoid of wisdom or adequately wise. He could be devoid of wisdom only by complete ignorance of philosophy and a total deprivation of the

28 *Summa theologiae*, 1–2, q. 66, a. 5, ad 4m.

donum sapientiae given in some measure to all along with sanctifying grace. He could be adequately wise only if he already enjoyed the beatific vision which alone is proportionate to the reality which theology would elucidate. In his intermediate position between wisdom and folly, he must take every precaution to arrive at the basic theoretical elements and all of them in as accurate a formulation as he can attain. But the greater his mastery of his subject, the keener will be his realization of the difficulty of this task and the profounder will be his gratitude that God has vouchsafed us not only a revelation of supernatural truth but also a divinely assisted teaching authority that is not chary in its use of the evangelical *Est, Est* and *Non, Non.*[29]

The basic relation, then, of speculative theology to the teaching authority of the church is the subordination of both understanding and science to wisdom. It is a supernatural subordination that runs parallel to the natural subordination of *quid sit* to *an sit*, of speculation to judgment. It also is a subordination that complements a point already made. We have argued that the truth of the conclusions of the *ordo inventionis* and thereby the truth of the elements that enter into the *ordo doctrinae* rest upon the truth of the assent of faith. We have now to notice that the *ordo doctrinae* by its selection of related basic terms adds a further synthetic element. Because that selection and its consequences are not evident, the mysteries remain 'hidden behind the curtain of faith and enveloped, as it were, in mists.'[30] Because the theologian is aware of his inescapable limitations, he propounds even his clearest theorems as merely probable. Because his clearest theorems are only probable, he is ever ready to leave an ultimate judgment upon them to the further exercise of faith that discerns in the church's dogmatic decisions the assistance of divine wisdom.

In conclusion, two further relations between the teaching authority of the church and speculative theology may be mentioned. On the one hand, the dogmatic pronouncements of the church draw upon the previous formulations of theologians, as might be illustrated ever more abundantly by running through the councils from Nicea to the Vatican. On the other hand, with each new dogmatic pronouncement the basis of the *via inventionis* receives an increment in clarity and precision that

29 Matthew 5.37.[8]
30 Concilium Vaticanum, sess. 3, c. 4: 'ipsius ... fidei velamine contecta et quadam quasi caligine obvoluta'; Denzinger, *Enchiridion symbolorum ...* 1796 (*DS* 3016).

is passed on to its conclusions to result in a corresponding increment in the exactitude of the *ordo doctrinae* and in the understanding of revelation.

5   Contemporary Methodological Issues

If Aristotelian and scholastic notions of science seem to me to be adequate[h] for a formulation of the nature of speculative theology both in itself and in its relations to revelation, to philosophy, and to the teaching authority of the church, still I should avoid the appearance of making exaggerated claims, and so I should acknowledge the existence of contemporary methodological issues[i] that cannot be dispatched in so expeditious a fashion.

In the first place, there is the problem of patterns of human experience, of the *Denkformen*.[j] Readers of the *Imitatio Christi* are familiar with the contrast between feeling compunction and defining it, between pleasing the Blessed Trinity and discoursing learnedly upon it. But the contrast to which I wish to draw attention is not between doing and merely knowing but between two types of knowing. Knowledge is involved not only in defining compunction but also in feeling it, not only in discoursing upon the Blessed Trinity but also in pleasing it. Still, these two types of knowledge are quite distinct, and the methodological problem is to define the precise nature of each, the advantages and limitations of each, and above all the principles and rules that govern transpositions from one to the other.

The significance of such transpositions is manifold.[k] They are relevant to the implementation of speculative theology in the apostolate and especially in Catholic education. Again, they are relevant to a study of Catholic tradition, for a great part of the evidence for the truths of faith, as they are formulated learnedly today, is to be found in documents not only written in a popular style but also springing from a mind that conceived and judged not in the objective categories of scholastic thought but in the more spontaneous intersubjective categories of ordinary human experience and ordinary religious experience. In the third place, such transpositions are relevant within the methodology of speculative theology itself. Just as the equations of thermodynamics make no one feel warmer or cooler and, much less, evoke the sentiments associated with the drowsy heat of the summer sun or with the refreshing coolness of evening breezes, so also speculative theology is not immediately relevant to the stimulation of religious feeling.[l] But unless this fact is acknowledged explicitly and systematically, there arises a constant pressure in favor of theological tendencies that mistakenly reinforce the light of faith and intelligence with the warmth of less austere modes of thought. Moreover, such tendencies, pushed to the limit, give rise to the intense and attractive but narrow theologies that would puff up to the dimension of the whole some part or aspect of Catholic tradition or Catholic experience; and by a natural reaction such exaggerations lead traditional thinkers to denigrate all scientific concern with the experiential modes of thinking in living.[m] To strike a balance one might say, I think, that because the particular and concrete is known by man only through sense and imagination and feeling, the theologian must seek to understand and appreciate the apostolic kerygma, the charisms of the early church, the *gnôsis* of Alexandria, the literary modes of patristic thought, the vitality of the liturgy, the role of personal confrontation, the momentousness of personal engagement.[n] Still, a human apprehension of the particular and concrete is never an apprehension of the whole. To know God and all things in their relations to God the human mind must effect the difficult shift from the familiar categories of intersubjective living to the objective categories in which the notion of being is potentially both completely universal and completely concrete.

In the second place, there is the problem of the relations between speculative and positive theology.[o] The Vatican Council spoke not only of an *intelligentia mysteriorum* but also of an individual and collective progress in the understanding, science, and wisdom with which the same revealed truths in the same sense are apprehended down the ages. On this identity St Pius x insisted in his condemnation of modernism; and the proof of this identity has been proclaimed the noblest task of the theologian by both Pope Pius ix and Pope Pius xii.[31] Still, it is one thing to be dedicated to the performance of one's duty, and it is another to discover the methodological principles on which that duty can be performed in a fully satisfactory fashion. An age of research has kept enriching us with ever further monographs on divisions and subdivisions and aspects of the doctrine of the Bible, the fathers, the scholastics, the *recentiores*,[p] the heretics, the councils, and the decisions of the Holy See. This flood tide of scholarly diligence yields a vast multiplicity. Yet if we ask how the multiplicity is to be reduced to unity, we are presented with

---

31 Pope Pius xii, *Acta Apostolicae Sedis* 42 (1950) 569, in the encyclical, *Humani generis*.

peculiar problems. For in the first place, the methods of scholarly research cannot guide the construction of a synthesis of the results of an enormous number of quite different researches. In the second place, specialists in particular fields are apt to boggle at any suggestion that nonspecialists settle what their results really mean and how they should be fitted together. In the third place, not only does there seem to be no one to perform the work of synthesis if both specialists and nonspecialists are excluded, but also the value of any synthesis would seem to be transitory since the conclusions of scholars today are always likely to be overruled by the conclusions of scholars tomorrow.

No doubt, the issue admits a *solvitur ambulando*. But the present question is a question of method, and perhaps the following observations will be found helpful. First, there seems to be room for a rough but serviceable distinction between two types of historical question.[q] Questions of the first type are not very relevant to theology; they are subject to the vicissitudes of developing scientific opinion; and they receive most light from the application of the methods of exact, positive research. On the other hand, questions of the second type are extremely relevant to theology; but they are little influenced by the cumulative work of scholars each adding fresh details and new aspects to the conclusions of their predecessors; and they tend to be settled now one way and now another not by scientific method but by the empiricist, naturalist, existentialist, idealist, relativist, or realist philosophy which individual scholars implicitly or explicitly invoke in their interpretation of the nature of scientific method and of the scientific attitude. Secondly, insofar as these two types of question can be distinguished with clarity and precision, one can affirm that just as reason is illuminated by faith so also method may be illuminated by faith; indeed, since method is simply reason's explicit consciousness of the norms of its own procedures, the illumination of reason by faith implies an illumination of method by faith. Thirdly, a study of scientific methods in their presuppositions and assumptions not only goes to the root of the matter (for the scientist is certain never of his conclusions but only of the validity of his method); it also provides the principles for a systematic critique and evaluation to which the results of scientific investigation have to be ready to submit. Fourthly, just as scientific method in the physical sciences is not a mere matter of measuring and curve fitting but employs these pedestrian techniques under the higher guidance supplied by relatively a priori differential equations, so there is no reason to suppose that scientific method in the historical sciences is free from higher-level controls and permanently dedicated to the exclusive production of unrelated monographs. Finally, if this component of historical method can be discovered, defined, and implemented, there would seem to be some probability that the rough yet serviceable distinction from which we began could be established in the light of clear and distinct ideas intrinsic to the field of methodological considerations.

Thirdly, there is the problem of the relations between speculative theology and the empirical human sciences.[r] Because speculative theology treats all things in their relations to God, it is acknowledged to be queen of the sciences. Because empirical human sciences are recent additions to the total range of human knowledge, the queen has been long accustomed to delegate the exercise of her functions to her handmaid, philosophy. But now there is a new situation. For human sciences are empirical inasmuch as they treat of man as in fact he is; man in the present order suffers from the effects of original sin and of personal sin, and only through supernatural grace does he escape the consequent darkening of his intellect and weakening of his will; it follows that the human issues of the present order cannot be satisfactorily subordinated to philosophy. If the human sciences were not empirical, if they studied human nature in the abstract, their subordination to philosophy would secure automatically their subordination to theology. But the fact is that the human sciences are empirical, that they are engaged in understanding all the data on man as he is, and that the only correct general form of that understanding is theological.

Now the issue I am raising has an enormous range of aspects, and perhaps to a majority of them methodological issues are not very relevant. But there does arise a point at which the methodological issue is relevant, and it may be illustrated concretely by supposing that a Catholic specialist in an empirical human science sees that his faith is relevant to the treatment of some problem and asks how he as a scientist is to make that relevance operative and fruitful.[32] Materially, the problem may be solved either by teaching the scientist theology or by teaching a theologian the science.[s] But that material solution is not practicable generally, and insofar as it works, it does so because the presence of the two disciplines in the same mind leads to an insight into their relations. Still,

32   An exceptional awareness of this type of problem is forced upon the Catholics of such a country as the United States, where the voluntary offerings of the faithful support some twenty Catholic universities.

the material solution gives a clue to the formal solution, namely, the systematic statement of the general content of the totality of such insights. Just as theology itself is a *scientia subalternata* resting on the understanding that is God, so also theology has to lead to an understanding of all things in their relation to God, and it is that understanding that will explain the measure and manner in which empirical human sciences are sub-alternate to theology. Finally, since the principles of empirical anthropology, psychology, sociology, pedagogy, medicine, economics, politics, and so forth, are not primitive propositions peculiar to each of those disciplines but methodical rules that are more or less common to all, it is primarily through the illumination of method by faith that theology has to exercise her queenly rule.

In the fourth and last place,[t] there is the problem illustrated by Fr Beumer's book. When he seeks a theologian that follows the doctrine of the Vatican Council on the nature of theology, he turns not to St Thomas but to M.J. Scheeben. He does so partly because of his interpretation of the *Summa theologiae* and partly because the Thomistic tradition seems to him to have been ever less interested in the Augustinian *intelligentia fidei*. I have disagreed rather emphatically with his first reason, but I should be implying that his preference for Scheeben was an impossibility if I did not meet his second reason with a distinction. On the one hand, then, I do not think a teacher can follow the *Summa* and fail to communicate some understanding of the faith to pupils that possess the requisite literary, philosophic, and historical knowledge. On the other hand, there seems no doubt that the opusculum, *De natura verbi intellectus*, has exerted a profound influence upon the Thomistic school, though in my opinion its doctrine conflicts with the doctrine of the certainly genuine works of Aquinas,[u] and its author gave the facts of human understanding no more recognition than did Duns Scotus.[33]

But behind such a historical accident there are deeper factors and they come to light as soon as one endeavors to explain the differences between the conceptualism of Scotus and, I believe, the quite distinct rational psychology of Aquinas. For then the issues of historical inter-

33 Perhaps the reader will find some evidence for this statement in my articles, 'The Concept of *Verbum* in the Writings of St. Thomas Aquinas,' *Theological Studies* 7 (1946) 349–92; 8 (1947) 35–79; 404–444; 10 (1949) 3–40; 359–93 [*Verbum*]. They were reviewed in *Bulletin thomiste* 8 (1951–53) 477–79, 740. I hope to publish shortly an examination of the theoretical issues entitled *Insight: A Study of Human Understanding* [CWL 3].

pretation are complicated by the self-knowledge of the interpreter, by his difficulty in grasping clearly and distinctly just what he is doing when he understands and conceives, reflects and judges. Nor is this difficulty to be overcome in any easy fashion, for it has all the complexity of the critical problem.

In other words, behind the difference of opinion between Mandonnet, who regarded the *De natura verbi intellectus* as doubtful or spurious, and Grabmann, who found no extrinsic evidence against its authenticity, there is the far deeper opposition that separates the constructive tendencies of intellectualism and the atomistic tendencies of conceptualism. Nor can one go to the root of that division without tackling the critical problem and, indeed, without conceiving the critical problem not as the easy question whether we know but as the real issue of what precisely occurs when we are knowing. Until that issue is settled in the luminous fashion that will make philosophy as methodical as science, there are bound to remain basic and unsolved problems of theological method.

In the light of this radical difficulty one comes to appreciate Fr Beumer's work in its real significance. He has appealed to an indisputable source. He has established solidly the meaning of the *intelligentia mysteriorum*. He has provided evidence that the intention of the Vatican Council was to speak of the nature of theology. Despite my complex reservations, his work is profoundly and practically significant.

9

Isomorphism of Thomist and Scientific Thought

Two sets of terms, say *A, B, C* ... and *P, Q, R* ... are said to be isomorphic if the relation of *A* to *B* is similar to the relation of *P* to *Q*, the relation of *A* to *C* is similar to the relation of *P* to *R*, the relation of *B* to *C* is similar to the relation of *Q* to *R*, etc., etc. Isomorphism, then, supposes different sets of terms; it neither affirms nor denies similarity between the terms of one set and those of other sets; but it does assert that the network of relations in one set of terms is similar to the networks of relations in other sets.

Our concern is briefly to indicate an isomorphism of Thomist and scientific thought. While there is no need to explain that by Thomist thought is meant the thought of St Thomas Aquinas, it may not be amiss to remark that by scientific thought is meant the thinking of the scientist as a scientist and not at all the excursions of scientists into philosophy. Again, while volumes might be written on Thomist thought alone or on scientific thought alone, our concern is with neither alone. Both are to be considered at once to bring to light an isomorphism, a protracted analogy of proportion,[a] that concentrates on a structural similarity to prescind entirely from the materials that enter into the structures. Finally, if this analogy is grasped, I think it will appear that the material differences are less significant than they seem to be when, as commonly occurs, the materials alone are considered and the structure is ignored.

First, then, let us note that the relation of hypothesis to verification is similar to the relation of definition to judgment. For the scientist's hypothesis of itself is merely an object of thought that, nonetheless, through verification becomes an object of scientific knowledge. In like manner a Thomist definition of itself is neither true nor false yet through judgment becomes an item of a true or false claim to knowledge of reality. It will be observed that (1) we are not saying that scientific hypothesis is the same as Thomist definition or that scientific verification is the same as Thomist judgment, but (2) we are affirming what a Thomist would name an analogy of proportion, namely, that scientific hypothesis stands to verification as Thomist definition stands to judgment.

Secondly, if we ask why scientific hypothesis needs verification and why Thomist definition needs judgment, we meet with similar answers. The scientist will insist that it is a mistake to try and base science on a priori necessities, that the one fruitful procedure is to scrutinize things as in fact they are, to discern in them what possibly may be their laws, to formulate these possibilities as mere hypotheses, and to submit such hypotheses to every test before placing any great reliance on them. The Thomist will reply in apparently a quite different manner. He will point out that definition stands to judgment as essence to existence, that a finite essence exists not necessarily but contingently, that divine wisdom can select any set of finite essences and arrange them in any of a vast variety of world orders while divine will is free to choose any whatever of the possible orders, and consequently that, while divine wisdom guarantees that there is a reason for everything, still in each case the ultimate reason must be the fact of divine free choice.[1] Plainly, the empirical character of science and the freedom of divine choice are two quite different things, yet there is a notable similarity between their functional significance in scientific and Thomist thought. The scientist has to verify his hypotheses because ultimately what counts is what in fact is so; and the Thomist has to pass judgment on definitions because ultimately what counts is what God chose to be so.

Thirdly, let us raise the question of origins. How does the scientist reach his hypotheses and how does the Thomist reach his definitions? The scientist will explain that commonly he begins from some problem, scrutinizes the relevant sensible data, selects their measurable features, plots the results of measurement on a graph, draws a smooth curve that approximately passes through all the points determined by the measurements, finds the mathematical formula that corresponds to the curve,

1   Thomas Aquinas, *Summa contra Gentiles*, 2, cc. 24, 26; 3, c. 97, §§ 13–17.

tests the formula by working out all its implications and comparing them with the results of further observation and experiment and, finally, if the formula passes the tests, announces it as a hypothesis. In his turn the Thomist will explain that a definition is an answer to the question, *Quid sit?*[b] What is it? He will recall that Socrates went about Athens asking such questions as, What is temperance? What is fortitude? What is justice? What is knowledge? He will add that Plato expressed the view that answers to such questions were based upon a recollection of eternal and immutable Forms or Ideas that subsist in some noetic heaven. Warming to his subject, he will point out how superficial it is to suppose that Aristotle merely transposed Plato's Forms from their abstract realm to an immanence in concrete, sensible objects. So far from meeting one myth with another, Aristotle set himself the task of finding out just what one means when one asks, 'What is it?' His conclusion was that 'What?' means 'Why?' Thus when one asks, 'What is an eclipse?' one really means, 'Why is the moon or sun darkened in this strange manner?'[2] Similarly, when one asks, 'What is a man?' one really means to point to a sensible object and inquire, 'Why is this a man?'[3] Accordingly, to define is to begin from sensible data and to discover why they are what they are, to discover their *causa essendi*, their form, their τὸ τί ἦν εἶναι, their *quidditas*, their essence. This is quite a cascade of terms but the marvel is that for so subtle a point there should be any terms at all. Moreover, as St Thomas pointed out, the trouble is that in the question, 'Why is this a man?' the 'this'[c] is ambiguous. For 'this' may refer to the supposit that is a man, and the reason why a supposit is of such a kind is an essence or quiddity. However, 'this' may refer simply to a set of sensitively apprehended materials, and the reason why materials have the being of a man is a *causa essendi* or form.[4] Now as a scientific hypothesis is not the same as a Thomist definition, so a scientific problem is not the same as a Thomist *quid sit*. Yet it is not difficult to discern another analogy of proportion. Just as the scientific problem leads to a scrutiny of sensible data that ultimately results in a hypothesis, so the Thomist question leads to a scrutiny of sensible data that ultimately results in a definition.

Fourthly, just as the Thomist definition abstracts from the material conditions of space and time that characterize its sensible origins, so according to the theories of special and of general relativity the math-

2 Aristotle, *Posterior analytics*, II, 2.
3 Aristotle, *Metaphysics*, VII, 17.
4 Thomas Aquinas, *In VII metaphys.*, lect. 17, 1667–68.

ematical expression of physical principles and laws is invariant with respect to inertial and, more generally, continuous transformations of spatiotemporal reference frames. Now abstraction and invariance are not exactly the same thing, for abstraction is predicated of the concept or inner word, while invariance is predicated of the mathematical expression of certain concepts or inner words. Still, expression and concept, outer and inner word, differ only as sign and signified, as effect and cause; and both Thomist abstraction and Einsteinian invariance affirm in different manners that the products of investigation are independent of the spatiotemporal conditions of their origins on the level of sense.

Fifthly, it is a commonplace that the scientist claims, not knowledge of the laws of nature, but the anticipation of an ever better approximation to such knowledge. For every formulation of natural law is open to revision; every duly established revision is regarded as a forward step in the advance of science; and so far from being dismayed, the scientist is apt to glory in this prospect of perpetual motion. Now it would be a most remarkable contrast if scientific scrutiny of sensible data could only approximate laws while Thomist scrutiny of sensible data hit off essential definitions with exactitude. But the fact is that the Thomist effort is marked with the same modesty as the scientific. We have to reason to reach the inner word of conception or definition.[5] There are many properties of sensible things that we do not know at all, and of those that do fall under our senses we usually cannot assign the exact reason.[6] In knowledge of truth all men are in process, for those that come after always add to the knowledge of those that went before, and so the beatitude that consists in the achievement of knowledge cannot belong to this life on earth.[7]

Sixthly, though scientist and Thomist both confess the limitations of their knowledge, it is no less true that both have quite precise ideas of what they seek to know. The scientist is out to determine the functions that will be satisfied by all possible measurements or enumerations, and this anticipation of an indeterminate function to be determined enables him to complement his a posteriori techniques of curve fitting with the rather a priori approach that consists in postulating invariance and in limiting the range of possibly relevant functions by arguing from differential and operator equations. In like manner, though the Thomist

5 *Super Ioannem,* 1, lect. 1, §26.
6 Thomas Aquinas, *Summa contra Gentiles,* 1, c. 3, §5.
7 Ibid. 3, c. 48, §12.

disavows knowledge of the essential definitions of the myriad species of things in this world, still he can establish that each thing has an essence, that the essence is a compound of form and matter, and that there is a real difference between essence and contingent existence. Now it would be plainly a mistake to identify the heuristic structure that results from scientific anticipations with the metaphysics that emerges from Thomist reflection. But at least it is remarkable that the scientist conceives as his ideal goal knowledge of theories verified in any number of different instances and that the Thomist will add that by verification the scientist knows contingent existence, by theories he knows essences and forms, and by appealing to instances he acknowledges matter as well as form and existence.

Seventhly, in the thought of St Thomas the notion of object[d] is defined by its causal relations to potency and act. Potencies are either passive or active. The object of a passive potency is its mover, and so colors are the objects of sight because they move eyes to the act of seeing. The object of an active potency is its term or end, and so the objects of imagination are the images that imagination produces and the things that the images are intended to represent.[8] But the peculiarity of human intelligence is that it has objects of both types.[9] There is the object as mover that is the 'quiddity or nature existing in corporeal matter,'[10] the object that is 'known first and known *per se*,'[11] 'the first thing we understand in the cognitional activity proper to this life,'[12] the object grasped in images as examples,[13] the object that must be grasped if anything at all is to be understood in this life.[14] Still, though the object as mover is restricted to the intelligibility immanent in sensible presentations, nonetheless the object as end is being in its full sweep,[15] and this object is known to us through the *media in quibus* of inner words,[e] of definitions and enunciations.

Now the scientist does not assert with St Thomas that 'images are related to intelligence as objects in which it considers, one way or another,

8 Thomas Aquinas, *Summa theologiae*, 1, q. 77, a. 3; see also q. 85, a. 2, ad 3m.
9 Ibid. q. 85, a. 2, ad 3m.
10 Ibid. q. 84, a. 7: 'quidditas sive natura in materia corporali existens.'
11 Ibid. q. 85, a. 8: 'primo et per se cognitum'; see also q. 87, a. 3.
12 Ibid. q. 88, a.3: 'primum autem quod intelligitur a nobis secundum statum praesentis vitae.'
13 Ibid. q. 84, a. 7.
14 Ibid.
15 Ibid. q. 79, a. 7.

as represented perfectly or as not represented, everything that falls within its range. Hence, when the imagination is prevented from functioning, the intelligence is prevented from functioning too, and this totally, even in regard to the knowledge of God ... '[16] But if one follows Einstein's rather celebrated advice[f] to cognitional theorists, one will pay very little attention to what scientists say and a great deal to what they do. For the history of scientific discovery, from Archimedes' inspiration to weigh the gold crown in water to Bohr's planetary model of the atom, has been but a long series of instances of what St Thomas, and before him Aristotle, meant by intellect's grasp of εἶδος or species[g] in phantasm: 'the faculty of understanding grasps the forms in images.'[17] 'Our faculty of understanding abstracts the intelligible forms from images insofar as it considers things according to the common aspects of their nature, but also it grasps the forms in the images, for it has no capacity whatever for understanding, not even for understanding the things from which it abstracts the forms, except by turning to images.'[18]

Further, while this immanence of intelligibility in the sensible has been a potent factor in the traditional attachment of scientists to a mechanist view of reality, the outstanding fact of the contemporary scientific situation is that this deep-rooted tendency is now being overcome by the inner development of science itself. From the days of Galileo the real object of the scientist was thought to be some imaginable stuff or particle or radiation that moved imaginably in some imaginable space and time. But relativity has eliminated the imaginability of scientifically conceived space and time; and quantum mechanics has eliminated the imaginability of basic processes. Whether he likes it or not, the scientist has transcended imagination. He can describe his present activity as determining the symbols that mathematically link given sets of pointer readings with other, future sets. But he cannot avoid asking himself what he knows

16 *Super Librum Boethii De Trinitate*, q. 6, a. 2, ad 5m: 'phantasmata comparantur ad intellectum ut obiecta, in quibus inspicit omne quod inspicit vel secundum perfectam repraesentationem vel secundum negationem. Et ideo quando phantasmatum cognitio impeditur, oportet totaliter impediri cognitionem intellectus etiam in divinis ... '
17 Aristotle, *De anima*, III, 7, 431b 2: τὰ μὲν οὖν εἴδη τὸ νοητικὸν ἐν τοῖς φαντάσμασι νοεῖ.
18 Thomas Aquinas, *Summa theologiae*, 1, q. 85, a. 1, ad 5m: 'Intellectus noster et abstrahit species intelligibiles a phantasmatibus, inquantum considerat naturas rerum in universali; et tamen intelligit eas in phantasmatibus, quia non potest intelligere etiam ea quorum species abstrahit, nisi convertendo se ad phantasmata.'

when he thus determines symbols; and it is the Thomist that has the answer to his question. For mathematical symbols are the outer words that signify inner words of conception and judgment; and the inner words are the *media in quibus* being, the object as end of human intelligence, is known.

Eighthly, let us ask why Thomist and scientific thought are isomorphic. Why do both begin from questions or problems concerning sensible data? Why do both inquiries issue in abstract definitions or invariantly expressed hypotheses that respectively stand in need of judgment or verification because of the absolute significance of fact? Why are both so modest in their claims to definitive knowledge? Why do Thomist metaphysics and scientific method anticipate similar structures in what is to be known through affirmed definitions and verified hypotheses?

Clearly, it is not enough to say that both types of thought proceed from the same human mind, for it is quite easy to point to a variety of philosophies that proceed from the human mind without exhibiting any notable isomorphism with scientific thought. The answer, then, must envisage the human mind under some precise aspect; and the relevant aspect, I submit, is neither truth nor certitude nor deduction nor necessity nor universality nor conception nor inquiry nor intuition nor experience nor a priori synthesis nor apperceptive unity nor description nor phenomenology nor induction nor, indeed, any mere combination of these. The relevant aspect is understanding.

For, in the first place, as far as Thomism is concerned, we have St Thomas' explicit statement on the issue. ' ... the human soul understands itself by its understanding,[i] which is its proper act, perfectly demonstrating its power and its nature.'[19] For the human soul knows itself not by its essence,[20] not through its habits,[21] but by reflecting on its acts of understanding,[22] and it is through a scrutiny of acts of understanding that the nature of the human mind and all its virtualities can be demonstrated perfectly.

In the second place, just as understanding is the key[j] that unlocks the secrets of the human soul, so also it is the key to scientific procedure.

19 Ibid. q. 88, a. 2, ad 3m: ' ... anima humana intelligit se ipsam per suum intelligere, quod est actus proprius eius, perfecte demonstrans virtutem eius et naturam.'
20 Ibid. q. 87, a. 1.
21 Ibid. a. 2.
22 Ibid. a. 3.

The scientist's goal is a goal of understanding, namely, the complete explanation of all phenomena. Because the scientist seeks understanding, he adverts to problems. Because understanding grasps intelligibility in sensible data, he observes and measures and experiments. Because understanding conceptualizes what it grasps in sensible data, the scientist formulates hypotheses. Because in sensible data understanding grasps not necessities but possibilities, the hypotheses stand in need of verification. Because such possibilities abstract from the material conditions of space and time, the mathematical expression of hypothetical laws proves invariant under transformations of coordinates. Because relevant data may be overlooked, even verified hypotheses are open to revision. Because every revision is simply a repetition of the same general process of experience, of hypothesis, and of verification, the structure of scientific knowledge is a constant, and that methodical constant squares with the Thomist metaphysical constant of potency, form, and act. Because, besides the moving object of understanding, the quiddity or species or εἶδος emergent in sensible or imagined objects, there also is the end or goal that is being in its full sweep, contemporary science finds itself compelled to relinquish its traditional naive realism and to come to grips with philosophic issues.

Ninthly, if the isomorphism of Thomist and scientific thought is grounded in the human mind as a faculty of understanding, then the material differences between Thomist and scientific thought are to be explained by the respectively different manners in which each derives from understanding. Thus St Thomas reflected on the act of understanding itself to reach a rational psychology of fundamental generality in harmony with an equally fundamental metaphysics. In contrast, scientists make no attempt to reflect on their acts of understanding; but they perform such acts in great numbers, in a vast variety of fields of inquiry, in historically developing sequences over long periods of time; not only do they perform the acts but also concretely, *exercite et non signate*,[k] they work out the real implications of the acts; and so they bring to light in their practice a methodical structure that is isomorphic with the conclusions of Thomist reflection and analysis.

Such, I believe, is the isomorphism of Thomist and scientific thought. Its implications are quite simple. On the one hand, the acts of understanding on which St Thomas reflected were acts possible in his medieval milieu; but many further acts are possible at the present time, and it is by bringing to light the enrichment they offer that contemporary

Thomists can carry out the Leonine program of *vetera novis augere et perficere*. On the other hand, His Holiness, Pope Pius XII, has invited scientists to seek the unity of all scientific knowledge[l] in a philosophy;[23] but scientific certainty regards not the changing content of theories but the permanent structure of method; and so one might suggest that scientists will find the philosophy they seek by reflecting on their method and through its structure arriving at the corresponding, isomorphic epistemology and metaphysics.[24]

23 *L'Osservatore Romano*, 25 aprile, 1955.
24 Perhaps I should note that I have treated the idea contained in this paper on the historical side in a series of articles in *Theological Studies* (1946–49) [*Verbum*] and on the theoretical side in a forthcoming work to be entitled *Insight*.

10

Insight:
Preface to a Discussion

When the Reverend President of the American Catholic Philosophical Association so generously invited me to address you, he asked me to speak on my book, *Insight*. Since then, to my deep regret, I have had to drop both my original hope to be present at this meeting and, as well, my original plan to correlate personal development with philosophic differences.[a] I must be content to provide a preface for a discussion, and to this end I have selected three questions that my book seems to have raised and, in any case, may possess an intrinsic interest of their own. They regard (1) the primacy of the ontological,[b] (2) the finalistic notion of being, and (3) knowledge of concrete, actual existence.

1   Ontological or Cognitional Primacy?

The most shocking aspect of the book, *Insight*, is the primacy it accords knowledge. In the writings of St Thomas, cognitional theory is expressed in metaphysical terms and established by metaphysical principles.[1] In *Insight*, metaphysics is expressed in cognitional terms and established by cognitional principles. The reversal appears complete. If Aquinas had things right side up – and that is difficult to deny – then I have turned everything upside down.

   1 There are, of course, exceptions. For example, ' ... hoc quilibet in se ipso experiri potest, quod quando aliquis conatur aliquid intelligere, format aliqua phantasmata sibi per modum exemplorum, in quibus quasi inspiciat quod intelligere studet' (*Summa theologiae*, 1, q. 84, a. 7 c.).

In attenuation, I should like to urge that even Aquinas occasionally turns things upside down. He wrote:

> ... anima humana intelligit se ipsam per suum intelligere, quod est actus proprius eius, perfecte demonstrans virtutem eius et naturam.[2]

This I should be inclined to translate:

> ... the human soul understands itself by its understanding, which is its proper act, perfectly demonstrating its power and its nature.

But however the passage is translated, it seems clear that a psychological act, named *intelligere*, is the basis of a perfect demonstration of the nature and the power of the human soul. Now power and nature are metaphysical entities. To demonstrate them perfectly involves one in a long list of metaphysical theorems. Yet we have Aquinas' own word for it that a perfect demonstration of these metaphysical entities may be derived from a consideration of *intelligere*, the proper act of the human soul.

Further, I do not feel that I am arguing from a stray sentence. It is Aristotelian and Thomist doctrine that knowledge of objects precedes knowledge of acts, that knowledge of acts precedes knowledge of potencies, that knowledge of potencies precedes knowledge of the essence of the soul.[3] Nor does contemporary scholasticism adopt a different procedure. It appeals to the potency, intellect, to distinguish the human soul from the brute. It appeals, if not to the act of understanding, then to the universal concept, to obtain knowledge of the potency, intellect.

Further, this clear-cut instance of the primacy of the cognitional fits in with a larger doctrine. There is a standard Aristotelian and Thomist distinction between what is first *quoad se* and what is first *quoad nos*. If one asks for what is first *quoad se*, for ontological causes, the essence of the soul grounds the potencies, the potencies ground the acts, and the acts ground knowledge of objects. But if one asks for what is first *quoad nos*, for cognitional reasons, the order is inverted: knowledge of objects

---

2 Ibid. q. 88, a. 2, ad 3m.
3 Aristotle, *De anima*, II, 4, 415a 16–22. Thomas Aquinas, *Sententia libri De anima*, 2, lect. 6, §304; *Summa theologiae*, 1, q. 87, aa. 1–3, and loca parallela. [Henceforth our reference to the Commentary on the *De anima* will be in the form, *In II De anima*.]

grounds knowledge of acts, knowledge of acts grounds knowledge of potencies, knowledge of potencies grounds knowledge of the essence of the soul.

On this showing, then, the ontological and the cognitional are not incompatible alternatives but interdependent procedures. If one is assigning ontological causes, one must begin from metaphysics; if one is assigning cognitional reasons, one must begin from knowledge. Nor can one assign ontological causes without having cognitional reasons; nor can there be cognitional reasons without corresponding ontological causes.

Moreover, this interdependence is not limited to the particular case of the human soul. It is universal from the very nature of rational and objective knowledge. Thus many of you would agree that Aquinas added existence, the *actus essendi*, to Aristotle's ontological causes; but you also would contend that, corresponding to this ontological cause, there is a cognitional reason, the judgment of existence. Again, Aristotle affirmed matter and form as ontological causes; but Aristotle did not affirm these ontological causes without having cognitional reasons, namely, sense and insight into phantasm.[4]

Finally, not only is there interdependence; it also is true that development must begin from the cognitional reasons. What began with Aristotle was, not form, but knowledge of form. What began with Aquinas was, not existence, but knowledge of existence. In like manner, any genuine development in Aristotelian and Thomist thought, if conducted on Aristotelian and Thomist principles, will originate in a development in man's understanding of the material universe;[5] from a developed

4 See *Metaphysics*, VII, 17; Bernard Lonergan, 'The Concept of *Verbum* in the Writings of St. Thomas Aquinas,' *Theological Studies* 7 (1946) 359–72 [*Verbum* 11–25]. Might I take this occasion to note that the pages on *quod quid est, quidditas* ('The Concept of *Verbum* ...' 370–72 [*Verbum* 23–25]) were far too much influenced by such statements as ' ... quidditatis esse est quoddam esse rationis' (*Super 1 Sent.*, d. 19, q. 5, a. 1, ad 7m) and 'Intellectus ... duplex est operatio. Una qua format simplices rerum quidditates; ut quid est homo, vel quid est animal ... ' (*De veritate*, q. 14, a. 1 c.). On *quidditas*, the proper object of intellect, see 'The Concept of *Verbum* ... ,' *Theological Studies* 10 (1949) 18–28 (in the fourth article, 'Verbum and Abstraction' [*Verbum* 158–68]).

5 Thomas Aquinas, *Summa theologiae*, 1, q. 87, a. 3 c.: ' ... id quod primo cognoscitur ab intellectu humano est huiusmodi obiectum [*natura* rei materialis]; et secundario cognoscitur ipse actus quo cognoscitur obiectum; et per actum cognoscitur ipse intellectus, cuius est perfectio ipsum

understanding of material things it will proceed to a developed understanding of human understanding; and from a developed understanding
of human understanding it will reach a clearer or fuller or more methodical account of both cognitional reasons and ontological causes.

With such a development the book, *Insight*, is concerned. Since St
Thomas wrote, there has piled up a heap of disputed questions[c] that St
Thomas himself never treated directly and explicitly. Since he wrote,
there has occurred a notable development in man's understanding of
the material universe. Since he wrote, there has arisen an array of disciplines with new problems that press upon the Catholic philosopher
and especially the Catholic theologian. Since he wrote, the human situation has changed profoundly in many ways. To meet these issues fairly
and squarely, I think it is necessary *yet not enough* to select a minimum
number of certitudes on which all agree, to strive for a thorough knowledge of medieval thought, to deduce new conclusions from old premises.
What our time demands of us is more; it asks us, I believe, to know and
to implement Aristotelian and Thomist method, to acknowledge in man's
developed understanding of the material universe a principle that yields
a developed understanding of understanding itself, and to use that developed understanding of human understanding to bring order and
light and unity to a totality of disciplines and modes of knowledge that
otherwise will remain unrelated, obscure about their foundations, and
incapable of being integrated by the queen of the sciences, theology.

2   The Finalistic Notion of Being

My second topic has to do with the notion of being, and I shall begin
with a problem. You will agree, I believe, that there is one and only one
ens per essentiam, that it is not an immediate object of our knowledge in
this life, that the only immediate objects of our present knowledge are
entia per participationem. It follows that our intellectual knowledge of being
cannot result from abstraction of essence. For if from a horse I abstract
essence, what I abstract is the essence, not of being, but of horse; if from
a man I abstract essence, what I abstract is the essence, not of being, but
of man; and the same holds for every other immediate object of our

---

intelligere. Et ideo Philosophus dicit quod obiecta praecognoscuntur
actibus, et actus potentiis.' [The phrase in square brackets was inserted
by Lonergan.]

present knowledge. No being by participation can yield us knowledge of the essence of being, because no being by participation has the essence of being; and what is true of essence, equally is true of quiddity, nature, species, and form. A being by participation no more has the quiddity of being, the nature of being, the species of being, the form of being, than it has the essence of being.

Now this fact gives rise to a problem. What differentiates intellect from sense is precisely its grasp of essence or, if you prefer, its grasp of quiddity or nature or species or form. But in this life we do not grasp the essence or quiddity or nature or species or form of being. How then can we have any intellectual notion, any intellectual concept, any intellectual knowledge of being? Indeed, to put the problem with the sharpness that is essential, how is it that we have precisely such an intellectual notion of being that (1) we can conceive the *ens per essentiam* and (2) we can pronounce the only beings that we do know directly to be merely *entia per participationem*?

Further, this problem of the notion of being is not unique, isolated, unparalleled. If in this life we cannot know God by his essence, it also is true that we know the essences of material things only rarely, imperfectly, doubtfully. If our knowledge of essence is so rare and imperfect, should we not conclude either that Aristotle and Aquinas were mistaken in characterizing human intellect by knowledge of essence or, perhaps, that we have not intellects in the full sense of that term?

Many of you, I feel, will incline to the latter alternative. Human intellect is *in genere rerum intelligibilium ut ens in potentia tantum*,[6] it belongs to the realm of spirit merely as potency. Its knowing is process. It is not some simple matter of grasping essence and affirming existence. It is the prolonged business of raising questions, working out tentative answers, and then finding that these answers raise further questions. Dynamism, process, finality are fundamental features of our intellects in this life. Hence, knowledge of things by their essences is for us, not an accomplished fact, but only the goal, the end, the objective of a natural desire.[7]

6 Ibid. a. 1 c.
7 The paradox might be put in other terms. Thus we cannot think without concepts. Yet Aquinas holds that concepts proceed from acts of understanding (ibid. q. 27, a. 1 c.) and that in order to reach understanding we have to think: ' ... cum volo concipere rationem lapidis, oportet quod ad ipsam ratiocinando perveniam' (*Super Ioannem*, 1, lect. 1, § 26). The

Moreover, according to Aquinas, the object of the natural desire of our intellects includes the *ens per essentiam*. When we learn of God's existence, spontaneously we ask what God is; but to ask what something is, releases a process that does not come to rest until knowledge of essence is attained; therefore we have a natural desire to know God by his essence.[8]

By such reasoning I was led in *Insight* to affirm that our natural intellectual desire to know was a natural intellectual desire to know being. The desire, precisely because it is intelligent, is a notion.[d] But the notion is not any innate idea or concept or knowledge. It is a desire for ideas, for concepts, for knowledge but, of itself, it is merely discontented ignorance without ideas, without concepts, without knowledge. Again, it is not a postulate. Postulates are parts of hypothetical answers, but the desire to know grounds questions. Nor is there any need to postulate questions. They are facts.

What is the issue here? I think it both very simple and very fundamental. If intellect is not characterized by its capacity to grasp essence, then I believe that one parts company from Aristotle and Aquinas and, as well, from any adequate account of the nature of human intelligence. If, on the other hand, intellect is characterized by its capacity to grasp essence, then the fact that our knowledge of essences is so slight can be met only by a full recognition of the essentially dynamic character of our intellects and, in particular, of our notion of being.

3   Knowledge of Concrete, Actual Existence

My third topic had to do with the objective universe of being. According to *Insight* this universe is to be known by the totality of true judgments and it is not to be known humanly[9] without true judgments. Four main questions arise. First, is this universe of being the real world? Secondly, is it concrete? Thirdly, is it the actually existing universe, or merely an essentialist universe? Fourthly, how can concrete, actual existence be known on the account of knowledge offered by *Insight*?

First, then, is this universe of being the real world?[e] Clearly, if by the

---

sole exception to this necessity of reasoning is natural knowledge (ibid.); and natural knowledge is of *ens* and such principles as the principle of contradiction (*Summa contra Gentiles*, 2, c. 83, §31). Compare the notion of heuristic structure in *Insight*, passim.

8 *Summa theologiae*, 1–2, q. 3, a. 8 c.; *Summa contra Gentiles*, 3, cc. 25–63.
9 See *Insight* 414.

real world one means what is to be known by the totality of true judgments and not without true judgments, then by definition the universe of being and the real world are identical in all respects. However, it frequently happens that the expression, the real world, is employed in quite a different sense. In this sense each of us lives in a real world of his own.[f] Its contents are determined by his *Sorge*, by his interests and concerns, by the orientation of his living, by the unconscious horizon[g] that blocks from his view the rest of reality. To each of us his own private real world is very real indeed. Spontaneously it lays claim to being the one real world, the standard, the criterion, the absolute, by which everything is judged, measured, evaluated. That claim, I should insist, is not to be admitted. There is one standard, one criterion, one absolute, and that is true judgment. Insofar as one's private real world does not meet that standard, it is some dubious product of animal faith[h] and human error. On the other hand, insofar as one's private real world is submitted constantly and sedulously to the corrections made by true judgment,[10] necessarily it is brought into conformity with the universe of being.

Secondly, is this universe of being, known by true judgment, the concrete universe? I should say that it is. To know the concrete in its concreteness is to know all there is to be known about each thing. To know all there is to be known about each thing is, precisely, to know being. For me, then, being and the concrete are identical terms.[k]

However, this view of the concrete has a presupposition. It presupposes that concepts express insights[l] and that insights grasp forms immanent in sensible presentations. To put the matter the other way about, it presupposes that the sensible has been intellectualized through schemes, sequences, processes, developments. On that supposition, human knowledge forms a single whole, and the totality of true judgments is necessarily knowledge of the concrete. On the other hand, if one ignores or neglects insight, then human knowledge splits into two parts.[11] Concepts are related to sensible presentations only as universals to particulars. Of

10 I am inclined to believe, however, that this constant and sedulous correction does not occur without a specifically philosophic conversion[i] from the *homo sensibilibus immersus* to *homo maxime est mens hominis* (Thomas Aquinas, *Summa theologiae*, 1–2, q. 29, a. 4 c.). This existential aspect of our knowing is the fundamental factor in the differentiation of the philosophies in *Insight*.[j]

11 It does so because none of us reach the totality of true judgments. What determines our view of the universe of being is our grounded anticipation of that totality.

themselves, concepts and judgments are abstract, and to reach the concrete there has to be added an unspecified series of internally unrelated sensible presentations. On this view, which wholeheartedly I reject, it is paradoxical to maintain that the totality of true judgments is knowledge of the concrete. On this view, knowledge of the concrete is reached by adding to knowledge of the abstract the humanly unattainable totality of sensitive perceptions.

Thirdly, is this concrete universe essentialist, or is it actual and existent? This question arises, I suspect, because there are two ways of analyzing judgments and, consequently, two ways of refuting essentialism.[12]

Thus one may argue that, while some judgments are merely a synthesis of concepts (a horse is a quadruped), still there are other judgments that involve a simple act of positing or rejecting (this horse exists). On the basis of this analysis, one will proceed to stress the extreme importance of the latter type of judgment and arrive, eventually, at a rejection of essentialism.

On the other hand, one may maintain that every judgment involves a simple act of positing or rejecting, that every human judgment in this life rests, in the last analysis, upon contingent matters of fact, that no synthesis of concepts, of itself, constitutes a judgment. On this view, on its cognitional side, there can be no human knowledge of real possibility or of real necessity without matter-of-fact judgments; and on its ontological side there can exist no real necessities without existing essences and no real possibilities without existing active or passive potencies.

You will find that in *Insight* this radical rejection of essentialism is worked out in detail. Judgment is, not synthesis, but positing or rejecting synthesis.[13] This positing or rejecting rests on a virtually unconditioned, that is, on a conditioned that in fact happens to have its conditions fulfilled.[14] Hence, a necessary nexus does not suffice for an analytic principle; the terms of the principle, in their defined sense, must also occur in concrete judgments of fact.[15] It follows that not only our knowledge of the concrete universe but even our knowledge of metaphysics is just factual.[16] Finally, the theory is sufficiently refined to do justice to

---

12 The ontological parallel is the question of the necessary and sufficient constitutive principles of subsistence. See my *De constitutione Christi ontologica et psychologica* (Rome: Gregorian University Press, 1956 [CWL 7]).

13 *Insight* 271–78.[m] On Aristotle 366.

14 Ibid. chapter 10 and p. 653.

15 Ibid. 306.

16 Ibid. 393.

the problems raised by symbolic logic, by mathematics, by the probable principles employed in the natural sciences,[17] and by ontological arguments for God's existence.[18]

Fourthly, how is concrete, actual existence known? Now if one asks for the ontological cause of knowledge of existence, clearly one must appeal to the existence of the thing immanent in the thing. On the other hand, if one asks for the cognitional reason justifying our claim to know existence, that reason is a true judgment of the type, This exists. For truth is the medium in which being is known; truth formally is found only in judgment; and existence is the act of being.

Next, how does one know that the judgment, This exists, is true? Here one is asking, not for an ontological cause, but for a cognitional reason. The only possible answer is that, prior to the judgment, there occurs a grasp of the unconditioned. For only the unconditioned can ground the objectivity of truth, its absolute character, its independence of the viewpoints, attitudes, orientation of the judging subject.

Thirdly, in what does this grasp of the unconditioned consist? It is not a grasp of the formally unconditioned, of an unconditioned that has no conditions whatever, of God himself. It is a grasp of a virtually unconditioned, of an unconditioned that has conditions which, however, in fact are fulfilled. Thus the question, Does it exist? presents the prospective judgment as a conditioned. Reflective understanding grasps the conditions and their fulfilment. From that grasp there proceeds rationally[19] the judgment, It does exist.

Fourthly, what are the conditions? Let us take an example. Suppose that on this table there is a small but very restless dog, moving about, demanding attention, whimpering, making a nuisance of himself. However, that supposition merely provides an ontological cause. What is first in our knowledge is a stream of sensible presentations. That stream might be organized or unorganized in a variety of manners. It might give rise

17 Ibid. 304–15.
18 Ibid. 670–71.
19 On rational procession, see Lonergan, 'The Concept of *Verbum* ... ,' *Theological Studies* 7 (1946) 380–91 [*Verbum* 33–45]; 10 (1949) 370–79 [*Verbum* 195– 206]; and my *Divinarum personarum conceptio analogica* (Rome: Gregorian University Press, 1957) 53–54, 57–61. [The same page numbers obtain for the 1959 edition; in 1964, the same press published a revised edition as *De Deo trino*, Vol. 2; here see pp. 66–68, 70–74; note the emendations, pp. 73–74 (CWL 9).]

to the reaction described by Sartre in *La Nausée*, or to a vital adaptation
if the dog suddenly barked or snapped at one, or to any degree of seeing
without noticing, noticing without attending, or attending that issued
forth into any of a wide variety of psychological processes. However,
you are philosophers. The presentations to you are organized by detached, intellectual inquiry. You verify that they cannot be classed as
illusory[n] or hallucinatory. You attend to them, not as kinds of data, but
in their concrete individuality.[o] In this stream of individual data, despite
their spatial and temporal multiplicity, you grasp an intelligible unity, a
single whole, an identity that unites what in space is here and there and
what in time is then and now. From that insight there proceeds the
concept of a thing. You revert from the concept to the data to conceive
the particular object of thought, this thing. In fact, all this supposing
has yielded merely an object of thought. But if the supposing all were
true, then all of you would be certain of the dog's real, actual existence.
Why? Because I have been listing conditions[20] of concrete, actual existence, and you have seen that, if the conditions were fulfilled, an affirmation of concrete, actual existence could not be avoided rationally.

Still, you will ask, just where did existence come in? Was it some one
of the data, or was it their totality? No, any and all the data are quite
compatible with phenomenalism, pragmatism, existentialism; but none
of these philosophies include Aquinas' *actus essendi*. Did, then, existence
come in with the insight, or with the concept, or with the particularized
concept? No, idealists and relativists know all about insights, concepts,
and their particularization; and to suppose that these activities yield more
than an object of thought is simply essentialism in its radical form. But,
then, what can be the origin of the notion of existence, if neither sense
nor understanding suffices? I think that, if you will go back over the
process just described, you will see that the notion of existence emerged
with the question whether the particularized concept, this thing, was
anything more than a mere object of thought. In other words, just as
existence is the act of being, so the notion of existence is the crowning
component in the notion of being. But the notion of being is our desire
to know, our drive to ask questions. The crowning question is the question for reflection, *An sit?* Is that so? An affirmative answer to that

20 For further relevant conditions, see *Insight* on the notion of the thing
(chapter 8), on the correctness of concrete insights (283–87), on such a
judgment of fact as the absence of illusion (280–83).

question posits a synthesis. Through the positing, the 'Yes,' the '*Est,*' we know existence and, more generally, fact.[21] Through the synthesis that is posited, we know what exists or, more generally, what exists or occurs.

What is the issue here? It is a simple and straightforward question of fact.

Is it a fact that our intellectual knowledge includes an apprehension, inspection, intuition, of concrete, actual existence?[p] Or is it a fact that our intellectual knowledge does not include an apprehension, inspection, intuition, of concrete, actual existence?

On the former alternative, a judgment of existence is simply a recognition of what we already know. Hence, on this view, in its basic instance, it is not through true judgment that we reach knowledge of existence, but it is through knowledge of existence that we reach true judgment.

On the latter alternative, however, we first reach the unconditioned, secondly we make a true judgment of existence, and only thirdly in and through the true judgment do we come to know actual and concrete existence. On this view, it is only through the actuality of truth that we know the actuality of being; and truth is reached, not by intuiting actual, concrete existence, but by a reflective grasp of the unconditioned.

Such, I believe, is the issue. Moreover, while I have no doubt that it is a momentous issue with repercussions throughout the whole of one's philosophic attitude, while I am aware that it is a decisive issue in a judgment on my book, *Insight,* I must also say that attention to the consequences can obscure the stark simplicity of the issue itself.[q] So I put it to you quite simply, What are the facts? Is there or is there not a human, intellectual intuition of concrete, actual existence?

I thank you.[r]

---

21 See Thomas Aquinas, *Summa theologiae,* 1, q. 54, a. 1 c.: 'Actio enim est proprie actualitas virtutis; sicut esse est actualitas substantiae seu essentiae.' See *Insight* 83, 248, 437, on existence and occurrence. While existence is prior *quoad se,* occurrence is prior *quoad nos.* To cover both terms *Insight* uses the names, fact, factual. On fact, 331.

11

Christ as Subject:
A Reply

A few years ago I yielded to necessity and put together for my students some supplementary notes in speculative Christology.[1] This booklet happens to have come to the attention of the Reverend A. Perego,[a] s.j., and he has offered the readers of *Divinitas* a presentation and a critical evaluation of my views on the consciousness of Christ.[2]

As the position imputed to me, both in the presentation and in the critical evaluation, is one that I fail to distinguish from heresy, I feel called upon to supplement Fr Perego's animadversions and, at the same time, to correct his imputation.

My notion of the subject and of consciousness is alleged to be incomprehensible, and so I shall offer a simplified version of the matter and a solution of the arguments presumably thought to be decisive.

The intimate relation between the articles of faith and theological thought[b] appears to me to be slighted, and so I shall reiterate in simple terms my conviction that the physical pain endured by Jesus Christ has a significant bearing on theological accounts of the consciousness of Christ.

My remarks, then, come under three headings: (1) A Misrepresentation; (2) The Notion of the Subject; (3) Christ as Subject. To these I

---

1 *De constitutione Christi ontologica et psychologica* (Rome: Gregorian University Press, 1956; 2nd ed., 1958) [3rd ed., 1961; 4th ed., 1964 (CWL 7)].
2 Angelo Perego, 'Una nuova opinione sull'unità psicologica di Cristo,' *Divinitas* 2 (1958) 409–24.

append a brief conclusion, and readers wishing to know at once where I stand should make a beginning where I end.

1   A Misrepresentation

According to Fr Perego I hold the remarkable view that in Christ, on-tologically and psychologically, there is a real duality of subject, *ego*, and *principium quod*, and no more than an abstract unity. This is so odd that, perhaps, I had best quote the various passages in which this interpre-tation takes shape and is exploited. At the bottom of page 412 there occurs the sentence, which for convenient reference may be named quo-tation *A*. It reads:

> If in fact the subject is considered in abstraction from the natures in which it subsists and from the consciousnesses by which it is manifested, we have to admit a *single* 'I' in Christ, because there is only the single person of the Word and no other; but insofar as the 'I' is referred instead to the nature in which it subsists, and to the consciousness by which it is manifested, we have to distin-guish two 'I's' – one divine and the other human.[3]

The pattern seems clear: one in the abstract, two in the concrete. This is followed immediately at the top of page 413 by the complementary statement, quotation *B*, which reads:

> And the same must be said of the *principium quod* of the opera-tions of Christ. If the person of the Word is considered without reference to the natures in which it subsists, we must say that in Christ there is one *principium quod*; but if instead we take ac-count of the nature in which it subsists, we must affirm that in Jesus the *principium quod* is double (pp. 116–117).[3*]

3 ' ... Se si considera infatti il soggetto come astratto dalle nature in cui sussiste e dalle coscienze con cui si manifesta, si deve ammettere in Cristo un *unico* "io," perchè non è altro che l'unica persona del Verbo; in quanto invece l'"io" è riferito alla natura, in cui sussiste, e alla coscienza, con cui si manifesta, si debbono distinguere *due* "io"; quello divino e quello umano.' Italics are Fr Perego's.

3* 'E lo stesso si deve dire del *principium quod* delle operazioni di Cristo. Se la persona del Verbo è considerata come non riferita alle nature in cui sussiste, si deve dire che in Cristo c'è un unico *principium quod*; se

The pattern has recurred: one in the abstract, two in the concrete. Next we are told (quotation *C*): 'it is a mere abstraction to consider the person of the Word without reference to its natures (p. 118).'⁴ There follows an inference, indicated by the word, *consegue*, where the minor premise seems to be supplied by quotations *A* and *B* and the major by quotation *C*. One of the conclusions (quotation *D*) reads:

> ... the duality in Christ of the *principium quod*, of the subject and of the 'I,' whether in the ontological order or in the psychological, corresponds to the reality, while on the contrary their unique-ness is nothing but an abstraction founded on another abstrac-tion, namely, on the 'person of the Word considered simply as such' (pp. 117, 118 and elsewhere).⁵

Once more the pattern: one in the abstract, two in the concrete. Ac-cordingly, in Christ, on the view imputed to me, in both the ontological and the psychological order, there is a real duality of *principium quod*, subject, and *ego*, and the only unity is one abstraction founded on an-other. Perhaps it is superfluous for me to prove that, between such a view and Nestorius' *persona unionis*, the differences are negligible. If ontologically the only unity of the *principium quod* and the subject is just

---

invece si tien conto della natura, in cui sussiste, si deve affermare che in Gesù il *principium quod* è duplice (pp. 116–117).'

4 Ibid. 413: 'è pura astrazione pensare la persona del Verbo senza riferi-mento alle sue nature (p. 118).' I had advanced (p. 118) that abstractions neither exist nor operate. This truism is thought by Fr Perego to be 'di fondamentale importanza per cogliere il pensiero del Lonergan sull'"io" di Cristo' (p. 413). I should say that what is held by everyone is of no im-portance whatever for understanding any specific type of thinking. What is significant lies in the imputations contained in quotations *A* and *B*.

With regard to quotation *C*, note that a concept cannot be abstracted from its meaning; one cannot mean 'subsistens distinctum in natura in-tellectuali' and exclude the connotation *in obliquo* of 'natura.' Secondly, one can mean 'person' without connoting two natures. Thirdly, in God *quod est* and *quo est* differ only *secundum modum significandi*. Fourthly, the mystery of the Blessed Trinity adds further complexities. Fifthly, what I discussed on my pp. 117–18 was the notion not of person but of *principium*.

5 Ibid. 413: ' ... la dualità in Cristo del *principium quod*, del soggetto e dell'"io," sia nell'ordine ontologico come in quello psicologico, corris-ponde alla realtà, mentre invece la loro unicità non è che un'astrazione, fondata su di un'altra astrazione, cioè sulla *persona Verbi nude spectata* (pp. 117, 118 ed altrove).'

an abstraction, then the unity of the person is just an abstraction; if the unity of the person is just an abstraction, our Lady is not the Mother of God.[c]

The imputation recurs at the bottom of page 415. After presenting my view that there is a single subject of both the divine and the human consciousness in Christ, the writer adds (quotation *E*):

> ... However, that holds 'according to the abstract consideration of the mind' (p. 118), since, if the conscious subject in Christ is considered with reference to the nature in which it subsists, then we have to say that the person of the Word *qua* subsisting in the divine nature and operating with the uncreated consciousness, constitutes the divine 'I,' which is not to be confused with the human 'I' (pp. 116–17).[6]

Naturally enough, this imputation is repeated once more when a *valutazione critica* of my position is attempted. So from page 423 there comes quotation *F*. It reads:

> Finally, we have to draw attention to this, that, while Lonergan on the one hand affirms the uniqueness of the psychological and ontological subject in Christ when he considers the divine person abstractly, that is, without reference to its two natures, on the other hand, when he considers the person in the concrete, with reference to its two natures, he introduces a true and proper psychological duality into the Savior.[7]

So much for the statements I believe in need of explicit correction.

6 Ibid. 415–16: ' ... Ciò però vale *secundum abstractam mentis considerationem* (p. 118), perchè, se il soggetto conscio in Cristo è considerato secondo il riferimento alla natura in cui sussiste, allora si deve dire che la persona del Verbo in quanto sussistente nella natura divina ed operante con la coscienza increata costituisce l'"Io" divino, da non confondersi con quello umano (pp. 116–117).'
7 Ibid. 423: 'Infine si deve rilevare che, mentre il Lonergan afferma da una parte l'unicità del soggetto ontologico e psicologico in Cristo, considerando la persona divina astrattamente, cioè senza riferimento alle sue due nature, dall'altra parte, considerandola in concreto, come riferita alle sue due nature, introduce nel Salvatore una vera e propria dualità psicologica.'

In speaking of Christ one may refer to the person, *principium quod*, subject, or *ego*, in four manners. Thus, one can speak (I do not say, *think*) of the person or *principium quod* (1) with both natures, (2) with the divine nature, (3) with the human nature, or (4) with neither nature. Similarly, one can speak of the subject or *ego* (1) with both the divine and the human consciousness, (2) with the divine consciousness, (3) with the human consciousness, or (4) with neither the divine nor the human consciousness.

The reader will be familiar with the fourth of these manners: it is the view imputed to me. But he will be far more familiar with the first manner: it is Chalcedon's

> ... we all with one voice profess our faith in one and the same Son, our Lord Jesus Christ, the same one perfect in deity and the same one perfect in humanity, truly God and truly man ...'[8]

Nor will a theologian be any less familiar with the second and third manners, for there is in common use the distinction between *Christus ut Deus* and *Christus ut homo*.

Now, on the strength of the references given in quotations *B* and *E*, let us turn to page 116 in my booklet and read:

> Therefore, insofar as the same subject is manifested to itself through the divine consciousness as well as through the human consciousness, there is simply one 'I' in Christ just as there is one person.
>
> But insofar as 'I,' or the psychological subject, not only denotes the subject itself but also implies a relation to the nature and the consciousness of which it is the subject, then, since there are two natures and two consciousnesses in Christ, we have to distinguish in Christ between the 'I as divine,' which is manifested to itself according to its infinite perfection, and the 'I as human,' which experiences itself according to the limitations of the as-

---

8 Denzinger, *Enchiridion symbolorum* ... 148: ' ... unum eundemque confiteri Filium et dominum nostrum Iesum Christum consonanter omnes docemus, eundemque perfectum in deitate, et eundem perfectum in humanitate, Deum verum et hominem verum ... ' [The Schönmetzer edition (301) has a slightly different phrasing.]

sumed nature. Of course, to make this distinction is merely to transfer to the psychological field the familiar distinction between Christ as God and Christ as man.[8*]

I submit that the first paragraph, 'Therefore, insofar as ... ,' does not abstract from both the divine and the human consciousness, that on the contrary it includes both. Hence, so far from employing the abstract, fourth manner imputed to me, I employ the concrete manner evident in the decree of the Council of Chalcedon. There is, then, a discrepancy between quotation A and my text. Similarly, there is a discrepancy between the conclusion, given in quotation D, and my text. In like manner, there is a discrepancy between quotation F and my text.

Again, I submit that *simpliciter* is opposed to *secundum quid*. There is, then, a discrepancy between my 'unum "ego" simpliciter' and, on the other hand, the 'secundum abstractam mentis considerationem' of quotation E.

If now we turn to the second paragraph, 'But insofar as ... ,' we find it explicitly stated that my 'ego ut divinum' and 'ego ut humanum' are to be taken in the same sense as 'Christus ut Deus' and 'Christus ut homo'. But no one fancies that the latter distinction implies 'due Cristi, quello divino e quello umano' [two Christs, one divine and the other human]. By parity of argument, no one should fancy that the former distinction means 'due "io"; quello divino e quello umano' [two 'I's,' one divine and the other human], as stated in quotation A, inferred in quotation D, put in other words in quotation E, and applied to the subject in quotation F.

So much for the first of the apparent minor premises. Let us now direct our attention to the other minor represented apparently by quo-

---

8* 'Quare inquantum idem subiectum sibi innotescit tum per conscientiam divinam tum per conscientiam humanam, unum "ego" simpliciter in Christo est sicut et una persona.

'Inquantum autem "ego," seu subiectum psychologicum, non solum ipsum subiectum dicit sed etiam habitudinem importat ad naturam atque conscientiam cuius subiectum est, cum in Christo duae sint naturae atque conscientiae, ideo in Christo distinguendum est inter "ego ut divinum" quod sibi secundum infinitam suam perfectionem innotescit et "ego ut humanum" quod se experitur secundum limitationes naturae assumptae. Quae sane distinctio nihil est aliud quam ad campum psychologicum eam transferre distinctionem quae inter Christum ut Deum et Christum ut hominem notissima est.'

tation *B*. If one turns, on the strength of the references supplied, to pages 117 and 118 of my booklet, one may read:

> In Christ, God and man, there are without mixture and without change two natures and two operations, and on this basis we think of (1) the divine nature as *principium quo* of the divine operation, and (2) the human nature as *principium quo* of the human operation.
>
> But in the same Christ, God and man, there is only one person who performs both divine and human operations, and so on the basis of this unity of person there is to be admitted only one *principium quod* of activity, namely, the divine person itself.
>
> When this is grasped and firmly held, we may go on to ask whether that *principium quod* is to be conceived as the divine person simply as such, while we prescind from each nature, or is to be conceived as the divine person insofar as it subsists in a nature.[8**]

Here, clearly enough, after speaking in the first, concrete manner of the one person that operates both *divina* and *humana* and so is a single *principium quod*, there is raised the question of the fourth manner. Is this one *principium quod* to be conceived in abstraction from both natures? The answer follows on page 118:

> The answer is that the *principium quod* of activity is always the person with reference to a nature; hence the one exercising the

---

8** 'In Christo Deo et homine sunt inconfuse et immutabiliter tum duae naturae (*DB* 148) tum duae operationes (*DB* 292), et secundum hoc significantur (1) divina natura ut principium quo operationis divinae et (2) humana natura ut principium quo operationis humanae. [*DB* is the standard abbreviation for the Bannwart edition of Denzinger, *Enchiridion symbolorum* ... The corresponding numbers in *DS* are 301 and 557.]

'At in eodem Christo Deo et homine invenitur una tantum persona quae operetur tum divina tum humana, et ideo secundum hanc personae unitatem agnoscendum est unum tantum principium quod operatur, nempe, ipsa divina persona.

'Quibus perspectis atque firmiter retentis, quaeritur utrum illud principium-quod concipiendum sit tamquam ipsa divina persona nude spectata cum praecisione ab utraque natura an concipiendum sit tamquam ipsa divina persona prout in aliqua subsistit natura.'

activity is always either Christ as God or Christ as man; or, in other words, it is always the divine person either as subsisting in the divine nature or as subsisting in the human nature.[8***]

There follow three arguments to prove the contention that the *principium quod* is not to be taken in abstraction from both natures.

Now I submit that to attribute to me the position that the one *principium quod* in Christ is just an abstraction is to attribute to me a view that (1) I explicitly reject and (2) I give three arguments for rejecting. There is, then, a discrepancy between my text and quotation *B*, between my text and the conclusion given in quotation *D*, and between my text and the reference to page 118 given in quotation *E*.

Further, when I say that 'the one exercising the activity is always either Christ as God or Christ as man,' I am employing language that is familiar to every theologian. That expression does imply a duality, not however in the *principium quod*, but in the *principia quibus*. There is, then, a discrepancy between my text and the imputation of a double *principium quod* in the statement given in quotation *B*. There is a similar discrepancy between my text and the duality of the *principium quod* concluded in quotation *D*.

To complete the picture, let us note that, when in quotation *E* the reader is assured that the single subject of both the divine and human consciousness is just an abstraction, the reader of the corresponding passage in my booklet is assured of the contradictory. Having treated the divine consciousness of Christ on pages 100–106 and the human consciousness of Christ on pages 106–124, I began my answer to the question of one subject of both the divine and human consciousness with the remark that follows:

> ... after the consideration by turns of Christ insofar as he is God and Christ insofar as he is man, a consideration that studied one aspect while prescinding from the other, we have now to undertake the concrete consideration in which we study Christ as he really is, namely, at the same time both God and man.[9]

[8***] 'Respondetur principium quod operatur semper esse personam cum respectu ad naturam; unde operans semper est aut Christus ut Deus aut Christus ut homo; vel iterum operans semper est persona divina aut qua subsistens in divina natura aut qua subsistens in humana natura.'
  [9] *De constitutione Christi* 125–26: '... post considerationem praecisivam in qua successive agitur de Christo in quantum est Deus et de Christo

Since quotation *F* is adorned with no references, its value would seem to derive simply from the evidence provided by quotations *A*, *B*, *D*, and *E* with their references to my pages 116–18. There is, however, in quotation *D* a further, if vague, reference to *altrove*. It perhaps may be met in a more simple fashion than quotations from every relevant sentence in my booklet. The author of some reflections on my views in the *Revue thomiste* had little use for my metaphysical and psychological opinions. Nonetheless, he felt able to write: 'He firmly defends the psychological unity of Christ, and there one can have a sense of agreement with him.'[10]

To conclude, the view imputed to me in the quotations I have given is about as different as possible from what I actually state. I consider (1) Christ as both God and man, (2) Christ as God, and (3) Christ as man. I exclude a consideration of the *principium quod* considered apart from both natures. On the contrary, on the view attributed to me, there vanishes the consideration of Christ as both God and man; there is substituted the abstraction I reject; and for my legitimate prescinding, parallel to 'Christ as God' or to 'Christ as man,' there is introduced a real duality of the *principium quod*, subject, and *ego*.

Some reader, however, may wish to raise a question. It is one thing to be conscious of oneself as God; it is quite another to be conscious of oneself as man. How, then, is it that divine consciousness and human consciousness can reveal one and the same subject?

If the hypothetical reader wishes an explanation of the mystery, he is asking too much. If he will be content with an imperfect analogy, that can easily be supplied. It is one thing to enjoy a good dinner; it is quite another to be flogged; but the same individual can first enjoy the one and then undergo the other. In brief, consciousness reveals not only acts and states but also the subject, and while acts and states vary, the subject remains consciously the same.

The difficulty, however, may be pressed. On my view the meaning of such names as *subject, principle*, includes a relation. If I speak of subject, I mean subject of consciousness. If I speak of principle, I mean principle of operation. If, then, it is one thing to be the subject of divine con-

---

inquantum est homo, institui oportet considerationem concretam in qua de Christo agitur prout re vera est, nempe, simul et Deus et homo.' In the paragraphs preceding quotation *E*, Fr Perego twice referred to my p. 126.

10 Jean-Hervé Nicolas, 'Chronique de théologie dogmatique,' *Revue thomiste* 57 (1957) 386: 'Il défend fermement l'unité psychologique du Christ, et là on peut se sentir d'accord avec lui.'

sciousness and another to be the subject of human consciousness, it follows that there are really two subjects. *A pari*, it follows that the principle of divine and human operations is really two principles.

The answer is, *Non sequitur*. Relatives are not multiplied by the multiplication of correlatives. The father of two sons is not two fathers; similarly, he is not one father in the abstract and two in the concrete; he is just one father. Again, the teacher of one hundred pupils is not one hundred teachers; similarly, he is not one teacher in the abstract but in the concrete one hundred teachers, drawing one hundred salaries, and enjoying one hundred paid vacations. Concretely, he is one and only one teacher.

2   The Notion of the Subject

The notion of the subject is difficult, recent, and primitive.[d]

It is difficult. St Thomas once remarked that everyone knows he has a soul, yet even great philosophers go wrong on the nature of the soul. The same is true of the subject. Everyone knows he is a subject, and so everyone is interested in the consciousness of Christ. Not everyone knows the nature of the subject, and so there is a variety of opinions.

The notion is also recent. If one wishes to find out what a soul is, one has only to read St Thomas. If one wishes to find out what a subject is, it is not enough to read ancient or medieval writers. They did not treat the matter explicitly. They did not work out systematically the notion of the subject. They did not integrate this systematic notion with the rest of their philosophic and psychological doctrine.[11]

---

11 I should say that Aristotle, St Augustine, St Thomas had an extraordinary grasp of the facts of consciousness. But I should not offer to prove this to people that have no grasp of the facts, no sense of history, and no inclination to transcend the merely verbal intelligence that, it seems, an electronic calculator successfully simulates. Thus St Augustine is fully aware that the *mens* is present to itself prior to any inquiry into itself (*De Trinitate*, x, ix, 12; PL 42, 980), but it would be an awkward task to show that Augustine's *mens* is coincident with our term, subject. St Thomas in a single article asks whether *intellective soul* knows itself, fixes his principles by discussing *intellect*, draws his conclusions with respect to concrete *men*, and amplifies them by speaking of the Augustinian *mens* (*Summa theologiae*, 1, q. 87, a. 1). No doubt, St Thomas is aware of his floating terminology (ibid. q. 79, a. 1, ad 1m); but a reader has to use his own judgment to reach a determinate meaning. Again, St Thomas knows precisely what psychological presence is (*Summa contra Gentiles*, 3, c. 46,

In the third place, the notion is primitive. It cannot be reached merely by combining other, better known concepts. It can be reached only by directing one's attention to the facts and to understanding them correctly. Nor is this enough. A difficult, recent, and primitive notion is not theologically useful until it has been transposed into the classical categories of scholastic thought;[e] and obviously such a transposition supposes some research into the exact meaning and the latent potentialities of classical writers such as St Thomas.

Needless to say, I did not attempt all this in a set of notes for theological students. I had explored Thomist intellectual theory in a series of articles published in *Theological Studies*.[12] I had explored the complex speculative issues in a book, *Insight*.[13] In my *De constitutione Christi* I was simply making available in Latin and for my students the conclusions I had reached in other studies.

My procedure was to present two opposed notions of consciousness: the first I named *conscientia-experientia*, and I employed it as the basis of my view of the consciousness of Christ; the second I named *conscientia-perceptio*, and I employed it to account for the opinions of those with whom I happened to disagree. Since the former met dogmatic requirements and the latter, I believed, did not, there seemed to me no need to leave the properly theological level of thought and to enter into philosophic and psychological questions.

Still, what precisely is the difference between the two positions, between consciousness conceived as an experience[f] and consciousness conceived as the perception of an object? In my booklet I set forth these differences at length (130–34), but for present purposes it will be suf-

---

§6), but this does not prevent him from using the term, presence, in an ontological sense; and a recognition of this fact depends upon the reader's knowledge of consciousness rather than on Aquinas' statements. Again, Augustinian presence differs from the factual and normative judgments distinguished in *De Trinitate*, IX, vi, 9 (PL 42, 965–66); Aquinas refers to this distinction in drawing his own between particular and universal knowledge of the soul (*De veritate*, q. 10, a. 8 c.); but in St Thomas there is a far sharper distinction between presence and universal knowledge than between presence and particular knowledge.

12 'The Concept of *Verbum* in the Writings of St. Thomas Aquinas,' *Theological Studies* 7 (1946) 349–92; 8 (1947) 35–79; 404–44; 10 (1949) 3–40; 359–93 [*Verbum*]. This is applied to Trinitarian theory in my notes, *Divinarum personarum conceptio analogica* (Rome: Gregorian University Press, 1957; 2nd ed., 1959). [See also *De Deo trino*, Vol. 2.]

13 *Insight: A Study of Human Understanding.*

ficient, perhaps, to select the fourth difference (*ad*) out of six, namely, that if consciousness is conceived as an experience there is a psychological subject, while if consciousness is conceived as the perception of an object there is no psychological subject. To establish this point I shall begin by indicating one manner in which the notion of *conscientia-perceptio* may arise; I shall next point out the defect in this notion; thirdly, I shall indicate the essentially opposed character of *conscientia-experientia*; and finally I shall turn to Fr Perego's objections.

Consider, then, the two propositions, John knows his dog, John knows himself. In both, the subject is John. In the first, the object is John's dog. In the second, the object is John himself. It follows that knowing is of two kinds: there is direct knowing in which the object is not the subject; there is reflexive knowing in which the object is the subject. Name reflexive knowing consciousness. Define the subject as the object of consciousness. Then it cannot be disputed, it seems, that consciousness is a reflexive knowing, for in consciousness the knower himself is known; and it cannot be disputed, it seems, that the subject is the object of consciousness, for whatever is known is an object. Nothing, it seems, could be simpler or clearer or more evident.

Still, it may be well to attend to a difficulty that could be raised. A cognitive act exercises no constitutive effect upon its object;[g] it simply reveals what the object already is; it exercises no transforming power over the object in its proper reality, but simply and solely manifests what that proper reality is. Accordingly, if consciousness is knowledge of an object, it can have no constitutive effect upon its object; it can only reveal its object as it was in its proper reality prior to the occurrence of the cognitive act or function named consciousness.

Thus, to illustrate this aspect of *conscientia-perceptio*, if without consciousness John is simply a prime substance (such as this man or this horse) then by consciousness John is merely revealed to himself as a prime substance. Again, if without consciousness John has no other psychological unity beyond the unity found in the objects of his knowledge, then by consciousness John is merely manifested as having no psychological unity beyond the unity found in the objects of his knowledge. Again, if without consciousness John cannot possibly be the conscious subject of physical pain, then by consciousness John is merely manifested as being incapable of suffering. Similarly, if without consciousness John cannot be the consciously intelligent or the consciously rational or the consciously free or the consciously responsible principle of his own intelligent, rational, free, or responsible acts, then by consciousness as knowledge of an object John merely knows himself as neither consciously intelligent, nor consciously rational, nor consciously free, nor consciously responsible.[h]

My difficulty, then, with the simple, clear, and evident view, which I named *conscientia-perceptio*, is that it is *simpliste*. It takes account of the fact that by consciousness the subject is known by the subject. It overlooks the fact that consciousness is not merely cognitive but also constitutive. It overlooks as well the subtler fact that consciousness is cognitive, not of what exists without consciousness, but of what is constituted by consciousness. For consciousness does not reveal a prime substance; it reveals a psychological subject that subsequently may be subsumed, and subsumed correctly, under the category of prime substance. Similarly, consciousness does not reveal the psychological unity that is known in the field of objects; it constitutes and reveals the basic psychological unity of the subject as subject. In like manner, consciousness not merely reveals us as suffering but also makes us capable of suffering; and similarly it pertains to the constitution of the consciously intelligent subject of intelligent acts, the consciously rational subject of rational acts, the consciously free subject of free acts, and the consciously responsible subject of responsible acts.

How, then, can one account for this constitutive function of consciousness? One cannot reject the principle that knowing simply reveals its object; one cannot suppose that knowing exercises a constitutive effect upon its object. It is true that the mode of the knowing may and does differ from the mode of the reality known. But it is fantastic to suggest that knowing an object changes the mode of reality in the object.

The alternative, I suggest, is to deny that consciousness is a matter of knowing an object; the alternative is to deny that only objects are known; the alternative is to reject the tacit assumption that *unumquodque cognoscitur secundem quod est obiectum*, and to put in its place the familiar axiom that *unumquodque cognoscitur secundum quod est actu*. On the basis of this axiom, one can assert that whenever there is a *sensibile actu* or an *intelligibile actu*, an object is known; and whenever there is a *sensus actu* or an *intellectus actu*, the subject and his act are known. On this view the subject in act and his act are constituted and, as well, they are known simultaneously and concomitantly with the knowledge of objects; for the *sensibile actu* is the *sensus actu*, and the *intelligibile actu* is the *intellectus actu*. Again, on this view the object is known as *id quod intenditur*, the subject

is known as *is qui intendit*, and the act is known both as the *intendere* of
the subject and the *intendi* that regards the object.[14]

On this position, which for other reasons I named *conscientia-experientia*, the constitutive as well as the cognitive aspects of consciousness are
satisfied. For cognitive acts certainly constitute a prime substance as
actually knowing sensible and intelligible objects; on the view I favor,
they also constitute the prime substance as consciously sentient, consciously intelligent, consciously the one principle of many acts, consciously rational when one act supplies the known reason that motivates
another act, consciously free when one act is the principle of other
alternative acts, consciously responsible when the consciously free subject
knows by other acts the consequences of his free choices.[15]

Such, then, is one difference between *conscientia-perceptio* and *conscientia-experientia*. It remains that we listen to Fr Perego's objections.

First, ' ... above all one fails to understand what consciousness conceived as experience is, this consciousness which grounds a confused

14 Consciousness, accordingly, is not to be confused with reflexive activity.
The ordinary operations of intellect are attending, inquiring, understanding, conceiving, doubting, weighing the evidence, judging. Their
objects may be either the self or other things. In the former case they
are named reflexive; in the latter, direct. This difference is not formal
but material; in both cases the formal objects are *ens, quidditas, verum*.
Now by *both* direct and reflexive operations the subject in act is constituted and known, not as object, but as subject; this constitutive knowing
and being known is consciousness. Hence, in direct activity the subject
is known once, and as subject; but in reflexive activity the subject is
known twice, as subject by consciousness, and as object by the reflexive
activity. Finally, there is a functional relation between consciousness
and reflexive activity: just as the data for direct activity are supplied by
sense, so the data for reflexive activity are supplied by consciousness.
Hence, just as I think of 'this' by a backward reference to sense,[i] so I
think of 'I' by a backward reference to the conscious subject; in both
cases one is thinking of the particular; and we think of particulars, not
because we understand particularity, but because our inquiry and understanding suppose and regard data. Similarly, just as our judgments
about material things involve a verification of concepts in the data of
sense, so our judgments about our feelings, our minds, our wills involve
a verification of concepts in the data of consciousness. It was this parallelism in function that led me to speak of *conscientia-experientia*.
15 This is summary. Basic notions are developed leisurely in *Insight*
320–28, 611, 613. See the notion of *emanatio intelligibilis* in *Divinarum
personarum conceptio analogica* 57–61 [revised in *De Deo trino*, Vol. 2,
70–74], and subsequently passim. Contemporary discussions of the subject's consciousness of freedom, notably when enduring torture on
moral grounds, are celebrated.

notion on the side of the subject without that subject becoming an object and term of consciousness ... '15*

Reply: I grant that there is no cognitional act without a content. I grant that there is no cognitional act without an object. I grant that there is no cognitional act without a term. I deny that the sole content of a cognitional act is its object.

My position cannot be understood if it is true to say that whatever is known is an object. Again, my position cannot be understood if it is true to say that *unumquodque cognoscitur secundum quod est obiectum*. I deny, however, that either of those assertions is true. I should say that *unumquodque cognoscitur secundum quod est actu*. Further, I should say that one and the same act is at once the act of the object and the act of the subject; inasmuch as there is a *sensibile actu* or an *intelligibile actu*, an object is known; inasmuch as there is a *sensus actu* or an *intellectus actu*, the subject in act and his act are constituted and known. Nor do I believe that Fr Perego can prove this position to be a contradiction in terms.

Moreover, while I do not believe that St Thomas worked out a theory of the subject and consciousness, still one can learn a thing or two from him. He holds that intellective soul knows itself by its act. He holds that that act supposes a *species* received in possible intellect. He holds that *actus specificantur per obiecta*. He does not hold that the *species* of the act, by which intellective soul knows itself, is abstracted from the soul or a similitude of the soul.[16] One might infer that, according to St Thomas, when intellective soul knows itself by its act, the relevant act has an object and that object is not the subject.

Secondly, I had explained that consciousness is knowledge of the sub-

15* '... non si riesce anzitutto a comprendere che cosa sia la coscienza-esperienza, che fonda una notizia confusa *ex parte subiecti*, senza che tale soggetto sia oggetto e termine della medesima ... ' (418).

16 *De veritate*, q. 10, a. 8, ad 5m (2ae ser. – in contrarium): '... anima non cognoscitur per aliam speciem abstractam a se, sed per speciem obiecti sui, quae fit forma eius secundum quod intelligit actu.'

Ibid. ad 9m: '... anima non cognoscitur per speciem a sensibus abstractam, quasi intelligatur species illa esse animae similitudo; sed quia naturam speciei considerando, quae a sensibilibus abstrahitur, invenitur natura animae in qua huiusmodi species recipitur, sicut ex forma cognoscitur materia.'

Summa theologiae, 1, q. 87, a. 1 c.: 'Si igitur intellectus humanus fieret actu per participationem formarum intelligibilium separatarum, ut Platonici posuerunt, per huiusmodi participationem rerum incorporearum intellectus humanus seipsum intelligeret.'

ject *sub ratione experti* and not *sub ratione entis, vel quidditatis, vel veri*. Fr Perego concludes that, on my view, consciousness cannot be intellectual.[17]

Reply: I grant that any object known by intellect is known *sub ratione entis, quidditatis, veri*. I deny that what is known by intellectual consciousness is known under those formalities. My reason is simply that consciousness is knowledge, not of the objects of acts, but of the acts themselves and their subject.[18]

Thus any object to which intellect attends falls under the *intentio entis intendens*. That intending is conscious; it is simply the wonder Aristotle said was the beginning of all science and philosophy. Still, it is one thing to wonder about sensible objects: it is quite another to wonder about intellectual wonder itself. Only in this second case does our own *intentio entis intendens* fall under our own *intentio entis intendens*; and only then is it considered *sub ratione entis*.

Again, what we understand and conceive is known *sub ratione quidditatis*. Such understanding and conceiving are conscious. But it is only when we understand and conceive understanding and conceiving that we know understanding and conceiving *sub ratione quidditatis*. Hence St Thomas insisted that it is one thing to know our souls by their presence and quite another to know the nature of soul.

Finally, what we rationally affirm is known *sub ratione veri*. That rational affirming is conscious. But that consciousness is not a rational affirming of rational affirming.

17 Perego 418: ' ... non si riesce anzitutto a comprendere che cosa sia la coscienza-esperienza, che fonda una notizia confusa *ex parte subiecti*, senza che tale soggetto sia oggetto e termine della medesima, e senza che sia raggiunto in nessuna maniera e misura *sub ratione quidditatis, veri et entis*. Si tratta forse di una speciale facoltà, diversa dall'intelletto, di una specie di senso radicale del soggetto, oppure di una specie di sentimento fondamentale di sapore rosminiano?'
18 Consciousness is true knowledge of what has a quiddity and is a being, but it is not knowledge under the formalities of being, quiddity, truth. Inasmuch as it constitutes in act what it knows, it recalls Aquinas' remark that the light of agent intellect is known *per se ipsum* (*De veritate*, q. 10, a. 8, ad 10m, 2[ae] ser. – in contrarium). Finally, inasmuch as it constitutes in act what it knows, it enjoys a natural infallibility which, however, has the indistinctness of the preconceptual (see *Summa contra Gentiles*, 3, c. 46, §6) and cannot be preferred by man as intelligent and rational to what is known intelligently and rationally under the formalities of being, quiddity, truth. Such a (nonrational) preference is the error of subjectivist tendencies recently denounced in H. Duméry.[j] The total negation of the subject is, of course, just the opposite error which, by its

Thirdly, Fr Perego contends that according to the explicit doctrine of St Thomas human psychological and moral consciousness is exclusively a matter of intellectual acts.[19]

Reply: I grant that moral consciousness is principally intellectual.[k] I grant that psychological consciousness is intellectual as well as sensitive. I grant that St Thomas denies reflection to sense, but I am not so certain that he denies consciousness to sense. He wrote: 'Sense ... does indeed begin to turn back to its essence, because it not only knows the sensible object, but also knows itself to be sensing; still, the return is not complete, because sense does not know its own essence.'[20] He also wrote: ' ... it belongs to the same faculty to see a color and to see the modification produced [in sight] by the color, to see the thing that is actually the object of sight and to see the seeing of that object. Hence that faculty by which we see that we see is not extrinsic to the seeing faculty, but differs from it only by a mental distinction.'[21] Above all, since Christ suffered physical pain, it is to be noted that pain is an 'experienced perception of injury'[22] and that 'pain ... begins in injury to the body and terminates in apprehension by the sense of touch, and therefore pain is in the sense of touch, as in the apprehending faculty.'[23] This seems to me very much like *conscientia-experientia*: the pain is in the sense of touch; the pain is, not in the whip that is felt by the sense of touch, but in the subject that feels the whip; it is *ut in apprehendente* [as in the apprehending faculty].

I suggest, then, there is some reason for doubting that St Thomas

wholesale incomprehension of issues, evokes and provokes exaggerated subjectivist views.

19 Perego 418: 'Su questo punto S. Tommaso è perfettamente esplicito. Secondo la dottrina dell'Angelico, la coscienza psicologica umana e quella morale, lungi dall'essere facoltà speciali, non sono che *atti dell'intelletto* ...' Italics Fr Perego's. I would draw attention to the 'non sono che.'

20 *De veritate*, q. 1, a. 9 c.: 'Sensus ... redire quidem incipit ad essentiam suam, quia non solum cognoscit sensibile, sed etiam cognoscit se sentire; non tamen completur eius reditio, quia sensus non cognoscit essentiam suam.' Here the reason why sense cannot reflect fully is said to be drawn from Avicenna.

21 *In III De anima*, lect. 2, §591: ' ... eiusdem virtutis est, videre colorem et immutationem quae est a colore, et visum in actu et visionem eius. Potentia ergo illa, qua videmus nos videre, non est extranea a potentia visiva, sed differt ratione ab ipsa.' See the parallel drawn between sense and intellect, ibid. lect. 9, §724.

22 *De veritate*, q. 26, a. 9 c.: 'experimentalis perceptio laesionis.'

23 Ibid. a. 3, ad 9m: 'dolor ... incipit a laesione corporis, et terminatur in apprehensione sensus tactus, propter quod dolor est in sensu tactus ut in apprehendente.'

absolutely excluded sensitive consciousness. In any case, whatever may be the difficulties of Thomist exegesis,[24] I feel that the issue in itself is quite clear. Pains are not objects of sense, *sensibilia propria*.[m] There are no unconscious pains. The subject of the pain feels the pain. The subject of the pain is not unconscious but conscious. His consciousness does not consist in reflecting on his pains; he has to feel them before he can reflect on them; if it is not *he* that does the feeling, if what he feels is not pain, then he has no pains to reflect on.

Fourthly, Fr Perego urges, 'St Thomas is explicit also in asserting a real distinction in human knowing between the direct cognitive act and the reflexive cognitive act which pertains to consciousness. He writes: "It is one act by which the intellect perceives a stone and another by which it understands itself to perceive a stone." '[25]

Reply: I have no doubt about the real distinction between the two acts. I grant the legitimacy of naming the first act direct and the second reflexive. I fail to see the explicit evidence for naming the second act *coscienziale* [pertaining to consciousness] or for suggesting that the first act is not *coscienziale*.

Further, I do not believe that a denial of consciousness in direct acts

24 Besides dependence on Avicenna (see above, note 20), Proclus' theorems relating reflexion with subsistence and incorporality must be noted. They came to St Thomas primarily through the *Liber de causis* (see *Super Librum De causis*, lect. 7, §§187–95; lect. 15, §§310–11). Clearly neo-Platonist views on the duality and imperfection of knowledge with the consequent distinction between the One and Mind (Plotinus, *Enneads*, v, vi, 1–3, & 6) were bound to conflict with the Aristotelian doctrine that knowing is an identity[l] in act of subject and object. This conflict comes out clearly in *Summa theologiae*, 1, q. 14, a. 2, where Aristotelian doctrine dominates the response in the *corpus*, the *Liber de causis* provides the first objection, and the *ad 1m* reduces 'return to one's essence' to a mode of speech that simply means 'subsistent.' Still, what perhaps is basically a neo-Platonist view seems attributed to Aristotle in the *Summa theologiae* (1, q. 87, a. 3 obiectio 3[a]); the Commentary on Aristotle's *De anima* may have been expecting to find it in Aristotle (*In III De anima*, lect. 2, §584), and remarks that it has not yet been found (ibid. lect. 3, §599). A recent study is by Michael Stock, 'Sense Consciousness according to St. Thomas,' *The Thomist* 21 (1958) 415–86; on the subject of sense consciousness, 481–86.

25 Perego 419: 'S. Tommaso è anche esplicito nello asserire la distinzione reale tra l'atto umano conoscitivo diretto e quello coscienziale riflesso. "Altro è l'atto, scrive egli, con cui l'intelletto percepisce una pietra, ed altro è quello con cui comprende di percepire una pietra." ' *Summa theologiae*, 1, q. 87, a. 3, ad 2m.

can be reconciled with affirmations that we experience what seem to be direct acts. St Thomas wrote:

> ... anyone can experience in himself the following, that when he tries to understand something, he forms images for himself by way of examples, and in these he inspects, as it were, what he is striving to understand.[26]

> ... for man abstracts the intelligibles from images and receives them into his mind in their actuated state; for in no other way would we have come to knowledge of these acts than by experiencing them in ourselves.[27]

> ... according to the opinion of Aristotle, which is more in accord with our experience ... according to the way of knowing that we experience.[28]

Fifthly, Fr Perego shifts his ground. Modern authors, anticipated by Suarez, distinguish between a direct consciousness had in the very exercise of sensitive and rational acts and, on the other hand, a formal reflexion that occurs in intellect alone. Only in the latter, he urges, is the subject known as subject, and so only the latter is human consciousness properly so called. This formal reflexion, he believes, must consist in a 'second or reflexive intention of the mind, by which we turn fully back to ourselves, and behold our existence and our modifications in their presence to us.' Consequently, he concludes, consciousness must be a *cognitio* and a *perceptio* with a proper term and content.[29]

26 *Summa theologiae*, 1, q. 84, a. 7 c.: ' ... hoc quilibet in se ipso experiri potest, quod quando aliquis conatur aliquid intelligere, format aliqua phantasmata sibi per modum exemplorum, in quibus quasi inspiciat quod intelligere studet.' It would seem difficult to suppose that by a first act we try to understand and by a second act experience ourselves trying to understand, etc.

27 *Summa contra Gentiles*, 2, c. 76, §17: ' ... homo enim abstrahit a phantasmatibus, et recipit mente intelligibilia in actu; non enim aliter in notitiam harum actionum venissemus nisi eas in nobis experiremur.'

28 *Summa theologiae*, 1, q. 88, a. 1 c.: ' ... secundum Aristotelis sententiam quam magis experimur ... secundum modum cognitionis nobis expertum.'

29 Perego 419–20: 'secunda seu reflexa mentis intentio, qua in nos plene redimus, ac nostram exsistentiam nostrasque modificationes praesentialiter intuemur.'

Reply: I have no doubt that consciousness has a content; I defined it as 'an internal experience, in the strict sense of the word, experience, of the self and of its acts.'[30] I grant that all cognitive acts have terms, but I believe they also have principles, and I should say that consciousness is of the principle not the term. Also, I have no doubt that Suarez is correct in distinguishing between *cognoscere proprie*, where one cognitive act is the object of another, and *cognoscere minus proprie*, where each cognitive act is known by the very exercise of the act itself. Further, I think I have good reasons for being more precise and saying *sub ratione entis, quidditatis, et veri* instead of *proprie*, and saying *sub ratione experti* instead of *minus proprie*. Finally, I have no doubt that consciousness is a *cognoscere sub ratione experti*.

I should say, however, that in direct consciousness not only acts are known *sub ratione experti* but also the subject. I should add that in direct consciousness the subject is known not as object but as subject, for these acts already have their own objects, and *ex hypothesi* these objects are not the subject. On the other hand, I should say that the superfluous[31] intuition postulated by Fr Perego has as its object the subject and so knows the subject not as subject but as object.

Sixthly, Fr Perego feels that I am somewhat confused in my thinking when I claim that (1) consciousness is had in all sensitive and intellectual acts and (2) consciousness is a presupposition of reflexive activities.[32]

Reply: I think that one will find my position clearer when one discovers that one need not assume that only objects are known. Meanwhile, the following passage, which I transcribe from a recent article by Prof. Georges Van Riet, may be found helpful:

> In our opinion, every conscious activity is necessarily present to itself[n] in an unreflected way, or, as Sartre writes it, is conscious

30 *De constitutione Christi* 83: 'sui suorumque actuum experientia stricte dicta atque interna.'

31 If direct consciousness already exists, as Fr Perego admits (419), then the existence and modifications of the subject are known already. Nor does reflexive activity consist in an intuition. It consists in acts of advertence (named reflexion, introspection) and in the two ordinary operations of intellect by which one reaches particular and universal answers to factual (*an sit*) and explanatory (*quid sit*) questions. It follows that the postulated intuition is superfluous. It suffers other obvious drawbacks as well, for it seems to yield false information to Fr Perego about the subject and his consciousness. While one is postulating, since it costs nothing, one might as well postulate an infinite series of intuitions each with the function of checking whether the previous one is correct.

32 Perego 421.

(of) itself. What characterizes this consciousness (of) self is the fact that it is still unexpressed; it is presence to self, not knowledge of self; it does not use concepts, or judgments, or words; it is silent, it does not speak. From the moment it reflects, it speaks; to reflect is in fact to elucidate through expression; the fruit of reflexion is the judgment. The paradox of human consciousness, which is incarnate and not angelic, is that even the elucidating act is unreflected for itself, conscious (of) self. It expresses something not reflected on, something lived or perceived, it does not express itself. Only a new act of reflexion will elucidate it by giving it expression, but this new act will in its turn still be unreflected.[33]

Seventhly, Fr Perego feels that not only the distinction but also the relation between consciousness and reflexive activity is obscure.[34]

Reply: Let us begin by putting the difficulty clearly. The data of consciousness are not imaginable. But St Thomas holds that no mere man in this life can understand anything at all at any time without conversion to phantasm.[35] How can one get intellect to operate with respect to data that are not imaginable?

Recall that acts are known by their objects, potencies by their acts, and the essence of the soul by its potencies.[36] There exists, then, an associative train linking imaginable objects with conscious experiences. It is by ex-

33 Georges Van Riet, 'Idéalisme et Christianisme: A propos de la "Philosophie de la Religion" de M. Henry Duméry,' *Revue philosophique de Louvain* 56 (1958) 403–404: 'A notre avis, toute activité consciente est nécessairement présente à soi de façon irréfléchie ou, selon la graphie de Sartre, consciente (de) soi. Ce qui caractérise cette conscience (de) soi, c'est d'être encore inexprimée; elle est présence à soi, non connaissance de soi; elle ne se sert pas de concepts, de jugements, de mots; elle est silencieuse, elle ne parle pas. Dès qu'elle réfléchit, elle parle; réfléchir, c'est en effet élucider en exprimant; le fruit de la réflexion est le jugement. Le paradoxe de la conscience humaine, qui est incarnée et non pas angélique, c'est que même l'acte élucidant est pour lui-même irréfléchi, conscient (de) soi. Il exprime un irréfléchi, un vécu ou un perçu, il ne s'exprime pas lui-même. Seul un nouvel acte de réflexion l'élucidera en l'exprimant, mais ce nouvel acte demeurera à son tour irréfléchi.'

34 Perego 421.

35 *Summa theologiae*, 1, q. 84, a. 7 c. Do not confuse conversion to phantasm, which is indispensable for understanding anything whatever, with reflexion on phantasm, which is needed for intellectual knowledge of the singular.

36 Thomas Aquinas, *In II De anima*, lect. 6, §§ 304–308.

ploiting that link that intelligence investigates the nature of sense, imagination, intellect, will, and the soul.

This, of course, is no more than a general directive, but it is easy to see that no more than a general directive can be given. Just as a blind man cannot understand a disquisition on colors, so a person with no experience of direct understanding cannot be expected to reach by introspection an understanding of what direct understanding is; and similarly a person without experience of introspective understanding cannot be expected to reach by an introspection of the second order an understanding of what introspective understanding is. One must begin from the performance, if one is to have the experience necessary for understanding what the performance is. Hence, if anyone cares for clarity on this issue, he can begin from the statement, 'non si riesce a comprendere' [one fails to understand]. He can contrast that experience of not understanding with other experiences in which he felt he understood. Then he can turn his efforts to understanding his experiences of understanding and not understanding. Finally, when proficient at introspective understanding, he can move to the higher level and attempt to understand his successful and unsuccessful efforts at introspective understanding.

I have dwelt on this point, because I believe it of utmost importance. We have seen that St Thomas prefers Aristotle's cognitional theory because it accords with experience. We have seen that St Thomas considered it to be a matter of experience that we (1) try to understand, (2) form relevant images, (3) inspect solutions in the images, (4) receive the intelligible in act, (5) abstract from phantasm.[37] But this is far from the whole story. Aristotelian and Thomist intellectual theory is essentially a matter of understanding experience. St Thomas wrote:

> The species therefore of the thing understood in act is the species of the understanding itself; and so it is that understanding can understand itself through this species. Thus the philosopher in an earlier passage studied the nature of possible intellect by studying the very act of understanding and the object that is understood.[38]

37 See above at notes 26–28.
38 *In III De anima*, lect. 9, §724: 'Species igitur rei intellectae in actu est species ipsius intellectus; et sic per eam se ipsum intelligere potest. Unde et supra Philosophus per ipsum intelligere et per illud quod intelligitur, scrutatus est naturam intellectus possibilis.'

By the act of understanding and by the εἶδος, the τὸ τί ἦν εἶναι, the αἴτιον τοῦ εἶναι, grasped by understanding in sensible data, Aristotle worked out the nature of possible intellect.[39] Without repeating the Aristotelian process in oneself, one may use the words *intelligere* and *quid sit*, but one does not know what they mean. Further, one has not a proper grasp of the nature and virtue of the human soul. Aquinas also wrote:

> ... the human soul understands itself by its understanding, which is its proper act, perfectly demonstrating its power and its nature.[40]

There is little in philosophy or in speculative theology that ignorance in these matters does not corrupt.

Eighthly, Fr Perego insinuates that if certain expressions of mine are taken literally, they would imply pantheism, the denial of natural theology, and the denial of a natural, human beatitude.[41]

Reply: The fact is that in his exposition, page 416, lines 6 to 24, Fr Perego begins with a misstatement; he shifts from Italian to Latin to repeat his misstatement; the Latin is part of a sentence in my booklet, with the significant difference that that part by itself is false, while my statement is true. Next, instead of showing some concern for the *sensus auctoris*, he proceeds to insinuate that I omit what I do not omit. On the basis of this insinuated omission there arise the alleged consequences of pantheism, the denial of natural theology, and the denial of a natural human beatitude. Finally, he handsomely refuses to believe that I mean what he concludes from the statement he falsely imputed to me.

Now there is no need to demonstrate *twice* that Fr Perego's presentation of another's views can leave something to be desired. The interest of the present misrepresentation lies in the fact that, if it bore any relation to my text, it could arise only from three simultaneous and incompatible misinterpretations. One might deny the unrestricted range of human

---

39 See ibid. lect. 7, on possible intellect, lect. 8 on its object, lect. 9 on self-knowledge. For 'magnitudini esse' and 'carni esse,' the whole of Aristotle's Book VII in the *Metaphysics* is relevant. At least do not omit chapter 17.

40 *Summa theologiae*, 1, q. 88, a. 2, ad 3m: ' ... anima humana intelligit se ipsam per suum intelligere, quod est actus proprius eius, perfecte demonstrans virtutem eius et naturam.' Contrast with the Thomist procedure, which rests on experience of understanding, the analogous notion of intellectᵒ formed on the basis of sense knowledge (intellect is a spiritual eye) with differences deduced from the existence of universals.

41 Perego 416. Contrast *De constitutione Christi* 9–10, §§1-2.

intellect as intellect, and so deny the possibility of natural theology. One might deny the natural limitation of human intellect as human, and so conclude to pantheism. But no one would simultaneously deny both. Moreover, it is only by affirming both that there arises any problem about natural human beatitude.

Ninthly, a hypothetical reader may interpose that he too finds quite odd my meaning when I employ such terms as *intelligere, quidditas, quid sit, quidditative,* and even *ens.*

Reply: The act that occurs when the teacher teaches and the learner learns is from the teacher and in the learner; it is named understanding, *intelligere.* It occurs frequently in the intelligent and rarely in the slow-witted. When it has occurred, one finds things clear; when it has not, one finds things obscure; thus one and the same mathematical theorem can be a masterpiece of elegance to one man and an insoluble puzzle to another. Further, once a man has understood, he no longer needs the teacher; he can operate on his own; he can repeat similar and cognate acts of understanding with ease, promptitude, and pleasure; he has an acquired habit.

The object of the act of understanding is the intelligible; the intelligible is expressed in concepts, but its basic occurrence is prior to the occurrence of the concept. When one finds things obscure, one cannot conceive them, define them, think them; they are for one, unless one is modest, inconceivable, indefinite, unthinkable. Hence, before one can conceive, one must understand; and, of course, unless one is rash, before one can judge, one must both understand and conceive.

The intelligible, grasped by human understanding, is known in the sensible, in what is imagined; it is the ground of universal concepts; nonetheless, it is related intrinsically to the concrete. Such intelligible-in-the-sensible is the *proper object* of human intellect; it is proper in two senses: first, in the sense that man in this life understands no intelligible whatever except as a derivative of that proper object, and secondly, in the sense that no pure spirit has as its proper object, its basic source of all intelligibility, the intelligible-in-the-sensible.

Besides the proper object of human intellect, there is its formal object. The proper object pertains to human intellect as human, as specifically different from other types of intellect. The formal object pertains to human intellect as intellect, as having something in common with every type of intellect. This formal object of intellect is being, where being means everything. The fact that being, everything, is the formal object of human intellect cannot be demonstrated by showing that man does understand everything. But it is clear from the fact that man wants to understand everything about everything, that to answer any number of questions is only to invite more questions, that man's intellect does not come to a complacent stop until it understands everything about everything. Again, the same point can be made negatively. If the formal object of human intellect were not being, then it would be some genus; and if it were a genus, then intellect would be completely confined to that genus, as sight is to color, and hearing is to sound; but human intellect is not completely confined to any genus; it can raise questions about absolutely everything that exists or even could exist, and so it cannot be completely confined to some single genus.

Now human intellect is not the only intellect. Each different type of intellect has its own proper object. But there can be only one intellect in which the proper object is also the formal object. For when the proper object is also the formal object of an intellect, then its natural act of understanding is infinite; it understands in act itself and, as well, everything else that does exist or could exist; such unrestricted understanding must be God, the principle and end of all actual being and, as well, the ground of all possible being.

There results the well-known paradox of finite intellect. Because its formal object is being, it is orientated towards infinite understanding; and without this orientation, it would not be an intellect. Because it is finite, it cannot be infinite understanding; for that would be a contradiction in terms; and so its proper object must differ from its formal object. Further, it cannot be said that finite understanding, while it is not infinite, nonetheless has an exigence for the infinite. If one says 'exigence,' one means necessity or one means nothing; but so far from being necessary, it is impossible for the finite either to be or to become the infinite; what necessarily is infinite, already is infinite; and what is not infinite cannot become infinite, for the infinite cannot become. Nor does the revealed mystery of the vision of God change things in the least, for not even the beatific vision of Christ is an act of understanding everything about everything;[42] and so not even in Christ is the alleged exigence fulfilled.

If the meaning of the foregoing has been understood,[43] it is not difficult

42 Thomas Aquinas, *Summa theologiae*, 3, q. 10, a. 2 c. See *De veritate*, q. 20, a. 5.

43 In itself it is not difficult. Historically, however, a theory of intellect

to learn the words. One has only to read St Thomas and understand what is said. An intellect completely in act with respect to being is God.[44] The proper object of our intellects is 'quidditas sive natura in materia corporali existens'.[45] God is not a material substance, and so we do not know *quid sit Deus*.[46] God is being, and since we do not know *quid sit Deus*, we do not know *quid sit ens*; in both cases our knowledge is analogical.[47] We naturally desire to know *quid sit Deus*; actually knowing it, however, is perfect beatitude, natural to God alone, beyond the natural capacity and the natural will of any possible creature.[48]

Tenthly, to return from the hypothetical reader to Fr Perego, he advances that there is an obscurity in my view of the relationship between Christ's human consciousness and Christ's beatific vision.[49]

Reply: I grant that the relationship is quite obscure if one is unfamiliar with the meaning of the question, *quid sit*, and also with the admiration that is the origin of all science and all philosophy. Otherwise, the relationship is plain as a pikestaff. By consciousness we are aware of ourselves but we do not understand our natures; because we know ourselves only *sub ratione experti*, we wonder what we are; and that wonder gives place to knowledge when we understand *quid sit homo*. But Christ as man was similar to us in all things save sin. He was aware of himself by consciousness, yet by that consciousness he did not know *quid sit*; moreover, since he had two natures, he had a twofold wonder, *quid sit homo* and *quid sit Deus*; the answer to the second was the beatific vision.

---

based upon the experience of the act of understanding had to struggle against another theory in which the basic element is, not understanding, but the universal concept. When coherent, as in Scotus,[p] such a theory is easily distinguished from the doctrine of Aristotle and of St Thomas. But between the two pure forms, there is a great variety of intermediate and incoherent blends; and this creates confusion.

44 *Summa theologiae*, 1, q. 79, a. 2 c.

45 Ibid. q. 84, a. 7 c.

46 Ibid. q. 1, a. 7, ad 1m; q. 2, a. 2, ad 2m; q. 3 init.; q. 12, a. 12 c. and ad 1m; a. 13, ad 1m; q. 13, a. 8, ad 2m; and passim.

47 The conceptualist tendency emphasizes the distinction between univocal and analogous concepts; the intellectualist emphasizes the distinction between quidditative and analogous knowledge.

48 *Summa theologiae*, 1, q. 12, aa. 1, 4, 5; q. 62, aa. 2, 4; 1–2, q. 3, a. 8; q. 5, a. 5; *Summa contra Gentiles*, 3, cc. 25–63. I cannot here undertake an exegesis of these passages; on the other hand, I think it prudent to state my own position, namely, that all true statements about the beatific vision are strictly theological, all strictly theological statements presuppose the articles of faith, and no strictly theological argument proceeds in the light of merely natural reason.

49 Perego 421.

Let us end this section on the notion of the subject. My contention was that consciousness is not only cognitive but also constitutive of the subject. My contention was that an adequate account of consciousness is had by making more explicit the familiar Aristotelian-Thomist doctrine of the identity in act of subject and object.[50] Perhaps the reader will agree with me when I say (1) that Fr Perego does not seem to know what consciousness is and (2) that his many objections are just *solubilia argumenta*.

3   Christ as Subject

The function of theology is to state clearly and unequivocally the full meaning of the articles of faith. The theology of Christ as subject includes an explicitation of the article of the creed, that 'Jesus Christ, his only Son, our Lord ... suffered under Pontius Pilate.' Consider, then, the following series of questions and answers that, were they not so elementary and so obvious, might be included in a catechism.

Q.   Who suffered under Pontius Pilate?
A.   Jesus Christ, his only Son, our Lord.
Q.   Did he himself suffer, or was it somebody else, or was it nobody?
A.   He himself suffered.
Q.   Did he suffer unconsciously?
A.   No, he suffered consciously. To suffer unconsciously is not to suffer at all. Surgical operations cause no pain, when the patient is made unconscious by an anesthetic.
Q.   What does it mean to say that he suffered consciously?
A.   It means that he himself really and truly suffered. He was the one whose soul was sorrowful unto death. He was the one who felt the cutting, pounding scourge. He was the one who endured for three hours the agony of the crucified.
Q.   Do you mean that his soul was sorrowful but he himself was not sorrowful?
A.   That does not make sense. The Apostles' Creed says explicitly

50 The pure case of the identity is the familiar tag, 'in his quae sunt sine materia idem est intelligens et intellectum.' Aristotle, *De anima*, III, 4, 430a 3–4; see Thomas Aquinas, *Summa theologiae*, 1, q. 14, a. 2. If I may hazard a surmise, I should say that the discovery of the subject, attributed to German idealism and subsequent philosophies, was simply an unbalanced effort to restore what implicitly existed in Aristotle and St Thomas but had been submerged by the conceptualist tendency mentioned above.

that Jesus Christ, his only Son, our Lord, suffered under Pontius Pilate.

Q.   Do you mean that his body was scourged and crucified but he himself felt nothing?

A.   No, he felt all of it. Were our bodies scourged and crucified, we would feel it. His was scourged and crucified. He felt it.

Q.   Is not Jesus Christ God?

A.   He is.

Q.   Do you mean that God suffered?

A.   In Jesus Christ there is one person with two natures. I do not mean that the one person suffered in his divine nature. I do mean that the one person suffered in his human nature.

Q.   It was really that divine person that suffered though not in his divine nature?

A.   It was. He suffered. It was not somebody else that suffered. It was not nobody that suffered.

Such is the doctrine we have all believed from childhood. Still, as an object of faith, it is apprehended, not in terms of an understanding of the nature of the subject and of consciousness, but in the more elementary fashion that rests on our own experience of ourselves as subjects and as conscious. There remains, then, the theologian's task, and it consists simply in making explicit what already is implicitly believed.[51]

Moreover, for present purposes there is no need for the theologian to master accurately what is meant by the consciously intelligent, consciously rational, consciously free, consciously responsible subject. His introspection can be limited to the simplest and most obvious of all instances, the suffering of physical pain. Can anyone suffer physical pain without being the subject of the pain? Can anyone suffer unconsciously?

---

51 It should seem contrary to faith to hold that it was not the only Son of God the Father that suffered but a human soul, a human body, a human consciousness, or a human subject not identical with the Son of God; again, the same is to be said of a view that maintained that, while in Christ's passion there was real human suffering, still there was no sufferer; again, the same is to be said of a view that Christ suffered unconsciously. However, as I noted (*De constitutione Christi* 109), the novelty of the question requires that one distinguish between the intention of Catholic authors and the statements they make because of an inadequate grasp of the nature of the subject and of consciousness.

Can one be the conscious subject of physical pain without being constituted as conscious subject? Can one be constituted as conscious subject
if one is merely known to an ontological self as an object, where that
knowing involves no real modification in the object? I find the answers
to these questions obvious.

It follows, then, since Jesus Christ, his only Son, our Lord, suffered
physical pain, therefore he was constituted as the conscious subject of
physical pain.

It follows *a pari* that the Word as man was the conscious subject of all
his human acts, for he was similar to us in all things save sin. For if
Christ was the conscious subject of physical pain, surely he also was the
conscious subject of looking and listening, of imagining Solomon in all
his glory and seeing the lilies of the field, of the acts of his *scientia beata,
infusa, acquisita,* of the free and responsible acts of will by which he
merited our salvation.

So simple a solution does not please Fr Perego, and he objects that
Christ as man cannot be a conscious subject in virtue of the hypostatic
union as such.[52]

I grant the contention and deny its supposition. My argument for the
human consciousness of Christ was drawn, not from the hypostatic union
as such, but from the definition of Chalcedon, *per omnia nobis similem
absque peccato.*[53] If Christ was similar to us *in all things,* then he did not
spend his entire life in a state of coma or of dreamless sleep.

Further, I wish to deny what the argument insinuates, namely, that
by the hypostatic union Christ was not constituted as potentially a conscious subject. By that union the Word was made flesh, and the Son was
really and truly a man. A man, by the mere fact that he is a man, is able
to see, hear, feel, understand, judge, will, enjoy, suffer; *eo ipso,* he is able
to be the conscious subject of these activities.

52 Perego 421.
53 *De constitutione Christi* 110. Observe there and on the following page the
    immediate application to the sufferings of Christ. This argument is
    not weakened in any way by mistaken views on the explicit doctrine of
    St Thomas regarding sense consciousness and the reflexive character
    of consciousness; similarly, it is not weakened by unsuccessful attempts
    to assert that consciousness properly so called is a reflexive intellectual
    intuition. On the contrary, the dogmatic fact demands recognition, and
    if a theory of consciousness is incompatible with it, then the theory
    has to be corrected.

But Fr Perego has a further objection. Such acts involve no actuation in the intentional order with respect to the Word. Therefore, they cannot constitute the Word as conscious of himself, a divine person.[54]

I distinguish. There is no actuation in the intentional order with respect to the Word as object, as *id quod intenditur*, I transmit. There is no actuation in the intentional order with respect to the Word as subject, as *is qui intendit*, I deny.[55]

Finally, Fr Perego objects that if Christ as man, in exercising his sensitive and intellectual acts, is conscious of himself, a divine person, then these acts must be supernatural.[56]

Either this is *ignoratio elenchi*, or else Fr Perego is introducing a new principle that he has not proved.

It is *ignoratio elenchi*, if Fr Perego fancies that I hold the Word as man to be conscious of himself inasmuch as he knows himself as object.

On the other hand, if Fr Perego is objecting against the Word's self-awareness as subject, he has yet to prove that *actus specificantur per subiectum*. The Word himself is God and stands in no need of a supernatural elevation; by the *gratia unionis* the Word is a man and a potential conscious subject of a human consciousness, and the *gratia unionis* is already entitatively supernatural; to demand a further supernatural elevation of the acts exercised by the Word presupposes what has not been proved, namely, that acts are specified by their subject.

Conclusion

A subject is a conscious person. A person is conscious by being the *principium quod* of acts of sense or intellect. Insofar as there is in man a *sensibile actu*, there is by that very act a *sensus actu* and a *subiectum actu*; insofar as there is an *intelligibile actu*, there is by that very act an *intellectus actu* and a *subiectum actu*. Finally, the *subiectum actu* is the *principium quod* of the act.

There follows an *analogia fidei*: a parallelism is to be recognized between ontological and psychological statements about the incarnate Word.[q] The main parallel statements are that, as there is one person with a divine and a human nature, so there is one subject with a divine and a

54 Perego 422–23.
55 Fifteen further difficulties along this line are solved, *De constitutione Christi* 111, 120–24.
56 Perego 423.

human consciousness. As the person, so also the subject is without division or separation. As the two natures, so also the divine and the human consciousness are without confusion or interchange. As the person, so also the subject is a divine reality. As the human nature, so also the human consciousness is assumed. As there is a great difference between 'being God' and 'being a man,' so also there is a great difference between 'being conscious of oneself as God' and 'being conscious of oneself as man.' As the former difference is surmounted hypostatically by union in the person, so the latter difference is surmounted hypostatically by union in the subject. As the two natures do not prove two persons, so the divine and the human consciousness do not prove two subjects.

The two sides of the parallelism have not, at present, the same theological note. The ontological side was developed centuries ago, and it has the authority of the decrees of Chalcedon and of the Third Council of Constantinople as understood by all Catholic theologians. The psychological side is an opinion on a question raised by contemporary theology; still, this opinion has in its favor arguments that seem rather peremptory.

First, one cannot accept 'eundemque perfectum in deitate, et eundem perfectum in humanitate' in an ontological sense to the exclusion of a psychological sense. The councils do not make any such reservation. On the contrary, they seem to me to exclude any such reservation (1) by the word *perfectum*, (2) by the phrase *per omnia nobis similem absque peccato*, and (3) by speaking of two wills and two operations. Now if the foregoing distinction between the ontological and the psychological is excluded, then the councils define both sides of my parallelism. Further, while all theologians do not as yet recognize this, that hesitancy arises simply because theology develops in time, with the theology of the ontology of Christ preceding the theology of the psychology of Christ.

Secondly, the article of the Apostles' Creed which I have stressed has a clear meaning in the minds of all the faithful including the theologians *qua fideles*. That clear meaning seems to me to exclude in rather peremptory fashion theories of the subject and of consciousness that, instead of explaining what everyone believes, not only seem to be reluctant to consider an article of faith with a clear connotation of consciousness but also seem to be incapable of being reconciled with what everyone believes.

Thirdly, the account of consciousness which my position presupposes fits easily into the framework of Aristotelian and Thomist thought. Moreover, while I have here given an argument drawn from the constitutive function of consciousness, I do not rest my case on that argument; my case rests on the facts of consciousness, and they are extremely numerous, extremely complex, and far too delicate to be exposed when one has to deal with somewhat unperceptive charges of incomprehensibility.

12

Openness and Religious Experience

1 The theme suggested to me[a] includes such heterogenous elements that I can do no more than set down certain headings which, perhaps, will be found suggestive.

2 How should I conceive *philosophy of religious experience?*

I should say that it involves (1) a material component, viz., 'religious experience,' and (2) a formal component, viz., 'philosophy of ... '[b]

In other words I should defend the existence of a discipline, viz., 'philosophy of ... ,' which with minor adaptations to diverse materials may be extended into any of the particular departments such as (1) philosophy of nature, (2) philosophy of science, (3) philosophy of man, (4) philosophy of history, (5) philosophy of the state, (6) philosophy of education, (7) philosophy of spirit, (8) philosophy of religion, etc.

With respect to each and all of its particularizations, 'philosophy of ... ' determines (1) basic terms, (2) basic correlations, (3) a basic orientation.

In illustration, I should say that my book, *Insight*, may be taken as a 'philosophy of ... ' In it the basic terms are empirical, intellectual, and rational consciousness; and I should note that as levels of consciousness they are immediate in their content though mediated[c] by reflection in their formulation.

The basic correlations are the relations of empirical to intellectual consciousness and of empirical and intellectual consciousness to rational consciousness. I note that these relations are isomorphic with the relations of potency, form, and act in the Aristotelian-Thomist tradition.

The basic orientation,[d] finally, is the pure, detached, disinterested, and unrestricted desire to know. I should note that this desire, when it is functioning, is no less immediate than the levels of consciousness when they are functioning.

3 Openness[e] as (1) fact, (2) achievement, (3) gift.

Openness as a fact is the pure desire to know. It is, when functioning, immediately given. It is referred to by Aristotle when he speaks of the wonder that is the beginning of all science and philosophy.[f] It is referred to by Aquinas when he speaks of the natural desire to know God by his essence.

Openness as an achievement has two aspects. In its more fundamental aspect it regards the subject, the νόησις, the *pensée pensante*. Here stages towards its acquisition are communicated or objectified in precepts, methods, criticism. Achievement itself arises when the actual orientation of consciousness coincides with the exigences of the pure, detached, disinterested, unrestricted desire to know.

But openness as achievement also has a consequent aspect that regards the object, the νόημα, the *pensée pensée*. For the pure desire to function fully, to dominate consciousness, there are needed not only precepts, methods, criticism, but also a formulated view of our knowledge and of the reality our knowledge can attain. Thus I should maintain that the crop of philosophies produced since the Enlightenment are not open to revealed truths because they possess no adequate account of truth.

I have spoken of openness as (1) fact and (2) achievement.

As fact, it is an intrinsic component in man's makeup. But as fact it does not consistently and completely dominate human consciousness.

It is a fact to which man has to advert, which he has to acknowledge and accept, whose implications for all his thinking and acting have to be worked out and successfully applied to actual thinking and actual acting.

Hence, besides openness as primordial fact, there also is openness as achievement. The history of religion, of science, of philosophy in all their vicissitudes is the history of such achievement.

But there is also openness as a gift, as an effect of divine grace.

Man's natural openness is complete. The pure desire is unrestricted. It inquires into everything, and asks everything about everything.

The correlative to the pure desire is 'being,' *omnia*, at once completely universal and completely concrete.

Nonetheless, there is a contrast, almost an antinomy, between the primordial fact and achievement, for the primordial fact is no more than a principle of possible achievement, a definition of the ultimate horizon that is to be reached only through successive enlargements of the actual horizon.

But such successive enlargements only too clearly lie under some law of decreasing returns. No one ever believed that the world would be converted by philosophy. In the language at once of scripture and of a current philosophy, man is fallen. There is then a need of openness as a gift, as an effect of grace, where grace is taken as *gratia sanans*.

Further, the successive enlargements of the actual horizon fall into two classes. There are the enlargements implicit in the very structure of human consciousness, the enlargements that are naturally possible to man. But there is also an ultimate enlargement, beyond the resources of every finite consciousness, where there enters into clear view God as unknown, when the subject knows God face to face, knows as he is known. This ultimate enlargement alone approximates to the possibility of openness defined by the pure desire; as well, it is an openness as a gift, as an effect of grace and, indeed, of grace not as merely *sanans* but as *elevans*, as *lumen gloriae*.

4 Openness and religious experience.[g]

The three aspects of openness are to be related. Openness as fact is for openness as gift; and openness as achievement rises from the fact, and conditions and, at the same time, is conditioned by the gift.

But openness as fact is the inner self, the self as ground of all higher aspiration.

Openness as achievement is the self in its self-appropriation and self-realization.

Openness as gift is the self entering into personal relationship with God.

Because these three are linked in the historical unfolding of the human spirit, they reveal how religious experience holds a fundamental place primarily in man's making of man[h] but no less in the reflection on that making that is philosophy or, indeed, 'philosophy of ... '

13

Metaphysics as Horizon

I   Coreth's *Metaphysik*

Fr Coreth, ordinary professor of metaphysics at the University of Innsbruck,[a] has given us not only a text by a professor but also a work by a philosopher.[1] The professorial hand is evident in the abundant *Zusätze* that in finer print recall historical antecedents and the contemporary setting. The philosophic mind is revealed in the sweep and subtlety of an argument that develops a unified understanding of being through a study of the being of man, the being of things, and the being of God.

The great merit of the work, in negative terms, is its clean break from the Wolffian tradition.[b] By being is meant, not what can be, but what is. By general metaphysics is understood, not a study of some prior realm of possibilities, but an understanding of actual existents. There is analogy not only of being but also of the transcendentals, and as the being of the subject grounds the account of the being of things, so the self-realization of the subject in inquiring, knowing, and willing grounds the account of the unity, ontic truth, and ontic goodness of things. If there is no omission either of the analysis of the finite existent or of the categories of material being, still the fact that the first analogate in our

---

1 Emerich Coreth, *Metaphysik. Eine methodisch-systematische Grundlegung* (Innsbruck-Vienna-Munich: Tyrolia-Verlag, 1961). [A second edition, with minor changes and different pagination, was published in 1964. References here are to the 1961 edition.]

analogous knowledge of being is human existence, inevitably is reflected in an account of personal being, of morality, community, historicity, and religion. In brief, the transition from being as what can be to being as what is has been carried through in its full implications. When being is the existent, when our knowledge of being is analogous, the object of the science of being has to be the set of existents, and the unity of the science can be only analogical.

Still, however familiar are these premises, and indeed however classical is Fr Coreth's doctrine, the result is a new look. For Fr Coreth is not merely breaking from the Wolffian tradition but also implementing the insights of Fr Joseph Maréchal. In this, of course, Fr Coreth reserves the right to go his own way. As he points out (12), what has come from Fr Maréchal is not a school but a movement, not a set of ready-made opinions repeated in unison by members of a uniform group, but a basic line of thought that already has developed in various manners and still continues to do so.

The substance of Fr Coreth's development can best be approached through a consideration of his method. This he deduces from the assumption that metaphysics is the *Gesamt- und Grundwissenschaft*: it is total, for being includes everything; it is basic, for it accepts no presuppositions that it itself does not justify. Its method, accordingly, will have to be a mediation of immediate knowledge (68–69, 233). Though a subordinate use of synthetic-inductive and analytic-deductive procedures is granted (88–91), still such mediate knowledge cannot meet the main issues, for it has presuppositions (61–64). On the other hand, immediate knowledge in its immediacy will not do, for simply to assert the evidence of one's fundamental metaphysical views only provokes the answer, *Quod gratis asseritur, gratis negatur* (67). It remains that the main method in metaphysics is a mediation of the immediate. There exists a latent metaphysics, present and operative in all our knowing; it is the metaphysical *Ureinsicht* in its immediacy; but it has to be thematized and made explicit, to be brought out into the open in accurately defined concepts and certain judgments (68–69). The main task of the metaphysician is not to reveal or prove what is new and unknown; it is to give scientific expression to what already is implicitly acknowledged without being explicitly recognized (93).

The proper tool in this mediation of the immediate is the rejection of the counterposition. Explicit judgments can contradict the latent metaphysics that they presuppose; but one has only to bring this contradiction to light, for the explicit judgment to be evident nonsense, and for its opposite to be established (68). Such a procedure Fr Coreth names transcendental method:[d] its basis lies, not in the content of the judgment, but in the conditions of its possibility (69); and he does not hesitate to assert that 'transcendental method, as we understand it, is not only the fundamental method that is demanded by the nature of metaphysics as basic science; it is also, one might venture to say, the integral method that takes over all other methods which, standing in isolation from one another, are insufficient, takes them over and, while respecting their legitimate concerns, sublates them into a higher unity.'[2]

Such a tool, clearly, needs a point of application, and this Fr Coreth finds in the concrete, conscious, active reality of the subject asking a question. To doubt questioning is to involve oneself in a counterposition, and so questioning is beyond the doubter's capacity to doubt coherently. Presuppositionless metaphysics, accordingly, begins from questioning: not from the appearance of it, nor from the concept of it, nor from judgments about it, but from the performance, the *Vollzug* (77–80). Linking such performance with conditions of possibility is the *Auslegung* in a sense carefully differentiated from that of Husserl and Heidegger (76, 91–94).

After the foregoing, merely introductory, discussion of method, the argument proper begins. No doubt, the proper place to begin is at the beginning, but some say one issue and others say another is the proper beginning. So there is a question about the beginning and, indeed, no matter where one starts, one starts from some question. For Fr Coreth, then, questioning itself is the beginning.

What is the condition of the possibility of questioning? In other words, what is the essence of questioning, what is found in every question to constitute it, not as question about this rather than about that, but simply as questioning? It is claimed that the condition of the possibility of any and all questions is an awareness that goes beyond the already known to an unknown to be known (130).

2 Ibid. 88: 'Die transzendentale Methode, wie wir sie verstehen, ist nicht nur die fundamentale Methode, die vom Wesen der Metaphysik als Grundwissenschaft gefordert ist; sie ist auch, wenn wir so sagen dürfen, die integrale Methode, die alle anderen, isoliert genommen unzureichenden Methoden in ihrem berechtigten Anliegen aufnimmt und in eine höhere Einheit aufhebt.'

What is this awareness of? At least, it is of the questionable, for if nothing were questionable, there could be no questions. But, further, the questionable is unrestricted: to propose a limit to questioning is to raise the question of the legitimacy of asking questions beyond the limit; and raising this question is already beyond the limit. In other words, to limit questioning lands one in a counterposition. Finally, as the questionable is unrestricted, so it is somehow one. For the condition of the possibility of questioning is always the same going beyond the already known to an unknown that is to be known; it follows that the questionable, of which questioning is aware, must be as much one as the awareness that constitutes questioning.   ⌐ = the *unity* of them & *being*

Still, what is it that is questionable, unrestricted, one? It is being. Being is the questionable: it is the great unknown, that all our questions are about (quid *sit*? an *sit*?) and never exhaust; it is unrestricted, for apart from being there is nothing; finally, it is one, for despite all other differences every instance of being is.

But we say 'is' and 'is not' in such different ways: we say there 'is' a moon; but we also say there 'is' a logarithm of the square root of minus one. In brief, there is a realm of absolute and unrestricted validity in which things 'are' *simpliciter*, and there are other realms in which they 'are' indeed but still are merely logical,[e] merely mathematical, merely hypothetical, merely phenomenological, and so on. Which is the realm that is the condition of the possibility of asking questions? Plainly, we ask questions with respect to all realms, but the realm of being that is the condition of questioning is the one that must be presupposed for there to be the others. When one states that a statement is merely logical, one means that really and truly it is merely logical. It follows that one cannot suppose that all statements are merely logical, for then it would be merely logical that they are merely logical, and it would be impossible to say that any really and truly is merely logical. The same holds for the merely hypothetical, the merely phenomenal, and any other restricted or qualified realm. By the same stroke any and every form of idealism is excluded. The possibility of questioning is being, and this being is   ✓ being in its unqualified sense, *An-sich-Sein*. 'From this it follows that there never is and never can be a closed "inner area" of transcendental subjectivity, for subjectivity in its very performance is already "outside" in the realm of being-in-itself in general which transcends subjectivity. Performance is constituted in its nature and its possibility by its horizon, but the horizon in which subjectivity realizes itself is always the horizon of being-in-itself in general.'[3]

2   Kant, Gilson, Coreth

Now we might continue to follow Fr Coreth's argument. We should learn that questioning not only is about being but is itself being, being in its *Gelichtetheit*, being in its openness to being, being that is realizing itself through inquiry to knowing that, through knowing, it may come to loving. This being of the questioning questioner is the latent metaphysics from which explicit metaphysics is derived; and in explicit metaphysics it is the primary analogate through which other being as being is understood.

However, as we cannot reproduce the book, it will be more profitable to locate it. If the more obvious location would be in the German philosophic tradition, with which Fr Coreth has the familiarity of one born on the spot, it will be more helpful, I think, to turn to the contemporary scholastic milieu, to which Fr Coreth also belongs. Accordingly, I shall select for purposes of contrast Prof. Gilson's *Réalisme thomiste et critique de la connaissance* (Paris, 1939). It is true, of course, that that book is not the whole of Prof. Gilson, and that Prof. Gilson is not the only opponent of Fr Maréchal. It remains that Prof. Gilson's book is still influential[f] (*Theological Studies* 22 [1961] 561) and that our purpose is not a survey of contemporary scholasticism but an introduction to Fr Coreth's thought. Our question is, then, In what manner do Kant, Prof. Gilson, and Fr Coreth differ?

2.1 Content and Performance

First, then, it is to be noted that the operative moment in Fr Coreth's use of transcendental method cannot occur in a Kantian context. For that operative moment lies in a contradiction not between content and content but between content and performance;[g] but a Kantian context

3 Ibid. 193: 'Daraus folgt, dass es einen geschlossenen "Innenraum" der transzendentalen Subjektivität niemals gibt noch geben kann, da die Subjektivität in ihrem Vollzug immer schon "draussen" ist beim An-sich-Sein überhaupt, das sie selbst übersteigt. Der Vollzug ist in seinem Wesen und seiner Möglichkeit konstituiert durch seinen Horizont; der Horizont aber, in dem die Subjektivität sich vollzieht, ist immer schon der Horizont des An-sich-Seins überhaupt.'

is a context of contents that does not envisage performances. Thus there is no explicit contradiction in the content of the statement, We are under an illusion when we claim to know what really is. On the other hand, there is an explicit contradiction in the reflective statement, I am stating what really and truly is so when I state that we are under an illusion whenever we claim to know what really and truly is so. However, the content of the explicitly contradictory statement adds to the content of the first what is found implicitly in the first, not as content, but as performance. Now to bring to light such contradictions is the operative moment in Fr Coreth's use of transcendental method. But such an operative moment cannot occur in a Kantian context for, while Kant envisages an *Ich denke* as a formal condition of the possibility of objective contents being thought, still he cannot find room for a concrete reality intelligently asking and rationally answering questions. In brief, phenomena appear, but they do not perform; and transcendental conditions of possibility within a transcendental logic do not transcend transcendental logic.

If the point has been explained, it will be well to apply it. Kant, then, acknowledges the need of the concept of noumenon as a *Grenzbegriff*: such a concept is of no use to him in knowledge of things, for he knows no noumena; but the same concept is essential to him, if he is to state the limitations of our *Anschauung*, if he is to state that we perceive not noumena but phenomena (*Kritik der reinen Vernunft* [= KRV] B 310–11). Now Fr Coreth would not claim that this passage in the *Kritik* is contradictory, for a passage is just a sequence of contents. He would claim that it is contradictory when the performer is added. For what the performer wants to assert is that really and truly our *Anschauung* is not of what really and truly is and, nonetheless, that we cannot know what really and truly is. This contradiction lies, not in the content uttered by the mind, but in the mind that utters the content, and not in a formal entity that merely thinks thoughts, but in a concrete intelligence that by its performance means and by its uttered contents denies that we know what really and truly is so.

2.2 Kant and Gilson

Secondly, if now we turn to a comparison of Prof. Gilson's position with Kant's, the differences appear massive. Kant is a critical idealist; Prof. Gilson is neither critical nor an idealist. But so radical an opposition does not preclude all similarity, for Prof. Gilson's door to his real world is perception, and Kant's door to his world of appearances is *Anschauung*.[h]

For Kant, the judgment that seven and five are twelve is synthetic and a priori. Still, it is only a posteriori, by an empirical *Anschauung*, that Kant knows five books in one pile on his desk, seven in another, and so necessarily twelve in all. Moreover, this function of *Anschauung* is universal. *Anschauung* is the one means by which our cognitional operations are related immediately to objects (KRV, A 19, B 33). Judgment is only a mediate knowledge of objects, a representation of a representation (KRV, A 68, B 93). Reason is never related right up to objects but only to understanding and, through understanding, to the empirical use of reason itself (KRV, A 643, B 671).

Of the pivotal importance of empirical *Anschauung* in his system, Kant was fully aware. It was his refutation of pure reason, for concepts and, along with them, principles can refer to objects and so can possess objective validity only through *Anschauung*. Of themselves, no matter how a priori they may be, they are the mere play of imagination and understanding (KRV, B 301). But what condemns pure reason, by the same stroke condemns realism. For the only *Anschauung* we enjoy is sensitive; sense does not know noumena; and so our concepts and principles have no reference to noumena. Human cognitional activity is confined to phenomena.

Prof. Gilson is equally convinced that perception is the one manner in which cognitional activity attains objectivity. He differs from Kant, not on the question of principle, but on the question of fact. He maintains an immediate realism and, as he very acutely remarks in his *Réalisme thomiste*, 'Kant himself maintains an immediate realism with regard to the existence of a Kantian external world.'[4] Accordingly, there are two questions. What is Prof. Gilson's fact? Does this mean that the whole issue turns upon a fact?

Prof. Gilson's fact is not the exact opposite of Kant's. Kant asserts that sense does not apprehend noumena, and Prof. Gilson is far from asserting that sense does apprehend noumena. His assertion is that over and above sensitive perceptions and intellectual abstractions there exists

4 Etienne Gilson, *Réalisme thomiste et critique de la connaissance* (Paris: Vrin, 1939) 176: 'Kant lui-même ... soutient un réalisme immédiat de l'existence d'un monde extérieur kantien.' [An English translation of Gilson's book has just been published (San Francisco: Ignatius Press, 1987), but the translations in this chapter are our own.]

an intellectual vision of the concept of being in any sensible datum. Moreover, he adds, it is the concept of being, seen in this manner, that is predicated in perceptual judgments of existence. Thus, 'the apprehension of being by intellect consists in a direct *vision* in any sensible datum whatever of the concept of being.'[5] Again, 'When the concept of being is, on the contrary, abstracted from a concrete existent perceived by the senses, the judgment predicating being of this existent attributes being to it ... as "seen" in the sensible datum from which the concept of being was abstracted.'[6] So much for the matter of fact.

But how does it come about that Prof. Gilson differs from Kant on a question of fact and not, as Fr Coreth, on a question of principle? The reason is very simple. Prof. Gilson does not advert to Fr Coreth's principle and, indeed, could not admit it without changing his own principles.

For Prof. Gilson idealism does not necessarily involve a contradiction. He denies flatly that he ever held critical idealism to be contradictory (160, note). He asserts that, once Berkeley's starting point is admitted, one cannot find a contradiction from one end of his work to another (195). He maintains that, if one starts from critical premises, then one may conclude to existence, but the concluded existence will be merely a postulate or merely a predicate (183).

Now if idealism is possible, there exists the problem of the bridge. Abstract concepts of *l'être en général* and of existence are one thing. Concrete, actual, extramental existence is another. To think the former is one thing. To know the latter is another. There has to be some ground, some principle, some evidence, if idealism is to be rejected, if it is to be claimed that we not merely think about immanent objects but also know extramental realities (see 185).

Further, the needed ground, principle, evidence cannot be reached by a deduction. If the premises are understood in a realist sense, then realism is not proved but presupposed. If the premises are understood in a nonrealist sense, then the conclusion has to be understood in the same sense, and so realism is not concluded. Realism must be immediate truth.

5 Ibid. 215: ' ... l'appréhension de l'être par l'intellect consiste à *voir* (his italics) directement le concept d'être dans n'importe quelle donnée sensible.'
6 Ibid. 225–26: ' ... lorsque le concept d'être est au contraire abstrait d'un existant concret perçu par le sens, le jugement qui prédique l'être de cet existant le lui attribue ... comme "vu" (his quotation marks) dans le sensible donné dont il l'abstrait.'

Moreover, this immediate truth cannot be anything proper to intellect, any innate knowledge, any a priori. When Prof. Gilson adduces the axiom, *Nihil in intellectu nisi prius fuerit in sensu*, he claims that it is to be taken with absolute universality and that it is to be applied with full rigor. No exception is to be admitted, not even for being and the principle of contradiction (200).

It follows that realism is possible if and only if we *perceive* reality. Some ground for it is needed, for idealism is possible. That ground cannot be a deductive conclusion. It cannot be innate or a priori knowledge. Therefore it must be a posteriori. On this point Prof. Gilson is explicit in a manner calculated to leave no loopholes. 'Thus, no matter what way we may put the question to realism, no matter how profoundly we may inquire of it, How do you know a thing exists? its answer will always be, By perceiving it.'7

However, if Prof. Gilson agrees with Kant in holding that objectivity is a matter of perception, if he differs from Kant in holding that de facto we have perceptions of reality, one must not think that he attempts to refute Kant by appealing to a fact that Kant overlooked. Prof. Gilson's realism is dogmatic; the course he advocates is ' ... the blunt reaffirmation of the dogmatic realism whose validity was denied by Kant's critique.'8

This does not mean that Prof. Gilson has no reasons for being a realist. He was a realist before he began philosophy. His study of philosophy, so far from leading him to abandon realism, has only confirmed his original convictions. For him the history of philosophy moves about an axis, and the axis is sanctioned by a Herodotean law of compensation. This axis is realism, and its sanction is that 'When a man refuses to think as a realist where he ought to do so, he condemns himself inevitably to think as a realist where he ought not to do so.'9

Prof. Gilson's dogmatism, if I understand him, is that the whole is prior to the parts, that realism is a whole, prior to its parts, and so incapable of being assembled by starting from some part and step by step adding on the others. We have already noted the proof that realism cannot be proved deductively. But the opposite procedures of advancing

7 Ibid. 203: 'Ainsi, de quelque manière et à quelque profondeur de plan que nous lui posions la question: comment savoir qu'une chose existe? le réalisme répond: en la percevant.'

8 Ibid. 163: ' ... la réaffirmation brute du réalisme dogmatique dont la valeur a été niée par la critique de Kant.'

9 Ibid. 228: 'Lorsqu'un homme refuse de penser en réaliste où il faut, il se condamne inévitablement à penser en réaliste là où il ne faut pas.'

inductively or constructively, if not demonstrably impossible, certainly bristle with difficulties. In any case, Prof. Gilson does not attempt them. His fact of intellectual perception is not conceived independently of his Thomist system. It is not investigated simply in terms of psychological introspection and analysis. On the contrary, Prof. Gilson does not believe metaphysicians should attempt to do psychology (125). He asserts a general osmosis between sense and understanding, but leaves it to psychologists to work out the details (207). He indicates the area in which the perceptual judgment of existence is to be found, but he makes no effort to survey, explore, and work out a detailed report (225). Prof. Gilson's fact is not a manifest datum, accessible to anyone, and by its sheer givenness imposed on any and every philosopher. On the contrary, its givenness is vague and its accessibility is restricted. And even were its givenness precise and its accessibility universal, that would not prevent the Kantian from placing the perceived existence in the category not of noumena but of phenomena. 'That is why in the last analysis you do not accept any part of realism as long as you do not accept it whole and entire.'[10]

2.3 Gilson and Coreth

Thirdly, to complete our circle of comparisons, we must now turn to Prof. Gilson and Fr Coreth. Here we are met with massive similarities, and it is the difference that requires clarification. For both are realists: they acknowledge the real existence of minerals, plants, animals, men, and God. Both are immediate realists: though Fr Coreth mediates this immediacy, still for him no less than for Prof. Gilson realism is immediate truth. In both immediate realisms an a posteriori component is recognized: neither attempts to restore the pure reason that Kant undertook to refute. Not only are both Thomists, but also both are quite convinced of the priority of metaphysics over everything in general and over cognitional theory most particularly. Finally, as realism for Prof. Gilson is a whole, as his thinking deals with philosophies as wholes, so too for Fr Coreth the priority of the whole over the parts is cardinal.

The basic difference is that, while Prof. Gilson's immediate realism cannot be mediated and so is dogmatic, Fr Coreth's immediate realism

10 Ibid. 224: 'C'est pourquoi, en fin de compte, on ne prend rien du réalisme tant qu'on ne le prend pas tout entier.'

not only can be but also is mediated. For Prof. Gilson realism is a whole that one must accept or reject, and with this Fr Coreth agrees. For Prof. Gilson realism is a whole that cannot be assembled step by step with every step guaranteed as alone rational, and with this Fr Coreth flatly disagrees. His transcendental method is essentially the method for explicitating the whole: for transcendental method ascertains conditions of possibility, and the first and foremost of all conditions of possibility is the whole itself.

Let us attempt to get clear this point about a philosophy as essentially a whole. Aristotle and Aquinas distinguish the expert and the wise man: the expert orders everything within a restricted domain; the wise man orders everything. Further, to call a congress of all experts representing all restricted domains does not secure the presence of a wise man, for none of the experts knows the relations between the restricted domains. Knowledge of the whole, then, is distinct from knowledge of the parts, and it is not attained by a mere summation of the parts. The very fact that the expert restricts his domain implies that he also restricts the number of aspects under which he considers the objects within his domain; as the restrictions are removed, further aspects come to light; only when all restrictions are removed do all aspects come to light; and once all restrictions are removed, there can be no ulterior and higher viewpoint from which new aspects come to light with a consequent revision and reordering of previous acquisition. So the unrestricted viewpoint is ultimate and basic: it is wisdom and its domain is being.

Now it is technically simpler to express the foregoing in terms of 'horizon.'[i] Literally, a horizon is a maximum field of vision from a determinate standpoint. In a generalized sense, a horizon is specified by two poles, one objective and the other subjective, with each pole conditioning the other. Hence, the objective pole is taken, not materially, but like the formal object *sub ratione sub qua attingitur*; similarly, the subjective pole is considered, not materially, but in its relation to the objective pole. Thus the horizon of pure reason is specified when one states that its objective pole is possible being as determined by relations of possibility and necessity obtaining between concepts, and that its subjective pole is logical thinking as determining what can be and what must be. Similarly, in the horizon of critical idealism, the objective pole is the world of experience as appearance, and the subjective pole is the set of a priori conditions of the possibility of such a world. Again, in the horizon of the expert, the objective pole is his restricted domain as attained by

accepted scientific methods, and the subjective pole is the expert practicing those methods; but in the horizon of the wise man, the philosopher
of the Aristotelian tradition, the objective pole is an unrestricted domain,
and the subjective pole is the philosopher practicing transcendental
method, namely, the method that determines the ultimate and so basic
whole.

Now, to connect the foregoing with a point made earlier, the fact of
horizon explains why realism and, generally, a philosophy cannot be
proved deductively. The reason is that horizon is prior to the meaning
of statements: every statement made by a realist denotes an object in a
realist's world; every statement made by an idealist denotes an object in
an idealist world;[j] the two sets of objects are disparate; and neither of
the two sets of statements can prove the horizon within which each set
has its meaning, simply because the statements can have their meaning
only by presupposing their proper horizon. Further, what is true of
statements is equally true of the statement of problems and of the statement of solutions; problems and solutions are what they are only in
virtue of the horizon in which they arise; they cannot be transported
intact into a different horizon. So we arrive in general terms and on the
level of principle at the type of point that was made in a specific form
by Prof. Gilson when he claimed: 'I have never maintained that critical
idealism is contradictory; what is contradictory is critical realism or, more
precisely still, wishing to pose the problem of critical idealism within the
perspective of Thomist realism. My thesis says no more than that.'[11]

However, if Fr Coreth grants that statements have a meaning only
within a horizon, how can he escape the dogmatism that Prof. Gilson
believes inevitable? The answer is that he begins, not from statement,
but from a performance, a *Vollzug*, asking questions. It is a performance
that begins early in childhood and is continued even by an Aquinas until
a higher form of knowledge supervenes. No doubt, that performance
will be interpreted or overlooked in different manners when assumed
within different horizons; but it is given to be interpreted or overlooked
whether or not it is assumed. Nor can any doubt be entertained about
the fact of the performance. To doubt questioning is to ask whether

---

11   Ibid. 160–61, note: 'Jamais je n'ai soutenu que l'idéalisme critique fût
     contradictoire; ce qui est contradictoire, c'est le réalisme critique, ou,
     plus précisément encore, c'est de vouloir poser le problème de l'idéal-
     isme critique dans la perspective du réalisme thomiste. A cela se limite
     ma thèse.'

questions occur. The condition of the possibility of doubting is the occurrence of questioning. Fr Coreth, then, begins from a clearly known,
universally accessible, indubitable occurrence. ✓

Now that occurrence is also the subjective pole in the horizon he is
mediating. It determines its correlative objective pole, which like questioning is one and unrestricted. Its name is being; for being is one, since
every being *is*; and being is unrestricted, for apart from being there is
nothing. ✓

Now the determination of the two poles is the determination of a
horizon, and it is easy to see that Fr Coreth's horizon is total and basic.
It is total, for beyond being there is nothing. It is basic, for a total horizon
is basic; it cannot be transcended, gone beyond, and so it cannot be
revised.

But further, for Fr Coreth being is precisely what St Thomas meant
by being. For as intended in questioning, being is unrestricted. In that
premise there is already included the conclusion that *esse de se est illimitatum*, whence it will follow that finite being is a compound of essence
and existence and that every *ens* is an *ens* by its relations to *esse*.

From this it would seem to follow that being for Fr Coreth and being
for Prof. Gilson must be exactly the same. For Prof. Gilson also means
by being what St Thomas meant. It remains that this identification is
not without its difficulties, for if the objective pole in Fr Coreth's horizon
is the same as the objective pole in Prof. Gilson's, the subjective poles
are manifestly different.

Thus Fr Coreth would accept the principle, *Nihil in intellectu nisi prius
fuerit in sensu*. But he would have to distinguish, say, between the way
there is nothing in a box and the way there is nothing in a stomach.
When there is nothing in a box, a box does not feel empty; when there
is nothing in a stomach, the stomach does feel empty. Human intelligence
is more like a stomach than like a box. Though it has no answers, and
so is empty, still it can ask questions.

Further, for Prof. Gilson being (225) or the concept of being (215,
226) is 'seen' in the data of sense. But for Fr Coreth being is what is
asked about with respect to the data of sense. So far from being seen in
data, being for Fr Coreth is what is intended by going beyond the data.
For questioning goes beyond an already known to an unknown that is
to be known: for Fr Coreth the already known is the datum, and the
unknown to be known is being.

Again, for Prof. Gilson, our knowledge of being is a posteriori: abstract concepts of being and existence are had by abstracting from sense; and to reach the concrete there is added to the abstractions his intellectual vision. But for Fr Coreth, being is an a priori, i.e., the intention of being in questioning bears no resemblance to sensitive or empirical knowledge. What is perceived is not unknown, not to be known, but already known. But being as intended in questioning is the exact opposite of the object of perception: it is not already known; it is unknown; it is to be known. In other words, the analysis of questioning forces one to conceive human intelligence, not on the analogy of sense, but properly in terms of intelligence itself.

Moreover, we have seen that Fr Coreth rejects the idealist's acceptance of idealism as contradictory, that Prof. Gilson regards idealism as non-contradictory, that consequently he is left with a problem of a bridge from a concept of *l'être en général* to an *existence concrète, actuelle, extra-mentale*, and that, inevitably enough, this bridge has to be an intellectual perception of existence. This narrative, it would seem, enables us to pick the exact point at which Prof. Gilson and Fr Coreth part company. Both agree that idealism is noncontradictory. But where Fr Coreth maintains that the idealist's acceptance of idealism is contradictory, and so eliminates the problem of the bridge, Prof. Gilson acknowledges a problem of a bridge and so arrives at his need for an intellectual perception of being. Hence, being can be a priori for Fr Coreth, because for him the idealist is involved in self-contradiction; but being must be a posteriori for Prof. Gilson, because for him idealism is not self-contradictory.

Finally, there remains the question how Fr Coreth and Prof. Gilson both arrive at the same objective pole, being in the Thomist sense, when their subjective poles are mutually exclusive. The explanation would seem to be that, if Prof. Gilson does not thematize questioning, nonetheless he asks questions and so intends what is intended in questioning; further, while Prof. Gilson asserts an intellectual perception of existence, still he is careful to integrate this perception within the structure of Thomist cognitional theory, and so is able to shift from a theory of being as something seen in data to a theory of being as something affirmed in perceptual judgments of existence. Hence, inasmuch as Prof. Gilson asks questions and gives rational answers, his position coincides with that of Fr Coreth, and as the subjective poles are the same so the objective poles are the same. On the other hand, if Prof. Gilson were to operate simply and solely with a concept of being that can be 'seen' in any sensible datum, not only would his subjective pole differ from Fr Coreth's but also it would be impossible for him to reach being in the Thomist sense as his objective pole; for being as object of perception is being in which essence and existence are only notionally distinct. ✓

2.4 Kant, Gilson, Coreth

Fourthly, we have been comparing Kant, Prof. Gilson, and Fr Coreth two at a time; there remain a few questions that are best put with respect to all three at once.

First, then, despite his use of such terms as 'transcendental' and 'a priori,' Fr Coreth is completely in agreement with Prof. Gilson's contention that ' ... what is contradictory ... is wishing to pose the problem of critical idealism within the perspective of Thomist realism.'[12] Indeed, Fr Coreth excludes as impossible within his horizon not only critical idealism but any idealism and along with them Prof. Gilson's perceptionism. For him there can be no problem of the 'extramental,' of getting outside the mind, for as soon as a question is asked, being is intended, being includes everything, and so everything already is within the mind's intention: ' ... subjectivity in its very performance is already "outside" in the realm of being-in-itself in general.'[13]

Secondly, does Fr Coreth perceive being or does he not? I think his answer would be that (1) being is not known without perceptions, (2) being is not known by perceptions alone, and (3) by the light of intelligence we know whether or not what we perceive is. In other words, he would not say with Prof. Gilson that we know being by perceiving it; and he would say with St Thomas: ' ... what those words of Augustine mean is this, that we should not expect to derive truth entirely from the senses. We also need the light of agent intellect; through this we attain to unchangeable possession of truth about changeable things, and distinguish the things themselves from their likenesses.'[14]

Thirdly, Fr Coreth would agree with Prof. Gilson's statement: ' ... the

12 Ibid. 160–61: ' ... ce qui est contradictoire, ... c'est de vouloir poser le problème de l'idéalisme critique dans la perspective du réalisme thomiste.'
13 Coreth, *Metaphysik* 193: ' ... die Subjektivität in ihrem Vollzug immer schon "draussen" ist beim An-sich-Sein überhaupt.'
14 *Summa theologiae*, 1, q. 84, a. 6, ad 1m: ' ... per illa verba Augustini datur intelligi quod veritas non sit totaliter a sensibus exspectanda. Requiritur enim lumen intellectus agentis, per quod immutabiliter veritatem in rebus mutabilibus cognoscamus, et discernamus ipsas res a similitudinibus rerum.'

transcendental viewpoint of a priori conditions for the object of knowledge is ignorant by definition of the empirical problem of the existence
in themselves of the objects known.'[15] He would point out, however,
that Prof. Gilson is speaking of Kantian thought, and he would indicate
the two essential differences between his approach and Kant's. First, his
transcendental inquiry is, not into the a priori conditions of cognitional
objects, but into the a priori conditions of questions. Kant wrote an
Erkenntniskritik: the conditioned is the objective pole, the condition is the
subjective pole. Fr Coreth is writing a metaphysics: his subjective pole,
questioning, is the conditioned; and his objective pole, being, is the
condition. Hence, Fr Coreth's transcendental inquiry is just the inverse
of Kant's. Secondly, Kant's a priori is in the essentialist order, and so,
as we have seen, it is solely through *Anschauung* that it can have any
objective reference or any objective validity; further, since this *Anschauung* is not of noumena, there cannot arise within the Kantian approach any question of the *existence en soi* of the objects known in Kant's
world as appearance. But what follows from Kant's a priori does not
follow from Fr Coreth's. Fr Coreth's is being as unrestricted, the whole
of all that is; within being there is already included *An-sich-Sein*. Not only
does *An-sich-Sein* lie within Fr Coreth's transcendental viewpoint, but
also from that very fact it follows that Fr Coreth's treatment of objectivity
differs totally from Kant's and, indeed, from that of any perceptionist.
For Kant cognitional operations can be related to objects only through
Anschauung, so that perception has to be the constitutive principle of
objectivity. For Fr Coreth the constitutive principle of objectivity is the
question: questioning immediately intends being; data are referred to
being as what questions are about; answers are referred to being as
answers to questions. Fr Coreth's position on objectivity is the inverse
of the Kantian position; it also is the inverse of the perceptionist position,
which relates our cognitional operations to reality, not through the intention of being in the question, but through sense.

3   Position on Coreth

At the end of this attempt to locate Fr Coreth's position within the
scholastic context, I must note that my operation is not altogether in
accord with Fr Coreth's exclusion of an *Erkenntniskritik*, his aim of pre-

15 Gilson, *Réalisme thomiste* ... 177: ' ... le point de vue transcendental des
    conditions *a priori* de l'objet de connaissance ignore, par définition, le
    problème empirique de l'existence en soi des objets connus.'

suppositionless metaphysics,[k] his projected inclusion within metaphysics of an *Erkenntnismetaphysik*. The fact is, of course, that while I consider Fr Coreth's metaphysics a sound and brilliant achievement, I should not equate metaphysics with the total and basic horizon, the *Gesamt- und Grundwissenschaft*.[l] Metaphysics, as about being, equates with the objective pole of that horizon; but metaphysics, as science, does not equate with the subjective pole. In my opinion Fr Coreth's subjective pole is under a measure of abstraction that is quite legitimate when one is mediating the immediacy of latent metaphysics, but is to be removed when one is concerned with the total and basic horizon. In the concrete, the subjective pole is indeed the inquirer, but incarnate, liable to mythic consciousness, in need of a critique that reveals where the counterpositions come from. The incarnate inquirer develops in a development that is social and historical, that stamps the stages of scientific and philosophic progress with dates,[m] that is open to a theology that Karl Rahner has described as an *Aufhebung der Philosophie*. The critique, accordingly, has to issue in a transcendental doctrine of methods with the method of metaphysics just one among many and so considered from a total viewpoint. For latent in the performance of the incarnate inquirer not only is there a metaphysics that reveals the objective pole of the total horizon but also there is the method of performing which, thematized and made explicit, reveals the subjective pole in its full and proper stature. Still, it is difficult to disagree completely with Fr Coreth, for in my disagreement I am only agreeing with his view that what has come from Fr Maréchal is, not a set of fixed opinions, but a movement; indeed, I am only asking for a fuller sweep in the alternations of his dialectic of *Vollzug und Begriff*.

14

Cognitional Structure

Let me begin by expressing my appreciation and gratitude to *Continuum* for its hospitality, to Fr Crowe for his initiative[a] and organizational labors, to the contributors for their serious interest in my writings.

I had thought, when consenting to undertake the present task, that I might most usefully address myself to an effort to come to grips with the thought of the other contributors. But I was informed that that could not be arranged. There was, of course, no lack of devotion to dialogue. But there did exist the mysterious complexities of editing and publishing by a fixed date the labors of many authors. Into these mysteries I was not to attempt to penetrate. I was to sit down at once, select a topic, and write on it.

I have chosen cognitional structure[b] as my topic, partly because I regard it as basic, partly because greater clarity may be hoped for from an exposition that does not attempt to describe the ingredients that enter into the structure, and partly because I have been told that my view of human knowing as a dynamic structure has been pronounced excessively obscure.

1 Dynamic Structure

A whole, then, has parts. The whole is related to each of the parts, and each of the parts is related to the other parts and to the whole.

Not every whole is a structure. When one thinks of a whole, there may come to mind some conventional quantity or arbitrary collection whose parts are determined by an equally conventional or arbitrary division. In such a case, e.g., a gallon of milk, the closed set of relations between whole and parts will be a no less arbitrary jumble of arithmetic ratios. But it may also happen that the whole one thinks of is some highly organized product of nature or art. Then the set of internal relations[c] is of the greatest significance. Each part is what it is in virtue of its functional relations to other parts; there is no part that is not determined by the exigences of other parts; and the whole possesses a certain inevitability in its unity, so that the removal of any part would destroy the whole, and the addition of any further part would be ludicrous. Such a whole is a structure.

The parts of a whole may be things, bricks, timbers, glass, rubber, chrome. But the parts may also be activities, as in a song, a dance, a chorus, a symphony, a drama. Such a whole is dynamic materially. But dynamism may not be restricted to the parts. The whole itself may be self-assembling,[d] self-constituting; then it is formally dynamic. It is a dynamic structure.

2   Human Knowing as Dynamic Structure

Now human knowing involves many distinct and irreducible activities: seeing, hearing, smelling, touching, tasting, inquiring, imagining, understanding, conceiving, reflecting, weighing the evidence, judging.

No one of these activities, alone and by itself, may be named human knowing. An act of ocular vision may be perfect as ocular vision; yet if it occurs without any accompanying glimmer of understanding, it is mere gaping; and mere gaping, so far from being the beau ideal of human knowing, is just stupidity. As merely seeing is not human knowing, so for the same reason merely hearing, merely smelling, merely touching, merely tasting, may be parts, potential components, of human knowing, but they are not human knowing itself.

What is true of sense is no less true of understanding. Without the prior presentations of sense, there is nothing for a man to understand; and when there is nothing to be understood, there is no occurrence of understanding. Moreover, the combination of the operations of sense and of understanding does not suffice for human knowing. There must be added judging. To omit judgment is quite literally silly: it is only by judgment that there emerges a distinction between fact and fiction, logic and sophistry, philosophy and myth, history and legend, astronomy and astrology, chemistry and alchemy.

Nor can one place human knowing in judging to the exclusion of experience and understanding. To pass judgment on what one does not understand is, not human knowing, but human arrogance. To pass judgment independently of all experience is to set fact aside.

Human knowing, then, is not experience alone, not understanding alone, not judgment alone; it is not a combination of only experience and understanding, or of only experience and judgment, or of only understanding and judgment; finally, it is not something totally apart from experience, understanding, and judgment. Inevitably, one has to regard an instance of human knowing, not as this or that operation, but as a whole whose parts are operations. It is a structure and, indeed, a materially dynamic structure.

But human knowing is also formally dynamic. It is self-assembling, self-constituting. It puts itself together, one part summoning forth the next, till the whole is reached. And this occurs, not with the blindness of natural process,[e] but consciously, intelligently, rationally. Experience stimulates inquiry, and inquiry is intelligence bringing itself to act; it leads from experience through imagination to insight, and from insight to the concepts that combine in single objects both what has been grasped by insight and what in experience or imagination is relevant to the insight. In turn, concepts stimulate reflection, and reflection is the conscious exigence of rationality; it marshals the evidence and weighs it either to judge or else to doubt and so renew inquiry.

Such in briefest outline is what is meant by saying that human knowing is a dynamic structure. Let us briefly note its implications.

First, on the verbal level, it implies a distinction between 'knowing' in a loose or generic sense and 'knowing' in a strict and specific sense. Loosely, any cognitional activity may be named knowing; so one may speak of seeing, inquiring, understanding, thinking, weighing the evidence, judging, as each an instance of knowing. Strictly, one will distinguish animal, human, angelic, and divine knowing, and one will investigate what in each case is necessary and sufficient for an instance of knowing.

Secondly, the view that human knowing is a dynamic structure implies that human knowing is not some single operation or activity but, on the contrary, a whole whose parts are cognitional activities.

Thirdly, the parts of a structure are related to one another, not by similarity, but functionally. As in a motorcar the engine is not like the tires and the muffler is not like the differential, so too in human knowing, conceived as a dynamic structure, there is no reason to expect the several cognitional activities to resemble one another. It follows that a study of human knowing cannot safely follow the broad and downhill path of analogy. It will not do, for instance, to scrutinize ocular vision and then assume that other cognitional activities must be the same sort of thing. They may turn out to be quite different and so, if one is to proceed scientifically, each cognitional activity must be examined in and for itself and, no less, in its functional relations to other cognitional activities. This third conclusion brings us to the question of consciousness and self-knowledge, which calls for another section.

3   Consciousness and Self-knowledge

Where knowing is a structure, knowing knowing must be a reduplication of the structure. Thus if knowing is just looking, then knowing knowing will be looking at looking. But if knowing is a conjunction of experience, understanding, and judging, then knowing knowing has to be a conjunction of (1) experiencing experience, understanding and judging, (2) understanding one's experience of experience, understanding, and judging, and (3) judging one's understanding of experience, understanding, and judging to be correct.

On the latter view there follows at once a distinction between consciousness and self-knowledge.[f] Self-knowledge is the reduplicated structure: it is experience, understanding, and judging with respect to experience, understanding, and judging. Consciousness, on the other hand, is not knowing knowing but merely experience of knowing, experience, that is, of experiencing, of understanding, and of judging.

Secondly, it follows that all cognitional activities may be conscious yet none or only some may be known. So it is, in fact, that both acts of seeing and acts of understanding occur consciously, yet most people know what seeing is and most are mystified when asked what understanding is.

Thirdly, it follows that different cognitional activities are not equally accessible.[g] Experience is of the given. Experience of seeing is to be had only when one actually is seeing. Experience of insight is to be had only when one actually is having an insight. But one has only to open one's eyes and one will see; one has only to open and close one's eyes a number of times to alternate the experience of seeing and of not seeing. Insights, on the other hand, cannot be turned on and off in that fashion. To have an insight, one has to be in the process of learning or, at least, one has to reenact in oneself previous processes of learning. While that is not peculiarly difficult, it does require (1) the authenticity that is ready to get down to the elements of a subject, (2) close attention to instances of one's own understanding and, equally, one's failing to understand, and (3) the repeated use of personal experiments in which, at first, one is genuinely puzzled and then catches on.

Fourthly, because human knowing is a structure of different activities, experience of human knowing is qualitatively differentiated. When one is reflecting, weighing the evidence, judging, one is experiencing one's own rationality. When one is inquiring, understanding, conceiving, thinking, one is experiencing one's own intelligence. When one is seeing or hearing, touching or tasting, one is experiencing one's own sensitivity. Just as rationality is quite different from intelligence, so the experience of one's rationality is quite different from the experience of one's intelligence; and just as intelligence is quite different from sensitivity, so the experience of one's intelligence is quite different from the experience of one's sensitivity. Indeed, since consciousness is of the acting subject *qua* acting, the experience of one's rationality is identical with one's rationality bringing itself to act; the experience of one's intelligence is identical with one's bringing one's intelligence to act; and the experiencing of one's sensitivity is identical with one's sensitivity coming to act.

Fifthly, then, experience commonly is divided into external and internal. External experience is of sights and sounds, of odors and tastes, of the hot and cold, hard and soft, rough and smooth, wet and dry. Internal experience is of oneself and one's apprehensive and appetitive activities. Still, if the meaning of the distinction is clear, the usage of the adjectives, internal and external, calls for explanation. Strictly, only spatial objects are internal or external and, while external experience may be of spatial objects, it itself is not a spatial object and, still less, is internal experience. Accordingly, we must ask what is the original datum that has been expressed by a spatial metaphor;[h] and to that end we draw attention to different modes of presence.

There is material presence, in which no knowing is involved, and such is the presence of the statue in the courtyard. There is intentional presence, in which knowing is involved, and it is of two quite distinct kinds. There is the presence of the object to the subject, of the spectacle to the spectator; there is also the presence of the subject to himself, and this is not the presence of another object dividing his attention, of another spectacle distracting the spectator; it is presence in, as it were, another dimension, presence concomitant and correlative and opposite to the presence of the object. Objects are present by being attended to; but subjects are present as subjects, not by being attended to, but by attending. As the parade of objects marches by, spectators do not have to slip into the parade to become present to themselves; they have to be present to themselves for anything to be present to them; and they are present to themselves by the same watching that, as it were, at its other pole makes the parade present to them.

I have been attempting to describe the subject's presence to himself. But the reader, if he tries to find himself as subject, to reach back and, as it were, uncover his subjectivity, cannot succeed. Any such effort is introspecting, attending to the subject; and what is found is, not the subject as subject, but only the subject as object; it is the subject as subject that does the finding. To heighten one's presence to oneself, one does not introspect; one raises the level of one's activity.[i] If one sleeps and dreams, one is present to oneself as the frightened dreamer. If one wakes, one becomes present to oneself, not as moved but as moving, not as felt but as feeling, not as seen but as seeing. If one is puzzled and wonders and inquires, the empirical subject becomes an intellectual subject as well. If one reflects and considers the evidence, the empirical and intellectual subject becomes a rational subject, an incarnate reasonableness. If one deliberates and chooses, one has moved to the level of the rationally conscious, free, responsible subject that by his choices makes himself what he is to be and his world what it is to be.

Sixthly, does this many-leveled subject exist? Each man has to answer that question for himself. But I do not think that the answers are in doubt. Not even behaviorists claim that they are unaware whether or not they see or hear, taste or touch. Not even positivists preface their lectures and their books with the frank avowal that never in their lives did they have the experience of understanding anything whatever. Not even relativists claim that never in their lives did they have the experience of making a rational judgment. Not even determinists claim that never in their lives did they have the experience of making a responsible choice. There exist subjects that are empirically, intellectually, rationally, morally conscious. Not all know themselves as such, for consciousness is not human knowing but only a potential component in the structured whole that is human knowing. But all can know themselves as such, for they have only to attend to what they are already conscious of, and understand what they attend to, and pass judgment on the correctness of their understanding.

4   The Epistemological Theorem

At this point one may ask why knowing should result from the performance of such immanent activities as experiencing, understanding, and judging. This brings us to the epistemological theorem,[j] namely, that knowledge in the proper sense is knowledge of reality or, more fully, that knowledge is intrinsically objective, that objectivity is the intrinsic relation of knowing to being, and that being and reality are identical.

The intrinsic objectivity of human cognitional activity is its intentionality. Nor need this intentionality be inferred, for it is the dominant content of the dynamic structure that assembles and unites several activities into a single knowing of a single object. Human intelligence actively greets every content of experience with the perplexity, the wonder, the drive, the intention, that may be thematized by (but does not consist in) such questions as, What is it? Why is it so? Inquiry through insight issues forth in thought that, when scrutinized, becomes formulated in definitions, postulates, suppositions, hypotheses, theories. Thought in turn is actively greeted by human rationality with a reflective exigence that, when thematized, is expressed in such questions as, Is that so? Are you certain? All marshaling and weighing of evidence, all judging and doubting, are efforts to say of what is that it is and of what is not that it is not. Accordingly, the dynamic structure of human knowing intends being. That intention is unrestricted, for there is nothing that we cannot at least question. The same intention is comprehensive, for questioning probes every aspect of everything; its ultimate goal is the universe in its full concreteness. Being in that sense is identical with reality: as apart from being there is nothing, so apart from reality there is nothing; as being embraces the concrete totality of everything, so too does reality.

This intrinsic relation of the dynamic structure of human knowing to being and so to reality primarily is not *pensée pensée* but *pensée pensante,* not *intentio intenta* but *intentio intendens,* not νόημα but νόησις. It is the originating drive of human knowing. Consciously, intelligently, rationally it goes beyond: beyond data to intelligibility; beyond intelligibility to truth and through truth to being; and beyond known truth and being to the truth and being still to be known. But though it goes beyond, it does not leave behind. It goes beyond to add, and when it has added, it unites. It is the active principle that calls forth in turn our several cognitional activities and, as it assembles them into single instances of knowing, so it assembles their many partial objects into single total objects. By inquiry it moves us from sensing to understanding only to combine the sensed and understood into an object of thought. By reflection it moves us from objects of thought through rationally compelling evidence to judgments about reality. From the partial knowledge we have reached it sends us back to fuller experiencing, fuller understanding, broader and deeper judgments, for what it intends includes far more than we succeed in knowing. It is all-inclusive, but the knowing we achieve is always limited.

As answers stand to questions, so cognitional activities stand to the intention of being. But an answer is *to* a question, because it and the question have the same object. So it is that the intrinsic relation of the dynamic structure of human knowing passes from the side of the subject to the side of the object, that the *intentio intendens* of being becomes the *intentio intenta* of this or that being. So the question, What's this? promotes the datum of sense to a 'this' that has a 'what-ness' and 'is.' The promotion settles no issues, but it does raise issues. It is neither knowledge nor ignorance of essence and existence, but it is the intention of both. What the essence is and whether that essence exists are, not answers, but questions. Still, the questions have been raised, and the very fact of raising them settles what the answers will have to be about. The *intentio intendens* of the subject summons forth and unites cognitional activities to objectify itself in an *intentio intenta* that unites and is determined by the partial objects of the partial activities. As the *intentio intendens* of the dynamic structure, so the corresponding *intentio intenta* of the structured cognitional activities is intrinsically related to being and reality.

It remains that the two relations are not identical. The *intentio intendens* is not knowing but merely intending: it is objectivity in potency. But the *intentio intenta* resides not in mere intending but in structured activities of knowing: it is objectivity in act. Moreover, objectivity in act, because it resides not in a single operation but in a structured manifold of operations, is not some single property of human knowing but a compound of quite different properties. Empiricists have tried to find the ground of objectivity in experience, rationalists have tried to place it in necessity, idealists have had recourse to coherence. All are partly right and partly wrong, right in their affirmation, but mistaken in their exclusion. For the objectivity of human knowing is a triple cord; there is an experiential component that resides in the givenness of relevant data; there is a normative component that resides in the exigences of intelligence and rationality guiding the process of knowing from data to judging; there finally is an absolute component that is reached when reflective understanding combines the normative and the experiential elements into a virtually unconditioned, i.e., a conditioned whose conditions are fulfilled.

The objectivity of human knowing, then, rests upon an unrestricted intention and an unconditioned result. Because the intention is unrestricted, it is not restricted to the immanent content of knowing, to *Bewusstseinsinhalte*; at least, we can ask whether there is anything beyond that, and the mere fact that the question can be asked reveals that the intention which the question manifests is not limited by any principle of immanence. But answers are *to* questions, so that if questions are transcendent, so also must be the meaning of corresponding answers. If I am asked whether mice and men really exist, I am not answering the question when I talk about images of mice and men, concepts of mice and men, or the words, mice and men; I answer the question only if I affirm or deny the real existence of mice and men. Further, true answers express an unconditioned. Mice and men are contingent, and so their existence has its conditions. My knowing mice and men is contingent, and so my knowing of their existence has its conditions. But the conditions of the conditioned may be fulfilled, and then the conditioned is virtually an unconditioned; it has the properties of an unconditioned, not absolutely, but de facto. Because human knowing reaches such an unconditioned, it transcends itself. For the unconditioned *qua* unconditioned cannot be restricted, qualified, limited; and so we all distinguish sharply between what is and, on the other hand, what appears, what seems to be, what is imagined or thought or might possibly or probably be affirmed; in the latter cases the object is still tied down by relativity to the subject; in the former the self-transcendence of human knowing has come to its term; when we say that something is, we mean that its reality does not depend upon our cognitional activity.

The possibility of human knowing, then, is an unrestricted intention that intends the transcendent, and a process of self-transcendence that reaches it. The unrestricted intention directs the process to being; the attainment of the unconditioned reveals that at some point being has been reached. So, quite manifestly, a grasp of dynamic structure is essential to a grasp of the objectivity of our knowing. Without the dynamism one may speak of concepts of being, affirmations of being, even the idea of being; but unfailingly one overlooks the overarching intention of being which is neither concept nor affirmation nor idea.[1] Again, without the structure there is no place for three quite different elements of objectivity and no thought of a third resulting from a reflective understanding of the other two; yet the empiricists are right in their insistence on data, for in the givenness of data resides the experiential component of objectivity; there is something to the idealist insistence on coherence, for in the directive exigences of intelligence and rationality there resides the normative component of objectivity; and there is something to the rationalist insistence on necessity, for a conditioned whose conditions are fulfilled is virtually an unconditioned, and reflective understanding grasps such a virtually unconditioned whenever it finds the fulfilment of conditions in the data of sense or consciousness and, at the same time, derives from normative objectivity the link that binds conditions with conditioned.

5   Counterpositions Criticized

The alternative to distinguishing is confusion.[k] We have been engaged in distinguishing between human knowing and its component elements and between the objectivity of human knowing and the objectivity proper to different components in human knowing. When, however, the distinctions are not drawn, confusion easily if not inevitably occurs.

From the viewpoint of the validity of human knowing, such confusions may be divided into two classes that are dialectically related. The naive realist correctly asserts the validity of human knowing, but mistakenly attributes the objectivity of human knowing, not to human knowing, but to some component in human knowing. The idealist, on the other hand, correctly refutes the naive-realist claim that the whole objectivity of human knowing is found in some component of human knowing, but mistakenly concludes that human knowing does not yield valid knowledge of reality. The strength of the naive-realist position is its confidence in the validity of human knowing; its weakness is its inability to learn. On the other hand, the strength of the idealist position is the sharpness

---

1 By an 'idea' is meant the content of an act of understanding; hence the idea of being is the content of the act that understands being; as being is unrestricted, so the act must be unrestricted. The idea of being, then, is the divine essence *qua species intelligibilis* of divine understanding.

with which it refutes the mistaken claims of naive realists; its weakness is its inability to break completely with the confusions introduced by naive realism.

If theoretically this dialectical process could begin from any confusion, commonly its starting point is the myth that knowing is looking. Jack or Jill is invited to raise a hand and to look at it. The hand is really out there; it is the object. The eye, strangely, is not in the hand; it is some distance away in the head; it is the subject. The eye really sees the hand; it sees what is there to be seen; it does not see what is not there to be seen. That is objectivity.

Once the essence of objectivity has been grasped in this dramatic instance, there follow generalization and deduction. The generalization contains two elements, one positive, and the other negative. The positive element in the generalization is that any cognitional activity that sufficiently resembles ocular vision *must* be objective; for if it sufficiently resembles ocular vision, one can grasp the essence of objectivity in it no less than in ocular vision; and an activity that possesses the essence of objectivity *must* be objective. The negative element is that any cognitional activity that does not sufficiently resemble ocular vision *cannot* be objective; for it lacks what is essential to objectivity; of itself, therefore, any such activity is merely immanent; it may have some subordinate or derivative role to play in human knowing, particularly when knowing is not immediate but mediate; but from the nature of the case it can make no proper contribution to the objectivity of human knowing, for of itself it has nothing to contribute.

The positive and negative elements of the generalization provide a basis whence one can deduce what human knowing must be and what it cannot be. With such premises to hand, one does not have to bother too much about cognitional fact. The analogy of ocular vision reveals what intellectual activity must be like if it is objective; it must be like seeing. Even if introspection discovers no intellectual activity that resembles seeing, still some such activity really must exist; for if it did not, then our intellectual activity would be merely immanent, and idealism would be correct; but the conclusion is false, and therefore the premise must be false. Again, no serious difficulty arises from the fact that introspection brings to light intellectual activities that do not resemble seeing; it is true that such activities make no contribution of their own to the objectivity of human knowing; they are not constitutive of our immediate knowledge or our knowledge by acquaintance; but they can perform some useful function in the subordinate and derivative parts of our knowing, in our mediate knowledge or our knowledge by description. Just what these functions are, of course, is somewhat obscure; but we may with confidence look forward to the time when sound and sane study and research will have cleared up these extraordinarily difficult and complicated problems. In the meantime, however, we have complete certitude with regard to the essentials of the matter. Knowing, if objective, is like seeing. We know that we know, and so, in some analogous sense of the word, see, we see our knowing. We know the truth of our knowing; but truth is the correspondence of the knowing to the known; therefore, in some analogous sense of the word, see, we see the correspondence of our knowing to the known. Finally, science is of the universal; but scientific knowledge is at least possible; therefore, in some analogous sense of the word, see, we see universals.

The idealist is not impressed. He feels that the distinction between appearance and reality has been overlooked. By appearance he does not mean any illusion or hallucination. He means precisely what Jack or Jill really does see: the shape of an outstretched hand, its color, the lines that mark it, its position out there in front of the head. He is willing to add what Jack and Jill do not see: the feelings inside the hand and the conjunction in ordinary experience of the feelings with the visible object. All of that is not reality but appearance. And by reality he means what is meant by Jack, Jill, and the naive realist. Such is his thesis, and he argues as follows.

When I lift a lump of lead, I may report either that the lead is heavy or that the lead feels heavy. When I gaze out my window at a green field, I may report either that the field is green or that the field looks green. Such alternative reports are not equivalent. When I say 'is heavy' or 'is green,' I am using language that purports to report the real properties of real things. When I say 'feels heavy' or 'looks green,' I am not committing myself to any statement about the objective properties of things but, on the contrary, am limiting my statement to impressions made on me. Hence it is quite possible for one to say that, while he does not know whether or not the field really is green, at least it appears green to him. Knowledge of appearance, then, is one thing; and knowledge of reality is another.

Now what does Jack know when he looks at his hand? What does Jill know when she looks at hers? Two answers are possible, so Jack may say that his hand *is* out there in front of his face, and Jill may say that her hand at least *seems* to be out there in front of her face. Nor is the difference between the two answers difficult to detect. When Jack says 'is,' he is not reporting what he knows by sight alone; he also has made a judgment; he has added *Denken* to *Anschauen*. When Jill says 'seems,' she is limiting her report to what is known by sight alone; the act of reporting involves thought and judgment; but what is reported is simply and solely what is known by her seeing, the appearance of a hand in front of her face.

No less than the naive realist, the idealist is capable of generalization and deduction. As sight, so also hearing, smelling, tasting, touching are constitutive, not of knowledge of reality, but only of knowledge of appearances. What is true of outer sense also is true of inner sense: by our consciousness we know, not our reality, but only its appearance. Hence, when we inquire, understand, think, we have only appearances to investigate, to understand, to think about. When we judge, our judgments must be based, not on things themselves, but only on their appearance. There is no way in which knowledge of reality could creep into our cognitional operations. Hence all our statements must be modified with the qualification, 'as far as appearances go.' To say that men commonly do not add that qualification or that they are not ready to admit it even when its necessity is demonstrated, is just another way of saying that they suffer from a transcendental illusion.

As the idealist was not impressed by the naive realist, so the critical realist is impressed neither by the one nor by the other. Against the naive realist of the type in question he maintains that the essence of the objectivity of human knowing does not stand revealed in seeing or in any other single cognitional operation. His reason is simple: first, human knowing is not some single operation but a structure of several operations; secondly, the objectivity of human knowing is not some single property but a combination of distinct properties that reside severally in distinct operations. Further, he contends that intellectual operations are not similar to sensitive operations, that the objectivity of intellectual operations is not similar to the objectivity of sensitive operations, and that to demand similarity as an a priori condition of the possibility of objective intellectual operations is to demand that rational psychology be reduced to a *terra incognita*. Intellectual operations are related to sensitive operations, not by similarity, but by functional complementarity; and intellectual operations have their objectivity, not because they resemble ocular vision, but because they are what ocular vision never is, namely, intelligent and rational.

Against the idealist of the type in question the critical realist maintains that sense does not know appearances. It is just as much a matter of judgment to know that an object is not real but apparent, as it is to know that an object is not apparent but real. Sense does not know appearances, because sense alone is not human knowing, and because sense alone does not possess the full objectivity of human knowing. By our senses we are given, not appearance, not reality, but data. By our consciousness, which is not an inner sense, we are given, not appearance, not reality, but data. Further, while it is true enough that data of sense result in us from the action of external objects, it is not true that we know this by sense alone; we know it as we know anything else, by experiencing, understanding, and judging. Again, it is not true that it is from sense that our cognitional activities derive their immediate relationship to real objects; that relationship is immediate in the intention of being; it is mediate in the data of sense and in the data of consciousness inasmuch as the intention of being makes use of data in promoting cognitional process to knowledge of being; similarly, that relationship is mediate in understanding and thought and judgment, because these activities stand to the originating intention of being as answers stand to questions.

Finally, against both the naive realist and the idealist of the types in question, the critical realist urges the charge of picture thinking. Why does the naive realist ground objective knowledge of reality in looking, perceiving, *Anschauung*? Why does the idealist assert that it is by *Anschauung* that our cognitional activities have their immediate relationship to objects?[2] It is because their world is a picture world. If their world were the universe of being, they would agree that the original relationship of cognitional activity to the universe of being must lie in the intention of being. But their world is a picture world; the original relationship of cognitional activity to the picture is the look; and so it is in looking that the naive realist finds revealed the essence of objectivity, and it is in *Anschauung* that the critical idealist places the immediate relation of cognitional activity to objects. There exists, then, something like a for-

2 On *Anschauung* in Kant I may perhaps refer to my note in *Gregorianum* 44 (1963) 310–11. It was reprinted the following year in the spring issue of *The Current* (Harvard-Radcliffe Catholic Club), Vol. 5. [Lonergan is referring to paragraphs that appear on pp. 193–94 in this collection.]

getfulness of being. There exists in man a need for an intellectual conversion *ex umbris et imaginibus in veritatem.*

6   Knowing and Living

The forgetfulness of being, manifested by naive realists and idealists,[1] has brought about a semantic reversal. Subjectivity once was a pejorative term;[m] it denoted a violation of the normative exigences of intelligence and rationality. But it has come to denote a rejection of misconceived objectivity and a reaffirmation of man's right to be himself even though he cannot untie the hard and intricate knots of philosophy.

This new usage is not without its own myth, in which Jack and Jill are concerned, not with their hands, but with one another. They look, of course, but much more they talk. They are not merely objects, but also subjects: an 'I' and 'thou' that add up to the single personal total of 'us' talking about 'ourselves' and what 'we' have done and shall do.

Objectivity, as misconceived, is transcended. The problem of the bridge from 'in here' to 'out there' tends to vanish when the whole stress falls on the interpersonal situation,[n] the psychic interchange of mutual presence, the beginnings of what may prove to be a lifelong union.

Objectivity, as correctly conceived, is by no means rejected. For Jack and Jill are not characters out of a social worker's casebook. They are neither unperceptive, nor stupid, nor silly. If they were, acquaintance would not blossom into friendship, nor friendship into intimacy.

Still, this recognition of objectivity is only implicit, and, above all, it is not objective knowing but human living[o] that is the main point. To understand the myth, one has to move beyond strictly cognitional levels of empirical, intellectual, and rational consciousness to the more inclusive level of rational self-consciousness.[p] Though being and the good are coextensive, the subject moves to a further dimension of consciousness as his concern shifts from knowing being to realizing the good. Now there emerge freedom and responsibility, encounter and trust, communication and belief, choice and promise and fidelity. On this level subjects both constitute themselves and make their world. On this level men are responsible, individually, for the lives they lead and, collectively, for the world in which they lead them. It is in this collective responsibility for common or complementary action that resides the principal constituent of the collective subject referred to by 'we,' 'us,' 'ourselves,' 'ours.'

The condition of possibility of the collective subject is communication, and the principal communication is not saying what we know but showing what we are. To say what one knows presupposes the labor of coming to know. But to show what one is, it is enough to be it; showing will follow; every movement, every word, every deed, reveal what the subject is. They reveal it to others, and the others, in the self-revelation that is their response, obliquely reveal to the intelligent subject what he is. In the main it is not by introspection but by reflecting on our living in common with others that we come to know ourselves.

What is revealed? It is an original creation. Freely the subject makes himself what he is; never in this life is the making finished; always it is still in process, always it is a precarious achievement that can slip and fall and shatter. Concern with subjectivity, then, is concern with the intimate reality of man. It is concern, not with the universal truths that hold whether a man is asleep or awake, not with the interplay of natural factors and determinants, but with the perpetual novelty of self-constitution, of free choices making the chooser what he is.

Further aspects of the significance of subjectivity are endless, for the intimate reality of man grounds and penetrates all that is human. But the point to be made here is, not to go on insisting on this significance which, commonly enough, is recognized, but to draw attention to a real danger inherent in the semantic reversal that we have noted. For the danger is that the values of subjectivity in its more recent sense will be squandered by subjectivity in its prior and pejorative sense. Unless the two meanings are sharply distinguished, praise of subjectivity seems to imply a condemnation of objectivity. But condemnation of objectivity induces, not a merely incidental blind spot in one's vision, but a radical undermining of authentic human existence.

It is quite true that objective knowing is not yet authentic human living; but without objective knowing there is no authentic living; for one knows objectively just insofar as one is neither unperceptive, nor stupid, nor silly; and one does not live authentically inasmuch as one is either unperceptive or stupid or silly.

It is quite true that the subject communicates not by saying what he knows but by showing what he is, and it is no less true that subjects are confronted with themselves more effectively by being confronted with others than by solitary introspection. But such facts by themselves only ground a technique for managing people; and managing people is not treating them as persons. To treat them as persons one must know and one must invite them to know. A real exclusion of objective knowing, so far from promoting, only destroys personalist values.

It is quite true that concern for subjectivity promotes as much objective knowing as men commonly feel ready to absorb. Authentic living includes objective knowing, and far more eagerly do human beings strive for the whole than for the part. Nonetheless it remains that the authentic living of anyone reading this paper, though it must start at home, cannot remain confined within the horizons of the home, the workshop, the village. We are citizens of our countries, men of the twentieth century, members of a universal church. If any authenticity we achieve is to radiate out into our troubled world, we need much more objective knowing than men commonly feel ready to absorb.

Conclusion

To resume, I have attempted (1) to state what is meant by a dynamic structure, (2) to indicate that human knowing is a dynamic structure, (3) to reveal the difference between consciousness and self-knowledge, (4) to conclude that the objectivity of human knowing is, not a single property of a single operation, but a triad of properties found in distinct operations, (5) to contrast this view of objectivity with views derived from picture thinking, and (6) to add a note on the relations between the dynamic structure of objective knowing and the larger dynamic structure that is human living.

15

Existenz and Aggiornamento

To speak of *Existenz*, on being oneself,[a] is to speak in public about what is private, intimate, more intimate perhaps than one has explicitly conceived. Such existential speaking cannot be tidily tucked away into a category: at once it is psychological, sociological, historical, philosophic, theological, religious, ascetic, perhaps for some even mystical; but it is all of them because the person is all and involved in all.

At the same time, it is not personal in a merely individual sense: it is not exhibitionism on the part of the speaker; it is not exhortation, a domestic exhortation[b] in place of a lecture, for those that listen. It is what the Germans call a *Besinnung*,[c] a becoming aware, a growth in self-consciousness, a heightening of one's self-appropriation,[d] that is possible because our separate, unrevealed, hidden cores have a common circle of reference, the human community, and an ultimate point of reference, which is God, who is all in all, τὰ πάντα ἐν πᾶσιν ϑεός.[e]

1   The Subject[f]

1 The first distinction is between substance and subject.[g] When one is sound asleep, one is actually a substance and only potentially a subject. To be a subject, one at least must dream. But the dreamer is only the minimal subject: one is more a subject when one is awake, still more when one is actively intelligent, still more when one actively is reasonable, still more in one's deliberations and decisions when one actively is responsible and free.

Of the human substance it is true that human nature is always the same; a man is a man whether he is awake or asleep, young or old, sane or crazy, sober or drunk, a genius or a moron, a saint or a sinner. From the viewpoint of substance, those differences are merely accidental. But they are not accidental to the subject, for the subject is not an abstraction; he is a concrete reality, all of him, a being in the luminousness of being.

Substance prescinds from the difference between the opaque being that is merely substance and the luminous being[h] that is conscious. Subject denotes the luminous being.

2 The being of the subject is becoming. One becomes oneself. When I was a child, I was a subject; but I had not yet reached the use of reason; I was not expected to be able to draw reasonably the elementary distinctions between right and wrong, true and false. When I was a boy, I was a subject; but I was a minor; I had not reached the degree of freedom and responsibility that would make me accountable before the law. The self I am today is not numerically different from the self I was as a child or boy; yet it is qualitatively different. Were it not, you would not be listening to me. Were you yourselves not, I would not be talking to you in this way.

3 The subject has more and more to do with his own becoming. When an adult underestimates a child's development and tries to do for the child what the child can do for itself, the child will resent the interference and exclaim, 'Let me do it.' Development is a matter of increasing the number of things that one does for oneself, that one decides for oneself, that one finds out for oneself. Parents and teachers and professors and superiors let people do more and more for themselves, decide more and more for themselves, find out more and more for themselves.

4 There is a critical point in the increasing autonomy of the subject. It is reached when the subject finds out for himself that it is up to himself to decide what he is to make of himself.[i] At first sight doing for oneself, deciding for oneself, finding out for oneself, are busy with objects. But on reflection it appears that deeds, decisions, discoveries affect the subject more deeply than they affect the objects with which they are concerned. They accumulate as dispositions and habits of the subject; they determine him; they make him what he is and what he is to be.

The self in the first period makes itself; but in a second period this making oneself is open-eyed, deliberate. Autonomy decides what autonomy is to be.

The opposite to this open-eyed, deliberate self-control is drifting. The drifter has not yet found himself; he has not yet discovered his own deed, and so is content to do what everyone else is doing; he has not yet discovered his own will, and so he is content to choose what everyone else is choosing; he has not yet discovered a mind of his own, and so he is content to think and say what everyone else is thinking and saying; and the others too are apt to be drifters, each of them doing and choosing and thinking and saying what others happen to be doing, choosing, thinking, saying.

I have spoken of an opposite to drifting, of autonomy disposing of itself, of open-eyed, deliberate self-control. But I must not misrepresent. We do not know ourselves very well; we cannot chart the future; we cannot control our environment completely or the influences that work on us; we cannot explore our unconscious and preconscious mechanisms. Our course is in the night; our control is only rough and approximate; we have to believe and trust, to risk and dare.

5 In this life the critical point is never transcended. It is one thing to decide what one is to make of oneself: a Catholic, a religious, a Jesuit, a priest. It is another to execute the decision. Today's resolutions do not predetermine the free choice of tomorrow, of next week or next year, of ten years from now. What has been achieved is always precarious: it can slip, fall, shatter. What is to be achieved can be ever expanding, deepening. To meet one challenge is to effect a development that reveals a further and graver challenge.

2   One's World

As the subject develops, his world changes. Note the difference between 'his world' and 'the world'; 'the world' is what is there to be known, and that is unchanged by its being known. But the subject's world is correlative to the subject: it may be a world that is mostly fantasy; it may be the real world; but its *differentia* is that it is the world in which the subject actually lives and develops.

A first world is the world of immediacy: it is the world of the infant, the world of what is felt, touched, grasped, sucked, seen, heard; it is the world to which the adult returns when with an empty head he lies in the sun; it is the world of immediate experience, of the given as given, of image and affect without any perceptible intrusion from insight or concept, reflection or judgment, deliberation or choice; it is the world of pleasure and pain, hunger and thirst, food and drink, surrender, sex, and sleep.

A second world is the world mediated by meaning,[j] and it has two forms. Initially it is an extension of the world of immediacy, a revelation of a larger world than the nursery, that comes through pictures, speech, stories, that is of incredible extent and variety. But initiation into the world mediated by meaning gradually leads to the discovery of the difference between fact and fiction, between what is just a story and what really and truly is so. The necessity of that distinction reveals that the world mediated by meaning is not just the sum of all worlds of immediacy: the world of grownups, the world of literature and science, philosophy and history, religion and theology, is not a world apprehended by infantile procedures. It is a universe of being, that is known not just by experience but by the conjunction of experience, understanding, and judgment.

The difference between the world of immediacy and the world mediated by meaning is the source of the critical problem of philosophers.[k] The world mediated by meaning is for the naive realist just an abstraction. For the idealist it is the only world we know intelligently and rationally, and it is not real but ideal. For the critical realist[l] it is the world we know intelligently and rationally, and it is not ideal but real; the world of immediacy is only a fragment of the real world.

A third world is not only mediated but also constituted by meaning.[m] Language is constituted by meaning: it is not just articulated sound; it has to have meaning; and the meaning can be incorporated in print no less than in sound.

But not only language is constituted by meaning. Human acts have meaning in their constitution: they include acts of will; will is rational appetite, an appetite that follows intellect;[n] and what intellect knows, it knows by meaning, by asking and answering questions.

Human acts occur in sociocultural contexts; there is not only the action but also the human setup, the family and mores, the state and religion, the economy and technology, the law and education. None of these are mere products of nature: they have a determination from meaning; to change the meaning is to change the concrete setup. Hence there is a radical difference between the data of natural science and the data of human science. The physicist, chemist, biologist verifies his hypotheses in what is given just as it is given. The human scientist can verify only in data that besides being given have a meaning.[o] Physicists, chemists, engineers might enter a court of law, but after making all their measurements and calculations they could not declare that it was a court of law.

I have spoken of the self-constituting subject and his world. The two are correlative, not only by definition inasmuch as I have distinguished *the* world and *his* world, but also because the free and responsible self-constituting subject can exist only in a freely constituted world. The world of immediacy is not freely constituted; the world mediated by meaning is not freely constituted; but the world constituted by meaning, the properly human world, the world of community, is the product of freely self-constituting subjects. To exclude freedom is to exclude *Existenz*.[p] John XXIII affirmed that freedom is constitutive of human nature.

For what is community?[q] It is not just a number of men within a geographical frontier. It is an achievement of common meaning, and there are kinds and degrees of achievement. Common meaning is potential when there is a common field of experience, and to withdraw from that common field is to get out of touch. Common meaning is formal when there is common understanding, and one withdraws from that common understanding by misunderstanding, by incomprehension, by mutual incomprehension. Common meaning is actual inasmuch as there are common judgments, areas in which all affirm and deny in the same manner; and one withdraws from that common agreement when one disagrees, when one considers true what others hold false and false what they think true. Common meaning is realized by will, especially by permanent dedication, in the love that makes families, in the loyalty that makes states, in the faith that makes religions. Community coheres or divides, begins or ends, just where the common field of experience, common understanding, common judgment, common commitments begin and end.

The common meanings constitutive of communities are not the work of isolated individuals nor even of single generations. Common meanings have histories: they originate in single minds; they become common only through successful and widespread communication; they are transmitted to successive generations only through training and education. Slowly and gradually they are clarified, expressed, formulated, defined, only to be enriched and deepened and transformed, and no less often to be impoverished, emptied out, and deformed.

As it is only within communities that men are conceived and born and reared, so too it is only with respect to the available common meanings of community that the individual becomes himself. The choice of roles between which he can choose in electing what to make himself is no larger than the accepted meanings of the community admit; his capacities for effective initiative are limited to the potentialities of the community for rejuvenation, renewal, reform, development. At any time in any place what a given self can make of himself is some function of the heritage or sediment of common meanings that comes to him from the authentic or unauthentic living of his predecessors and his contemporaries.

3   Authenticity of the Subject and His World

The question of authenticity[r] is twofold: there is the minor authenticity of the subject with respect to the tradition that nourishes him; there is the major authenticity that justifies or condemns the tradition itself. The first passes a human judgment on subjects; the second is the judgment of history and ultimately the judgment of divine providence upon traditions.

As Kierkegaard asked whether he was a Christian, so divers men can ask themselves whether or not they are genuine Catholics or Protestants, Moslems or Buddhists, Platonists or Aristotelians, Kantians or Hegelians, artists or scientists, etc. They may answer that they are, and be correct in their answers. But they can also answer affirmatively and still be mistaken. In that case there will exist a series of points in which what they are coincides with what the ideals of the tradition demand, but there will be another series in which there is a greater or less divergence. These points of divergence are overlooked: whether from a selective inattention or a failure to understand or an undetected rationalization. What I am is one thing, what a genuine Buddhist is[s] happens to be another, and I am unaware of the difference. My unawareness is unexpressed; I have no language to express what I really am, so I use the language of the tradition I unauthentically appropriate, and thereby I devaluate, distort, water down, corrupt, that language.

Such devaluation, distortion, corruption, may occur only in scattered individuals. But it may occur on a more massive scale, and then the words are repeated but the meaning is gone. The chair is still the chair of Moses, but it is occupied by the scribes and Pharisees. The theology is still scholastic, but the scholasticism is decadent. The religious order still reads out the rules and studies the constitutions, but one doubts whether the home fires are still burning. The sacred name of science is still invoked, but one can ask with Edmund Husserl whether any significant scientific ideal remains, whether it has not been replaced by the conventions of a clique. Then the unauthenticity of individuals generates the unauthenticity of traditions. Then if the subject takes the tradition as it exists for his standard, he can do no more than authentically realize unauthenticity.

The word *aggiornamento*, minted by John XXIII and retained by Paul VI, is not entirely outside the range of the present reflections, for the problem set the church by the modern world is at once massive and profound. The modern world is in advance of its predecessors in its mathematics, its natural sciences, its technology, its history, its human sciences, its method of philosophy, and the wealth, variety, and penetration of its literary potentialities. It holds within its grasp what lay beyond the horizon, the comprehension, the capacity for expression, of Hebrew and Greek, Hellenistic and medieval, Renaissance and Reformation, Counter-Reformation and Enlightenment man. From that enormous development the church has held off: it could praise the ends; it could not accept the means; and so it could not authentically participate in the process that eliminated the standardized man of classicist thought and ushered in the historical consciousness[t] of today.

Modern man has created his states and his sciences, his philosophies and his histories, his cultures and his literatures, on the basis of absolute autonomy. There is human intelligence, human reasonableness, human responsibility, and that is all there is. To speak of God is at best irrelevant; to turn to God – except by way of political gesture or emotional outlet – is to sacrifice the good we know and by our own resources can attain.

Karl Jaspers repeats from Kierkegaard, or perhaps from Nietzsche, that unless I sinned, I could not be myself. The sin of modernity[u] is not any sin of frailty, any transient lapse, any lack of advertence or consent. It is the fully deliberate and permanently intended determination to be oneself, to attain the perfection proper to man, and to liberate humanity from the heavy hand of ecclesiastical tradition, ecclesiastical interference, ecclesiastical refusal to allow human beings to grow and be themselves.

The word *aggiornamento* has electrified the world, Catholic and non-

Catholic, because it seems to imply a rejection of classicism, a rejection of the view that human nature is always the same, a rejection of the view that any change is only an incidental modification introduced to meet a merely accidental difference in circumstances. It opens, or seems to open, the door to historical consciousness, to the awareness that men individually are responsible for their lives and collectively are responsible for the world in which they live them.

It would be a long and very complex task to list all the ways in which change – *aggiornamento* – is possible and permissible and desirable, and all the other ways in which it is not. To do so would be beyond the scope of the present discussion. The present question rather is what kind of men we have to be if we are to implement the *aggiornamento* that the Council decrees, if we are to discuss what future decrees are to be desired, if we are to do so without doing more harm than good, without projecting into the Catholic community and the world any unauthenticity we have imbibed from others or created on our own. In brief, we have to ask what it is for a Catholic, a religious, a priest, to be himself today. There is the modern secularist world with all its riches and all its potentialities. There is the possibility of despoiling the Egyptians. But that possibility will not be realized unless Catholics, religious, priests, exist, and exist not as drifters but creatively and authentically.

Being oneself is being, and by being is not meant the abstract but the concrete. It is not the universal concept, not nothing, of Scotus and Hegel, but the concrete goal intended in all inquiry and reflection. It is substance and subject: our opaque being that rises to consciousness and our conscious being by which we save or damn our souls. That conscious being is not an object, not part of the spectacle we contemplate, but the presence to himself of the spectator, the contemplator. It is not an object of introspection, but the prior presence that makes introspection possible. It is conscious, but that does not mean that properly it is known; it will be known only if we introspect, understand, reflect, and judge. It is one thing to feel blue, and another to advert to the fact that you are feeling blue. It is one thing to be in love, and another to discover that what has happened to you is that you have fallen in love. Being oneself is prior to knowing oneself. St Ignatius said that love shows itself more in deeds than in words; but being in love is neither deeds nor words; it is the prior conscious reality that words and, more securely, deeds reveal.

That prior opaque and luminous being is not static, fixed, determinate, once for all; it is precarious; and its being precarious is the possibility not only of a fall but also of fuller development. That development is open; the dynamism constitutive of our consciousness may be expressed in the imperatives, Be intelligent, Be reasonable, Be responsible;[v] and the imperatives are unrestricted – they regard every inquiry, every judgment, every decision and choice. Nor is the relevance of the imperatives restricted to the world of human experience, to the *mundus aspectabilis*; we are open to God. Implicit in human inquiry is a natural desire to know God by his essence; implicit in human judgment about contingent things there is the formally unconditioned that is God;[w] implicit in human choice of values is the absolute good that is God.

In Christ Jesus we are not only referred to God, as to some omega point, but we are on our way to God. The fount of our living is not *erôs* but *agapê*, not desire of an end that uses means but love of an end that overflows. As God did not create the world to obtain something for himself, but rather overflowed from love of the infinite to loving even the finite – *Deus suam gloriam non quaerit propter se, sed propter nos* (*Summa theologiae*, 2–2, q. 132, a. 1, ad 1m): the glory of the Father is the excellence of the Son, and the excellence of the Son is the excellence of the adoptive sons[x] – as Christ in his humanity did not will means to reach an end, but possessed the end, the vision of God, and overflowed in love to loving us, so too those in Christ participate in the charity of Christ: they love God *super omnia* and so can love their neighbors as themselves; they participate in that charity because they are temples of Christ's Spirit, members of his body, adopted children of the Father whom Christ could name *Abba*; the risen Lord, the *Kurios* of things invisible and visible, has bought them at a great price; he possesses them; [*Quicumque*] *Spiritu Dei aguntur, ii sunt filii Dei* [All who are led by the Spirit of God are sons of God (Romans 8.14)].

But this being in Christ Jesus may be the being of substance or of subject. Inasmuch as it is just the being of substance, it is known only through faith, through affirming true propositions, meditating on them, concluding from them,[y] making resolutions on the basis of them, winning over our psyches, our sensitive souls, to carrying out the resolutions through the cultivation of pious imagination and pious affects, and multiplying individual effort and strength through liturgical union. Inasmuch as it is just the being of substance, it is being in love with God without awareness of being in love. Without any experience of just how and why, one is in the state of grace or one recovers it, one leaves all things to follow Christ, one binds oneself by vows of poverty, chastity, and obedience, one gets through one's daily heavy dose of prayer, one longs for the priesthood and later lives by it. Quietly, imperceptibly, there goes forward the transformation operated by the *Kurios*, but the delicacy, the gentleness, the deftness, of his continual operation in us hides the operation from us.

But inasmuch as being in Christ Jesus is the being of subject, the hand of the Lord ceases to be hidden. In ways you all have experienced, in ways some have experienced more frequently or more intensely than others, in ways you still have to experience, and in ways none of us in this life will ever experience, the substance in Christ Jesus becomes the subject in Christ Jesus. For the love of God, being in love with God, can be as full and as dominant, as overwhelming and as lasting an experience as human love.[z]

Being in Christ Jesus is not tied down to place or time, culture or epoch. It is catholic with the catholicity of the Spirit of the Lord. Neither is it an abstraction that dwells apart from every place and time, every culture and epoch. It is identical with personal living, and personal living is always here and now, in a contemporary world of immediacy, a contemporary world mediated by meaning, a contemporary world not only mediated but also constituted by meaning.

In personal living the questions abstractly asked about the relations between nature and grace emerge concretely in one's concern, one's interests, one's hopes, one's plans, one's daring and timidity, one's taking risks and playing safe. And as they emerge concretely, so too they are solved concretely. Such concrete solutions, whether doing a job or exercising a personal role, divided from the viewpoint of the challenge to which Pope John XXIII initiated a response,[aa] may be solutions thought out in Christ Jesus for an archaic world that no longer exists or for a futurist world that never will exist;[bb] they may be thought out for the world that is now but only at the price of not being thought out in Christ Jesus; they may be for the world that is now and thought out in Christ Jesus.

Our time is a time for profound and far-reaching creativity. The Lord be with us all – *ad maiorem Dei gloriam*[cc] – and, as I have said, God's own glory, in part, is you.

16

Dimensions of Meaning

I   Meaning and the World of the Subject

My topic is meaning,[a] and at first sight at least it seems to be a very secondary affair. What counts is reality. What is of primary moment is, not the mere meaning, but the reality that is meant.

This contention is quite correct, quite true, as far as it goes. But it is involved, I think, in an oversight. For it overlooks the fact that human reality, the very stuff of human living, is not merely meant but in large measure constituted through acts of meaning. This, if you will bear with me, I now shall endeavor to explain.

Insofar as one is lost in dreamless sleep, or lies helpless in a coma, then meaning is no part of one's being. As long as one is an infant, etymologically a nontalker, one is busy learning to develop, differentiate, combine, group[b] in ever broader syntheses one's capacities for operation in the movements of head and mouth, neck and arms, eyes and hands, in mastering the intricacies of standing on one's feet, then of tottering from one spot to another. When first hearing and speech develop, they are directed to present objects, and so meaning initially is confined to a world of immediacy, to a world no bigger than the nursery, and seemingly no better known because it is not merely experienced but also meant. Then, to all appearances, it is quite correct to say that reality comes first and meaning is quite secondary.

But as the command and use of language develop, there comes a reversal of roles. For words denote not only what is present but also what is absent, not only what is near but also what is far, not only the past but also the future, not only the factual but also the possible, the ideal, the ought-to-be[c] for which we keep on striving though we never attain. So we come to live, not as the infant in a world of immediate experience, but in a far vaster world that is brought to us through the memories of other men, through the common sense of the community, through the pages of literature, through the labors of scholars, through the investigations of scientists, through the experience of saints, through the meditations of philosophers and theologians.

This larger world, mediated through meaning, does not lie within anyone's immediate experience. It is not even the sum, the integral, of the totality of all worlds of immediate experience. For meaning is an act that does not merely repeat but goes beyond experiencing. What is meant is not only experienced but also somehow understood and, commonly, also affirmed. It is this addition of understanding and judgment that makes possible the larger world mediated by meaning, that gives it its structure and its unity, that arranges it in an orderly whole of almost endless differences: partly known and familiar, partly in a surrounding penumbra of things we know about but have never examined or explored, partly in an unmeasured region of what we do not know at all. It is this larger world mediated by meaning that we refer to when we speak of the real world, and in it we live out our lives. It is this larger world mediated by meaning that we know to be insecure, because meaning is insecure, since besides truth there is error, besides fact there is fiction, besides honesty there is deceit, besides science there is myth.

Beyond the world we know about, there is the further world we make. But what we make we first intend. We imagine, we plan, we investigate possibilities, we weigh pros and cons, we enter into contracts, we have countless orders given and executed. From the beginning to the end of the process, we are engaged in acts of meaning; and without them the process would not occur or the end be achieved. The pioneers in this country found shore and heartland, mountains and plains, but they have covered it with cities, laced it with roads, exploited it with their industries, till the world man has made stands between us and a prior world of nature. Yet the whole of that added, manmade, artificial world is the cumulative, now planned, now chaotic product of human acts of meaning.

Man's making is not restricted to the transformation of nature, for there is also the transformation of man himself. It is most conspicuous, perhaps, in the educational process, in the difference between the child

beginning kindergarten and the doctoral candidate writing his dissertation. But the difference produced by the education of individuals is
only a recapitulation of the longer process of the education of mankind,
of the evolution of social institutions, and of the development of cultures.
Religions and art forms, languages and literatures, sciences, philosophies, the writing of history, all had their rude beginnings, slowly developed, reached their peak, perhaps went into decline and later underwent
a renaissance in another milieu. And what is true of cultural achievements, also, though less conspicuously, is true of social institutions. The
family, the state, the law, the economy, are not fixed and immutable
entities. They adapt to changing circumstance; they can be reconceived
in the light of new ideas; they can be subjected to revolutionary change.
Moreover – and this is my present point – all such change is in its essence
a change of meaning: a change of idea or concept, a change of judgment
or evaluation, a change of the order or the request. The state can be
changed by rewriting its constitution; more subtly but no less effectively
it can be changed by reinterpreting the constitution or, again, by working
on men's minds and hearts to change the objects that command their
respect, hold their allegiance, fire their loyalty. Community is a matter
of a common field of experience, a common mode of understanding, a
common measure of judgment, and a common consent. Such community
is the possibility, the source, the ground, of common meaning; and it is
this common meaning that is the form and act that finds expression in
family and polity, in the legal and economic system, in customary morals
and educational arrangements, in language and literature, art and religion,
philosophy, science, and the writing of history.

At this point, permit me to resume what I have been trying to say. I
have been meeting the objection that meaning is a merely secondary
affair, that what counts is the reality that is meant and not the mere
meaning that refers to it. My answer has been that the functions of
meaning are larger than the objection envisages. I would not dispute
that, for the child learning to talk, his little world of immediacy comes
first, and that the words he uses are only an added grace. But as the
child develops into a man, the world of immediacy shrinks into an in-
conspicuous and not too important corner of the real world, which is a
world we know only through the mediation of meaning. Further, there
is man's transformation of his environment, a transformation that is
effected through the intentional acts that envisage ends, select means,
secure collaborators, direct operations. Finally, besides the transforma-

tion of nature, there is man's transformation of man himself; and in this second transformation the role of meaning is not merely directive but also constitutive.

2   Control of Meaning

I might go on to enlarge upon the constitutive functions of meaning, and many profound themes might be touched upon. For it is in the field where meaning is constitutive that man's freedom reaches its high point. There too his responsibility is greatest. There there occurs the emergence of the existential subject, finding out for himself that he has to decide for himself what he is to make of himself. It is there that individuals become alienated from community, that communities split into factions, that cultures flower and decline, that historical causality exerts its sway.

But I propose to use the little that has been said and the much that I hope has been suggested merely as a springboard. I have been endeavoring to persuade you that meaning is an important part of human living. I wish now to add that reflection on meaning and the consequent control of meaning are still more important. For if social and cultural changes are, at root, changes in the meanings that are grasped and accepted, changes in the control of meaning mark off the great epochs in human history.[d]

2.1 Classical Control: Functioning and Breakdown

The classical expression of the effort to control meaning is found in the early Platonic dialogues. There Socrates is represented as putting very simple questions, listening patiently to answers, and invariably showing that none of the proffered answers was satisfactory. The questions were not abstruse. On the contrary they were of the type that anyone of average common sense, let alone any Athenian, would feel that he could answer. What is courage? What is self-control? What is justice? What is knowledge? After all, no one is going to say that he has no notion of the difference between courage and cowardice, or that he does not know what is meant by self-control, or that he has never been able to figure out what people mean by justice, or that knowledge and ignorance are all one to him. But if everyone naturally felt he could answer Socrates' questions, no one was able to give the kind of answer that Socrates wanted. For Socrates wanted universal definitions, brief and exact statements that fitted every case of courage and, at the same time, fitted nothing except courage; or that fitted every case of self-control and nothing but self-control; that applied to each and every instance of justice and only to justice.

Now, whatever the profundities of Platonism, at least we can all see for ourselves that Socrates carried out on the Athenians an experiment that bears on meaning. The result of the experiment was quite clear. There are at least two levels to meaning. There is the primary, spontaneous level, on which we employ everyday language. There is a secondary, reflexive level, on which we not merely employ but also say what we mean by everyday language. On the primary, spontaneous level, the Athenians were quite at home; they knew perfectly well the difference between courage and cowardice, between self-control and self-indulgence, between justice and injustice, between knowledge and ignorance; they were in no way inclined to confuse one with the other, or to get mixed up in their use of words. But paradoxically this did not enable them to proceed to the secondary, reflexive level, and work out satisfactory definitions of courage and self-control, of justice and knowledge. On the contrary, definition was a new idea; Socrates had to explain repeatedly what a definition was; again and again he would show that a good definition had to be *omni et soli*, had to apply to every instance of the defined and to no instance of something else. The Athenians understood what he meant, but they could not produce the definitions. Socrates himself knew what he meant, but he too could not produce the definitions. He was the wisest of men, according to the Delphic oracle, but the grounds for this accolade were ironical: he was the wisest because he at least knew that he did not know.

No doubt, you will want some better authority than the Delphic oracle before you will be convinced that Socrates was really wise. After all, is there any point to this mediation of meaning, this proceeding from a primary level on which we all know well enough what we mean, to a secondary level on which we discover that we have the greatest difficulty in saying what exactly we do mean? Does it not seem to be an idle waste of time, an excessive effort devoted to useless subtlety? At first sight, one might answer, 'Yes.' But on second thoughts, perhaps, one will say, 'No.' And there are very good grounds for adding second thoughts. Anthropologists[e] will assure you that primitive men are as intelligent and as reasonable as the rest of us in the practical affairs of life, in their hunting and fishing, in their sowing and reaping, in any activity from which there follow ascertainable and palpable results. Yet, despite their intelligence and reasonableness, it remains that all their activities and all their living are penetrated, surrounded, dominated by myth and magic.[f] Moreover, what is true of primitives also is true, though in a modified manner, of the ancient high civilizations, of Babylon, Egypt, and Crete, of the ancient settlements along the Indus and Hoang-ho, of the Incas and Mayas in South and Central America. In those civilizations large-scale enterprises were common: there were great works of irrigation, vast structures of stone or brick, armies and navies, complicated processes of bookkeeping, the beginnings of geometry, arithmetic, astronomy. The poverty and weakness of the primitive had been replaced by the wealth and power of the great state. The area over which man exercised his practical intelligence had been increased enormously. Yet myth and magic remained to penetrate, surround, dominate both the routine activities of daily life and the profound and secret aspirations of the human heart.

Now myth and magic are both instances of meaning. Myth is a declarative meaning; magic is an imperative meaning. But the declaration of myth is mistaken, and the command of magic is vain. Both have meaning, but the meaning is meaning gone astray. The prevalence, then, of myth and magic among primitives and its survival even in the ancient high civilizations reveal the importance of the Socratic enterprise. The mediation of meaning is not idle talk but a technique that puts an end to idle talk; it is not a vain subtlety but a cure for a malady to which all men are prone. Just as the earth, left to itself, can put forth creepers and shrubs, bushes and trees, with such excessive abundance that there results an impenetrable jungle, so too the human mind, led by imagination and affect and uncontrolled by any reflexive technique, luxuriates in a world of myth with its glories to be achieved and its evils banished by the charms of magic. So it is that in Western culture, for the past twenty-four centuries, the movement associated with the name of Socrates and the achievement of fourth-century Athens have been regarded as a high point, as a line of cleavage, as the breaking through of a radically new era in the history of man.

I have been repeating to you, in my own manner, something like the contention put forward by the German existentialist philosopher, Karl Jaspers, in his work, *The Origin and Goal of History*. According to Jaspers, there is an axis on which the whole of human history turns; that axis lies between the years 800 and 200 B.C.; during that period in Greece, in Israel, in Persia, in India, in China, man became of age; he set aside the dreams and fancies of childhood; he began to face the world as perhaps it is.

But if I have been repeating another's view, I have had an ulterior purpose that regards neither primitives nor Greeks but ourselves. For the Greek mediation of meaning resulted in classical culture and, by and large, classical culture has passed away. By and large, its canons of art, its literary forms, its rules of correct speech, its norms of interpretation, its ways of thought, its manner in philosophy, its notion of science, its concept of law, its moral standards, its methods of education, are no longer accepted. What breathed life and form into the civilization of Greece and Rome, what was born again in a European Renaissance, what provided the chrysalis whence issued modern languages and literatures, modern mathematics and science, modern philosophy and history, held its own right into the twentieth century; but today, nearly everywhere, it is dead and almost forgotten. Classical culture has given way to a modern culture, and, I would submit, the crisis of our age is in no small measure the fact that modern culture has not yet reached its maturity. The classical mediation of meaning has broken down; the breakdown has been effected by a whole array of new and more effective techniques; but their very multiplicity and complexity leave us bewildered, disorientated, confused, preyed upon by anxiety, dreading lest we fall victims to the up-to-date myth of ideology and the hypnotic, highly effective magic of thought control.

The clearest and neatest illustration of the breakdown of classical culture lies in the field of science. It is manifest, of course, that modern science understands far more things far more fully than did Greek or medieval science. But the point I would make is not quantitative but qualitative. The significant difference is not more knowledge or more adequate knowledge but the emergence of a quite different conception of science itself. The Greek conception was formulated by Aristotle in his *Posterior Analytics*; it envisaged science as true, certain knowledge of causal necessity. But modern science is not true; it is only on the way towards truth. It is not certain; for its positive affirmations it claims no more than probability. It is not knowledge but hypothesis, theory, system, the best available scientific opinion of the day. Its object is not necessity but verified possibility: bodies fall with a constant acceleration, but they could fall at a different rate; and similarly other natural laws aim at stating, not what cannot possibly be otherwise, but what in fact is so. Finally, while modern science speaks of causes, still it is not concerned with Aristotle's four causes of end, agent, matter, and form; its ultimate objective is to reach a complete explanation of all phenomena, and by such explanation is meant the determination of the terms and intelligible relationships that account for all data. So for each of the five elements constitutive of the Greek ideal of science, for truth, certainty, knowledge, necessity, and causality, the modern ideal substitutes something less arduous, something more accessible, something dynamic, something effective. Modern science works.

Now this shift in the very meaning of the word, science, affects the basic fabric of classical culture. If the object of Greek science was necessary, it also was obvious to the Greeks that in this world of ours there is very much that is not necessary but contingent. The Greek universe, accordingly, was a split universe: partly it was necessary and partly it was contingent. Moreover, this split in the object involved a corresponding split in the development of the human mind. As the universe was partly necessary and partly contingent, so man's mind was divided between science and opinion, theory and practice, wisdom and prudence. Insofar as the universe was necessary, it could be known scientifically; but insofar as it was contingent, it could be known only by opinion. Again, insofar as the universe was necessary, human operation could not change it; it could only contemplate it by theory; but insofar as the universe was contingent, there was a realm in which human operation could be effective; and that was the sphere of practice. Finally, insofar as the universe was necessary, it was possible for man to find ultimate and changeless foundations, and so philosophy was the pursuit of wisdom; but insofar as the universe was contingent, it was a realm of endless differences and variations that could not be subsumed under hard and fast rules; and to navigate on that chartless sea there was needed all the astuteness of prudence.

The modern ideal of science has no such implications. We do not contrast science and opinion; we speak of scientific opinion. We do not put theory and practice in separate compartments; on the contrary, our practice is the fruit of our theory, and our theory is orientated to practical achievement. We distinguish pure science and applied science, applied science and technology, technology and industry; but the distinctions are not separations, and, however great the differences between basic research and industrial activity, the two are linked by intermediate zones of investigation, discovery, invention. Finally, if contemporary philosophic issues are far too complex to be dealt with in the present context, as least we may say that philosophy has invaded the field of the concrete, the particular, and the contingent, of the existential subject's decisions and of the history of peoples, societies, and cultures; and this entry of philosophy into the realm of the existential and the historical not merely extends the role of philosophic wisdom into concrete living but also, by that very extension, curtails the functions formerly attributed to prudence.[8]

Nor it is only from above that prudence is curtailed: its province is also invaded from below. We do not trust the prudent man's memory, but keep files and records and develop systems of information retrieval. We do not trust the prudent man's ingenuity, but call in efficiency experts or set problems for operations research. We do not trust the prudent man's judgment, but employ computers to keep track of inventories and to forecast demand. We do not rely on the prudent man's broad experience, but conduct fact-finding surveys and compile statistics. There is as great a need as ever for memory and ingenuity, judgment and experience; but they have been supplemented by a host of devices and techniques, and so they operate on a different level and in a different mode; while the old-style prudent man, whom some cultural lag sends drifting through the twentieth century, commonly is known as a stuffed shirt.

2.2 Modern Control: Functioning and Problems

I have been indicating, very summarily, how a new notion of science has undermined and antiquated certain fundamental elements of classical culture. But besides the new notion itself, there is also its implementation. A new notion of science leads to a new science of man. Classically orientated science, from its very nature, concentrated on the essential to ignore the accidental, on the universal to ignore the particular, on the necessary to ignore the contingent. Man is a rational animal, composed of body and immortal soul, endowed with vital, sensitive, and intellectual powers, in need of habits and able to acquire them, free and responsible in his deliberations and decisions, subject to a natural law which, in accord with changing circumstances, is to be supplemented by positive laws enacted by duly constituted authority. I am very far from having exhausted the content of the classically orientated science of man, but enough has been said to indicate its style. It is limited to the essential, necessary, universal; it is so phrased as to hold for all men whether they are awake or asleep, infants or adults, morons or geniuses; it makes it abundantly plain that you can't change human nature; the multiplicity and variety, the developments and achievements, the breakdowns and catastrophes of human living, all have to be accidental, contingent, particular, and so have to lie outside the field of scientific interest as classically conceived. But modern science aims at the complete explanation of all phenomena, and so modern studies of man are interested in every human phenomenon. Not abstract man but, at least in principle, all the men of every time and place, all their thoughts and words and deeds, the accidental as well as the essential, the contingent as well as the necessary, the particular as well as the universal, are to be summoned before the bar of human understanding. If you object that such knowledge is unattainable, that the last day of general judgment cannot be anticipated, you will be answered that modern science is, not a ready-made achievement stored for all time in a great book, but an ongoing process that no library, let alone any single mind, is expected to encompass. And even though this ongoing process never can master all human phenomena, still by its complete openness, by its exclusion of every obscurantism, modern study of man can achieve ever so much more than the conventional limitations of classically orientated human studies permitted.

From the modern viewpoint classical culture appears as a somewhat arbitrary standardization of man. It distinguished the literal and the figurative meanings of words and phrases, and it conveyed more than a suggestion that literal meaning is somehow first, while figurative meaning is a dress or ornament that makes the literal meaning more striking, more vivid, more effective. Perhaps it was Giambattista Vico in his *Scienza nuova* that first put forward the contrary view by proclaiming the priority of poetry. In any case his contention is true in the sense already indicated: it is only through uncounted centuries of development that the human mind eventually succeeds in liberating itself from myth and magic, in distinguishing the literal truth from figurative expression, in taking its stand on what literally is so, and in rationalizing figures of speech by reducing them to the categories of classical rhetoric. But this achievement, if a necessary stage in the development of the human mind, easily obscures man's nature, constricts his spontaneity, saps his vitality, limits his freedom. To proclaim with Vico the priority of poetry[h] is to proclaim that the human spirit expresses itself in symbols before it knows, if ever it knows, what its symbols literally mean. It is to open the way to setting aside the classical definition of man as a rational animal and, instead, defining man with the cultural phenomenologists as a symbolic animal or with the personalists as an incarnate spirit.[i]

So the twentieth century has witnessed a rediscovery of myth, and the rediscovery has taken many forms. With Freud one may find in contemporary human living the terrifying figures of family relationships set forth in the Theban cycle of the Greek tragedians. With Jung one may plunge to the primal archetypes and the symbols of transformation attributed to a collective unconscious. With Ludwig Binswanger and Rollo May one may distinguish the dreams of night, occasioned by somatic disturbance, and the dreams of morning when the existential subject, not yet awake and himself, still is already busy with the project that shapes both him himself and his world. With Gilbert Durand one may explore the whole realm of everyday, omnipresent metaphor, and place this vast and complex manifold in a dialectical sequence by relating it to the three dominant reflexes connected with keeping one's balance, swallowing one's food, and mating. One may go on to explore the arts of Madison Avenue in democracies, or of the ministries of culture in totalitarian states. One can join the literary critics that articulate the psychic mechanisms underneath the glossy surface of poetry's immortal lines. One can turn to the liturgists and the historians of religions to search, with Mircea Eliade, for a crosscultural language that is prior to manmade languages and independent of them. One can read the Old Testament as a reinterpretation of the symbols of Babylon and Canaan and, with Paul Ricoeur, discern the dialectic in which older and less adequate symbols of guilt are complemented, corrected, modified, and still retained in combination with newer ones.

From the affect-laden images within us and from the many interpretations that illuminate them, one may turn outward to the phenomenology of intersubjectivity. Human communication is not the work of a soul hidden in some unlocated recess of a body and emitting signals in some Morse code. Soul and body are not two things but coprinciples in the constitution of a single thing. The bodily presence of another is the presence of the incarnate spirit of the other; and that incarnate spirit reveals itself to me by every shift of eyes, countenance, color, lips, voice, tone, fingers, hands, arms, stance. Such revelation is not an object to be apprehended. Rather it works immediately upon my subjectivity, to make me share the other's seriousness or vivacity, ease or embarrassment, joy or sorrow; and similarly my response affects his subjectivity, leads him on to say more, or quietly and imperceptibly rebuffs him, holds him off, closes the door.

As phenomenology explores the whole drama of our interpersonal relations, so too it takes its stand within us, within that volume (defined by the nude statue) of sensing, feeling, reaching, longing space which is a human body, to make thematic our perceiving, the preconceptual activities of our intellects, the vertical liberty[j] by which we may emerge out of prevoluntary and prepersonal process to become freely and responsibly, resolutely yet precariously, the persons we choose to be.

Still, what are we to choose to be? What are we to choose to make of ourselves? In our lives there still comes the moment of existential crisis when we find out for ourselves that we have to decide for ourselves what we by our own choices and decisions are to make of ourselves, but the psychologists and phenomenologists and existentialists have revealed to us our myriad potentialities without pointing out the tree of life, without unraveling the secret of good and evil. And when we turn from our mysterious interiority to the world about us for instruction, we are confronted with a similar multiplicity, an endless refinement, a great technical exactness, and an ultimate inconclusiveness.

When the educated, or the cultured, or the gentlemanly, or the saintly man was standardized by classical culture, then it was recognized that definitions were to be explained but not disputed. Today terms are still defined, but definitions are not unique: on the contrary, for each term there is a historical sequence of different definitions; there is a learned explanation for each change of definition; and there is no encouragement for the sanguine view that would exclude further developments in this changing series.

What is true of definitions is also true of doctrines. They exist, but they no longer enjoy the splendid isolation that compels their acceptance. We know their histories, the moment of their births, the course of their development, their interweaving, their moments of high synthesis, their periods of stagnation, decline, dissolution. We know the kind of subject to which they appeal and the kind they repel: Tell me what you think and I'll tell you why you think that way. But such endlessly erudite and subtle penetration generates detachment, relativism, scepticism. The spiritual atmosphere becomes too thin to support the life of man.

Shall we turn to authority? But even authorities are historical entities. It is easy enough to repeat what they said. It is a more complex task to say what they meant. There are indeed areas in which problems of interpretation do not occur. Euclid's *Elements* were written some twenty-three centuries ago, and, while one has to study to understand him, still, once one has understood, there exists no problem about his meaning. There is no hermeneutic literature on Euclid. But on Plato and Aristotle, on St Paul and St John, on Augustine and Aquinas, on Kant and Hegel, there are endless works of commentary, interpretation, exegesis, explanation; and there is no expectation that this stream will dry up, that a final word will be spoken.

In brief, the classical mediation of meaning has broken down. It is being replaced by a modern mediation of meaning that interprets our dreams and our symbols, that thematizes our wan smiles and limp gestures, that analyzes our minds and charts our souls, that takes the whole of human history for its kingdom to compare and relate languages and literatures, art forms and religions, family arrangements and customary morals, political, legal, educational, economic systems, sciences, philosophies, theologies, and histories. New books pour forth annually by the thousands; our libraries need ever more space. But the vast modern effort to understand meaning in all its manifestations has not been matched by a comparable effort in judging meaning. The effort to understand is the common task of unnumbered scientists and scholars. But judging and deciding are left to the individual, and he finds his plight desperate. There is far too much to be learnt before he could begin to judge. Yet judge he must and decide he must if he is to exist, if he is to be a man.

Conclusion

Many among you will find this picture too bleak. Many, especially, will point out that I have said nothing about the Catholic faith, Catholic philosophy, Catholic theology. On these, then, a word must be added.

The crisis, then, that I have been attempting to depict is a crisis not of faith but of culture. There has been no new revelation from on high to replace the revelation given through Christ Jesus. There has been written no new Bible, and there has been founded no new church, to link us with him. But Catholic philosophy and Catholic theology are matters, not merely of revelation and faith, but also of culture.[k] Both have been fully and deeply involved in classical culture. The breakdown of classical culture and, at last in our day, the manifest comprehensiveness and exclusiveness of modern culture confront Catholic philosophy and Catholic theology with the gravest problems, impose upon them mountainous tasks, invite them to Herculean labors. Indeed, once philosophy becomes existential[1] and historical, once it asks about man, not in the abstract, not as he would be in some state of pure nature, but as in fact he is here and now in all the concreteness of his living and dying, the very possibility of the old distinction between philosophy and theology vanishes. What is true of that distinction is true of others. What is true of distinctions also is true of each of the other techniques that mark the style and fashion the fabric of our cultural heritage. Classical culture cannot be jettisoned without being replaced; and what replaces it cannot but run counter to classical expectations. There is bound to be formed a solid right that is determined to live in a world that no longer exists. There is bound to be formed a scattered left, captivated by now this, now that new development, exploring now this and now that new possibility. But what will count is a perhaps not numerous center, big enough to be at home in both the old and the new, painstaking enough to work out one by one the transitions to be made, strong enough to refuse half measures and insist on complete solutions even though it has to wait.

Lexicon of Latin and Greek Words and Phrases

Shorter Latin Words and Phrases

(Translation here is generally rather literal. Words and phrases commonly found in English dictionaries – a priori, de facto, non sequitur, etc. – are not included.)

a pari: with equal force (used of an argument)
ab esse ad posse valet illatio: there is a valid inference from fact to possibility
actio: action, activity
actio est in passo: the activity is in the recipient
actio physica: physical action
activitas: activity, action
actus: act, activity, reality
actus essendi: the act of being, existing
actus huius ut ab hoc: an act of this being, inasmuch as it is from this being
actus per se apti ad prolis generationem: acts suited by their nature to generate offspring
actus specificantur per obiecta: acts are specified by their objects
actus specificantur per subiectum: acts are specified by their subject
ad maiorem Dei gloriam: to the greater glory of God
ad mentem divi Thomae: in conformity with the mind of St Thomas
agere: to act, activity
agere in virtute alterius: to act in the power of another
amor amicitiae: the love of friendship (i.e., of friends for one another)
amor concupiscentiae: the love of desire (i.e., the love that desires)
an sit? quid sit? is it? what is it?
analogia fidei: the analogy of faith

appetibile apprehensum movet appetitum: the desirable thing that is apprehended moves the appetite

appetitus tendit in bonum sibi conveniens: appetite is drawn to the good that
suits it (is proper to it)

argumenta convenientiae: arguments (based on what is) fitting

bonum est sui diffusivum: the good is creative of further good; see Lonergan
(chapter 2, 30): 'productive of further instances of the good'

causa, causae: cause, causes

causa/ratio cognoscendi, essendi: the cause/reason of knowing, of being

Christus ut Deus, ut homo: Christ as God, as man

civitas terrena: the earthly city (realm)

cognitio: knowledge

cognoscere: to know, knowing

cognoscere minus proprie: knowing, less properly so called

cognoscere proprie: knowing, properly so called

cognoscere sub ratione experti: to know under the aspect of (attaining) the
experienced

concursus immediatus: immediate union in acting (co-activity)

concursus simultaneus: simultaneous union in acting

conscientia: consciousness

conscientia-experientia: consciousness as experience

conscientia-perceptio: consciousness as perception

Constitutio de fide catholica: Constitution on the Catholic Faith

contingens ut in maiori parte: happening for the most part

contingens ut in minori parte: happening less often

corpus caeleste: heavenly body

crede ut intelligas: believe that you may understand

cuius gratia: that for the sake of which

Deus est subiectum huius scientiae: God is the subject of this science

Deus operatur in omni operatione naturae et voluntatis: God is active in
every activity of nature and of will

Deus suam gloriam non quaerit propter se, sed propter nos: God seeks the
divine glory, not on account of the divine self, but on our account

dictum de omni et nullo: 'what is true of a class of objects is true of all the
members of that class' [thus, Lonergan (chapter 1, 13); but the phrase is not
literally translatable]

differentia: (specific) difference

dimidium animae suae: the very half of his/her soul

divina, humana: divine things, human things
donum intellectus: the gift of understanding
donum sapientiae: the gift of wisdom

elevans: elevating (grace)
ens: being (i.e., a being)
ens per essentiam: being whose essence is being
entia per participationem: beings that participate in being
eo ipso: by that very fact
esse: to be, being
esse de se est illimitatum: being of itself is unlimited
est: it is
eundem perfectum in humanitate: the same (one) perfect in humanity
eundemque perfectum in deitate: and the same (one) perfect in deity
ex hypothesi: by hypothesis
ex simplici voluntate ... ex ordine etiam aliarum causarum: (depending) simply on the will (of God) ... (depending) also on a concatenation of other causes
ex umbris et imaginibus in veritatem: out of shadows and figures into the truth
exercite et non signate: present in performance but not made thematic
excusatio matrimonii et copulae: a reason excusing marriage and sexual intercourse

finis operantis: the end of the one acting; Lonergan (chapter 2, 28 note 34): 'motive'
finis operis: the end of the work/act/thing; Lonergan (chapter 2, 28): 'objective ordination'
finis qui: the end which (attracts)
finis quo: the mode in which the end (attracts);   Lonergan (chapter 2, 19): 'the mode of motivation or termination.'
forma fluens: a fluid form

gratia elevans: elevating grace
gratia sanans: healing grace
gratia unionis: the grace of union

hoc ad quod opus ordinatum est ab agente: that to which the work is directed by the one acting
honestum remedium concupiscentiae: the 'virtuous remedy for concupiscence' (Lonergan, chapter 2, 49)

humana, divina: human things, divine things

id a quo: that from which
id quod habet partes extra partes: that which has parts lying outside parts
id quod intenditur: that which is intended
ignoratio elenchi: ignorance of (the point of) the argument
immediatio suppositi: the immediacy of contact (between agent and recipient)
immediatio virtutis: the immediacy of power (power extending through a means to the recipient)
in aliis: in other things
in genere rerum intelligibilium ut ens in potentia tantum: (a thing that) in the genus of intelligible entities is like pure potency (in material entities)
in maiori parte, in minori parte: [see **contingens ut in ...**]
intellectus actu: actually understood (said of the object); the intellect in act (said of the faculty)
intellectus fidei: understanding of the faith
intellectus mysteriorum: understanding of mysteries
intellectus possibilis: intellect as receiving
intelligentia indivisibilium: understanding of simple (non-composite) beings
intelligentia mysteriorum: understanding of mysteries
intelligere: to understand, understanding
intelligere est pati: to understand is to receive (an effect)
intelligibile actu: actually intelligible
intendere: to intend, intending
intendi: to be intended, being intended
intentio entis intendens: intending intention of being
intentio intendens: intending intention
intentio intenta: intended intention
intus legere: to penetrate ('read' within)
ipsum agere: activity itself
ipsum esse: being itself
ipsum intelligere: understanding itself [**ipsum agere, ipsum esse, ipsum intelligere** may be used of God, but may also be used in a finite sense when the meaning is simply reflexive]
is qui intendit: the one who intends

lumen gloriae: light of glory

media in quibus: the mediating realities in which
mens: mind
minus proprie: less properly (speaking)
modus significandi: the mode of signifying

motor immobilis: immovable mover
motus: motion, change, activity
motus est in mobili: the motion (change) is in the changed entity
mundus aspectabilis: the visible world, universe
mutuum auxilium: 'mutual aid' (Lonergan, chapter 2, 49)

natura pura: pure nature
nexus mysteriorum inter se: the connection of the mysteries with one another
nihil aliud ... quam complacentia boni: nothing else than satisfaction with the good
nihil in intellectu nisi prius fuerit in sensu: there is nothing in the intellect unless it was first in sense
nihil in natura frustra: nothing in nature is in vain
nihil prius aut posterius: nothing prior or subsequent
nisus: striving

omni et soli: (applicable) to all instances and to them alone; Lonergan (chapter 16, 236): 'to every instance of the defined and to no instance of something else'
omnia: all things
omnia appetunt Deum: all things desire God
omnia intendunt assimilari Deo: all things have as their objective to become like God
omnia simul: all things at once
operatio: operation
ordo disciplinae: order of teaching, of presentation
ordo doctrinae: order of doctrine, teaching, presentation
ordo executionis, ordo intentionis: order of execution, order of intention
ordo inventionis: order of discovery
ordo universi: the order of the universe

per accidens, per se: (occurring) by chance, (occurring) as a rule
per omnia nobis similem absque peccato: like us in everything, (but) without sin
perceptio: perception
persona unionis: the person of the union
potentia activa: active potency
potentia agendi: power to act
potentia passiva: passive potency
praemotio physica: physical premotion
praestantia ontologica formae: the ontological superiority of the form
principia quibus: principles by which
principium quo: principle by which

principium quod: principle which
priora quoad nos: the things that are first in regard to us
priora quoad se: the things that are first in themselves
procedere: to proceed (from)
proprie: properly (speaking)
propter quid: that on account of which (i.e., the explanatory cause)

qua fideles: insofar as (they are) believers
quaestio, quaestiones: question, questions
quaestiones annexae: questions connected (with the main subject)
qui, quo: see **finis qui, finis quo**
quia sunt: that they are
quicumque Spiritu Dei aguntur, ii sunt filii Dei: whoever are led by the Spirit of God are the children of God
quid est? what is it?
quid sint? what are they? what might they be?
quid sit? what is it? what might it be?
quid sit Deus, ens, homo? what is (might be) God, being, man?
quidditas: the essence, quiddity (whatness)
quidditas rei materialis: the essence of a material thing
quidditas sive natura in materia corporali existens: an essence or nature existing in corporeal matter
quidditative: quidditatively, essentially
quo est omnia fieri: (that) by which it is (possible for us) to become all things
quoad exercitium actus: as regards the exercise of the activity
quoad nos, quoad se: in regard to us, in regard to themselves
quod gratis asseritur, gratis negatur: what is arbitrarily asserted may be arbitrarily denied
quod quid erat esse: what a thing was to be [the Ross translation of Aristotle has simply 'the essence']

ratio: reason (the reason for, the explanatory cause)
ratio/causa cognoscendi, essendi: the reason/cause of knowing, of being
recentiores: the more recent (writers)
relatio relationis est ens rationis: the relation of a relation is (not a real entity but) an entity of the mind (only)

sanans: healing (grace)
scientia: knowledge, science
scientia beata, infusa, acquisita: beatific, infused, acquired knowledge
scientia subalternata: a science subordinate (to another science)
secundum: according to

secundum abstractam mentis considerationem: according to the abstract consideration of the mind

secundum quid: from a particular viewpoint, according to some aspect

sensa: things sensed

sensibile actu: actually sensible (able to be sensed)

sensibilia propria: things that can be sensed in the proper meaning of the term, sensed

sensus actu: actually sensed

sensus auctoris: the meaning of the author

separatio a mensa et thoro: separation from bed and board (literally: table and bed)

simpliciter: simply (not from some particular viewpoint)

sistitur in primo: a halt is called at the first step

solubilia argumenta: solvable arguments

solvitur ambulando: the solution is found in the doing (i.e., by walking)

species: species, form

status quaestionis: state of the question

sub ratione entis: under the formal aspect of being

sub ratione entis, quidditatis, et veri: under the formal aspect of being, of essence, and of truth

sub ratione entis vel quidditatis: under the formal aspect of being or of essence

sub ratione experti: under the formal aspect of the experienced

sub ratione sub qua attingitur: under that aspect which the activity specifically regards

subiectum actu: actually a subject

super omnia: above all things

syllogismus faciens scire: a syllogism bringing knowledge to birth (making to know)

terra incognita: unknown land

totius vitae communio, consuetudo, societas: sharing, familiarity, companionship in the whole of life

unumquodque cognoscitur secundum quod est actu: everything (that is known) is known insofar as it actually is

unumquodque cognoscitur secundum quod est obiectum: everything (that is known) is known insofar as it is an object

utrum sit: whether it is

veritas logica consistit in adaequatione intellectus ad rem: logical truth consists in the correspondence of intellect to reality

veritas logica est formaliter in solo iudicio: logical truth is formally found only in the judgment

verum: the true, truth

vetera novis augere et perficere: to add to and perfect the old by means of the new

via affirmationis, negationis, et eminentiae: the way of affirmation, of negation, of eminence

via / ordo disciplinae, doctrinae: the order of teaching, doctrine, presentation

via / ordo inventionis: the order of discovery

'video meliora proboque ...': 'I see the better things and I approve of them (but) ...'

virtus divina creata: divine created power

virtus dormitiva: soporific influence

voluntas mota et non movens: a will that is moved but does not move (does not act causally)

Greek Words and Phrases

αἴτιον τοῦ εἶναι: the cause of (a thing) being (i.e., the cause that a thing is)

εἶδος: form

ἐνέργεια: 'operation' (Lonergan, 1967b: 102)

κοινωνία: community

νόημα: the understood (object)

νόησις: (the act of) understanding

συλλογισμὸς επιστημονικός: 'explanatory syllogism' (Lonergan, chapter 8, 118)

τὰ μὲν οὖν εἴδη τὸ νοητικὸν ἐν τοῖς φαντάσμασι νοεῖ: understanding grasps the intelligibles in (by insight into) phantasms

τὰ πάντα ἐν πᾶσιν θεός: God (is) all in all

τὸ τί ἦν εἶναι: the essence, what a thing was to be (*quod quid erat esse*)

Editorial Notes

The purpose of these notes is limited in many ways, three of which may be worth mentioning.

Their immediate reference is to Lonergan alone; they would illuminate his meaning through data on his history, on the context in which he wrote, on parallel or contrasting points made in his other writings. The purpose is not then encyclopedic. A simple example will show the difference. There is no note in chapter 1 on Porphyry's tree; important though that notion be for students of logic, they can look it up in standard encyclopedias. There *is* a note on Broadcast Bounty, which is of no importance whatever in the general history of thought, but is illuminating for the direction in which Lonergan's thought was moving at the time of this essay.

Secondly, the notes only here and there include references to materials in the Lonergan Archives. These references were suggested to me by Robert M. Doran, who has begun a computerized catalogue of the Archives papers. I consider it important to include them, as a means of alerting readers to the wealth of data available in these papers; but it will take decades to exploit that wealth, and meanwhile I make such notes as occur to me from my own study of Lonergan.

A third limitation is due to the early appearance of this volume in the set of Collected Works. When the set is complete, and an index to the complete set compiled, many of these notes will become superfluous. We therefore locate them at the end of the volume, allowing for their easy omission from later editions of Lonergan's own writings. The same limitation applies to the brief Index of Notes I have added, and to the list of Works Referred To. Need I say that the latter is not a bibliography, nor does the reference code I used correspond to that of the definitive bibliography that will appear in the Index volume of the Collected Works.

At the end of each note there is a number in square brackets; this refers the reader to the page of the text where the superscript for the note is to be found. References in these notes to *Collection*, unless otherwise stated, will be to pages of the present volume rather than to the 1967 edition.

1   The Form of Inference

'The Form of Inference' was published first in *Thought* (a Fordham University Quarterly) 18 (1943) 277–92. Lonergan was already making a name for himself with his articles in *Theological Studies* on the Thomist concept of operative grace, so it was understandable that the editors of *Thought* should ask him for a contribution, but perhaps puzzling that he should respond with an article on logic. The puzzle, however, evaporates on acquaintance with a previous history which can, at least partly, be documented.

When Lonergan was a philosophy student at Heythrop College, England (1926–29), he wrote several times for the student publication, *Blandyke Papers*. ('Publication' here means simply that the author, having had his article duly refereed, copied it by hand into a notebook which was left in a common room for perusal by the college 'public.')

Lonergan's first contribution, 'The Form of Mathematical Inference,' appeared in the January issue of 1928, and shows a remarkable grasp already of the idea he would characterize nearly twenty years later as 'insight into phantasm' (1946a: 372; 1967b: 25). The real forerunner, however, of the article in *Thought* was 'The Syllogism,' which was first read before the student Philosophy and Literature Society, Feb. 26, 1927, and published a year later in the *Blandyke Papers*, March 1928, 33–64.

This article, considerably rewritten, is surely the one that appeared fifteen years later in *Thought*, but there is also an intervening history that can be cautiously surmised. It is clear that the young Lonergan had a keen interest in logic; in particular, as he has more than once declared, he had made a close study of H.W.B. Joseph's *Introduction to Logic* (1974: 38, 263, 276). Further, we have found, scattered through the Lonergan Archives, seven legal-size pages which Lonergan had used as scrap paper but which clearly are pages 2, and 6 to 11, of an essay in the field of logic, and just as clearly belong in series with the essays of 1928 and 1943.

Now these 'Logic Fragments' (to give them a name) can be dated with considerable probability between 1933 and 1940. For one thing, the example of the 'stump orator ... [who] proposes his panacea for the depression' (10) puts the fragment in the period when 'the depression' was a stock phrase, and with some probability before the period when the war had made the phrase less of a writer's stock-in-trade. Further, there is an interesting change, for an example of a woman statesman, from Elizabeth in the 'Logic Fragments' (11) to Maria Teresa in the published article (14 in this volume). Now there is reliable hearsay that the essay in *Thought* had been written earlier, offered for publication and rejected, and then pulled out of the files on the request of *Thought* for a contribution. It is at least plausible, then, that Lonergan had offered the essay to an English editor, had had it returned, and later retouched it for an American readership. The likely period for this intermediate essay would be during his theology studies, 1933–37, when we know from his letters that he was expecting to specialize in philosophy, his ideas were proliferating, and he was putting them on paper with abandon.

The original publication divided the text by numbers, presumably Lonergan's own. We have retained the numbers, except for the Conclusion (Lonergan's number 5), but have added subtitles.

RELATED WRITINGS

'The Form of Mathematical Inference,' 1928a; 'The Syllogism,' 1928b; 'Mathematical Logic,' 1957c. For the relation of logic to Lonergan's wider cognitional theory, consult the indices (Logic; and cognate words) of *Insight: A Study of Human Understanding*, 1957a; *Method in Theology*, 1972; *A Second Collection*, 1974; *Understanding and Being*, 1980.

NOTES

a **Mr Joseph's thorough *Introduction to Logic***: the article in *Thought* uses the second edition of Joseph's book (1916, reprinted 1925, 1931, and again 1946, 1950, 1957); the references in the *Blandyke Papers* (1928a, 134; 1928b, 34 and passim) do not correspond to the second edition, but presumably to the first (1906). The 'Logic Fragments' also speak (9) of 'Mr Joseph's fine analysis of syllogism.' [3]

b **Newman ... the ... illative sense**: Newman had a profound influence on Lonergan, who as a student 'went through the main parts of ... *Grammar of Assent* six times' (1974: 38; see 263: 'I ... read several times the more theoretical passages'), and in particular likened the 'illative sense' to his own 'reflective understanding' (1967b: 47; 1974: 263, 273; 1980: 133, 318; see also 48 in this volume). [3]

c **a cumulation of probabilities – too manifold to be marshaled, too fleeting to be formulated**: compare J.H. Newman, *An Essay in Aid of a Grammar of Assent* (London: Longmans, Green and Co., 1930) 288, 'the cumulation of probabilities ... too fine to avail separately, too subtle and circuitous to be convertible into syllogisms.' [3]

d **Is the human mind a Noah's ark ...?**: the same image recurs later in the volume, but in another context, with Lonergan doubting 'that Plato's ideas are in the divine mind pretty much as the animals were in Noah's ark' (85 note 75). [4]

e **symbolism**: at this time Lonergan's chief interest in symbols regarded their fertile relation to the act of insight (96, 104–105; see also note *g* to chapter 6 below, on 'the symbolic image'); that interest endures in the book, *Insight* (1957a: 17–19) and in lectures on *Insight* (1980: 30–32); but other aspects, connected with myth and mystery, are also coming into focus at that time (1957a: chapter 17). [5]

f **the square root of 1764**: a favorite example of Lonergan's (1957a: 17), one he uses also when he would demonstrate the difference between merely following a mathematical rule of thumb and understanding the operation (1980: 64–65). [5]

g **Broadcast Bounty, Inc.**: in 1943 Lonergan was deep into his analysis of economics and drew examples from that field to a degree not found in either 'The Syllogism' of 1928 or the (intermediate?) 'Logic Fragments'; other examples are capitalists (11), employers (11), savings (13, 14), and property (13, 14). [7]

h **inductive conclusions**: whether at this time induction was a special problem to Lonergan is not clear to me; certainly, by the time he wrote *Insight*, he had found 'the transition ... from a particular case to the general case an almost automatic procedure of intelligence' (1957a: 288; see also 301). [16]

i **sensa**: this could be simply a typographical error for 'sense,' but it could also be an anglicizing of the Latin plural, on the analogy of 'data' three lines before ('from data through hypothesis to verified theory ... from sensa through intellection to judgment'); there may be an influence here from a phrase he used in the *Blandyke Papers*: 'resolutio facta ad sensum' (1928a: 127). So we leave the word as we found it. Incidentally, Lonergan later tended to avoid the term, intellection, finding it too much associated with a cognitional theory he opposed. [16]

j **a first step in working out an empirical theory of human understanding and knowledge**: how small a step it was may be judged from the two great steps of the *verbum* articles (1967b) and the book, *Insight* (1957a). [16]

2   Finality, Love, Marriage

'Finality, Love, Marriage' was first published in *Theological Studies* 4 (1943) 477–510, a journal then recently established at Woodstock College, Maryland, and the outlet two years earlier for Lonergan's series on operative grace in

St Thomas. Again, the choice of topic might puzzle the reader, but again also there is a history to explain the choice. Lonergan was during this time on the theology faculty at the College of the Immaculate Conception in Montreal, and in the year 1941–42 was assigned to teach a course on marriage (repeated in 1944–45). This course was the occasion, presumably, for his review of Dietrich von Hildebrand's *Marriage* in *The Canadian Register* (1942b). The review in turn provoked a little correspondence, and we have two letters of Lonergan from the exchange (1942c; 1942d). Further, his doctoral dissertation (1971) had familiarized him with the work on grace of H. Doms, to whose study of marriage he refers at the beginning of this article.

The topic was therefore one on which Lonergan had been working directly or indirectly – and working, as we should expect, at the most fundamental levels of thought. This article is, in fact, a mini-*Summa* of theology: a theology of creation in its outline of nature, civilization, and grace; a theology of history in its analysis of human process; a theology of culture and religion in its study of life, the good life, and eternal life; and, finally, in the context of all this, a theology of marriage. The real puzzle is not so much Lonergan's choice of topic, but the neglect of theologians to study his contribution, and mine the riches buried here.

At Lonergan's suggestion the editor of the 1967 volume made several verbal changes in the text of 1943; these have been retained in the present volume. The quotations from scripture seem to follow the Douai translation, but with variations that are perhaps Lonergan's own. The four main subtitles are those of the 1943 publication; further subtitles and all the numbers have been supplied by the present editors.

RELATED WRITINGS

Review of Dietrich von Hildebrand's *Marriage*, in *The Canadian Register* (Quebec edition), May 23, 1942, p. 5. Letter, ibid., June 6, p. 9. Letter, ibid., June 20, p. 9. There are also in the Archives unpublished materials of great interest for the present question. One item is a manila folder entitled 'De Matrimonio 1945' (Batch 2, Folder 37, in the preliminary cataloguing). It contains, among other things, nearly a hundred pages, mostly typed, that deal with the same questions as this chapter; it almost certainly pertains to the courses Lonergan taught on marriage, Montreal, 1941–42 and 1944–45. Another item is a sheaf of ten typed pages in a folder entitled 'Eucharistia' (Batch 2, Folder 33). It too deals with many of the questions of this chapter, and seems to belong to Folder 37 rather than to 33. – The special interest here of both these items is their relation to the notion of vertical finality, which Lonergan seems to have been working out during these years.

NOTES

a **Fr Ford**: Rev. John C. Ford, s.j., was for many years professor of moral theology at Weston College, seminary of the New England Province of Jesuits. He took account of 'Finality, Love, Marriage' in his 'Notes on Moral Theology, 1944,' in *Theological Studies* 5 (1944) 530–31, and voiced some 'strictures' (Lonergan's word to me on suggesting that I read Ford) on the position of the article. [18]

b **vertical finality**: an idea with a long and important history in Lonergan's work. Years later he wrote: 'On vertical finality see my papers, "Finality, Love, Marriage" and "The Natural Desire to See God." ' This remark is found in 'Mission and the Spirit' (1985: 33), and that article goes on from vertical finality to speak of emergent probability, referring the reader for that notion to the book, *Insight* (1957a). 'The Natural Desire to See God' is chapter 5 in the present volume. See also my notes on Dynamic; Open and intellectualist. [19]

c **Lennerz**: Rev. Heinrich Lennerz, s.j., was a professor at the Gregorian University in Rome while Lonergan was a student there, a theologian to whom he would later refer with considerable respect in his own professorial work. See also his word of thanks to Fr Lennerz in the Preface to his doctoral dissertation (1985a: 9). [20 note 10]

d **the notional distinction between *finis qui* and *finis quo***: on the previous page Lonergan speaks of the formal constituent of an end, 'the good as cause,' and adds that 'with regard to the formal constituent itself it is necessary to distinguish between *qui* and *quo*, between the good thing which is motive or term and the mode of motivation or termination.' All reality, he goes on, 'responds to God as absolute motive and tends to him as absolute term; but on each level it does so differently ... [according to] the mode of ... response, of ... orientation.' This distinction, which seems to be Lonergan's own, recurs in his later work, *De ente supernaturali*; there it is applied to the complex rational operations of the virtues, which attain God: *qui, obiectum quod*, but do so rationally: *obiectum quo* (1946b and 1973a: thesis 3a). [20]

e **the mists of Aristotelian science**: this phrase points to an ambivalence in Lonergan's relationship with Aristotle. First of all, his interest developed only slowly, going from Plato to Augustine to Aquinas and then to Aristotle (see also note *t* below). There is evidence indeed in the *Blandyke Papers* of a certain disdain for the latter (1928a: 128; 1928b: 34). But even when his appreciation had developed, perhaps through the influence of Aquinas, he seems to have distinguished three headings: (1) the content of Aristotle's science, (2) Aristotle's notion of what science is, and (3) Aristotle's great discovery of the act of insight. Lonergan's remark here on 'mists' refers to the content of the science; later in this volume (238) and increasingly as time goes on (1974: Index, under Aristotle; Modern) he will criticize the Aristotelian notion of science; but he will not criticize Aristotelian insight, which he is just now beginning to exploit in his *verbum* studies (1967b: 25–33), or the Aristotelian wonder which, he agrees, is the origin of all science and philosophy – as it is, likewise, of insight. [21]

f **organic evolution within limited ranges**: Lonergan's early views on evolution will have to be studied from the Archives, but the guarded language here may be a concession to the anti-evolution mentality still prevalent among Roman Catholics in 1943; see also the remark later in this chapter (43) on the 'measure of truth' in the theory of evolution. Lonergan's own theory, which will be worked out very thoroughly a decade later (1957a: Index, under Emergent Probability), is already forecast in his references here to modern statistical law and chance variation (22, note 16, and 85 – the latter locus a brief reference to biological evolution). [22]

g **obedientially**: a technical term to refer, for example, to the 'obedience' by which stones would, at God's command, become children of Abraham; see the reference later in the chapter (36) to obediential potency. Lonergan will analyze this notion in his *De ente supernaturali* (1973a: Thesis 4a); see also chapter 5 in the present volume. [22]

h **love**: this analysis acquires exceptional importance in hindsight from Lonergan's later work (1972: Index, under Love), where he regularly refers to the three types – religious love, domestic love, love of nation and humankind; but Lonergan never returned to the extended analysis he undertakes here. [23]

i **the complexity of the concrete**: there is a distinct evolution in Lonergan's thinking as he added scholarship to science, moving from focus on the universal and necessary to inclusion of the particular and concrete (1972: chapters on Interpretation, History), but the problem had existed earlier for him in regard to love and the good – see also in this volume his 'concrete and dynamic notion of the good' (108, and note *a* to chapter 7). Of course, even his necessary and universal science began with insight into 'this' image, 'these' data, that is, with the universal in the particular (1967b: 30, 151–52 and passim). See my notes on Historical consciousness; 'This.' [23]

j **For any activity is ... the act of a faculty**: Lonergan continued to use the language of 'faculty psychology' well into the 1960s, though in fact his approach as early as *Insight* had become that of intentionality analysis; see his remarks in *A Second Collection* (1974: 223, 277). [23]

k **friendship**: Lonergan's independent thinking will run more to terms like 'community'; see my note on that word (also 1972: Index). [25]

l **selfishness**: this account of selfishness may be incorporated into the later

idea, self-realization through self-transcendence, mentioned in The
Subject of 1968 (1974: 70, 75) and a regular theme of *Method* (1972:
Index, under Self-transcendence). [25]

m **idealism of ... aspiration ... sorry facts of ... performance**: to be related
to the moral impotence that figures so largely in Lonergan's theology
of divine grace (1971: Index, under Impotency; 1957a: 627–30); the
idea recurs in this volume (186–87). [26]

n **dialectical ... aspect of this tension**': an early reference to that notion of
dialectic which will become such a key term in Lonergan's developing
thought – see *Insight* (1957a: Index) and *Method* (1972: Index). Dialectic
had already figured in an important way in Lonergan's doctoral dissertation (1985a: 20–21), though only a trace of this appears in its original
publication (1971: 7). [26]

o **pseudorealist**: pseudorealism is to be distinguished from naive realism;
the latter is an epistemological term, the former is connected with the
rationalization of moral delinquency. See the remarks in this volume
(110) on " 'realist" views, in which theory is adjusted to practice and
practice means whatever happens to be done.' For Lonergan's own
epistemological realism see, also in this volume, the chapter on Cognitional Structure. [28]

p ***bonum est sui diffusivum***: the good spreads itself around, is creative of
other instances of the good – a principle deriving from Dionysius the
Areopagite and often quoted by Thomas Aquinas. [34]

q **great republic of culture**: to be related to the idea, set forth later in this
volume, of cosmopolis or 'cultural community' (109; see also 1957a:
Index, under Cosmopolis). Notice that 'organistic spontaneity' and 'mutual esteem and mutual good will' correspond well enough to the first
two terms of Lonergan's triad of 'life, the good life, and eternal life.'
But 'the great republic of culture' does not correspond exactly to the
'eternal viewpoint' he has just mentioned; perhaps, however, as a trans-
historical aspect of the good life, it provides an analogate for the eternal
viewpoint. [39]

r **what is prior *quoad se* is posterior *quoad nos***: a familiar principle in
Lonergan, related to his own pair, explanation and description (1957a:
Index, under Description), and applied to our knowledge of God in
'Theology and Understanding' (chapter 8 of this volume; see especially
117–27) and to knowledge of soul in '*Insight*: Preface to a Discussion'
(chapter 10 of this volume; see 143–44). The pair will later be identified
with the realms of theory and common sense, and then they turn out
to be only two of the realms Lonergan's differentiations of consciousness
will generate: 'Where we distinguish four realms of meaning, namely,
common sense, theory, interiority, and transcendence, an older theology

distinguished only two, common sense and theory, under the Aristotelian designation of the *priora quoad nos* and *priora quoad se'* (1972: 258). [45]

s **ordination of intercourse to conception ... a statistical law**: a principle that would assume great importance in Roman Catholic debates following the papal encyclical *Humanae vitae* a quarter of a century later. [46 note 73]

t **Augustine's 'Fecisti nos ad te, Domine ...'**: Thou hast made us for thyself, O Lord, and our hearts are restless till they rest in thee. Lonergan's interest in Augustine preceded his interest in Aquinas (1974: 38, 264–65), and he returned to an Augustinian emphasis in later life (for example, 1972: 39), but his relation to Augustine has been little studied. The developing complexity of his relation to Aquinas may be studied in his papers, 'The Future of Thomism' (1974: 43–53), and 'Aquinas Today: Tradition and Innovation' (1985b: 35–54). A revealing light on the relations he saw among his three great teachers (Aristotle, Augustine, and Aquinas) may be found in the Introduction to the *Verbum* book (1967b: vii–xv); it was written fifteen years after the publication of the original studies. [49]

u **the theorem of the supernatural**: a key concept in Lonergan's early theology of divine grace (1971: 13–19), and not abandoned later (1974: 131), though among other theologians the distinction of natural and supernatural was falling into disfavor.

v *natura pura*: a mental construct which, as Henri de Lubac was then engaged in demonstrating, theologians tended to turn into a distorting reality; Lonergan's views are set forth in chapter 5 of the present volume. [50 note 80]

w **virginity**: Lonergan's traditional position on virginity is not likely to find favor today, but I believe he would continue to uphold it. It is, however, to be understood in the context of his pluralism, which is even more applicable to vocations than to doctrines. The illuminating context is that of the realms and stages of meaning: 'religious expression will move through the stages of meaning and speak in its different realms ... Eastern religion stressed religious experience. Semitic religion stressed prophetic monotheism. Western religion cultivated the realm of transcendence through its churches and liturgies, its celibate clergy, its religious orders, congregations, confraternities' (1972: 114). [51]

x A note at the end of the article of 1943 ran as follows: 'In accordance with the author's wish, it is planned to make this article the starting point of a discussion, with a view to clarifying and developing its contribution to the theory of marriage. Comments from readers are invited. – EDITOR.' But on March 29, 1944, the Holy Office ruled as inadmissible

the opinion of recent writers who either denied that the generation
and education of children was the primary end of marriage, or taught
that secondary ends were not essentially subordinate to the primary. This
put an effective damper on discussion of the questions raised by Prof.
Doms and, as far as I know, the editor's suggestion was never followed
up. [52]

3   On God and Secondary Causes

This chapter of *Collection* was originally a book review, published therefore
without title, in *Theological Studies* 7 (1946) 602–13, as a study of Eduardo
Iglesias, *De Deo in operatione naturae vel voluntatis operante.* But since a good
part of the review is straightforward exposition of Lonergan's own views on
mediate causality, views that entered deeply into his work on the theology
of grace, it seemed worthy of inclusion in *Collection*, and I was able to bring
Lonergan to agree. The review appears now with the title I gave it in *Collection*.
All subtitles and their numbers are the work of the editors of the present
volume.

RELATED WRITINGS

Lonergan's interest in reviewing the Iglesias book was undoubtedly sparked
by its affinity to his own doctoral work, his study of operative grace in Thomas
Aquinas, rewritten and published in a series of articles a few years previously.
See especially the chapters (in the later book publication) on St Thomas'
Theory of Operation, and on Divine Transcendence and Human Liberty
(1971: chapters 4 and 5); sections of the review also relate to the chapter on
Habitual Grace as *Operans* and *Cooperans* (1971: chapter 3). Further, the expos-
itory part of the review is closely related to, is in fact little more than a translation of, a section of *De ente supernaturali*, Scholion III to Thesis 4a (1973a:
49–53), entitled 'De concursu divino'; this work was produced for his students
when Lonergan taught a course on divine grace in Montreal (fall semester,
1946). Finally, I may note a review Lonergan did of another book by Iglesias,
De Deo creationis finem exsequente, in *Theological Studies* 13 (1952) 439–41. Some
of the points made in 1946 are briefly repeated there. (The book itself, published in 1951, does not seem to take account of the 1946 review; at least it
does not list Lonergan in its index.)

NOTES

a   **the Thomist doctrine, *Deus operatur in omni operatione naturae et vol-
     untatis*:** God is active in every activity of nature and of will; I have not

found this statement verbatim in Aquinas, but the doctrine is surely his; see the *Indices ... occurrentium in Summa theologiae et in Summa contra gentiles ... extractum ex Tomo* XVI *editionis leoninae* (Rome: Apud Sedem Commissionis Leoninae, 1948), Index elementorum, under Deus – operatio. [53]

b **Stufler's position**: Rev. Johann Baptist Stufler, S.J., was for many years a professor of theology at Innsbruck. His work, especially the book, *Gott der erste Beweger aller Dinge* (Innsbruck, 1936), had come in for considerable criticism in Lonergan's doctoral dissertation (1971: Index, Stufler). [53]

c **mediate causality ... mediate cause**: these terms can cause confusion; 'mediate cause' is apt to be identified with 'intermediate cause,' but 'mediate causality' in Lonergan's use is not so much intermediate causality as it is the property of a cause that uses a mediating agent; thus, mediate causality is not saved if there is no influx from A to C, it is saved and increased if C depends more on A than on B – clearly, mediate causality is predicated of A, the first in the causal series, when A uses B as an intermediate cause. [54]

d **Durandus, Molina, and Bañez**: the same trio appear in *De ente supernaturali* (1973a: 50); for Lonergan's general views on Molina see his article, 'Molina, Luis de,' in the 14th edition of *Encyclopaedia Britannica* (1965c: 667–68). [54]

e **conditioned**: Lonergan uses this word in two contexts, which need to be distinguished here: that of the 'merely accidental series' and that of 'the proper causal series.' In the accidental series of Abraham, Isaac, and Jacob, Abraham is a condition but not a cause of Jacob, the conditioned. In the proper causal series of Lonergan, typewriter key, and paragraph, the typewriter key is also conditioned; but it is Lonergan's instrument, and is a cause of the paragraph when Lonergan applies it to its operation. Now Lonergan need not be the cause of the typewriter key, but when God uses an instrument, the case is different: God not only applies the created cause to its operation, but is also cause (and creator) of the cause.

On the metaphysical notion of application, see Lonergan's work on divine grace (1971: 72–80); for the empirical side of this metaphysical analysis, see his study of emergent probability (1957a: Index, under Emergent). [56]

f *Sistitur in primo*: freely rendered, the buck stops here – at the very start of the causal or logical series. [57]

g **'relatio relationis est ens rationis'**: the relation of a relation is (not a real entity but) an entity of the mind (only). [57]

h **either Thomist or Thomistic views**: Lonergan, as he will explain three

years later, uses 'Thomist' for what is of Thomas, 'Thomistic' for what
is of the school of Thomas (1967b: 142, note 6). [60]

i **Avicenna had combined neo-Platonist emanationism with Aristotelian
cosmic theory**: both of Lonergan's major Thomist studies contain references to Avicenna (1971: Index; 1967b: Index), but the pertinent source
for the present question is a collection of unpublished notes Lonergan
made in his dissertation research; there is a series on Aristotle's Hierarchy, Avicenna's Hierarchy, Hierarchy in St Thomas, and Systematiza-
tion of Hierarchy. The second in this series is only one page but begins
with the statement, 'Avicenna combines a Plotinian emanationism with
Aristotelian cosmic theory and Ptolemaic astronomy' (Lonergan
Archives). [61]

j *concursus immediatus*: immediate concurrence, in the sense of immediate
co-activity; Lonergan regularly left '*concursus*' in Latin, perhaps because
the English 'concurring' is so readily understood of agreement of minds
rather than of metaphysical cooperation in actions. [61]

k *voluntas mota et non movens*: the will as moved (by another agent) and
not (yet) exercising any causality of its own; it was important in Lonergan's metaphysics of the will that the first act of willing was passive and
therefore not free (see the next note). [63]

l **in later Thomist doctrine not only is such passivity incompatible with
freedom, but also ... the act of willing an end is not free**: for the
historical record it should be noted that a publisher's error made the
original text say the exact opposite, 'compatible' rather than 'incompatible.' [63]

m **the systematic refutation of *concursus simultaneus* and *praemotio physica***:
simultaneous coactivity and physical premotion describe respectively
the Molinist and Bannezian doctrines on God's way of exerting causality
with and/or on the human will. [64]

4   The Assumption and Theology

'The Assumption and Theology' was published first as a chapter in the symposium, *Vers le dogme de l'Assomption*. Journées d'études mariales (Montreal:
Fides, 1948) 411–24.

The symposium was a direct consequence of a letter which Pope Pius XII
wrote in 1946 to the bishops of the Roman Catholic church, asking their views
on the definition of the assumption of Mary, mother of Jesus, into heaven.
Archbishop Joseph Charbonneau of Montreal sponsored a theological congress
on the topic, Aug. 12–15, 1948. Lonergan's paper was presented in the
English-language section of the congress. The date (presumably, of composition) is given very exactly in the published form as 'July 15, 1948.' Further, the

Archives have various items relevant to this work: the bibliographic cards Lonergan used, and a folder, 'Assumption B.V.M.,' with his own typescript, annotated with instructions on how to deliver the paper (Batch 2, Folder 35).

Papal definition of the assumption as an article of faith followed in 1950, to the dismay of ecumenists in the Greek Orthodox and Protestant churches. To both groups the definition appeared as an exercise of Roman imperialism, and to Protestants an unseemly exercise also of Marian piety. Piety there is in Lonergan's paper; it appears in his very terminology – 'our good Lord,' 'best of sons' love for the best of mothers,' and his regular title for Mary, 'our Lady.' This is a point of some biographical importance, for we continue to find evidences of Lonergan's piety intermingled with his theology right to the end of his life.

The theological importance of the paper is found not so much in its position on Marian privilege as in its position on the development of doctrine. Lonergan has already moved far beyond logical deduction, and into the area of understanding; this he will expound more theoretically and at length in chapter 8 of the present volume, but the theory takes on meaning through this concrete application to development in our understanding of Mary's role. Later work will stress the role of differentiations of consciousness for development in general (1972: 139, 333, 352–53) and of 'human psychology and specifically the refinement of human feelings' (320) for development of the Marian doctrines.

In this paper Lonergan adheres closely to the Douai translation for his scriptural texts. Numbers and titles of the three main divisions are his own; we have added numbers and titles for the subdivisions.

RELATED WRITINGS

'A New Dogma' (1951a), an address on a Montreal radio station, following the papal definition. There is in the Archives an unpublished paper, *De argumento theologico ex sacra scriptura*, Gregorian University (1960b), which should be compared with the argument of this chapter.

NOTES

a **thesis defended at the ... Gregorian ... 1946**: the source referred to yields the information that this was a scholastic 'disputation,' that the defendant was the Salesian, Joseph Quadrio, a fourth-year student of theology, that objections were posed by Prof. Armando Fares of the Lateran University and Prof. Reginald Garrigou-Lagrange of the Angelicum (now St Thomas University). [69 note 11]

b **In the twenty-fourth chapter of St Luke**: one of Lonergan's favorite passages, used also in 'A New Dogma,' to illustrate development of understanding; it is interesting that in this very paper (77 note 32) he quotes John of St Thomas as appealing to the same Lucan source on the illumination of hidden revelation and the manifestation of hidden meaning – would this have influenced Lonergan's use? [70]

c **one has to get beyond conceptualism**: Lonergan was deep at this time into his writing of the *verbum* articles, a chief aim of which was to replace conceptualism with an authentic Thomist intellectualism (1967b: Index, Conceptualists; see also several loca in the present volume, 84–86, 132, 137–40). [77]

5   The Natural Desire to See God

'The Natural Desire to See God' was first published in the *Proceedings of the Eleventh Annual Convention of the Jesuit Philosophical Association*, Boston College, 1949, 31–43.

Again, there is a context. The very 'Catholic' philosophy of Maurice Blondel and the theological erudition of Henri de Lubac in his book, *Surnaturel*, had opened a new approach to the relation of natural and supernatural. Debate, aggravated by association of this question with that of the 'new theology' in general, was extremely lively, involving both philosophers and theologians. It happened that the President of the Jesuit Philosophical Association in 1949 was Rev. Gerard Smith, a close personal friend of Fr de Lubac, and he invited three theologians to address the Association on what he called 'one of the most important issues ever raised in the history of thought.' The three were Philip Donnelly, Bernard Lonergan, and Gustave Weigel. (Incidentally: Lonergan was one of the delegates nominated at the business meeting of the Association to succeed Fr Smith as President; he lost the election, no doubt to his immense relief.)

Lonergan had already given considerable thought to the questions raised by de Lubac. The Archives contain a folder, 'De Novissimis' (Batch 2, Folder 38), 27 typed pages dealing with the desire to see God and related questions; this almost certainly pertains to the Montreal courses on that topic, 1942–43 and 1945–46. Further, I have notes of one whole lecture, from his Toronto course on divine grace (1947–48), that was devoted to an analysis and critique of *Surnaturel*. But his paper before the Jesuit Philosophical Association entered only indirectly into the controversy, being a strictly theoretical presentation of his personal position on the natural desire to see God.

The numbers and titles of the three main divisions in the present publication are ours, but the 1967 *Collection* had numbered the objections he considered, and we have retained this feature as a subnumbering of the third division.

RELATED WRITINGS

De ente supernaturali, Thesis 4a, Scholion (De naturali desiderio videndi Deum per essentiam); this is a work of 1946, but in 1951–52 a note on the present question was added to the Scholion, and incorporated in later issues (1973a: 34–42, 84–86). *De sanctissima Trinitate: Supplementum quoddam* (1955a: 36–41 = §24, Appendix: De naturali desiderio intellectus). More remotely relevant: chapter 20 of *Insight* (1957a), called a 'deduction reminiscent of Blondel' in a review by W. Norris Clarke (*Theological Studies* 18 [1957] 629–32); and the 1968 paper, Natural Knowledge of God (1974: 117–33).

NOTES

a **desire to see God**: it is a kind of weathervane pointing to Lonergan's intellectualist approach during the 1950s that so many of his writings then (1953: 9; 1955a: 34; 1956: 17, 19; 1957a: 369; 1957b: 76, 265; etc.) refer to *Summa theologiae*, 1–2, q. 3, a. 8, where Thomas Aquinas asks whether human beatitude consists in seeing the divine essence, and speaks of a natural desire to know what God is; a little later in the present paper (83) Lonergan refers to Thomas on the question, though without specifying the passage in the *Summa*; in chapter 8 (118) he does refer to the *Summa*, but to 1, q. 12, a. 1 instead of 1–2, q. 3, a. 8 (see also 147, 186, 230). [81]

b **desires of human intellect**: this idea is to be related first to the pure desire to know, which was so dominant a notion in *Insight* (1957a: Index, under Desire), and then to the fuller dynamism of human spirit which we find in *Method* (1972: Index, under Dynamic, Dynamism – see also note *i* to this chapter). [81]

c **the basic questions, *an sit* and *quid sit***: the point had been made in the *verbum* articles (1967b: 12–16), where however the main concern was not so much to establish the pair of questions, as it was to transform 'what' questions into 'why' questions. Later Lonergan will add a third question to the Thomist pair (see my note on Levels), but throughout his career the question remained the operator of human development, the immediate expression of the dynamism of incarnate spirit. [81]

d ***via affirmationis, negationis, et eminentiae***: the traditional three ways of conceiving God – positively, transferring created perfections to the divinity; negatively, denying created imperfections; transcendently, understanding created perfections in an analogous and eminent sense. [82]

e **proportionate object ... adequate object**: Lonergan's distinction here between the proportionate object of intellect, which is the formal cause (specifying the essence of a material being), and the adequate object, which is being, simplifies and clarifies notions that had already appeared in the *verbum* articles (1967b: Index, under Object), and will reappear in the present volume. But though the idea is clear, the terminology is somewhat fluid; thus he will say in chapter 11 (176): 'Besides the proper object of human intellect, there is its formal object. The proper object pertains to human intellect as human ... The formal object pertains to human intellect as intellect ... This formal object of intellect is being.' The formal object of intellect is not, then, the formal cause of a material being. (Other passages in this volume on formal cause: 96–97, 135; see also note *j* to chapter 6.) [82]

f **the question, *quid sit Deus***': (1) to see God (note *a* above), (2) to know what God is, and (3) 'what Aquinas called "videre Deum per essentiam" ' (83) are simply three different ways of saying the same thing. [83]

g **discovery of the paradox**: see 87 below, 'any finite wisdom must expect paradox,' and 177, 'There results the well-known paradox of finite intellect ... orientated towards infinite understanding ... [but incapable of being] infinite understanding.' [84]

h **closed conceptualism ... open intellectualism**: this pair of terms originated in Lonergan's study of Thomist cognitional theory (1967b), but the vision has widened now to take in the alternative views of world order that result respectively from conceptualism and intellectualism. The former yields the 'static and essentialist view' that Lonergan has just described (84–85), but for the counterpart of an open intellectualism we may turn to *Insight*, a book Lonergan was just now starting to write, and read in chapter 15 (see also 695–96) his view of the dynamism of world process. It is worth noting that this dynamism was already explicit in the 1943 discussion of vertical finality (note *b* to chapter 2 above). [86]

i **dynamic**: it will be helpful to gather various related ideas into a pattern here; there is the dynamism of intellect (desire to know, open intellectualism, etc.), and there is the dynamism of world process (the vertical finality of chapter 2 above and of chapter 15 of *Insight*); there is the resulting world order that is 'an intelligible unity mirroring forth the glory of God' (85 above); and there is in human spirit a vertical liberty that extends the dynamism of intellect into the responsible and affective spheres (1972: 40, 122, 237–38, 240, 269). Finally, we may add the distinction of chapter 14 below (206) between the materially dynamic whole (a song, a dance, in which the parts are activities) and the formally dynamic whole in which the parts are self-assembling (as in cognitional structure – and, without doubt, in the total structure of incarnate spirit). [86]

j **existential**: the term, existential, is used here in the Thomist sense, as it will be in *Insight* (1957a: 248); it is only with the Boston College lectures of 1957 that Lonergan will give thorough treatment to modern existentialism (1957d; see also 1956: 14–19). [86]

6   A Note on Geometrical Possibility

'A Note on Geometrical Possibility' was first published in *The Modern Schoolman* 27 (1949–50) 124–38. There is a series of contexts which can be described with growing specificity. The original context is Lonergan's student interest in mathematics, especially in relation to cognitional theory, an interest documented by his contributions to the *Blandyke Papers* (1928a; 1929a; 1929b). The study of Thomist cognitional theory in the late 1940s (1967b) put the original interest into a new context. The present problem followed that study, providing an 'opportunity ... for working out a concrete application of the Thomist theory of intellect and science' (93 below); the link here is his acquaintance with the work of Peter Hoenen, which probably dates from the year Lonergan arrived at the Gregorian University in Rome for theology studies (1933) – Hoenen was a professor there and published his article on the origin of first principles in that year. Is there also an extrinsic context in the fact that *The Modern Schoolman* had published an extremely sharp attack on Lonergan three years earlier? The suggestion is that this article would then have a peace-making mission – a diplomatic possibility the mention of which is not out of place in this note on geometrical possibility.

The division titles are those found in the first printing; we have added the division numbers.

RELATED WRITINGS

'The Form of Mathematical Inference' (1928a). 'True Judgment and Science' (1929a). 'Infinite Multitude' (1929b). More specific references to the *verbum* articles, to *Insight*, and to the Halifax lectures of 1958 (*Understanding and Being*) will be given in the Notes. There is an unpublished draft of an English translation of Hoenen's relevant Latin writings at the Milltown Park Lonergan Center, Dublin.

NOTES

a   **five common notions**: some of Lonergan's readers have thought he erred here, but his text agrees with Heath's. Note his remark on the following page: 'It will be simpler to base the discussion on Euclid rather than his modern correctors.' [92]

b   **the so-called *quaestiones annexae***: so-called, that is, in seminary programs of studies, referring to questions of science connected with philosophy; the term seems to derive from the Roman directives for such studies – see *Acta Apostolicae Sedis* 23 (1931) 272, where the Congregation of Seminaries and Universities speaks of 'Quaestiones scientificae cum Philosophia coniunctae.' [93]

c **definitions ... nominal and essential**: these will become 'nominal and explanatory' in *Insight*, at which time also the category of 'implicit' definitions will be added (1957a: 10–13); see also *Understanding and Being* (1980: 52–54), and in both books compare nominal/explanatory with description/explanation. [94]

d **generalization, as distinct from universalization**: the ideas are clear, and the contrast is sharp, but as happens elsewhere the terminology is fluid. Generalization, as used here, is to be related to the commonsense generalizations of *Insight* (1957a: Index, under Generalization), and both are to be related to 'knowing that' (*scientia quia*, the work of the cogitative sense) as contrasted with 'knowing the reason why' (*scientia propter quid*, the work of understanding), as this pair is set forth in the *verbum* study (1967b: 30; see 39 on the cogitative sense). But Lonergan will often speak of generalizing when he is dealing with strictly explanatory understanding, *scientia propter quid,* and therefore with the universalization of the present passage. In fact, he had a kind of passion for generalizing in this sense; an instance is found in the first essay of this *Collection*, where he seeks the 'general form of all inference' (4), but better known are the generalized empirical method of *Insight* (1957a: 72, 243) and the generalized apologetic he finds in the dialectic of his *Method in Theology* (1972: 130). [95]

e **one cannot imagine a Euclidean point**: see also *Insight* (1957a: 7) and *Understanding and Being* (1980: 49, 71). [95]

f **necessary for intellect to convert to phantasm**: the expression is strange but the meaning is simple, namely, that intellect has a natural orientation to phantasm (image), turns to it for its object of study, and through an act of insight finds an intelligibility immanent in the image; the question had occupied Lonergan in his *verbum* studies (1967b: 158–62), during which his thought on the matter underwent a certain development (159, note 97). [96]

g **The solution ... is the symbolic image**: this image 'that stands for things it does not resemble' is regularly appealed to by Lonergan; as he says in *Insight*, 'Between the cart-wheel and the circle there is ... only an approximation' (1957a: 16, and see 17–19). See also *Understanding and Being* (1980: 30–32, 49, 71), and note *e* to chapter 1 above; but the treatment here (96 and 104–106 below) seems to be his most thorough discussion. [96]

h **They proceed from acts of understanding**: in the *verbum* studies it had been a major point, especially important of course for Trinitarian theology, that concepts and judgments are not a cognitional first but proceed consciously and rationally from insight; this was an essential point of Lonergan's campaign for a fertile intellectualism against a sterile conceptualism. [96]

i **the formal cause of the circle**: the circle is a favorite example for illustrating the occurrence of insight; see *Verbum* (1967b: 27–29), *Insight* (1957a: 7–13), and *Understanding and Being* (1980: 45–49). Here we find insight linked to the formal cause of a circle; current misunderstanding of formal causality is the reason Lonergan gives for not exploiting this link in *Insight* (1957a: 78). On formal cause see note *e* to chapter 5 above; on soul as formal cause: the *verbum* studies (1967b: 14–21), and *Understanding and Being* (1980: 33). [96]

j **scientific syllogism**: Aristotle's scientific syllogism had been studied in the *verbum* articles (1967b: 12–13, 23–24), and will figure in chapter 8 of the present volume (117–18), as well as in *Understanding and Being* (1980: 56–60); not, however, in *Insight*. [97]

k **Euclid's fifth postulate**: this 'parallel postulate' had a peculiar fascination for Lonergan; there is an obscure reference in the *Blandyke Papers* (1928a: 132), there were two earlier references in this essay (92, 95), and it will be discussed in *Understanding and Being* (1980: 30–32), if not in *Insight* (though straight angles are discussed there, 1957a: 10–11). The present discussion (99–101) is, however, his most thorough, so far as I know. The fascination has two sources. One is more theoretic: besides the general difficulty of transforming images into symbols ('Between the cart-wheel and the circle there is ... only an approximation' – note *g* above), there is the sheer impossibility of imagining infinity, though to the lay mind parallel lines meet at 'infinity.' The other source is historical: the influence on a new mathematics exerted by struggles with the parallel postulate (1980: 30–32). [99]

l **possibility**: we have a general discussion here of a question that had already arisen in chapter 5 in regard to the 'concrete possibility' of various world orders (88–91); a light on this complex matter is found in *Insight* – '... possibility is concrete. Logicians may say that a "mountain of gold" is possible if there is no intrinsic contradiction involved in supposing such a mountain. But, in fact, a mountain of gold is possible only if the means are available for acquiring enough gold ... for transporting it to a single place ...' (1957a: 337). This leads us to distinguish the immanent or intrinsic possibility (of a form or essence) from the external possibility (which requires agent and purpose). But intrinsic possibility, as the present chapter shows, requires the intelligibility both of the item in question and (when we are dealing with an accident) of a substance in which it may inhere; the latter in turn requires a world order, the possibility of which would be subject to the conditions discussed in chapter 5 above. [102]

m *veritas logica est formaliter in solo iudicio*: logical truth is formally found only in the judgment – a central point in both the *verbum* articles (1967b: 59–66) and *Insight* (1957a: chapter 9), though Lonergan would not use 'logical' to characterize the truth in question. [102]

n *veritas logica consistit in adaequatione intellectus ad rem*: logical truth consists in the correspondence of intellect to reality – the so-called 'correspondence' theory of truth which has raised the hackles of some philosophers, but for Lonergan means simply that the facts are what they are stated to be; the problem of some superlook comparing intellect and reality arises only when knowing is identified with looking (1957a: 634–35) – on which see 208, 214–19 in the present volume. [102]

o **Aristotle's** *intelligentia indivisibilium*: the *noêsis adiairetôn*, that is, understanding of the simple, of the noncomposite, of the unitary essence (*A Lexicon of St Thomas Aquinas*, ed. Roy J. Deferrari et al., Washington, D.C., 1948, under Intellegentia, gives Aristotle's *De anima*, III, 6, 430a 26, as source). [102]

p **the grasp of unity ... in empirical multiplicity**: there is a generic sense in which every insight grasps a unity in multiplicity, and that is the sense in question here; but there is also a particular sense in which a 'thing' is grasped as a 'unity-identity-whole,' and that is discussed in *Insight* (1957a: chapter 8). In one case multiple data are grasped in a single correlation, in the other multiple correlations (each a unification of data) are grasped as centered in one 'thing'; see 108 below in chapter 7, on 'the unities that are things and the ... correlations that explain their operations.' [102]

q **the unity of the unified**: the paragraph following this phrase is an epitome of what we might call the analogy of the intelligible, corresponding to what Lonergan elsewhere wrote on the analogy of intellect; where the latter analogy runs through human, angelic, and divine intellects (1955a: 30–31), the former runs from common matter to divine being. See also note *a* to chapter 9 below. [102]

r **the ground of possibility is intelligibility**: the question here is primarily of intrinsic possibility and therefore of immanent intelligibility (note *l* above), not of the possibility that requires external agents (though there too intelligibility is a condition). Here as always there is close correspondence between, along with the distinction of, the cognitional and the ontological: it is one question whether a thing can come to be (for that there must be intrinsic intelligibility), and another question whether I can affirm something to be (for that I first form an idea as a 'possible' explanation, and then ask the question of truth: Is it really the explanation?). [103]

s **sense and imagination**: there is a useful listing here of various terms describing images: formal, representative, virtual, and symbolic. The formal image seems equated with the representative which is required for insight; virtual ('as when Euclid only virtually imagines indefinitely produced straight lines') and symbolic ('as when Euclid imagines lines with breadth as well as length but understands them and thinks of them as without breadth') may 'fall short of representation' and so 'in the same measure ... fail to provide the agent objects that cause insights.' [104]

7 **The Role of a Catholic University in the Modern World**

'The Role of a Catholic University ...' was first published in French translation, in *Relations* 11 (1951) 263–65, in response to an invitation from the editor. The occasion was as follows: In 1952 Pax Romana was to meet successively at Toronto, Montreal, and Quebec, in order to discuss the very topic of this article. *Relations*, the Jesuit monthly in Montreal, devoting an editorial to the question, invited Lonergan to contribute a leading article in the same issue. At the time Lonergan was already hard at work on *Insight*, and so the present article, which was his response to the invitation, turns out to be an epitome of some of the chief ideas of that book. Translation, though undertaken by one of his own students, proved extraordinarily difficult – the following issue had to acknowledge an erratum – and Lonergan would often use this experience to illustrate the differences, in culture and thought patterns, between the English and the French.

The history of the English text has its own interest. The French had had subtitles for the six divisions. These were, presumably, editorial additions for, when Lonergan's English became available (mimeographed at the Xavier University institute on Philosophy of Education, 1959), the divisions were numbered but had no titles.

This 1959 text was the basis for the 1967 printing in *Collection*, and my copy shows the editorial changes, one of which, minor though it seem, is worth noting. Lonergan's first paragraph announced two main parts: 'I shall endeavor (1) to set forth a ... notion of the good and (2) to place within that frame-work both ... the modern world, and the Catholic University.' This I changed to 'I shall endeavor, first, to ... and, then, to ...' Presumably, I felt the conflict between the set of two numbers in the announcement and the set of six in the actual text. Still, my ploy reduced the sharpness of the main division, an effect I tried to restore by another slight change, inserting 'now' in the first line of section 4, where Lonergan had simply, 'This rough outline suffices for an adumbration of our basic terms ...' – The whole history may seem a fuss to some readers, but perhaps not to those who know how important it is to attend to Lonergan's distinctive manner of dividing his papers. With this *caveat* we feel justified in retaining the 1967 format, but have added our own subtitles.

RELATED WRITINGS

This short essay deals with a topic in which Lonergan was keenly interested, but strangely he published nothing else in his lifetime that took up the topic expressly. He did, however, authorize the editing of his course of lectures on the philosophy of education, given at Xavier University, Cincinnati, in the summer of 1959; see volume 10 of the Collected Works. The Archives also have notes of an unpublished lecture he gave in 1949, Towards a Definition of Education (Batch 2, Folder 55).

NOTES

a **a ... concrete and dynamic notion of the good**: the concrete and dynamic notion of being is familiar to readers of *Insight*; the full notion of the good was not worked out till the late 1960s; so this short passage is important for our perspective on Lonergan's development, showing his notion of the good as already 'concrete and dynamic' in 1951. See also my notes on Concrete, Dynamic. [108]

b **As human knowing rises on three levels, so also the good**: this is also the pattern in *Insight* (1957a: chapter 18), but later Lonergan will work out a notion of the good as a fourth level (responsibility, decision, the existential) which sublates the previous three; see *Method in Theology* (1972: chapter 2). Between these two books his usage of the term, level, is in transition (see 108, 219, 232–33 in the present volume). [108]

c **technological ... economic ... political**: a triad of terms familiar to readers of *Insight* (1957a: see especially chapter 7). [108]

d **As appreciation is a spring of action, so criticism is a source of restraint**: a kind of hermeneutics of recovery and hermeneutics of suspicion in the ethical sphere, and an orientation of considerable importance for the creative dialectic of values that is emphasized in Lonergan's later writings. Compare the recurring 'praise and blame' – for example, in *The Subject*: 'the incessant flow of praise and blame that makes up the great part of human conversation' (1974: 83). [109]

e **three levels of community**: two of these are very clear in *Insight*, the intersubjective and the civil (1957a: 212–14); the third is somewhat ob-. scured there by the long discussion of biases, progress and decline, etc. (but see 234 on what is needed to reverse the cycle of decline, and 236–42 on the role of culture in this reversal). The concept of community is enormously important for Lonergan, a fact that is missed in some criticism, probably because of his insistence on interiority. On community see also note *n* to chapter 14 below, and note *q* to chapter 15. [109]

f **cosmopolis**: see also note *q* to chapter 2 above, and of course *Insight* (1957a: 238–42); Lonergan did not create this term, but he gave it a meaning that has not been sufficiently studied. Incidentally, his typescript for *Insight* (Archives) show him changing the original capital to lower-case – as if to say that 'cosmopolis' should become a common noun in our language. [109]

g **development-and-decline**: a pair more familiar now as 'progress and decline' – on which see the indices of *Insight* and *Method*. [109]

h *video meliora proboque* **...**: this phrase from Ovid (*Metamorph.*, vii, 20–21, according to the Lewis and Short *Latin Dictionary* – deterior) is also quoted in *Insight* (1957a: 600), where the countering phrase, *Deteriora sequor*, is also given (inaccurately) and the notion of moral impotence is more fully set forth (627–30—see also 186–87 below); the present paragraph, with its ironic reference to 'realist' views, spells out the 'pseudo-realism' mentioned above (note *o* to chapter 2). [110]

i **a succession of lower syntheses**: an idea to which Lonergan repeatedly returned: in *Insight* (1957a: 231); *De ratione convenientiae* (1953: 8); etc. It is probable that in the more ecumenical spirit that prevailed after the Second Vatican Council he would modify the language he uses here, but his historical analysis still deserves pondering. [110]

j *virtus dormitiva*: an ironical reference to definitions that use other words but say nothing explanatory. [111]

k **moral precepts narrow down to lists of prohibitions**: Lonergan did not deny the difficulty of formulating a positive code of ethics – 'textbooks in moral theology ... can name all the evils to be avoided but get no further than unhelpful platitudes on the good to be achieved' (1985b: 104; and see 1984: 14–15) – but he seemed to regard a concrete notion of the good as of great importance in formulating a positive moral code. 'For the good is never an abstraction. Always it is concrete. The whole point to the process of cumulative insight is that each insight regards the concrete while the cumulative process heads towards an ever fuller and more adequate view. Add abstraction to abstraction and one never reaches more than a heap of abstractions. But add insight to insight and one moves to mastery of all the eventualities and complications of a concrete situation' (1985b: 104; and see 1984: 14–15). A clear and graphic passage: 'what moves men is the good, and good in the concrete ... If at one time law was in the forefront of human development, as one might infer from the language of the Deuteronomist, from the fervent praise of law in the Psalms, from the role of law in the history of the clarification of such concepts as justice, responsibility, guilt; still, at the present time it would seem that the immediate carrier of human aspiration is the more concrete apprehension of the human good effected through such theories of history as the liberal doctrine of progress, the Marxist doctrine of dialectical materialism and, most recently, Teilhard de Chardin's identification of cosmogenesis, anthropogenesis, and christogenesis' (1974: 6–7; see also 39–40). [111]

l **The supernatural virtues**: another notion to which Lonergan repeatedly returned is the double role of the theological virtues of faith, hope, and charity, that of orienting us to God, and that of modifying our relationship to the world (1957a: 741; 1972: 105, 117; 1974: 8). There is a useful analogy here with the ontological and economic Trinity: as we may think of the Three in their eternal being, but also of the Three in their dynamic entry into the created world, so faith, hope, and charity are in themselves a relation to God, but also they profoundly influence our living in this world. [112]

m **real principles ... are not enunciations in books but intelligences in act**: a remark that is orienting for the whole of *Insight*, where 'the aim is not to set forth a list of the abstract properties of human knowledge but to assist the reader in effecting a personal appropriation of the concrete, dynamic structure immanent and recurrently operative in his own cognitional activities' (1957a: xvii). [112]

n **a new and distinct problem of integration**: another recurring theme; see 130–31 in this volume; also *Method in Theology* (1972: 364–67), *A Second Collection* (1974: 29), *A Third Collection* (1985b: chapter 12). A useful heading under which to study this question in the later Lonergan is that of praxis. [113]

8 Theology and Understanding

'Theology and Understanding' was first published in *Gregorianum* 35 (1954) 630–48. Writing from Rome to the present editor on June 13, 1954, Lonergan gives the context and an overview of his article: 'I was pressed to review for Gregorianum J. Beumer's Theologie als Glaubensverständnis, and wrote an article 29 pages plus 2 of notes. Beumer argued for a theology based on the Vatican's intelligentia mysteriorum but interpreted Thomas in the light of the Thomistic tradition. He was the sort of meat that I love digesting. I was all for the Vatican, showed that Thomas knew a lot more about Glaubensverständnis than Beumer ever dreamed, and admitted that the probably spurious De Natura Verbi Intellectus had put the Thomistic school a bit off the track.'

The division numbering is that of the original printing. We have added the division titles.

RELATED WRITINGS

Most of Lonergan's works are in some degree related to this chapter, since its topic, theology precisely as understanding, was a major interest through much of his life. His work on method, however, during his professorship in Rome, 1953–65, is somewhat more immediately relevant. Succinct statements are incorporated into his theology proper; see the section, De intelligentia theologica, in his *De constitutione Christi ontologica et psychologica* (1956: Pars III), the section, De fine, ordine, modo dicendi, in his *Divinarum personarum conceptio analogica* (1957b: cap. I; see 1964a: II, cap. I), the sections, Introductio and Praemittenda, in his *De Deo trino*, Vol. I (1964a – see 1976 for English translation). Less succinct but opening a window to a mind at work are the courses of that period; they are still unpublished, but the Archives provide some record of three of them: *De systemate et historia, De intellectu et methodo, De methodo theologiae.*

NOTES

a **Johannes Beumer's** *Theologie*: Fr Beumer continued to write on the topics that were the concern of his book, but without ever taking account, so far as I know, of Lonergan's article. In particular he wrote (with Lodewijk Visschers) *Die theologische Methode* (Freiburg, 1972) for the *Handbuch der Dogmengeschichte*, but I have not found Lonergan listed in the extensive bibliographies on Die Hochscholastik (§8, 74–75), Die katholische Theologie [der Neuzeit] (§12, 104), or Das Erste Vatikanische Konzil (§13, 117). *Method in Theology*, however, is listed in the bibliography for Die theologische Methode in der Problematik von heute (§14, 126); but the single statement I have found on Lonergan is the unhelpful remark of note 7, p. 128: 'In der Kontroverse zwischen B.J.F. Lonergan and K. Rahner ... wird man wohl dem letzteren beipflichten müssen.' [114]

b **while the arrangement for teaching and learning begins from the theoretical elements**: readers of the original *Collection* should be alerted to the omission of this line from that edition (1967a: 127, last line; see the original, *Gregorianum* 35 [1954] 636, lines 2–3); I owe the correction to Robert Doran. [120]

c **P. Vanier**: Fr Paul Vanier belonged to the first generation of Lonergan's theological students; he was working on his doctorate at the College of the Immaculate Conception in Montreal while Lonergan was professor there, and the latter's influence was certainly important in Vanier's Trinitarian work. The same is true of the field of education which Vanier later took up; his early death cut short a promising career. [121 note 24]

d **rigorous proofs for Trinitarian theses**: at this time proofs still figured strongly in Lonergan's theology (though in speculative theology the goal remained understanding, not certitude); they by no means disappear in his later work, but he came to see that they are effective only within a horizon, and so selection of a horizon is the basic step – in other words, proofs work within a system, but one's horizon determines what the system will be. [122]

e **one dismisses *argumenta convenientiae* as proofs that do not prove**: these are theological arguments based on what is fitting, and as proofs, of course, they rate very low on the scale; but Lonergan's point is that they are not meant as proofs, they are rather the expression of theological understanding – in his book, then, they rate much higher. See his remark (124) on 'discriminating between arguments that settle matters of fact and arguments that throw some light on the nature of things'; the latter are *argumenta convenientiae*. Lonergan deals with them chiefly in the context of Christology; see, for example, his *De ratione convenientiae ...* (1953). [125]

f **wisdom**: the role assigned to wisdom shows a considerable development in Lonergan from the time of the *verbum* articles (1947: 52–61, 73–78; see 1967b: 66–75, 88–94) through *Insight* (1957a: 407–408) and *De intellectu et methodo* (unpublished course of 1959: 17–25), to what seems a startling disappearance of the word and concept from *Method in Theology*. But the function earlier assigned to wisdom remains; it is just that wisdom now resides in the community, and its organ is interdisciplinary. That future development is anticipated in this very chapter (130–31) when Lonergan all but uses the word, interdisciplinary, in regard to scientist and theologian. [125]

g **Matthew 5.37**: this text was rather a favorite of Lonergan; see also *The Way to Nicea* (1976: 10). [126 note 29]

h **Aristotelian and scholastic notions of science seem ... adequate**: note that this is said of speculative theology, and in a context where the accent is on the element of understanding. (See note *e* to chapter 2 above.) [127]

i **contemporary methodological issues**: this fifth section of the article is of major historical importance, for it gives us a privileged glimpse of the direction in which Lonergan's thinking is turning at this crucial time. [127]

j *Denkformen*: thought patterns, more familiar to Lonergan's readers under the headings of patterns of experience (*Insight*) and differentiations of consciousness (*Method*). [127]

k **The significance of such transpositions is manifold**: the notion of transposition was a major preoccupation of Lonergan at this time, but the focus of his study might seem to have been on transposition from scripture to dogmatic theology; it is useful therefore to have this illuminating and comprehensive paragraph which alerts us to the further transposition needed for 'the implementation of speculative theology in the apostolate and especially in Catholic education' – a continuing concern of Lonergan, one that will move to the fore in chapter 14 of *Method* (1972). See also note *o* below. [127]

l **religious experience ... religious feeling**: there is need of a study on the positive role of feeling even in the early Lonergan; otherwise, we seize on his negative remarks and then tend to make *Method* a complete about-turn (as I once did). On that positive role see, for example, chapter 17 of *Insight* (1957a), already written at the time of this article, and chapter 12, which followed soon after, of the present volume (see especially note *g* to that chapter). [127]

m **scientific concern with the experiential modes of thinking in living**: this phrase shows the three aspects we need to keep in mind for an adequate view of Lonergan – there is the experiential aspect of living which he shares with the human race, there are experiential modes of thinking, in which some have gifts denied to others (Lonergan was not a poet), and there is the pondering of these modes proper to one in the intellectual pattern of thinking (here we find Lonergan's favorite role). See also note *o* to chapter 14 below. [128]

n **the role of personal confrontation, the momentousness of personal engagement**: another indication that these categories figured explicitly in Lonergan's thinking long before *Method*. See also note *n* to chapter 14 below. [128]

o **relations between speculative and positive theology**: see note *k* above, on transposition from scripture to dogma; the relevant loca are in *Divinarum personarum* ... (1957b: 17–19 and passim), and in the extant notes of the courses, *De intellectu et methodo* and *De methodo theologiae* (1959b: 58–65 and passim; 1962: 48–60). See also note *g* to chapter 16 below. [128]

p *recentiores*: a term used in older theology manuals, generally indicating writers who are not merely more recent but also rather low on the totem pole of authorities. [128]

q **two types of historical question**: Lonergan does not offer names and definitions for these two types, but the second is obviously a question of philosophy ('settled ... by the ... philosophy which individual scholars ...

invoke'). A useful parallel is found in his later remarks on interpretation: 'interpretation is just a particular case of knowing, namely, knowing what is meant; it follows that confusion about knowing leads to confusion about interpreting' (1972: 154); and, 'Max Weber ... was led to distinguish between problems of empirical causation (How did Caesar die? ...) and ... problems of meaning (Why do people die? What sense is there to it?) ...' (1985b: 20). [129]

r **the relations between speculative theology and the empirical human sciences**: in the Halifax Lectures of 1958 Lonergan will call this 'the fundamental theological problem' today (1980: 117), but that remark needs exegesis. Perhaps one might come near Lonergan's maturer mind by thinking of theology's relation to scholarship (history and related fields) as the fundamental problem of the first phase, and of theology's relation to the empirical human sciences as fundamental in the second phase, where encounter with and feedback from the contemporary world are crucial (see *Method* for the distinction between sciences and scholarship, 1972: 233–34). His focus late in life on economics would vividly illustrate the second concern. [130]

s **solved either by teaching the scientist theology or by teaching a theologian the science**: as Lonergan goes on to say, this 'material solution is not practicable' and he will later give more attention to the interdisciplinary field as the place to look for a solution (1972: 22–23, 132–33, 366–67). See also note *f* above. [130]

t **In the fourth ... place**: this fourth problem is not named, but clearly (see 132) it requires a cognitional theory, leading to an epistemology, which leads in turn to a methodical philosophy – the three steps of *Insight* (1957a). [131]

u **its doctrine conflicts with the doctrine ... of Aquinas**: the *verbum* studies explain that this work 'forced older interpreters to take it as genuinely Thomist that the *verbum* was formed prior to any understanding' (1967b: 161). [131]

9   Isomorphism of Thomist and Scientific Thought

'Isomorphism of Thomist and Scientific Thought' was first published in *Sapientia Aquinatis*, Vol. I, Rome, 1955, 119–27, for the fourth international Thomistic congress. This series, organized by the Roman Academy of St Thomas, met first in the centennial year of 1925, again in 1936, and a third time in 1950. Three general themes were discussed at the 1955 meeting: comparisons of Thomist doctrine (1) with the present state of the sciences, (2) with Hegelian and Marxist dialectic, and (3) with the questions prompted by existentialism. Lonergan's paper fell under the first heading and gave him an opportunity to link his Thomist studies on cognitional theory (1967b) with his book, *Insight* (1957a).

Lonergan did not attend the congress, for it was held Sept. 13–17, and he was in Canada for the summer. But, as Fr Charles Boyer, General Secretary of the Congress, states in his 'Ad lectorem' (5), the papers in Vol. I were published in advance to promote discussion during the congress itself. Vol. II, published a year later, contains accounts of actual proceedings at the congress. Here the first 'relatio', on the first theme, was given by Fr M.L. Guerard des Lauriers, who presented in brief summary eleven of the papers submitted in advance (presentation of Lonergan's: 29–30), and raised some questions on these papers (brief references to Lonergan's; 34, 47). The report, however, of discussions on the first theme (229–62) does not show any reference to Lonergan's paper.

RELATED WRITINGS

The first two articles in the *verbum* series (1967b), and chapters 1–5 and 9–10 of *Insight* (1957a), still unpublished at the time of the congress. Relevant also, since this chapter finds two modes of knowing isomorphic, are the papers in which Lonergan deals with the isomorphism of three structures (cognitional theory, epistemology, and metaphysics): chapter 14 of the present volume, and 'De notione structurae,' *Apertura* 1 (May, 1964) 117–23.

NOTES

a **a protracted analogy of proportion**: Lonergan rarely discussed analogy itself, but it was a favorite device of his to trace an analogous concept through a series of analogates; see note *q* to chapter 6 above on the analogy of the intelligible. We may add these items for a partial list: the analogy of matter, in the *verbum* articles (1967b: 143–47); the analogy of intellect in his *De sanctissima Trinitate* (1955a: 30–31); the analogy of methods, in his *De constitutione Christi ...* (1956: 44–49). There are also unpublished lectures of 1963 on the analogy of meaning: Gonzaga University, Spokane, and Thomas More Institute, Montreal. But the present 'protracted' analogy is somewhat different; it is 'protracted,' not through a series of analogates, but through a series of similarities between two analogates. [133]

b **the question, *Quid sit*?**: the familiar pair of questions, *quid sit* and *an sit* (note *c* to chapter 5 above), structure much of the argument of this paper, though the second question is not quoted in the Latin. [135]

c **this**: scholastic philosophy discusses 'thisness' at considerable length, where Lonergan deals rather with the concrete 'this'. 'Thisness' would not in fact make sense to him, since '-ness' refers to a formal element, and what makes a thing 'this' is not form but potency. See also 150–51, 166 note 14, in this volume. [135]

d **the notion of object**: in Lonergan's metaphysical analysis there are two types of object, both defined by causal relations (object of active, object of passive potency); later he will be interested more in intentionality analysis than in metaphysical, and his notion of object will develop accordingly. See his paper, 'Natural Knowledge of God' (1974: especially 121–24). [137]

e *media in quibus* **of inner words**: the media of inner words in which (we know objects). But for Lonergan our cognitional activities have an immediate relationship to real objects in the intention of being; the relationship is mediate in data, understanding, thought, and judgment (see 218 in this volume). [137]

f **Einstein's rather celebrated advice**: one of Lonergan's favorite anecdotes; see also *Understanding and Being* (1980: 97). [138]

g εἶδος **or** *species*: Greek and Latin, respectively, for form, but for form as the intelligibility of data rather than as an ontological constituent of things. [138]

h *νοεῖ*: this quotation appears in Greek on the title page of *Insight* (1957a). Curiously, Lonergan originally wrote καί νοεῖ ὁ νοῦς τά εἴδη ἐν τοῖς φαντάσμασι; my memory now (over thirty years later) is that I informed him I could not find this wording in Aristotle, whereupon he substituted the words that now appear (he was in the habit of quoting Aristotle's Greek from memory!). [138 note 17]

i **... the human soul understands itself by its understanding**: Lonergan found this phrase of Thomas a piece of useful ammunition in argument with the Thomists; he quotes it in chapters 10 and 11 of this volume (143 – where we find the translation I have used – and 175). [139]

j **understanding is the key**: a remark that is itself the key to Lonergan. It would be pedantic to insist on that, but two points are worth making: the first, that Lonergan was onto the importance of understanding (without the precision that Thomism would later give him) from his student days at Heythrop College (1928a); the second, that studies of understanding continue to come out, thirty years later, without so much as a mention of *Insight: A Study of Human Understanding*. [139]

k *exercite et non signate*: present in performance but not made thematic. We might say that the aim of *Insight* is to have the readers appropriate *signate* what they use *exercite* in daily life. [140]

l **the unity of all scientific knowledge**: a lifelong quest of Lonergan's, in which the goal was sought first in a metaphysics (1957a: Index, under Metaphysics unifies ...) but later in a basic method – 'transcendental method offers a key to unified science' (1972: 24). [141]

10   *Insight*: **Preface to a Discussion**

'*Insight*: Preface to a Discussion' was first published in *Proceedings of the American Catholic Philosophical Association* 32 (1958) 71–81. The appearance of *Insight* in April of 1957 had brought an invitation from Fr Allan Wolter, the Association President, to address their meeting the following spring. Lonergan was agreeable and proposed to talk on Philosophic Difference and Personal Development. Under this heading he prepared a synopsis of the proposed talk and published it in *The New Scholasticism* 32 (1958) 97. Later, however, he changed his mind about the topic. One factor in his decision was surely his inability to attend the meeting, for he wrote on Dec. 18, 1957, to Fr Eric O'Connor: 'I have not yet had word whether I can go to Detroit for the Cath. Phil. Meeting at Easter. Consequently I have done nothing yet about writing the paper, since it would have to be very different if I were not there to ad lib and supplement.' When he did draft the paper the content was probably influenced also by the difficulties reviewers of *Insight* had raised, for he wrote to the present editor in a letter of Feb. 21, 1958: 'The paper will deal with three points: primacy of knowledge, dynamic notion of being, and concrete actual existence. I think N. Clarke's difficulties are fairly general.' Further correspondence I had with Lonergan at this time dealt with questions I thought might be raised at the convention (for when Lonergan found he could not attend in person, he asked me to read the paper in his stead), but the points made belong with the history of *Insight*. The appointed commentator was Fr Luke Burke, and various courteous questions followed from the floor, but it must have been disappointing to the members, as it was to Lonergan, that he could not be there in person.

    The subtitles and their numbers were added by the present editors, but correspond to the divisions announced in Lonergan's first paragraph.

RELATED WRITINGS

Besides *Insight* itself, there are the Halifax Lectures delivered that same summer but published much later (1980) – one might call them a book-length expansion of the paper – and '*Insight* Revisited' (1974: 263–78) written sixteen years later for the Jesuit Philosophical Association (curiously, Lonergan was not able to present that paper in person either). I should mention the large number of lectures on the book, given at various times and in various places, as well as a number of academic courses in various university settings, but discussion of these also belongs in the history, still to be written, of *Insight*.

NOTES

a **my original plan to correlate personal development with philosophic**

differences: that topic would have been a most natural development of *Insight*; furthermore, it would have been a natural follow-up of his 1957 course on Existentialism at Boston College, where precisely this problem was treated at length. [142]

b **the primacy of the ontological**: his letter to me had given 'primacy of knowledge' as the first topic; either phrase will do for asking which is primary, the ontological or the cognitional; as for the answer, 'the ontological and the cognitional are not incompatible alternatives but interdependent procedures' (114). Useful to evaluate this answer is *Understanding and Being*, where Lonergan says in effect: start where you please, but complete the circle, from cognitional to metaphysical and back to cognitional, or metaphysical to cognitional and back to metaphysical; further, one must go round the circle over and over, expanding and deepening one's understanding (1980: 220–21). Still, I do not think there is any doubt that, for Lonergan, the methodical way is to start with cognitional process; see his remark on Coreth and the latter's exclusion of an *Erkenntniskritik* (203–204 below). [142]

c **a heap of disputed questions**: it was a scandal to Lonergan that scholastics, and philosophers in general, had no method or anything analogous to a crucial experiment with which to solve their endless disputed questions; this had occupied him from the time of his doctoral dissertation, it was one of the chief motives impelling him to work on method, and it contributed, I surmise, to his original plan to talk on Philosophic Difference and Personal Development. (On the 'scandal' of disputed questions see *Method in Theology* (1972: 20–21.) [145]

d **The desire, precisely because it is intelligent, is a notion**: Lonergan, so far as I know, had not defined the term, notion, in *Insight*, but in a letter of Feb. 21, 1958, he said in the staccato style he sometimes adopted (and presumably in answer to a question from me): ' "Notion" in notion of being is very exceptional as basis of all heuristic structure. Not Hegelian influence; needed a word that would not necessarily suggest notion of being to be a concept; but the ground of all conceiving and affirming.' Also useful, though the transcript of the tape is not wholly trustworthy, is 'The Human Good,' where Lonergan, speaking of the notion of value, says: 'You see I use the word "notion" not uniformly, but at times, in a special sense. A notion. There are different types of questions in which we intend an object without knowing it. ... We are intending an intelligibility that we want to know but do not know, and that is a notion. These notions are not abstract. They are comprehensive' (1979: 117). Another very helpful locus occurs in the French translation of the *verbum* articles (not in the English), where Lonergan distinguishes '(1) notion,

(2) concept implicite, (3) connaissance, (4) idée et (5) théorie de l'être' (1966: 44, note 196). [147]

e **is this universe of being the real world?**: in *Insight* this is a central issue for the objectivity of our human knowing, and especially for our knowledge of God. But there the adversary is naive realism; here it is more directly existentialist *Sorge*, on which Lonergan had lectured the previous summer at Boston College. [147]

f **each of us lives in a real world of his own**: helpful here are the 1957 lectures on Existentialism, with their distinction between 'my' world and 'the' world; this may then be related to the distinction between the world of immediacy and the world mediated by meaning (224–25 in chapter 15 below), which pair in its turn is to be related to the actual and ultimate horizons of chapter 12 (187 below). To be noted: 'world' in this context is not that of 'world order' and 'world process' (chapter 5 above). [148]

g **horizon**: this is now emerging as a technical term. The short chapter, De ex-sistentia, in *De constitutione Christi*, did not use the word, or take up horizon as a theme (1956: 14–19). But it was a theme in the 1957 lectures on Existentialism, and of course in the 1963 study, 'Metaphysics as Horizon' (chapter 13 in this volume; see especially 198–99, 204; also 187 in chapter 12). For other data on this development, see Lonergan's Gregorian University courses: *De intellectu et methodo* (1959b: 42), and *De methodo theologiae* (1962: 3). [148]

h **animal faith**: a reference presumably to Santayana, who appears also in the Existentialism lectures (1957e: 66), as well as in a 1980 lecture of *A Third Collection* (1985: 210, 218). [148]

i **a specifically philosophic conversion**: Lonergan will declare in the St Michael's Lectures of 1972 that '*Insight* insists a great deal ... on the importance ... of intellectual conversion' (1973b: 12). One cannot deny that; still, *Insight* had not used this phrase, though Lonergan spoke at some length on 'Radical Intellectual Conversion' in the Thomas More Institute Lectures, Intelligence and Reality, of 1950–51 (1950c: 14), and this is surely either identical with, or a chief component of, the philosophic conversion mentioned here. The Christology of 1956 deals in an illuminating way with a 'conversio quaedam et intima et radicalis, conscia atque deliberata' which is clearly intellectual conversion, and is related to the conversion which is the work of grace (1956: 17–18, 19). One difference between 1950 and 1972: the 1950 lectures distinguish between incidental and radical intellectual conversion; in 1972 and *Method*, conversion by its very nature is radical (1972: Index, under Conversion). [148 note 10] j **This existential aspect of our knowing is the fundamental factor in the differentiation of the philosophies in _Insight_**: a topic that would have figured more prominently in the paper Lonergan originally proposed to give, as it did in the Halifax Lectures of the coming summer (1980: 18–21, and see that book's Index under Subject, also my note on Subject in the present volume). [148 note 10]

k **being and the concrete are identical terms**: to be related to Lonergan's campaign in _Insight_ to identify the real with being (1957a: 673, 676 and passim) and to reject the notion of knowing as taking a look (ibid., Index under Knowing and looking). See also my note on Concrete in this volume. [148]

l **concepts express insights**: or, proceed from understanding (see my note on Procession); this is another way of stating Lonergan's intellectualism, opposed to a conceptualism which derives concepts by a metaphysical process instead of consciously and rationally. [148]

m **_Insight_ 271–78**: Lonergan refers here to _Insight_, but a more explicit reference to this position is found in the _verbum_ articles (1967b: 48–49, 59). [149 note 12]

n **You verify that they cannot be ... illusory**: on the same page Lonergan refers, on 'judgment of fact as the absence of illusion,' to _Insight_, 280–83; but those pages deal with the general conditions of judgment, and not with absence of illusion in particular; for the latter, see 1980: 216–17. [151]

o **attend to them [presentations], not as kinds of data, but in their concrete individuality**: this is the procedure spelled out in _Insight_ for grasp of a 'thing' as unity-identity-whole (1957a: chapter 8), the very terms that occur in this passage ('an intelligible unity, a single whole, an identity that unites what in space is here and there and what in time is then and now. From that insight there proceeds the concept of a thing'). See also note _p_ to chapter 6 above. [151]

p **intuition, of concrete, actual existence**: the 'simple and straightforward question of fact,' whether there is an intuition of concrete, actual existence, will be the central issue between Gilson and Lonergan in chapter 13 below; Gilson is not mentioned here, but he had a great influence on many who attended this meeting, as Lonergan must have known. His own authority here would, of course, be Newman and the illative sense.

Lonergan's position on intuition is compactly stated in a letter of Sept. 14, 1973, to Louis Roy (whom I thank for this communication): 'In English "intuition" differs from "insight"; it grasps what is existing and present, as Scotus would say; "insight" merely grasps what might be relevant and is to be affirmed only if verified.' Such usage depends, however, on convention; the word's root (*intueor*, and compare *intelligere* = *intus legere*) does not require this convention; and Lonergan would (and sometimes did) substitute 'intuition' for 'insight.' (For more on intuition in this volume, see 172 note 31, and 201–202; also note *r* below, on the original conclusion to this chapter.)

I may note here that in the present context Lonergan used 'real' and 'concrete' interchangeably. Thus, on the preceding page he had spoken of 'real, actual existence' and immediately afterward of 'concrete, actual existence.' The *Collection* of 1967, perhaps with excessive fussiness, had tried to correct this. [152]

q **attention to the consequences can obscure the stark simplicity of the issue itself**: one of the consequences of Lonergan's position is stated very forthrightly that same summer in the Halifax Lectures, 'if one frankly acknowledges that intellect is intelligence [as opposed to taking a look], one discovers that one has enormous problems in epistemology' (1980: 20–21). See also note *k* to chapter 15 below. [152]

r **I thank you**: the present conclusion of the paper (the six short paragraphs beginning, 'What is the issue here?') is a revision of the original. I have a memo from Lonergan (undated but received prior to the convention of April, 1958), instructing me to delete the original conclusion and to substitute these six paragraphs. The deletion began – so I reconstruct the matter now – part way down the penultimate page, which therefore went to the printer with the deleted paragraphs crossed out. That part of the deleted material has been lost, but the last page of deleted material did not go to the printer; I have it still in my possession, and it reads as follows:

> makes no effort to endow people with the common sense needed to make judgements of concrete, actual existence, though it is concerned to eliminate from common sense the component of common nonsense with which it may be afflicted.[23] On the other hand, just as there is a very real problem of determining what exactly our knowledge is, so also there is a very real problem of determining what exactly one means by existence. The Thomist *esse* in the sense of *actus essendi*[24] is not the object of sensible presentation; it is not the object of Santayana's animal faith; it is not the object of Scotist and Ockhamist intuition; it is not Heidegger's *das Seiendes* or Sartre's *étant*; it lies beyond the horizon of phenomenalists and pragmatists, sensists and materialists, idealists and relativists; it is the *est* of *id quod est* and in the man, Jesus of Nazareth, it is the *ipsum esse* of God.[25] I thank you.

(A piece of incidental intelligence: the line, 'it is not the object of Scotist and Ockhamist intuition,' was inserted by hand – Lonergan's

afterthought when he had already typed the page. Notice that footnotes
22 to 25 have also been lost; presumably I simply crossed them off the
last page of Lonergan's typescript before sending it to the printer.) [152]

11   Christ as Subject: A Reply

'Christ as Subject: A Reply' was first published in *Gregorianum* 40 (1959)
242–70. As regards style and content it stands by itself in this collection, a
vehement refutation by Lonergan of an attack on his Christology. The topic,
subjectivity and consciousness in Christ, had emerged only in modern times,
and had slowly been taking shape in its Roman Catholic form, largely through
the work of such theologians as the Franciscan, Déodat de Basly, and the
Jesuit, Paul Galtier. Lonergan was rather slow to take up the question; it was
not treated in his Toronto course on Christology in 1948–49, and he provided
only a brief set of notes for his students the next time this treatise came up
there: *De conscientia Christi* (1952). He was busy, of course, working out in
Insight the theory of knowledge and consciousness (chapter 11) that would
enable him in due course to handle the question with competence. So in 1956
he produced his *De constitutione Christi ontologica et psychologica*, one of the
most neglected masterpieces of this century (1956), and this is the work that
came under attack by Fr Angelo Perego in the pages of *Divinitas*.

Of the special difficulties this chapter presented in editing the *Collection* of
1967, some have faded away while others have grown more acute. Thus in
1967, when the aim was to get some of Lonergan's ideas into circulation, I
expressed regret that the positive sections of the article could not be separated
from its vehement polemics; I do not see that as a difficulty today, when the
history of Lonergan's life and work is of general interest, and this episode is
part of that history. But the general difficulty mentioned in my Preface to this
volume, that of languages, is worse now than it was in 1967, and is especially
acute in this chapter: Lonergan's quotations switch back and forth between his
own Latin and Perego's Italian, while he carries on a running conversation
in English, not to mention some quotations here and there in French. To
translate is to lose the flavor, and maybe the force, of Lonergan's argument;
but to leave the original language is to lose many a reader, especially in the
Latin. The end result is naturally a compromise, adapting slightly that of the
1967 edition. The longer passages are translated in the text, with the original
transferred to footnotes (numbered so as to retain Lonergan's own usage –
hence 8*, 8**, etc., are introduced editorially), but for shorter phrases I rely
now on the Lexicon provided for this volume, eliminating most of the bumpy
parentheses of 1967. For the record note that Lonergan used the original
language in all his quotations, adding his own translation according to need.

A general note should be added on the words 'reflexion' and 'reflection.' The difference may at times be simply one of spelling. Still, Lonergan repeatedly uses 'reflexion' in this article, in contrast to the recurring 'reflection' elsewhere in his work, and this may indicate a certain nuance that editors should not tamper with; we have therefore left his spelling the way we found it.

The divisions and their titles are also Lonergan's, though he named his divisions Parts I, II, and III.

RELATED WRITINGS

Besides the related writings already mentioned (*De conscientia* ...; chapter 11 of *Insight*; *De constitutione* ...) see Lonergan's paper of Jan. 20, 1963, at the North American College, Rome, Consciousness and the Blessed Trinity; and the three editions of his theology manual, *De Verbo incarnato*, 1960, 1961, and 1964 (the latter showing considerable revision of his treatment of Christ's human knowledge).

NOTES

a **the Reverend A. Perego**: Fr Angelo Perego has continued to write in the theological journals, but I have not noticed any response on his part to this article of Lonergan's. [153]

b **The intimate relation between the articles of faith and theological thought**: this relation was *de rigueur* for Lonergan, from the beginning of his career to the end; indeed, at the time of this article he even conceives theology's function to be simply stating the meaning of the articles of faith (179); later, however, his *Method* will make room for limited participation by nonbelievers (the unconverted) in the first phase of theology (1972: 268), and will give theology as a whole a wider function, that of mediating between a religion and a culture. [153]

c **if the unity of the person is just an abstraction, our Lady is not the Mother of God**: an allusion to the Council of Ephesus (431), where the *theotokos* was the 'crucial experiment' – if Christ is a single person, that person is God, Mary is his mother, and she is therefore *theotokos*, God-bearing. [156]

d **The notion of the subject is difficult, recent, and primitive**: nevertheless, Lonergan finds the notion implicit in Augustine and Aquinas (179 note 50, below; see also 162 note 11). [162]

e **A ... notion is not theologically useful until ... transposed into ... scholastic thought**: despite his 1954 essay (chapter 8 above) Lonergan is still at this time dominated by the concept of theology as speculative. [163]

f **consciousness conceived as an experience**: Lonergan's technical definition in his *De constitutione Christi* ... was, 'Conscientia est sui suorumque actuum experientia stricte dicta atque interna' (1956: 83) – consciousness is internal experience, in the strict sense of experience, of oneself and of one's acts. Note here his repeated insistence that data of consciousness are an empirical source just as data of sense are – hence his term, generalized empirical method (1957a: 72, 243). It is impossible to exaggerate the theological consequences of this; they are simply enormous. It is the exclusion of the data of consciousness and restriction to the data of sense, to what is 'external,' that largely accounts for our failure to give the Holy Spirit the role that God intended in paralleling the mission of the Son with that of the Spirit.

It may help to anticipate a question readers could raise here. They will remember that elsewhere Lonergan distinguishes sharply between self-consciousness and self-knowledge; see, for example, *A Third Collection* (1985b: 57): ' ... inner experience ... is consciousness as distinct from self-knowledge.' Few have exact knowledge of their conscious activities, 'for while they are conscious, still that consciousness is not knowledge but only the infrastructure in a potential knowledge that few get around to actuating' (ibid. 58; see also note *f* to chapter 14 below). In the present chapter, however, Lonergan seems to insist on the cognitive function of consciousness.

The contradiction is only apparent. Knowledge is a compound of many activities: potential in experience, formal on the level of understanding, actual in judgment. There is therefore potential self-knowledge in experience of ourselves (consciousness), but actual self-knowledge only when we make a judgment on ourselves. It was important in this chapter for Lonergan to insist on the cognitive aspect of consciousness, even though the knowledge is only potential; and it was equally important elsewhere to insist that consciousness is not actual self-knowledge.

For development in Lonergan's notion of consciousness, see note *n* to this chapter below. [163]

g **A cognitive act exercises no constitutive effect upon its object**: that is, a cognitive act insofar as it is cognitive; Lonergan would not deny that the attempt to measure a quantity sometimes introduces agencies into the situation that change the quantity being measured. [164]

h **consciously intelligent ... rational ... free ... responsible**: this quartet of terms, used repeatedly at this time (passim in this chapter, and see 210, 222, 243 below), is to be compared with the three levels of *Insight* and the four levels of *Method* (see my notes on Levels); it divides the later fourth level into two parts, freedom and responsibility. [165]

i **I think of 'this' by a backward reference to sense**: see my note on 'This.' [166 note 14] j **subjectivist tendencies recently denounced in H. Duméry**: Lonergan combined great respect for Duméry's work with sharp criticism of his failure to account for objective truth; see his *De Verbo incarnato* (1964b: 15–16), also his *De Deo trino* (1964a, 1: 60, 274). [168 note 18]

k **I grant that moral consciousness is principally intellectual**: a concession that Lonergan might have qualified later when he developed more fully the existential factor (1968a). [169]

l **the Aristotelian doctrine that knowing is an identity**: a major point in Lonergan's *verbum* studies (1967b: 72, 186 and passim). [170 note 24]

m **objects of sense, *sensibilia propria***: this is Thomist usage, which Lonergan follows to the extent that he distinguishes sense and consciousness; see 218 below, 'consciousness ... is not an inner sense.' But data for understanding are found in both sense and consciousness (note *f* to this chapter). [170]

n **every conscious activity is ... present to itself**: it was just at this time that Lonergan began to explain consciousness as presence to oneself, where previously he had explained it as inner experience; so one is led to ask whether this quotation from Van Riet is the source of that important refinement. The complex facts do not allow a simple affirmative answer. First, there is already a fairly elaborate philosophy of presence in the earlier Trinitarian theology (1957b: 229–36, especially 230–32), though the context there is that of the presence of one person to another. Then, in the 1957 lectures on Existentialism, Lonergan begins to develop the difference between presence of one person to another and one's presence to self (1957e: 131–32, and see 82–86, 123–28). Thirdly, the Halifax Lectures in the summer of 1958 are quite explicit on consciousness as presence to oneself (1980: 16–17, 22, and passim). Now Van Riet's article was published that same summer, and it is just possible that Lonergan had read it before leaving Europe for Halifax, in which case it would have had a crystallizing effect on a process already well under way. A neat indication of the shift is found in the theses set at this time by Lonergan for the Gregorian University examinations on the incarnate Word: the 1958 thesis on the consciousness of Christ does not mention presence; the 1960 thesis, on the same dual consciousness, states that the person of the Word 'tum modo divino tum modo humano sibi praesens est.' (On the notion of presence in Augustine and Aquinas, see 162, note 11, of this volume.) [172]

o **the analogous notion of intellect**: the reader should not miss the strong contrast between a proper understanding of intellect, which is the Thomist way, and this 'analogous notion,' which is based on a supposed similarity with looking. [175 note 40]

p **When coherent, as in Scotus**: for all of Lonergan's sharp criticism of

Scotus, he respected his logical rigor, on which see also *Understanding and Being* (1980: 61); the incoherence, for Lonergan, lay in adopting Scotism while intending to be a Thomist – much Thomism he would call crypto-Scotism (1967b: 31, note 146). [178 note 43]

q **a parallelism is to be recognized between ontological and psychological statements about the incarnate Word**: a parallelism made thematic in the very title of the book, *De constitutione Christi ontologica et psychologica*, and brought into focus with extreme clarity in the section on the ontological and psychological kenosis of the Son of God (1956: 115). [182]

12   Openness and Religious Experience

'Openness and Religious Experience' was first published in *Il Problema dell'esperienza religiosa* (Brescia: Morcelliana, 1961) 460–62, written for a congress held at the Jesuit house of philosophy studies at Gallarate (near Milan). This congress, an annual event of considerable importance in Italy and beyond, had chosen philosophy and religious experience as its theme for 1960, and invited Lonergan to take part. His paper, again submitted *in absentia*, is brief (just a series of 'headings,' his opening sentence says), but it is packed with clues to his integral notion of nature and grace, and to the development of his thinking on religious consciousness.

The division numbers are all Lonergan's own.

RELATED WRITINGS

Relevant passages in Lonergan's dissertation, in his *De ente supernaturali*, in his *De sanctissima Trinitate*, and in *Insight*, will be indicated in individual notes; of general relevance is chapter 5 of this volume, on The Natural Desire to See God; also chapter 15, *Existenz* and *Aggiornamento*, in its study of the transition from substance to subject in Christ Jesus.

NOTES

a **The theme suggested to me**: Lonergan's correspondence with the congress organizers has not been found in the Archives, but in a letter to me, dated Dec. 22, 1959, he wrote as follows, 'Have been approached with question, Would I attend Gallarate meeting ...? Theme: philosophy and religious experience ... It is a first class meeting ... about number of 60 univ prof's. Very attractive. Have not yet decided.' [185]

b **philosophy of**: Lonergan had given considerable thought to what could be called a philosophy of science, a philosophy of education, a philosophy of history, and similar issues; it was only natural that the notion, philosopy of, should itself become a question to him; and, in fact, we have turned up a page in the Archives on just this heading (included in Vol. 10 of the Collected Works, *Topics in Education*). See also *De intellectu et methodo* (1959b: 47). [185]

c **immediate ... mediated**: this pair of terms referred, in Lonergan's 'metaphysical' period, to modes of causality (note *c* to chapter 3); then, in the thinking characteristic of *Insight*, the reference is to the immediacy of cognitional dynamism as contrasted with its (mediated) appropriation; a third reference, under the influence of intentionality analysis, will be to the worlds determined by patterns of meaning; add to the list the two phases of his theological method, mediating and mediated (1972: chapter 5). See also note *e* to chapter 9, note *c* to chapter 13, and notes *j* and *m* to chapter 15. [185]

d **basic orientation**: this is still characterized by the pure desire to know (of *Insight*), rather than by the 'undertow' of religious experience (of *Method*). [186]

e **openness**: see note *h* to chapter 5 above; there and in chapter 2 the term was used in the context of world process; the specific meaning now is the openness of human spirit and of the being which is its object, as set forth in *Insight* (1957a: chapter 12). See also chapter 15 in this volume (229–30) and *De intellectu et methodo* (1959b: 48). [186]

f **the wonder that is the beginning of all science and philosophy**: this notion from the beginning of Aristotle's *Metaphysics*, quoted so often by Lonergan, is regularly linked in his thinking with the Thomist natural light of intellect; then, in the lectures, Intelligence and Reality, we find a cryptic linking of Aristotle's agent intellect, Thomist light of intellect, and Kantian 'Original synthetic unity of apperception' (1950c: 15). [186]

g **religious experience**: clues to the history of this topic in Lonergan's thinking may be found in the grace course of 1946, where he speaks of awareness of the supernatural (1973a: 23–24, 30); in the usage of the *verbum* articles, where the sense is that of mystical experience (1967b: 92); in the section on Metaphysics, Mystery, and Myth of *Insight* (1957a: 531–49); and the 'ordinary religious experience' of chapter 8 above (127). But the concentration on doctrine that characterized the Roman Catholic church during the modernist scare inhibited development on religious experience, and Lonergan got round late to the question. [187]

h **man's making of man**: this idea, now coming into focus for Lonergan, is worked out in the lectures on Existentialism (1957d: passim, under such headings as On Being Oneself, The Self-Constituting Subject, etc.). See my notes on Existential, also 220 of chapter 14 in this volume ('the perpetual novelty of self-constitution'), 223–24 in chapter 15, and 233–34, 243–44 in chapter 16. [187]

13   Metaphysics as Horizon

This chapter was first published in *Gregorianum* 44 (1963) 307–18. It takes up again the question of fact posed at the end of chapter 10, 'Is there or is there not a human, intellectual intuition of concrete, actual existence?' This time, however, the context is provided by Fr E. Coreth, and the question is posed in terms of metaphysical method – terms certainly agreeable to Lonergan. A third question regards the extension of method to include the development of the inquiring metaphysician, and here Lonergan seems to ask for a dimension not included in Coreth's perspective.

Lonergan's correspondence with me at this time is illuminating for this chapter. In a letter of July 5, 1961, he advised: 'Get yourself a copy of E Coreth, Metaphysik ... It works out metaphysics from the basis of the question; very neat' – and he seemed pleased to be included in Coreth's Foreword as belonging to the Maréchal line. A letter of Dec. 11, 1962, speaks of doing a long review article on the book, and a letter of March 31, 1963, adds: 'My review article on Coreth took a month or so to get lined up and written. Delighted Lotz, O'Farrell, Alfaro. Lines up Gilson with Kant against Coreth (and incidentally myself). Have mailed you copies. Van Roo did 500 offprints for sale; so it is circulating among students.' Later that year (June 9, 1963), in replying to my request for an article in the *Festschrift* being prepared for him, he wrote: 'I shall write the contribution you desire: but I need time to think things out and luck to hit nails on the head (Metaphysics as Horizon had been cooking since Fay and Hawkins wrote).' – The reference here is to two reviewers who had written sharp criticisms of *Insight* a few years earlier.

Lonergan's only footnote to this article (publication data on Coreth's book) has been supplemented by notes 2–15, to which we have transferred foreign-language quotations translated now in the text. The references Lonergan left in his text remain there still. We have added the division numbers and titles.

RELATED WRITINGS

Relations ramify here, but I would list, as especially relevant, chapters 14–16 of *Insight* (1957a); 'Theories of Inquiry,' the 1967 talk to the American Catholic Philosophical Association (1974: 33–42); the 1973 paper, '*Insight* Revisited,' to the Jesuit Philosophical Association (1974: 263–78); 'Questionnaire on Philosophy' (1984b).

NOTES

a **Fr Coreth, ordinary professor of metaphysics at the University of Innsbruck**: Fr Emerich Coreth later contributed to a *Festschrift* for

Lonergan ('Dialectic of Performance and Concept,' *Spirit as Inquiry* [Chicago: Saint Xavier College, 1964]), as well as to the International Lonergan Congress of 1970 ('Immediacy and the Mediation of Being: An Attempt to Answer Bernard Lonergan,' *Language Truth and Meaning*, edited by Philip McShane [Dublin: Gill and Macmillan, 1972]). [188]

b **the Wolffian tradition**: Wolff was a kind of *bête noir* in Lonergan's writings. [188]

c **mediation of immediate knowledge**: on the general uses of mediate and immediate in Lonergan, see note *c* to chapter 12 above. The precise theme of mediation would be discussed in lectures at Gonzaga University, Spokane, this same year of 1963, when Lonergan would list as a source of his ideas, H. Niel, *De la médiation dans la philosophie de Hegel*, Paris, 1945. Fr Niel would later be influential in the decision to translate the *verbum* articles into French, and would himself contribute to the Lonergan *Festschrift* of 1964 ('The Old and the New in Theology,' *Spirit as Inquiry*, 1964). [189]

d **Such a procedure Fr Coreth names transcendental method**: here we discover an influence for Lonergan's decision, made apparently about this time, to speak of his own method as transcendental. Some steps in this development may be noted. There was a section in his *De constitutione Christi* called De methodorum analogia (1956: 44–49); it dealt with the analogy of philosophical and theological methods but did not take up transcendental method as a theme. Then there is an interesting development between 1959 and 1962 in the two courses, *De intellectu et methodo*, and *De methodo theologiae*. In the first Lonergan says he will talk 'de methodo generali,' giving general precepts that regard every science (1959b: 37) – this is transcendental in effect, but is not at this point given that name. Three years later, however, in *De methodo* he gives, among several characteristics of his method, that it is transcendental (1962: 6), adding at once the question, Is this transcendental method Kantian? For sources on this use of transcendental, he gives Coreth's book (which he had read by July of 1961), and an article by J. de Vries in *Scholastik*, 1961. For 'transcendental' in another context, see 83, 87, in this volume. [190]

e **a realm of ... merely logical [being]**: see '*Insight* Revisited,' where Lonergan affirms his dependence for this idea on Coreth – 'A point not made in *Insight* I have since learnt from Fr. Coreth. It regards spheres of being. Real being is known when the fulfilling conditions are data of sense or of consciousness. Restricted spheres of being are known when the fulfilling conditions are not data but some lesser requirement: the merely logical is what satisfies criteria of clarity, coherence, and rigor ... ' (1974: 274). Other restricted spheres are similarly described. (The language of the quotation is very much Lonergan's own; I presume that here, as elsewhere, to have 'learnt' from another means that the other was more Socratic midwife than direct teacher.) [191]

f **Prof. Gilson's book is still influential**: in support of this Lonergan *cites Theological Studies*; the reference is to an article by Fr Gerald A. McCool, 'The Philosophy of the Human Person in Karl Rahner's Theology,' 22 (1961) 537–62. Lonergan's personal copy of this issue is sidelined passim, and there is a double sideline at the relevant locus (561, note 31), which reads as follows: 'For a clear and forceful summary of the difficulties connected with the Maréchalian starting point and method in philosophy, see Etienne Gilson, *Réalisme thomiste et critique de la connaissance* ...' [192]

g **contradiction not between content and content but between content and performance**: a point Lonergan had already made with all clarity in *Insight*, though not in precisely these terms; see, for example, his remark on Hume, 'The intelligence and reasonableness of Hume's criticizing were obviously quite different from the knowledge he so successfully criticized' (1957a: 389), where the context is that of the positions and counter-positions. See also Existentialism (1957d: 19, 22) and *Understanding and Being* (1980: 38, 231). For a general view on contradiction within the thinking subject, we should note that, besides the contradiction in question here, between content and performance, there is also a contradiction between orientation and exercise, and this was a focus in the 1958 lectures: we default on rationality when, oriented rationally, we nevertheless judge wrongly, or refuse to judge at all (1980: 137). We should also distinguish these pairs from the pair, high aspiration and defective achievement, which refers more directly to the moral order (see note *m* to chapter 2 above). [192]

h **perception ... *Anschauung***: in this long exposition (193–97) of Kantian *Anschauung* and Gilsonian perception, Lonergan does not use the term, intuition, but his view of the claims made for intuition (see note *p* to chapter 10 above) would correspond to Gilson's claims for perception: 'the judgment ... attributes being ... as "seen" in the sensible datum' (195, translating Gilson's 'vu'). In 'Theology and Praxis' this is designated perceptualism; note also the remark, 'Fourteenth-century Scholasticism discussed with considerable acumen the validity of an intuition of what exists and is present ...' (1985b: 193). [194]

i **horizon**: the word had already acquired a technical sense for Lonergan (see note *g* to chapter 10 above), but we now have what may have been his first published exposition of the concept. [198]

j **every statement made by a realist denotes an object in a realist's world; every statement made by an idealist denotes an object in an idealist**

world: here we have in advance an explanation of the somewhat cryptic remark made in *Method* a few years later, 'An idealist never means what an empiricist means, and a realist never means what either of them means' (1972: 239); see also 'What in one [horizon] is found intelligible, in another is unintelligible' (1972: 236). On naive realism, idealism, and critical realism, see the thorough exposition and contrast of chapter 14 below (214–19). [199]

k **his aim of presuppositionless metaphysics**: Lonergan's position was indicated above (note *b* to chapter 10) – one can start with metaphysics, provided one goes round the circle of metaphysics and cognitional theory, but in the methodical approach the metaphysics is based on the cognitional theory. [204]

l **I should not equate metaphysics with the total and basic horizon, the *Gesamt- und Grundwissenschaft***: Lonergan, I believe, is in transition on this point; in *Insight*, metaphysics deals with the integral heuristic structure of proportionate being (1957a: 390–96); it is the highest viewpoint in human knowledge (394); it unifies other departments of knowledge (ix, xi, xxix, and passim). It is true that cognitional theory is the basis of his (methodical) metaphysics (xxix, 387–90 and passim), and would exercise the *Grund*-function, but at that time metaphysics would fulfil the *Gesamt*-function. The later Lonergan would, I think, somewhat modify that position. His final integral view seems better expressed in 'Questionnaire on Philosophy'; now total philosophy has four parts: cognitional theory, epistemology, metaphysics, and existential ethics (1984: 30, 32). Another clue to this development: *Insight*, at the time of its writing, was considered to deal with two questions: 'What is happening when we are knowing? ... What is known when that is happening?' (1957a: xxii). On reflection, some years later, Lonergan realized he had dealt with three questions: 'the procedure followed in *Insight* was to treat three linked questions: What am I doing when I am knowing? Why is doing that knowing? What do I know when I do it?' (1974: 37). The Questionnaire of 1976 should have led, I think, to a list of four questions, but Lonergan does not seem to have taken that step. (To be distinguished from the three questions above, which deal with relating knowledge to reality, are the three questions that lift the subject from level to level of consciousness: What? Is it? Ought I?)

Lonergan's changing viewpoint is especially illustrated in his view of theology: originally, he saw it as Thomas Aquinas did, under the heading of its object (God, and all things in relation to God); by the time he wrote *Method* he realized that the desired unity had to be found first on the side of the subject. [204]

m **a development that ... stamps the stages of ... progress with dates**: see his remark to Sebastian Moore, 'Concepts have dates' (*Compass: A Jesuit Journal*. Special Issue, Spring 1984, 9). See also in this volume (226 in chapter 15): 'Common meanings have histories.' The principle applies also in the field of ethics (consequently, I would add that values have dates too); see his 1967 Theories of Inquiry: 'I base ethics ... on invariant structures of ... knowing and ... doing ... this basis leaves room for a history and, indeed a development of morals' (1974: 39); likewise, his claim that his ethics is 'an ethics that, like the metaphysics, [is] explicitly aware of itself as a system on the move' (1974: 40). [204]

14   Cognitional Structure

'Cognitional Structure' was first published in *Spirit as Inquiry. Studies in Honor of Bernard Lonergan* (Chicago: Saint Xavier College, 1964) 230–42 (this was a special issue of *Continuum*, 2, where the pagination for the article was 530–42). Lonergan was to reach the age of sixty on Dec. 17, 1964, and the editor of *Continuum*, Justus George Lawler, invited me to edit a special issue of the journal for this occasion. Lonergan agreed to make a contribution of his own, and explains his choice in the opening lines of the paper.

A point of interest in regard to the title, *Spirit as Inquiry*: Lonergan himself suggested it, when I was pondering in his presence what the volume might be called; the phrase, spirit of inquiry, occurs in the *verbum* articles (1967b: 53). Incidentally, I believe a certain cadence is lost from the title when 'inquiry' is accented on the first syllable; Lonergan, whose pronunciation was formed by years of listening to reading at meals, accented it on the second.

Division numbers and titles are our addition, but correspond to the list in Lonergan's final paragraph.

RELATED WRITINGS

Various chapters of *Insight*, but especially 9–13 (1957a); the 1967 Response, reprinted as 'Theories of Inquiry' (1967e = 1974: 33–42); and above all 'De notione structurae' (1964c).

NOTES

a **to Fr Crowe for his initiative**: the chain of initiative started with Fr Michael Shields, then a theology student in Toronto, who suggested the idea to Dr Lawler; I came in only on the latter's invitation, and organized the contributors. [205]

b **cognitional structure**: Lonergan's interest in cognitional theory was of course longstanding, going back to his study of philosophy at Heythrop

College; in a letter from there to his Jesuit friend, Henry Smeaton, dated June 20 [1927], he remarks, 'The theory of knowledge is what is going to interest me most of all.' The notion of structure, however, as applying to knowledge, developed more slowly; it was certainly a focal idea when he wrote *Insight*, but in the *verbum* period, though he knew of 'levels of activity' (1967b: 65), he seemed to make structure more a metaphysical concern: The 'matters of fact that have been assembled ... find their systematic formulation and structural interrelation in terms of potency, habit, operation, action, passion, object, species' (1967b: 97). His interest in structuralism as a movement does not appear till 1978 when he gave a lecture under the title, 'What Is Claude Lévi-Strauss Up To?' [205]

c **internal relations**: on this concept see *Insight* (1957a: 343–44, 493–94). [206]

d **self-assembling**: an expression not found in the indices of previous works, though the idea is almost explicit in the dynamism which calls forth the cognitional operations in their natural sequence. To be related to this notion (possibly as source): the self-mediation of organic life, worked out in the 1963 lectures at Gonzaga University and Thomas More Institute (1984a: 6–12). [206]

e **not with the blindness of natural process**: here Lonergan extends to the whole self-assembling sequence the intelligence and rationality he had worked out years before, in sharp contrast with natural process, for the procession of inner word from insight (1967b: 33–34, 199–200). [207]

f **consciousness and self-knowledge**: the basic locus for clarifying these two quite different terms is chapter 11 of *Insight* (1957a), and the most important theological application is to the consciousness and self-knowledge of Christ (1956: Pars VI); much misunderstanding can be avoided by getting the terms straight in their distinction from and relation to one another. See also *Understanding and Being* (1980: chapter 6, part 1). [208]

g **different cognitional activities are not equally accessible**: this raises a serious pedagogical problem. For self-appropriation it is important that students exercise themselves (see on the next page the exhortation to 'the repeated use of personal experiments') on each of the four levels of consciousness; the advice is easy to follow on the first level, the level of attention, and on the second the teacher can readily propose questions for intelligence; but on the third level real exercises in judgment are not at all easy to invent, and on the fourth one may ask whether it is not a contradiction in terms to speak of exercises in responsibility that are merely for 'practice'; as for the fifth level, and the precept, 'Be in love,' is not my falling in love (and *a fortiori* my receiving of someone else's love) totally a gift? [208]

h **internal and external ... a spatial metaphor**: as with the 'upward' and 'downward' movements in human development, Lonergan constantly uses spatial metaphors, but only occasionally, as here, warns us that the expression *is* a metaphor. [209]

i **To heighten one's presence to oneself ... one raises the level of one's activity**: this exercise is distinguished from self-appropriation; one may heighten one's presence to oneself, as happens in the exercise of responsibility, without any effort whatever at self-appropriation. But see note *d* to chapter 15 below. [210]

j **the epistemological theorem**: these pages (211–14) are a splendid epitome of the position Lonergan had developed over the years; see *Verbum* (1967b: Index, under Criteriology, Critical), *Insight* (1957a: Index, under Knowing-Objectivity-Reality-Truth), *Understanding and Being* (1980: Index, under Epistemology). [211]

k **The alternative to distinguishing is confusion**: another splendid epitome (214–19), this time of Lonergan's views on two epistemologies that were his permanent adversaries, naive realism and idealism. See also chapter 13 of this volume. [214]

l **something like a forgetfulness of being ... The forgetfulness of being, manifested by naive realists and idealists**: what Lonergan meant by forgetfulness of being became clearer a decade later in his papers, 'Christology Today' (1985: 89), 'Questionnaire on Philosophy' (1984b: 14), and especially 'Theology and Praxis' (1985: 185, 193–94); from this last locus, one is led to define forgetfulness of being as 'forgetfulness of the inner light, the light that raises questions and, when answers are insufficient, keeps raising further questions ... the inner light of intelligence ... the inner light of reasonableness ... the inner light of deliberation' (193). [218-19]

m **Subjectivity once was a pejorative term**: Lonergan's thought on subjectivity began to come into focus only in the theological works of 1956 and 1957 (see especially *Divinarum personarum*, 1957b: 176–83 = 1964a: II, 196–204), and in the lectures on Existentialism of 1957. Full thematizing came in the 1968 lecture, The Subject (1974: 69–86). Nevertheless, *Insight* already has numerous references to subjectivity and, if the term is not well indexed in 1957, that failure is due to the indexer; compare the index to *Understanding and Being*, a book which covers the same ground at nearly the same time, but is indexed twenty years later. [219]

n **the interpersonal situation**: *Insight* (1957a: 731, note) postponed discussion of personal relations till they could be treated in theology; there are scattered references all through Lonergan's post-*Insight* writings to the interpersonal, including the last two chapters of this volume (see especially 226–27, 233–34, 242–43), but for a broader context I suggest attention to the second phase of theology and the downward movement of human development (handing on): these are especially dependent on community and the interpersonal. See also note *n* to chapter 8 above. [219]

o **human living**: another topic that Lonergan continually refers to but never thematized; there is great need of a thematic treatment that would bring his many differentiations of consciousness and their various specializations under the general heading of human living – otherwise the perpetual temptation is to associate human living with undifferentiated consciousness, and to regard the specializations as somewhat less than human. See also note *m* to chapter 8 above. On personal living and abstract questions, see the end of chapter 15 (231) below. [219]

p **beyond strictly cognitional levels of empirical, intellectual, and rational consciousness to the more inclusive level of rational self-consciousness**: there is considerable debate about the 'three levels' of Lonergan's *Insight* as contrasted with the 'four levels' of his *Method* (see my notes on Levels). Here we have a clear reference, antedating *Method* by several years, to rational self-consciousness as a new level beyond cognition. At the time of this paper, then, Lonergan is in transition (see in this volume 108, 219, 232–33), but has not reached the development of the later work; that development is clearly indicated by the change of nomenclature, when the level of rational self-consciousness becomes the level of responsibility and existential decision. [219]

15   *Existenz* **and** *Aggiornamento*

'*Existenz* and *Aggiornamento*' was first published in *Focus: A Theological Journal* 2 (1965) 5–14. This was a student publication at Regis College, deriving its name from the practice of having a focal essay round which student contributions might be grouped. When Lonergan gave this paper at the College on Sept. 14, 1964, the editor, Joseph Brzezicki, requested it for the focal essay of a future issue. Lonergan readily agreed, and supplied the typescript of his lecture. When the *Focus* article came out, it was sent to him in Rome for possible corrections before republication; he returned it promptly (his letter to me of March 18, 1965), and some slight changes in the *Collection* printing are presumably due to this revision.

Since the lecture was given to Jesuits, and was published first in a journal mainly for Jesuit students, it has a good many 'family' allusions. These have been allowed to stand, but I should note that the Archives contain a photocopy of the paper (from *Collection*), in which Lonergan had eliminated most of them and written in other changes as well. I have no clue to the purpose of this 'revised copy,' and it does not seem to have been published, so I reprint the paper as it appeared in *Collection*, but indicate in the notes some of the proposed 'revisions' that have more to do with general ideas.

Lonergan's original typescript is itself of absorbing interest, and cannot be studied in a paragraph. Here I note two points only. The first: the title is given as 'On Being Oneself (Christliche Existenz heute),' and Lonergan used 'On Being Oneself' as a running head throughout his typescript (pp. 2–6). The other: he numbered the whole paper from 1 to 12. Number 1 is our present pair of introductory paragraphs; numbers 2–6 are the present part 1, The Subject; numbers 7–8 part 2, One's World; numbers 9–12 are part 3, Authenticity of the Subject and His World. Fr Brzezicki thought this numbering gave the article a more technical appearance than suited his purpose, discussed a new format with Lonergan, showed him a new typing, and had it approved before Lonergan's departure for Rome later that same month. The three main divisions, however, with their titles, are from Lonergan himself; further, he has a marginal notation to the title of part 1: '5 main points.' *Focus* numbered these 1–5 (Lonergan's 2–6), and we have done the same in a subnumbering of part 1.

RELATED WRITINGS

The lecture stands at the beginning of a new phase in Lonergan's thinking, the fruit of the ideas emerging a decade earlier when he wrote 'Theology and Understanding.' It can be related to several chapters of *A Second Collection*, as well as to *Method in Theology*. Of particular relevance are: the Introduction to the book edition of the *verbum* articles (1967b: vii–xv) – note the revealing title, 'Subject and Soul,' which this Introduction receives in *Philippine Studies* 13 (1965) 576–85—and, of course, the 1968 lecture, The Subject (1974: 69–86; see especially 72–73 on subject and soul). Earlier writings pointing to the new trend are a section, De ex-sistentia, in the 1956 Christology (1956: 14–19), the section, Quaenam sit analogia subiecti temporalis et subiecti aeterni, in the 1957 Trinitarian theology (1957b: 176–84 = 1964a: II, 196–204), and the 1957 notes on Existentialism (1957d).

NOTES

a   *Existenz,* **on being oneself**: the 'revised copy' has crossed this out, and written instead 'religious experience.' [222]

b   **it is not ... a domestic exhortation**: a term used in religious families for the spiritual talk given regularly in the community, generally by one of the senior priests. Lonergan had given such talks himself, and one of these, The Mystical Body of Christ (Nov., 1951), is included in the Collected Works, Vol. 17. [222]

c **what the Germans call a *Besinnung***: crossed out in the 'revised copy.'

d **a heightening of one's self-appropriation**: see note *i* to chapter 14 above, on the difference between self-appropriation and raising the level of one's activity. It seems to me that the present text combines the two aspects: to reach the existential level is certainly a heightening of one's presence to oneself, and there is every reason to suppose that self-appropriation will aid the process. [222]

e τὰ πάντα ἐν πᾶσιν θεός: the reference is surely to 1 Corinthians 15.28, where however the text reads ἵνα ᾖ ὁ θεός τὰ πάντα ἐν πᾶσιν, that God may be all in all. Lonergan may well have written the Greek from memory. [222]

f **The Subject**: see my notes *g* and *i* below, also note *d* to chapter 11; recall that these divisions and subtitles are from Lonergan himself. [222]

g **substance and subject**: transition from substance to subject would be a rather good summary of Lonergan's own development at this time (see note *m* to chapter 14 above); the Archives supply documentary evidence of Lonergan's early interest in substance. [222]

h **opaque being ... luminous being**: Lonergan's early use of the metaphor of light was of course closely related to the Thomist natural light of intellect (1967b: Index, under Light), but the context has changed somewhat to that of meaning and self-appropriation; further, the term should be related to the *Gelichtetheit* of Coreth (192 above) and to the inner light that Lonergan discusses with Voegelin (1985: 193–196). [223]

i **a critical point in the increasing autonomy of the subject ... when the subject finds out ... that it is up to himself to decide what he is to make of himself**: see also 235 of this volume, on 'the existential subject, finding out for himself that he has to decide for himself what he is to make of himself'; this is the existential discovery (1972: 38), regarding the existential decision (1972: 121), etc. There is a section called The Existential Subject (1974: 79–84), in the lecture, The Subject, with the useful metaphor of 'the free and responsible subject producing the first and only edition of himself' (1974: 83). See my notes on Existentialism; Man's making of man; etc. [223]

j **world of immediacy ... world mediated by meaning**: see my notes on Horizon; Immediate; World; etc. Observe that the 'world mediated by meaning' later became the 'world mediated by meaning and motivated by value'; the change should follow logically on the 1968 lecture, The Subject, but there is a time lag in these matters, and it is only in the papers of *A Third Collection* (from 1974 on) that we find this development domiciled in Lonergan's writings. [225]

k **The difference between the world of immediacy and the world mediated by meaning is the source of the critical problem of philosophers**: crossed out in the 'revised copy'; but as the rest of the paragraph shows, Lonergan has not abandoned the position taken in the 'deleted' sentence. [225]

l **critical realist**: Lonergan makes his point now in terms of the two worlds, where earlier he had put it in terms of what intellect is (note *q* to chapter 10 above). [225]

m **A third world is not only mediated but also constituted by meaning**: the notion of meaning as an ontological constituent came strongly into Lonergan's thinking at this time (through the influence, I believe, of Dilthey); it has enormous potential in theology, for example, in joining new thought to traditional on the Eucharist. For the broader context of meaning, see note *a* to chapter 16. (The 'third world' here has nothing to do with the one the newspapers talk of; the latter, however, is a concern in Lonergan's writings on economics.) [225]

n **will is rational appetite, an appetite that follows intellect**: this is the language of faculty psychology, not much used by Lonergan in his later years. [225]

o **data that besides being given have a meaning**: the 1964 Georgetown University lectures speak of data (the field of natural sciences), data with a meaning (the field of human sciences), data with a meaning that is true and salvific – the field of the theologian dealing with revelation and dogma. (I owe this information to notes taken by Sister Rose Wilker.) [226]

p **To exclude freedom is to exclude *Existenz***: the 'revised copy' has 'personality' for '*Existenz*', and has the immediately following sentence (on John XXIII) crossed out. [226]

q **For what is community?**: Lonergan's interest in community was lifelong, but different contexts led to different approaches; in *Insight*, for example, in the context of dialectic, he would speak of the tension of community (1957a: 214 and passim); here, in the context of meaning, he speaks of what constitutes community. Note that there are four degrees of achievement of community, and that they correspond to what he will eventually call the four levels of consciousness. [226]

r **Authenticity**: another word that entered Lonergan's vocabulary as early as the Existentialism lectures (1957d: 25) and is now in 1965 recurrent. A close relative in *Insight* would be 'genuineness' (1957a: 475–78, 623–26) but the adequate forerunner there is perhaps not so much a single concept as it is response to the book's invitation, and fidelity to its moving viewpoint. [227]

s **what a genuine Buddhist is**: the logic of this phrase is to make Lonergan

a Buddhist; the 'revised copy' makes it read, 'what a genuine Catholic
or Buddhist is.' [227]

t **the process that eliminated the standardized man of classicist thought
and ushered in ... historical consciousness**: one of the most quoted
of Lonergan's ideas; I have not noticed any thematic treatment in his
writings prior to the 1966 address to the Canon Law Society of America
(1974: 1–9), but it is curious that a 1949 lecture in the Archives, Towards a Definition of Education (Batch 2, Folder 55), already speaks of
the errors of classicism. [228]

u **The sin of modernity**: Lonergan notes here a negative side to modernity,
but fundamentally his attitude is positive, if cautiously so; 'our disen-
gagement from classicism and our involvement in modernity must be
open-eyed, critical, coherent, sure-footed' – from the 1968 paper, Belief:
Today's Issue (1974: 98). [228]

v **the imperatives, Be intelligent, Be reasonable, Be responsible**: the first
listing I have noticed in Lonergan of what he will later call the transcendental precepts, and it is still only partial. [230]

w **Implicit in human inquiry is a natural desire to know God by his
essence; implicit in human judgment about contingent things there is
the formally unconditioned that is God**: on the natural desire to see
God, see my notes on Desire. Now, however, there is a further point of
some importance regarding the word, implicit. For some followers of
the Maréchal movement, God is co-affirmed in every affirmation. That
is not Lonergan's position; I have a record of a question I put to him
after this very talk, Is the existence of God implicit in every judgment?
His answer: No, but the *question* of God's existence is implicit. See also
Method (1972: 105): 'the question of God is implicit in all our questioning.' [230]

x **the excellence of the Son is the excellence of the adoptive sons**: the
published text, in both *Focus* and *Collection*, omits the words, 'of the Son
is the excellence,' but Lonergan has written them into the 'revised copy,'
and we include them now for they clearly belong. [230]

y **faith ... affirming true propositions ... concluding from them**: that this
is an inadequate view of faith is clear from the argument (see also the
following note), but that does not mean that Lonergan rejected conclusions from faith, much less that he rejected the element of truth in
the propositions of faith. [230]

z **the love of God, being in love with God, can be as full and as dominant ... an experience as human love**: here at once we have the remedy
for an inadequate notion of faith, a dynamism that takes us beyond
merely affirming true propositions and concluding from them. [231]

aa **divided from the viewpoint of the challenge to which Pope John XXIII initiated a response**: crossed out in the 'revised copy.' [231]

bb **an archaic world that no longer exists ... a futurist world that will never exist**: two aberrations that Lonergan had lined up in his 1957 Trinitarian theology (1957b: 38 = 1964a: II, 51). An early book review (of Francis Stuart Campbell, *The Menace of the Herd*) has these lines: 'the author is not immune from archaism: I use the word in Toynbee's sense who divided political thinkers, in times of crisis and disintegration, into futurists who wish to tear up everything by the roots ... and ... archaists who find the cause of all evils in the desertion of the ... good old ways ...' (1943c). Toynbee's influence on Lonergan is pervasive, and needs to be studied; curiously, a reference to Toynbee in *Theological Studies* 3 (1942) 578, note 230, was omitted from the publication in book form (1971: 144). [231]

cc ***ad maiorem Dei gloriam***: for the greater glory of God, unofficial Jesuit motto; though most bits of local color were crossed out in Lonergan's 'revised copy,' this one was retained. The original has simply the initials, A.M.D.G. – the usual Jesuit way of referring to the motto. [231]

16   Dimensions of Meaning

'Dimensions of Meaning' was first published in *Collection* (New York: Herder and Herder, 1967) 252–67. It had been an address in the Distinguished Lecture Series at Marquette University, May 12, 1965. At that time *Collection* was ready to go to press with fifteen chapters, but at the last minute and with the agreement of Fr Lonergan and Dr Lawler this lecture was added as chapter 16. Division numbers and titles have been added in the present edition.

RELATED WRITINGS

Besides the preceding chapter of this volume, one may list a lecture at the Thomas More Institute, 'Time and Meaning' (1975: 29–54); the 1966 paper, 'The Transition from a Classicist World-View to Historical-Mindedness' (1974: 1–9); and chapter 7 of *Method in Theology* (1972). Reference to some unpublished papers will be made in the notes.

NOTES

a **My topic is meaning**: note *m* to chapter 15 above dealt with meaning as constitutive, but the topic is broader now. Meaning had interested Lonergan early in his career. The introduction to his doctoral disserta-

tion shows his concern with discovering by inductive and scientific methods the meaning of Thomas Aquinas, in contrast to commentators who
'tell us that St. Thomas *must* mean this or that' (1985a: 12; the point
is made again in chapter 3 above: 60–61). In his review of von Hildebrand's book on the meaning of marriage, he complains that the author
is vague on the meaning of meaning: 'A book has been written on
"The Meaning of Meaning" and it concluded that "meaning" has over
eight hundred meanings. Which of these is meant by von Hildebrand,
what is a primary meaning, what would be a secondary meaning, are
so many questions conveniently left without an answer' (1942b). The
verbum articles concluded in 1949 with a little essay on the meaning
of an author and its interpretation (1967b: 215–20). Half a column was
needed to list the references to meaning in the Index of *Insight*. Despite
this build-up, the topic did not really come to center stage till the summer of 1962, when a lecture in his institute on the method of theology
(Regis College) was devoted to hermeneutics, and one later in the summer (at Regis again, and at Thomas More Institute) to time and meaning.
The next year his Gonzaga University lectures made meaning a major
topic, and this was followed by another lecture at Thomas More Institute
on the analogy of meaning. There was, then, a long and detailed history
preceding these last two chapters of *Collection*. [232]

b **develop, differentiate, combine, group**: this series surely shows the
influence of Piaget, who had figured prominently in Lonergan's education lectures of 1959 (CWL 10: chapter 8), but whose name had not
appeared in *Insight*, or in the 1958 lectures published as *Understanding
and Being*. [232]

c **not only the factual but also the possible, the ideal, the ought-to-be**:
Lonergan has a well-worked out parallel of the cognitional (three levels
of consciousness) and the ontological (three levels in the constitution
of proportionate being); it has often been asked what fourth level might
correspond ontologically to the intentional fourth level of value – there
seems to be the germ of an answer in the phrase, 'the possible, the ideal,
the ought-to-be.' [233]

d **changes in the control of meaning mark off the great epochs in human
history**: the notion of *control* of meaning is obviously of great importance for the understanding of this chapter, as well as for the structure
of history, but I do not think Lonergan ever thematized it. There are
abundant references to 'control' in the Index of *Insight*, and several in
the Index of *A Second Collection*, and these might give one a start on a
history of the term in Lonergan; further, since he cites Socrates here for
the 'classical expression of the effort to control meaning,' a study of his
references to that thinker should prove profitable. [235]

e **anthropologists**: see *Understanding and Being* (1980: 180), where there is more specific reference on this point to Malinowski and the Trobriand Islanders. [236]

f **myth and magic**: see *Insight* (1957a: 542, 547, and passim in chapter 17). [237]

g **this entry of philosophy into the realm of the existential and the historical ... curtails the functions formerly attributed to prudence**: nevertheless, at one point in his development (the 1962 course, *De methodo theologiae*), in his new attention to historical consciousness, Lonergan had found the old notion of prudence useful for understanding the particular and changeable with which history deals (1962: 27).

It is fitting that *Collection* should conclude with ideas that point to Lonergan's new historical consciousness. Not only does *A Second Collection* begin with a paper on 'The Transition from a Classicist World-View to Historical-Mindedness' (1974: 1–9), but Lonergan remarked, in a conversation late in life (March, 1980) that all his work had been introducing history into Catholic theology: J. Martin O'Hara, ed., *Curiosity at the Center of One's Life. Statements and Questions of R. Eric O'Connor* (Montreal: Thomas More Institute, 1987) 427. The remark is illuminating, though it may exaggerate a bit, as happens in conversation; it certainly should not be so interpreted as to omit the work of inculturation for which chapter 14 of *Method* provides such a solid basis. The orienting notion for an integral view is found in the two phases, mediating and mediated, of theological method. [240]

h **To proclaim with Vico the priority of poetry**: a useful passage to counteract a view commonly held of Lonergan as exclusively cerebral. [241]

i **the ... definition of man as a rational animal ... as a symbolic animal or ... as an incarnate spirit**: this series illustrates Lonergan's remark that concepts have dates (see note *m* to chapter 13 above); see also the remark (243 below), 'Today terms are still defined, but definitions are not unique: on the contrary, for each term there is a historical sequence of different definitions.' We might add to the series on man the concept of human beings as self-constituting subjects (see 266 above), and as self-completing animals – in the 1976 lectures on Religious Studies and Theology (1985b: 127, 141, 154, 159). But compare Lonergan's position on 'the explanatory definition of man' in the original, discarded Preface of *Insight* (1985c: 6). [242]

j **vertical liberty**: an early occurrence of a term that will assume considerable importance in *Method in Theology* (1972: 40, 122, 237–38, 240, 269). [243]

k **Catholic philosophy and Catholic theology are matters, not merely**

of ... faith, but also of culture: compare the first line of the Introduction to *Method*: 'A theology mediates between a cultural matrix and the significance and role of a religion in that matrix' (1972: xi). [244]

l **philosophy becomes existential**: see note *l* to chapter 13 above, on the addition of existential ethics to Lonergan's regular philosophic triad of cognitional theory, epistemology, and metaphysics. [245]

Works of Lonergan
Referred To in Editorial Notes

This is not a complete bibliography of Lonergan's works, and the code used (year, with letter added when necessary) is not the definitive one that we hope to draw up in the index volume to the Collected Works. It is simply a list of the works referred to in the Editorial Notes above. Some of these works are published, some are in the semipublished state of notes issued for students, some are not published in any sense, but all are available in the Library and/ or Archives of the Lonergan Research Institute, Toronto. Translations and various 'editions' are listed only insofar as they are pertinent to the notes, but we have indicated the volume number of the Collected Works in which each item is expected to appear.

1928a 'The Form of Mathematical Inference.' *Blandyke Papers*, No. 283 (Jan.), 126–37 (CWL 17).
1928b 'The Syllogism.' Ibid. No. 285 (March), 33–64 (CWL 17).
1929a 'True Judgment and Science.' Ibid. No. 291 (Feb.), 195–216 (CWL 17).
1929b 'Infinite Multitude.' Ibid. 217–20 (CWL 17).
1935 Review of L.W. Keeler, *The Problem of Error, from Plato to Kant. Gregorianum* 16, 156–60 (CWL 17).
1940 '*GRATIA OPERANS*: A Study of the Speculative Development in the Writings of St. Thomas of Aquin.' S.T.D. thesis, Gregorian University, Rome (CWL, volume not determined). Rewritten for publication: 1941, 1942a; 1971.
1941 'St. Thomas' Thought on *Gratia operans*' (first of four articles). *Theological Studies* 2, 289–324 (CWL 1).
1942a 'St. Thomas' Thought on *Gratia operans*' (second, third, and fourth of four articles). Ibid. 69–88, 375–402, 533–78 (CWL 1).

1942b Review of Dietrich von Hildebrand, *Marriage. The Canadian Register* (Quebec edition), May 23, p. 5 (CWL 17).

1942c Letter (on marriage). Ibid. June 6, p. 9 (CWL 17).

1942d Letter (on marriage). Ibid. June 20, p. 9 (CWL 17).

1943a 'The Form of Inference.' *Thought* 18, 277–92 (CWL 4).

1943b 'Finality, Love, Marriage.' *Theological Studies* 4, 477–510 (CWL 4).

1943c Review of Francis Stuart Campbell, *The Menace of the Herd. The Canadian Register* (Quebec edition), April 24, p. 5 (CWL 17).

1945 Thought and Reality. Lectures at Thomas More Institute, Montreal, 1945–46 (CWL 21).

1946a 'The Concept of *Verbum* in the Writings of St. Thomas Aquinas' (first of five articles). *Theological Studies* 7, 349–92 (CWL 2).

1946b *De ente supernaturali: Supplementum schematicum.* Notes for students, College of the Immaculate Conception, Montreal (CWL 16).

1946c Review of E. Iglesias, *De Deo in operatione naturae vel voluntatis operante. Theological Studies* 7, 602–13 (CWL 4).

1947 'The Concept of *Verbum* in the Writings of St. Thomas Aquinas' (second and third of five articles). *Theological Studies* 8, 35–79, 404–44 (CWL 2).

1948 'The Assumption and Theology.' In: *Vers le dogme de l'Assomption* (Journées d'études mariales). Montreal: Fides, 411–24 (CWL 4).

1949a 'The Concept of *Verbum* in the Writings of St. Thomas Aquinas' (fourth and fifth of five articles). *Theological Studies* 10, 3–40, 359–93 (CWL 2).

1949b 'The Natural Desire to See God.' *Proceedings of the Eleventh Annual Convention of the Jesuit Philosophical Association*, 31–43 (CWL 4).

1950a 'A Note on Geometrical Possibility.' *The Modern Schoolman* 27 (1949–50), 124–38 (CWL 4).

1950b *De scientia atque voluntate Dei: Supplementum schematicum.* Notes for students, Regis College (Christ the King Seminary), Toronto (CWL 16).

1950c Intelligence and Reality. Lectures at the Thomas More Institute, Montreal, 1950–51 (CWL 21).

1951a 'A New Dogma.' *The Canadian Messenger of the Sacred Heart* 61, 11–15 (CWL 17).

1951b 'Le rôle de l'université catholique dans le monde moderne.' *Relations* 11, 263–65, 320 (CWL 4).

1952 *De conscientia Christi.* Notes for students, Regis College, Toronto (CWL 16).

1953 *De ratione convenientiae eiusque radice, de excellentia ordinis, de signis rationis systematice et universaliter ordinatis, denique de convenientia, contingentia, et fine incarnationis: Supplementum schematicum.* Notes for students, Gregorian University (CWL 6).

1954 'Theology and Understanding.' *Gregorianum* 35, 630–48 (CWL 4).

1955a *De sanctissima Trinitate: Supplementum quoddam.* Notes for students, Gregorian University (CWL 6).

1955b 'Isomorphism of Thomist and Scientific Thought.' In: *Sapientia Aquinatis*, Vol. 1 (Communicationes IV congressus thomistici internationalis). Rome: Catholic Book Agency, 119–27 (CWL 4).

1956 *De constitutione Christi ontologica et psychologica supplementum confecit Bernardus Lonergan, S.I.* Rome: Gregorian University Press (CWL 7).

1957a *Insight: A Study of Human Understanding.* London: Longmans, Green and Co. (CWL 3).

1957b *Divinarum personarum conceptionem analogicam evolvit Bernardus Lonergan, S.I.* Rome: Gregorian University Press (CWL 9).

1957c Mathematical Logic. Notes for lectures, Boston College (CWL 18).

1957d Existentialism. Notes for lectures, Boston College; typescript made at Thomas More Institute, Montreal (CWL 18).

1957e Existentialism. Transcript of tape recording of lectures, Boston College; made by Nicholas Graham; available at Lonergan Research Institute, Toronto (CWL 18).

1958a 'Philosophic Difference and Personal Development.' *The New Scholasticism* 32, 97 (CWL 17).

1958b '*Insight*: Preface to a Discussion.' *Proceedings of The American Catholic Philosophical Association* 32, 71–81 (CWL 4).

1958c *Insight: A Study of Human Understanding.* Revised students edition. London: Longmans, Green and Co. (CWL 3).

1959a 'Christ as Subject: A Reply.' *Gregorianum* 40, 242–70 (CWL 4).

1959b *De intellectu et methodo.* Notes by students of theology course, Gregorian University (CWL 19).

1960a 'Openness and Religious Experience.' In: *Il Problema dell'esperienza religiosa* (Atti del XV Convegno del Centro di Studi Filosofici tra Professori Universitari). Brescia: Morcelliana, 460–62 (CWL 4).

1960b *De argumento theologico ex sacra scriptura.* Notes for faculty seminar, Gregorian University (CWL 17).

1961 *De Deo trino. Pars analytica.* Rome: Gregorian University Press (CWL 9).

1962 *De methodo theologiae.* Notes by students of theology course, Gregorian University (CWL 19).

1963 'Metaphysics as Horizon.' *Gregorianum* 44, 307–18 (CWL 4).

1964a *De Deo trino.* Vols. 1 (2nd ed.), 2 (3rd ed.). Rome: Gregorian University Press (CWL 9).

1964b *De Verbo incarnato* (3rd ed.). Rome: Gregorian University Press (CWL 8).

1964c 'De notione structurae.' *Apertura* 1 (May), 117–23 (CWL 6).

1964d 'Cognitional Structure.' In: *Spirit as Inquiry. Studies in Honor of Bernard Lonergan* (ed. Frederick E. Crowe). Chicago: Saint Xavier College, 230–42 (CWL 4).

1965a 'Subject and Soul.' *Philippine Studies* 13, 576–85 (CWL 2).

1965b '*Existenz* and *Aggiornamento*.' *Focus: A Theological Journal* 2, 5–14 (CWL 4).

1965c 'Molina, Luis de.' *Encyclopaedia Britannica* (14th edition), 667–68; 665–66 in 1967 printing (CWL 17).

1966 *La notion de verbe dans les écrits de saint Thomas d'Aquin*. Paris: Beauchesne.

1967a *Collection: Papers by Bernard Lonergan, S.J.* (ed. Frederick E. Crowe). New York: Herder and Herder (CWL 4).

1967b *Verbum: Word and Idea in Aquinas* (ed. David B. Burrell). Notre Dame: University of Notre Dame Press (CWL 2).

1967d 'The Transition from a Classicist World-View to Historical-Mindedness.' In: *Law for Liberty. The Role of Law in the Church Today* (ed. James E. Biech- ler). Baltimore: Helicon, 126–33 (CWL 11).

1967e 'Response.' *Proceedings of The American Catholic Philosophical Association* 41, 254–59 (CWL 11, under title, 'Theories of Inquiry').

1968a *The Subject*. Milwaukee: Marquette University Press (CWL 11).

1968b 'The Natural Knowledge of God.' *Proceedings of the Twenty-third Annual Convention of The Catholic Theological Society of America*, 54–69 (CWL 11).

1971 *Grace and Freedom: Operative Grace in the Thought of St. Thomas Aquinas* (ed. J. Patout Burns). London: Darton, Longman & Todd (CWL 1).

1972 *Method in Theology*. London: Darton, Longman & Todd (CWL 12).

1973a *De ente supernaturali: Supplementum schematicum*. Revised edition. Toronto: Regis College (CWL 16).

1973b *Philosophy of God, and Theology: The Relationship between Philosophy of God and the Functional Specialty, Systematics*. London: Darton, Longman & Todd (CWL 14).

1973c *Insight* Revisited (Paper for Discussion at the Thirty-fifth Annual Convention of the Jesuit Philosophical Association). Marquette University, Milwaukee (CWL 11).

1974 *A Second Collection: Papers by Bernard J.F. Lonergan, S.J.* (eds. William F.J. Ryan and Bernard J. Tyrrell). London: Darton, Longman & Todd (CWL 11).

1976 *The Way to Nicea: The Dialectical Development of Trinitarian Theology* (A translation by Conn O'Donovan from the first part of *De Deo trino*). London: Darton, Longman & Todd (CWL 9).

1979 'The Human Good.' *Humanitas* 15, 113–26 (CWL 14).

1980 *Understanding and Being* (eds. Elizabeth A. Morelli and Mark D. Morelli). New York and Toronto: Edwin Mellen (CWL 5).

1984a 'The Mediation of Christ in Prayer.' METHOD: *Journal of Lonergan Studies* 2/1, 1–20 (CWL 6).

1984b 'Questionnaire on Philosophy.' Ibid. 2/2, 1–35 (CWL 14).

1985a 'The GRATIA OPERANS Dissertation: Preface and Introduction.' Ibid. 3/2, 9–49 (CWL, volume not determined).

1985b *A Third Collection: Papers by Bernard J.F. Lonergan, S.J.* (ed. Frederick E. Crowe). New York: Paulist (CWL 13).

1985c 'The Original Preface of INSIGHT.' METHOD: *Journal of Lonergan Studies* 3/1, 3–7 (CWL 3).

Index to Editorial Notes

Index to Text

A posteriori, and *Anschauung*, 194; and immediate realism, 197. A. p. and a priori, for Coreth and Gilson, 200–201; in science, 136–37

A priori, Coreth and Kant, 203. Synthetic a. p., 194

Abbreviation, of symbolism, 5, 6. A. not employed in illative sense, 7

Absolute, of true judgment, 148. *See also* God

Abstract concept (unique) vs. sense data (multiple), 95–96, 97. A. lines and points, vs. image, 95–96. A. man of classical culture, 240–41. A. nature and finality, 22

Abstraction, and concept, 136; and definition, 135; and essence, 145. A. of forms from images, 138. A. and invariance, 135–36, 139, 140. A. and mediation of latent metaphysics, 204. A. of possibilities from space-time conditions, 140. A. unconscious for conceptualist, 85, 86

Accident, *see* Essence, Intelligibility, *Per se*, Substance

Act(s), consciously intelligent, rational, free, responsible, 165–66. Immanent a., 55. A. as *intendere* of subject and *intendi* of object, 166. Potency and a., 34 n. 60, 43; *see also* Potency, form, a. A. specified by object, 167. A. and verification, 140. *See also* Justification, Love, Object, Pure, Reality, Subject

Actio, 58–59. *A. in passo*, 57–58. *A. physica*, 59

Active voice, 57

Activity, raising level of, 210. Cognitional a., 206–209, 211–12

Actual grace, *see* Grace

Actuality and possibility, 102, 106

Actus (actu), *essendi*, 144, 151. *A. huius ut ab hoc*, 58. *Intellectus, intelligibile, sensibile, sensus actu*, 165, 167. *Unumquodque cognoscitur secundum quod est a.*, 165, 167. *See also Exercitium*

Adam, and Christ, 71–72; and Mary, 78, 79. Gifts of A. 26, 50 & n. 79. *See also* Fall

Advantage, private, *see* Good

Agapê, 230

know: a basic orientation, 186;
grounds questions, 147; not innate
idea, concept, knowledge, 147;
but a notion, 147; a notion of
being, 151; an openness, 186. *See
also* Fulfilment, Object

Determinism, 210

Development begins from cognitional
reasons, 144–45. D. and decline,
39, 109–110. D. of (obj.): Aristotelian and Thomist thought, 144–45;
doctrine, 69–70 n. 15, 71, 74–77;
philosophy and theology, 86; science, 74, 86, 104. D. of (subj.):
infant, 232; inquirer, 204; subject,
223–24, 230. *See also* Understanding, d. of

Dialectic: of development and decline, 39; of history, 109–110; of
multiple human appetites, 26; of
social conscience, 26–27; of *Vollzug
und Begriff*, 204

Dictum de omni et nullo, 13, 14, 15

Different, numerically, qualitatively,
223

Differential equations, 136

Dilemma, trilemma, tetralemma,
etc., 9

Discovery, scientific, 20

Disjunctive argument, 9

Dispositions of subject, 223

Distinguishing, alternative to confusion, 214

Distribution in syllogism, 10

Doctrine, and explanation in theology, 18. *See also* Development,
History, Teaching authority

Dogmatic realism (Gilson), 196, 199

Doms, H., 17 & n. 2, 18 nn. (3, 7),
21, 33 n. 53, 41 nn. 65–66, 45, 46
n. 73, 48 n. 75, 51 n. 82

Donnelly, P., 20 n. 11

Doucet, V., 81 n. 1

Dreaming, 210, 222. Dreams of night,
of morning, 242

Drifting, 224, 229

Drive of human intellect, *see* Desire

Druwé, E., 68 n. 8, 69 n. 11, 70 n. 15

Duméry, H, 168 n. 18

Durand, G., 242

Durandus, 54, 61, 62

Dynamism, of human intellect, *see*
Desire of h. i., Intellectualism,
Open; *also* Static. Upward d. of
universe, 18, 21–22, 22–23, 29, 31,
36, 37–48 passim, 49, 51; *see also*
Finality, vertical

Economy, domestic, 37. *See also*
Redemption, Technology

Education, Catholic, 108–113,
127–28. Child's e., 42, 46–47 & n.
74, 48–49, 51, 233–34. Human
e., 38. *See also* Marriage

Effect, 54, 56, 57

Ego (I) in Christ, *see* Christ

Egoism and altruism, 25; transcendence of, 25

Einstein, A., 136, 138

Eliade, M., 242

Emanatio intelligibilis, 166 n. 15

Emanationism, 61

Empirical, Aristotle's ethics as, 25. E.
aspect of good, 108. E. knowledge
vs. intellectual, 94–95. E. theory
of understanding and knowledge,
16

Empiricism, 212, 214

Enchiridion symbolorum, 18 n. 5, 27 n.
32, 34 n. 58, 73 n. 17, 75 n. 18,
114 n. 3, 126 n. 30, 159 n. 8**

End, absolute, horizontal, vertical, *see*
Finality, Term. Act as e., 43. E.
as apprehended, 59. E., and means,

fied theory, 16. H. and definition,
134–35; and form, 140; and formulation, 211; and verification, 16,
133–34, 139, 140, 226
Hypothetical argument, 8–10. H. a.
as compound, 9–10. H. a., and
dilemma, trilemma, tetralemma,
etc., 9; and disjunctive argument,
9; and illative sense, 7–8; and
interpretation of syllogism,
10–15 (connotational, 11–13; denotational, 10–11; d.-c., 13–15);
and *modus tollens*, 8–9; and nonsyl-
logistic formal inference, 8–10;
and reduction to syllogistic form,
3; and sorites, 9–10; and symbolism, 6; and syntax, 5. H. a. gives
ultimate unity to types of inference,
15–16. H. form contrasted with
syllogistic, 14. H. sorites, 9–10

I (ego), known as subject and as ob-
ject, 166 n. 14. I in Christ, *see* Christ
Id a quo, 54, 55, 59
Idea defined, 214 n. 1. I. of being,
214 n. 1. Ideas (Plato), 85, 135
Ideal entities (mathematics), 6
Idealism, 151, 212, 214. I. excluded,
191. German i., 179 note 50. I.
for Coreth, 201, 202; for Gilson,
195, 199, 201, 202. I., naive real-
ism, critical realism, 214–19
Identity in act of subject and object,
165–66, 179 & n. 50
If, 4
Iglesias, E., 53–65
Ignatius Loyola, St, 229
Illative sense, 3, 6–8, 48 n. 75
Illumination by faith, of method,
129–30; of reason, 124
Illusion, 151 & n. 20; transcendental
i., 83

Image, and concept, 95–96. Grasp of
forms in i., *see* Grasp. I. object of
imagination as active potency, 137.
I. required for understanding,
137–38. Types of i.: representative,
104–105, 106; symbolic, 95–96,
104–105; virtual, 104. *See also*
Phantasm
Imaginability and modern science,
138
Imaginable, limits of, 104. I. and
relativity, quantum mechanics,
138–39. *See also* Intelligible
Imagination, 137. I. and geometry,
95–96; and inquiry, 207; and intelligence, 138; and knowledge of
God, 138. Points, lines, and i.,
95–96. Theology and i., 128. I.
transcended in modern science, 138
Imitatio Christi, 127
Immanence, 213
Immediacy, world of, 224–25, 226
Immediate, 55, 62. I. experience, 233.
I. and mediated, 185, 186, 189,
197–98, 204; and mediated relation
of knowing to objects, 218. *See
also* Causality, *Immediatio*, Meaning,
World
Immediatio virtutis, suppositi, 46 n. 73,
55, 63
Immortality, 72, 78
Imperatives of consciousness, 230
Implication and affirmation, 73–74 n.
17. Implier, i., implied, 16. I. in
denotational coincidence, 10–11; in
illative sense, 7; in language, 4–5;
in syllogism, 6, 7. I. of revelation,
68–70; of scripture, 70–71, 74.
Types of i. (formal, material, scientific), 29 n. 34. *See also* Conclusions
Impotence, moral, 86
Incarnation, 22, 27